STUDIES IN
EARLY
CHRISTIANITY

A Collection of Scholarly Essays

edited by
Everett Ferguson
ABILENE CHRISTIAN UNIVERSITY

with
David M. Scholer
NORTH PARK COLLEGE AND THEOLOGICAL SEMINARY

and
Paul Corby Finney
CENTER OF THEOLOGICAL INQUIRY

A Garland Series

CONTENTS OF SERIES

VOLUME IV

Orthodoxy, Heresy, and Schism in Early Christianity

edited with introductions by

Everett Ferguson

Garland Publishing, Inc.
New York & London
1993

Library of Congress Cataloging-in-Publication Data

Orthodoxy, heresy, and schism in early Christianity / edited by Everett
Ferguson.
    p. cm. — (Studies in early Christianity ; v. 4)
    Includes bibliographical references.
    ISBN 0–8153–1064–1 (alk. paper)
    1. Church history—Primitive and early church, ca. 30–600.
2. Theology, Doctrinal—History—Early church, ca. 30–600.
3. Heresies, Christian—History—Early church, ca. 30 to 600.
I. Ferguson, Everett, 1933–   . II. Series.
BR166.O78 1993
273'.1—dc20   92–41867
                                        CIP

Printed on acid-free, 250-year-life paper
Manufactured in the United States of America

Contents

Series Introduction

Christianity has been the formative influence on Western civilization and has maintained a significant presence as well in the Near East and, through its missions, in Africa and Asia. No one can understand Western civilization and the world today, much less religious history, without an understanding of the early history of Christianity.

The first six hundred years after the birth of Jesus were the formative period of Christian history. The theology, liturgy, and organization of the church assumed their definitive shape during this period. Since biblical studies form a separate, distinctive discipline, this series confines itself to sources outside the biblical canon, except as these sources were concerned with the interpretation and use of the biblical books. During the period covered in this series the distinctive characteristics of the Roman Catholic and Eastern Orthodox Churches emerged.

The study of early Christian literature, traditionally known as Patristics (for the church fathers), has experienced a resurgence in the late twentieth century. Evidences of this are the flourishing of a new professional society, the North American Patristics Society, a little over twenty years old; the growing number of teachers and course offerings at major universities and seminaries; the number of graduate students studying and choosing to write their dissertations in this area; the volume of books published in the field; and attendance at the quadrennial International Conferences on Patristic Studies at Oxford as well as at many smaller specialized conferences. This collection of articles reflects this recent growing interest and is intended to encourage further study. The papers at the International Conferences on Patristic Studies from the first conference in 1951 to the present have been published in the series *Studia Patristica,* and interested readers are referred to these volumes for more extensive treatment of the topics considered in this series of reprints and many other matters as well.

The volumes in this series are arranged topically to cover biography, literature, doctrines, practices, institutions, worship, missions, and daily life. Archaeology and art as well as writings are drawn on in order to give reality to the Christian movement in its early centuries. Ample attention is also given to the relation of Christianity to pagan thought and life, to the Roman state, to Judaism, and to doctrines and practices that came to be judged as heretical or schismatic. Introductions to each volume will attempt to tie the articles together so that an integrated understanding of the history will result.

The aim of the collection is to give balanced and comprehensive coverage. Early on I had to give up the idealism and admit the arrogance of attempting to select the "best" article on each topic. Criteria applied in the selection included the following: original and excellent research and writing, subject matter of use to teachers and students, groundbreaking importance for the history of research, foundational information for introducing issues and options. Preference was given to articles in English where available. Occasional French and German titles are included as a reminder of the international nature of scholarship.

The *Encyclopedia of Early Christianity* (New York: Garland, 1990) provides a comprehensive survey of the field written in a manner accessible to the average reader, yet containing information useful to the specialist. This series of reprints of Studies in Early Christianity is designed to supplement the encyclopedia and to be used with it.

The articles were chosen with the needs of teachers and students of early church history in mind with the hope that teachers will send students to these volumes to acquaint them with issues and scholarship in early Christian history. The volumes will fill the need of many libraries that do not have all the journals in the field or do not have complete holdings of those to which they subscribe. The series will provide an overview of the issues in the study of early Christianity and the resources for that study.

Understanding the development of early Christianity and its impact on Western history and thought provides indispensable insight into the modern world and the present situation of Christianity. It also provides perspective on comparable developments in other periods of history and insight into human nature in its religious dimension. Christians of all denominations may continue to learn from the preaching, writing, thinking, and working of the early church.

Introduction

No topic has engaged scholarly discussions of Christian origins in the mid- and later twentieth century more intently than the relationship of orthodoxy and heresy. The older paradigm posited a uniform teaching at the beginning of the Christian movement, from which variant teachings and groups diverged. Modern studies, on the other hand, have emphasized the variety in the early Christian movement and concluded that orthodoxy was a later achievement, realized in the old catholic church that emerged from the second-century controversies with Gnosticism, Marcionism, and Montanism. It must be considered, however, that the establishment of creedal and institutional orthodoxy was possible in part because there was a core of common teachings and practices that went back to the early days of Christianity.

Everyone recognized the apostles and early disciples of Jesus as authoritative sources for his teachings. Hence, the dispute between what became the orthodox church and the heresies and schisms concerned what constituted apostolic faith and practice. The great church constructed a three-fold defense of its apostolicity. The important developments on these fronts occurred in the late second century, but the defenses were constructed out of materials already at hand in the church.

(1) What is the source of apostolic teaching? Where is it to be found? These questions raised the problem of the canon of scripture. Some aspects of this development were treated in Volume III. Marcion, by limiting the true teaching to his edition of Luke and the Pauline epistles, made acute the question of the exact limits of the canon. Other groups accepted only one Gospel, as some Jewish Christians in regard to Matthew. In other circles the authority of the writings of John was in dispute. These controversies illustrate the importance of defining the books where apostolic teaching was to be found. The orthodox canon was the result of insistence on the authority of books written by apostles or by early disciples active in their circles and circulated among the churches with their approval.

(2) What is the content of apostolic teaching? What is the standard of interpretation for what is written in the books accepted as authorita-

tive? Here we are brought to the formulation of the Rule of Faith (or Canon of Truth, as Irenaeus called it) and the Apostles' Creed. A summary content of the apostolic preaching became the rule by which the scriptures were to be interpreted. There were various wordings of the Rule of Faith, but it was essentially a summary of Christian affirmations about the nature of God, the facts of the career of Jesus, and the gift of the Holy Spirit and his work in the church. It served as a summary of the preaching, perhaps especially for the instruction of new converts.[1] This standard and not Gnostic mythology or some other teaching was the guide for the correct understanding of the scriptures. The Apostles' Creed, on the other hand, was the confession of faith made by new converts in connection with baptism. Since liturgical language tends toward uniformity, the creed did achieve rather early a virtual fixity of wording. In later legend it was said to have been actually composed by the apostles, but in origin it was intended as a summary of the faith taught by the apostles. The similarity of contents with the Rule of Faith is provided by the obvious connection between the faith preached and the faith believed.

(3) What is the channel of apostolic teaching? Where does one go to find the apostolic scriptures and their correct interpretation? The answer was that the right community was the church with its bishops and presbyters who held their position in succession from the apostles and who had continued the same teaching from apostolic times (see further Volume XIII). Apostolic succession, as presented by Irenaeus, became a powerful argument for the church as apostolic as opposed to the heresies and schisms that separated from it.

The great church, therefore, argued that it had an apostolic ministry, an apostolic faith or creed, and an apostolic canon of scriptures. Since canon and ministry are dealt with in other volumes in this series, the articles in this volume feature the other arguments used by the great church in its struggle with its opponents in order to achieve unity of belief: tradition, the Rule of Faith, and the Apostles' Creed.

It is generally agreed that catholic orthodoxy was well established by the end of the second century, and that the church of Rome occupied a place of central importance for the degree of doctrinal, organizational, and liturgical uniformity that was achieved. It seems appropriate, therefore, to open this volume with George LaPiana's article, which although now old, remains a classic treatment of the church at Rome at the end of the second century during the episcopate of Victor, whose efforts to achieve unity among the Christian communities in Rome brought it to leadership in the Christian world.

Then it seems appropriate to follow Volume III, which emphasized the place of the Bible in the church, with articles dealing with the norms of faith, including the Rule of Faith and the Apostles' Creed, which had a determinative role in how the Bible was understood and applied in the early church and whose normative character established catholic orthodoxy in its rivalry with various competing forms of the Christian message. Matching the institutional development was the recognition of norms of faith (see Mitros).

Other articles take up developments in regard to tradition.[2] Tradition was not used initially to refer to a different mode of transmission of apostolic teaching (oral, as opposed to written), but to refer to the fact of transmission (what was handed over). The apostolic teaching, both written and oral, was tradition, and the oral and written messages were two different modes of transmitting the same doctrine. Papias's preference for the "living voice" over written documents has often attracted attention of students of tradition in the early church. Walls argues that Papias meant no disparagement of apostolic writings (as in the later contrast between "scripture" and "tradition"), but had in mind non-apostolic or heretical writings. Papias appealed to the oral tradition in order to obtain proof of the genuineness of the contents of the books of scripture and to obtain interpretations of the meaning of these books. In fact, the very treatise from which the quotation about the "living voice" comes, *Exposition of the Oracles of the Lord*, instead of being a commentary on the oral gospel, may have been (according to a common usage of the word "oracles") a commentary on written documents.

In time, however, tradition came to be used for ecclesiastical customs and for teachings implicit but not explicit in scripture. The articles by R. P. C. Hanson, who wrote one of the major books on *Tradition in the Early Church*,[3] show the broadening of the concept of tradition. By the time of the Christological controversies of the fifth century, the ancient reliance on tradition was no longer sufficient.[4] Local traditions had fragmented the validity of the appeal to a uniform apostolic tradition.

The Rule of Faith (or of Truth) and the Apostles' Creed were part of tradition in the primary sense, or at least were efforts to summarize the tradition. Earlier studies often confused the *regula fidei* and the *symbolum apostolorum* because of their similar content. It now seems clear that they should be distinguished as to their function (as outlined above), and that this distinction explains why the former remained fluid in its terminology, whereas the latter had a certain fixity of wording from its beginning. Amundsen makes some important clarifications in the meaning of the terminology used by Irenaeus. Smulders elsewhere has summarized his argument that the Apostles' Creed from the beginning was a confession of faith.[5] The meaning of "symbol" is a "pact." Confessing the creed was entering into a covenant or pact with God and represented the identity of the person.[6]

Current scholarship is much occupied with the varied expressions given to the faith in the early centuries by those who professed to follow Jesus. Helmut Koester, from the standpoint of a New Testament scholar, has traced "trajectories" from the earliest disciples of Jesus through various early Christian documents to later movements.[7] His studies were prepared for by Walter Bauer, who advanced the view that heresy preceded orthodoxy, the latter resulting from reaction against heresy. That thesis has gained in popularity in recent years, in spite of important refutations of elements in Bauer's case.[8] Although the conclusions to be drawn from the phenomenon differ, the diversity in early Christianity is now an accepted axiom.

Attention is given in this volume to a sampling of expressions of Christian belief in the early centuries. Many others could be included. For instance, the origins of Docetism is a much discussed question.[9] Twentieth-century study of Marcion has been dominated by the work of Adolf von Harnack.[10] There are now efforts to break away from the hold Harnack's interpretation has had on interpretation, and May gives a good survey of the *status quaestionis*.

The major heresy confronting the church in the second century was Gnosticism. Its importance and the plethora of scholarly activities spurred by the new source material in the Nag Hammadi documents dictated that a separate volume (V) be devoted to this subject. One article here (Benoit) is devoted to Irenaeus, a crucial figure in the church's response to variant forms of Christianity. (The major Trinitarian and Christological controversies of the fourth and fifth centuries are also covered in a separate volume [IX]).

Much of the impetus for doctrinal development came from popular Christianity, not from the theologians. Carpenter's study of the third century shows this aspect. In addition to doctrinal differences, other factors—social, national, and personal—were at work in the early heresies and schisms, even as in the growth of orthodoxy. A. H. M. Jones argues, however, against the popular interpretation of the early heresies and schisms as merely disguised national or social movements. These factors must be considered and assessed in each instance of religious controversy and division. There were real doctrinal differences even where other considerations were present. No one factor explains every dispute.

Two schisms where social, cultural, and perhaps ethnic factors appear to have been significant were those involving Montanism in Asia Minor and Donatism in North Africa. Lawlor anticipated some recent studies in pointing out the error of assuming that Tertullian reflected original Phrygian Montanism.[11] On the distinctives of remarriage, fasting, and martyrdom, he seems to have been more rigorous and ascetic than the Phrygian Montanists, who were less ascetic than catholic Christians.[12] Even where disputes were sharp, there could be irenical aspects of the controversy.[13]

Notes

1. L. W. Countryman, "Tertullian and the Regula Fidei," *The Second Century* 2 (1982):208–227.

2. See Oscar Cullmann's article on "The Tradition," in A.J.B. Higgins, ed., *The Early Church: Studies in Early Christian History and Theology* (Philadelphia: Westminster Press, 1956): 59–99, reprinted in Volume III. For an Eastern Orthodox perspective on tradition see George Florovsky, "The Function of Tradition in the Ancient Church," *Greek Orthodox Theological Review* 9 (1963):181–200.

3. London: SCM, 1962.

4. See Robert Wilken, "Tradition, Exegesis, and the Christological Controversies," *Church History* 34 (1965):123–145, reprinted in Volume IX.

5. P. Smulders, "The *Sitz im Leben* of the Old Roman Creed," *Studia Patristica* 13 (1975):409–421.

6. H. Carpenter, "Creeds and Baptismal Rites in the First Four Centuries," *Studies in Early Christianity* Volume 11 (1993): 367–377.

7. James M. Robinson and Helmut Koester, *Trajectories through Early Christianity* (Philadelphia: Fortress, 1971); the article included in this volume is reprinted from this book (pp.114–157).

8. In addition to Norris, see H. E. W. Turner, *The Pattern of Christian Truth* (London: Mowbray, 1954); James F. McCue, "Orthodoxy and Heresy: Walter Bauer and the Valentinians," *Vigiliae Christianae* 33 (1979):118–130; G. Burke, "Walter Bauer and Celsus: The Shape of Late Second-Century Christianity," *The Second Century* 4 (1984):1–7; Tom Robinson, *The Bauer Thesis Examined: The Geog-*

raphy of Heresy in the Early Christian Church (New York: Edwin Mellen, 1988).

9. J. G. Davies, "The Origins of Docetism," *Studia Patristica* 6 (1962):13–35.

10. Now available in English: *Marcion: The Gospel of the Alien God* (Durham: Labyrinth, 1989).

11. For instance, William Tabbernee, "Early Montanism and Voluntary Martyrdom," *Colloquium* 17 (1985):33–43 and Ronald E. Heine, "The Role of the Gospel of John in the Montanist Controversy," *The Second Century* 6 (1987/88):1–19.

12. On women in Montanism see F. Klawiter, "The Role of Martyrdom and Persecution in Developing the Priestly Authority of Women in Early Christianity: A Case Study of Montanism," *Church History* 49 (1980):251–261, reprinted in Volume XIV.

13. J. Vodopivec, "Irenical Aspects of St. Augustine's Controversy with the Donatists," *Studia Patristica* 6 (1962):519–32.

THE ROMAN CHURCH AT THE END OF THE SECOND CENTURY

THE EPISCOPATE OF VICTOR, THE LATINIZATION OF THE ROMAN CHURCH, THE EASTER CONTROVERSY, CONSOLIDATION OF POWER AND DOCTRINAL DEVELOPMENT, THE CATACOMB OF CALLISTUS

GEORGE LA PIANA

HARVARD UNIVERSITY

DURING the latter part of the second century Irenaeus of Lyons, at the beginning of his treatise "Against All Heresies," did not hesitate to state with great emphasis that Christianity had fully succeeded in keeping intact the original Christian faith, in safeguarding the unbroken continuity of the apostolic tradition, and in maintaining the unity of belief and of sacramental practice throughout all the churches scattered in the Roman Empire.[1] One might easily remark that the very treatise which Irenaeus had set himself to write offered clear evidence that the Christian unity so emphatically affirmed by him did not really exist. Far from being united, Christianity was rent by serious doctrinal and disciplinary conflicts. Evidently Irenaeus was speaking of the oneness of the Christian faith without taking into account the divergent beliefs and practices of those groups which had been cut off from the communion of the Great Church. So understood his assumption was true: by the end of the second century the καθολικὴ ἐκκλησία did possess unity of essential belief and even a certain degree of uniformity in its organization and practice. How such a unity had been achieved

[1] Adv. Haer., i. 10, 2.

is one of the most important problems in the history of early Christianity.[2]

Christianity in its process of expansion appropriated from many environments and peoples a great variety of moral and doctrinal elements, of practices and popular traditions, of spiritual tendencies and religious experiences. Through this process of assimilation Christianity enriched its spiritual content and the church, which originally in the thought of its primitive members was but a temporary organization, a simple shelter for those who were to be saved in the imminent parousia, assumed gradually and consistently the character of a permanent organization. All kinds of doctrinal, religious, social, and political problems which in the beginning appeared of no importance to the Christians, and which could be overlooked or dealt with summarily, since all of them would be solved *en bloc* and forever by the parousia, began one by one to urge themselves upon the church and to come within its sphere of thought and influence.

These problems did not make their appearance abruptly or everywhere simultaneously among the Christian churches; they arose and found expression at different times and in different places, according to the local circumstances and to the

[2] B. H. Streeter, The Four Gospels, 1924, pp. 498 f., has called attention to the importance of this problem in connection with the diffusion and canonization of the books of the New Testament: "There is a problem in early Church history which few historians have frankly faced, and which those who have tried to date the books of the New Testament in an unreal abstraction from their environment in history have strangely felt themselves absolved from even raising. How are we to account for that broad general consensus on the main lines of belief and practice to be found, amid much local diversity, throughout the loose federation of communities known as the Catholic Church which appears all over the Roman Empire by the end of the second century?" After a long enumeration of the questions which agitated the Christian communities, and on which heresies and schisms arose, Streeter concludes: "It was the acceptance by the leading Churches at an early date of an authoritative Life of Christ, interpreted in the light of the great Epistles of Paul, that made it possible for some kind of unity in the direction of doctrinal development to be preserved." Undoubtedly it was so; it is obvious, however, that the common acceptance of a small body of authoritative literature, which was itself open to the most divergent interpretations, marks only the first step in circumscribing the tradition, and that it itself presupposes an instrument capable of using this tradition and fixing its interpretation for the purpose of securing the unity of doctrinal development. For such an instrument we must turn to the organization, since Christianity was from the beginning not a mere doctrine but also a church.

degree of intensity in the spiritual life of the various Christian communities. A different appreciation of the implications of the fundamental Christian beliefs provoked almost everywhere personal and group conflicts and awakened opposing tendencies and discordant traditions. Local and divergent solutions of the same problems whether of doctrine or of practice were adopted in various places in the name of the same Christian spirit and of the same apostolic tradition. On the other hand, the principle of the necessary unity of faith and practice was implicit in the Christian consciousness of possessing the sole and exclusive way of salvation. The need of uniform solutions was felt, and to satisfy this need an organization adequate to the task was gradually developed. It was through organization that Christianity saved the doctrinal tradition by creating in time a definite system of relations among the churches, which made it possible to achieve and to maintain for a long time a striking fundamental unity.

From the point of view of the study of this historical process, the history of the Church of Rome of the first three centuries has a unique importance. In that period, for many and various reasons, the Christian community of Rome was not only one of the largest, but also was highly representative of the various currents of thought, tradition, and practice of the whole Christian church. It is not an exaggeration to say that the Church of Rome became very early the great laboratory of Christian and ecclesiastical policy and that it contributed more than any other church to the practical solution of the most urgent problems and to the defeat of the internal forces which were leading Christianity to a complete disintegration.[3] The crucial period of the history of the Roman Church of preconstantinian times, the period which marks the culmination of its early development, is to be found in the years which run from the last quarter of the second century to the first decades of the

[3] I have outlined the main characteristics of the internal development of the Church of Rome in the early period, and the rise of the monarchical episcopate in that church, in three other publications (Il Problema della Chiesa Latina in Roma, Rome, 1922; La Successione episcopale in Roma e gli albori del Primato, Rome, 1922; 'La primitiva comunità cristiana di Roma e l'Epistola ai Romani,' Ricerche Religiose, Rome, May–July 1925), of which the present study is the continuation.

third. In this period the Church of Rome emerged from a long crisis to a new life, the most important and most significant features of which may be summarized as follows:

1. The monarchical form of the Roman episcopate overcame the last resistance of the local opposition, and at the same time a vigorous attempt was made to enforce within the Roman Christian community the principle of unity of faith and of doctrine and of uniformity in discipline and liturgical practices.

2. For the first time clear evidence appears that the Church of Rome did not hesitate to impose on other churches its own traditions, assuming thus the right to represent the genuine and authoritative tradition of Christianity.

3. The Church of Rome, in its determined effort to achieve internal unity and to gain cohesion, tried to overcome all kinds of divisive doctrinal and practical divergences by recourse not so much to theological debate and philosophical speculation as to disciplinary measures, which increased the power of its hierarchical organization and led gradually to the elimination of all groups and tendencies that could not be conquered or assimilated.

4. A general reconstruction of the system of ecclesiastical administration of the Roman Church took place in that period. Through favorable circumstances the Christian community as such acquired even the possession of cemeteries and meeting-places for the cult.

5. And finally, in this period the Church of Rome, which up to that time had the aspect of a community of Greek speech and traditions, gradually began to assume the character of a Latin church, different in many ways from the churches which had been established in the countries of the eastern Mediterranean basin.

The Latinization of the Roman Church is a fact of capital importance in the history of Christianity, and it is surprising that historians have paid little attention to the process out of which this church finally emerged as a Latin church.

, The last decades of the second century and the first years of the third are a turning-point in the history of Roman policy and institutions, just as they mark the beginning of a new period in the history of the Church of Rome.

The Antonine tradition, which through the system of adoption in the imperial succession had, at least in appearance, conciliated the seemingly irreconcilable principles of the *Romana libertas* and of the *imperium*, came to an end. Under the Severi the equestrian class and the provincial aristocracy were the object of great favors and acquired new distinction at the expense of the old Roman senatorial class. Many traditions which reserved to Romans or Italians the exclusive right to hold certain offices either in the army or in the administration were abolished; the provincials were gradually lifted to the level of the Romans and finally Roman citizenship was granted to all free men in the empire.[4]

The conception itself of the nature of the imperial authority began to undergo a gradual transformation, and the growth of the military and economic importance of the provinces and the realization of their vital function in the life of the empire fostered and made more requisite a new juridical development which aimed to stabilize the equilibrium of the Roman régime on a broader basis than the *jus* of the Quirites.[5] At the same

[4] To the old, but in many points still useful, book of Ceuleneer (Essai sur la vie et le règne de Septime Sévère, Bruxelles, 1880) have now been added the recent works of Platnauer (The Life and Reign of Septimius Severus, Oxford, 1918) and J. Hasabroek (Untersuchungen zur Geschichte des Kaisers Septimius Severus, Heidelberg, 1921), which reduce to more modest proportions the traditional opinion that Severus "was the principal author of the decline of the Roman Empire" (Gibbon, Decline and Fall, chap. v, at the end), and soften even the general assumption that Severus "planted the despotism of the East in the soil of the West" (Domaszewski, Gesch. d. röm. Reiches, II, p. 262). It is undeniable, however, that Septimius's reign marks a turning point in the history of the empire and of Roman institutions.

[5] On the transformation of the conception of the Imperium see the recent work of O. T. Schultz (Vom Prinzipat zum Dominatum. Das Wesen des römischen Kaisertums des dritten Jahrhunderts, Paderborn, 1919, pp. 21 ff.). The legislation of Severus is well analyzed by Ceuleneer (pp. 271–289) and by Platnauer (pp. 158–213). Platnauer remarks: "In general we notice the markedly milder character of the laws now framed; the growing feeling that human life is precious, as such, leads to a legislative humanitarianism, the more valuable in that it does not seem to degenerate into sentimentality" (p. 181). It is not surprising that the Roman juridical schools were willing to follow this new path. Roman jurisprudence ceased to be a closed field reserved to the followers of the narrow Quiritarian tradition. The new school which opposed the old-fashioned formalism could not ignore the new elements which had gained so much im-

5

time the tendency toward a more comprehensive religious syncretism increased in intensity, pervading even the fundamental political and religious conceptions of the Roman official cults, and the door was opened wide to the infiltration of new oriental and foreign traditions and practices which all worked together for the de-romanization of Rome and of Roman institutions.

A great factor in this process of transformation of the juridical, social, and religious life of the empire was the Roman population itself, a population cosmopolitan as well by origin as in character. All the provinces and all the cities were represented in Rome by immigrant groups and by their descendants, and all of them had imported and kept in Rome their traditions, their gods, their cults, and their associations. Even the Roman aristocracy had gradually filled its ranks with provincials who by the favor of the emperors had climbed up to the senatorial class, and through marriages and adoptions had often inherited the names and estates of the most famous ancient republican families, which for the most part had one after another come to an end.[6] The intense vital process of action and reaction between the capital and the provinces affected deeply the political, religious, and social life of Rome and of its cosmopolitan population.

Turning to the history of the Church of Rome during the same period the historian cannot fail to be impressed by the

portance in the social, economic, and political life of the empire. The period from Marcus Aurelius to the end of the Severan dynasty is the golden age of classical jurisprudence, and it is interesting to notice that many of the greatest jurists who most contributed to its development were men of provincial birth and of broad training. Such were Salvius Julianus, an African from Hadrumetum; Cervidius Scevola, a Greek; Aemilius Papinianus, probably an oriental related to Julia Domna; Domitius Ulpianus, who derived his origin from Tyre in Phoenicia; and, perhaps the greatest of all, Julius Paulus, who also is said to have been of Eastern origin.

[6] Nothing is more instructive as a sign of the gradual transformation of Roman institutions than to follow the history of the Roman senate and of its membership. To the well-known works of Bloch and Lécrivain (Bibliot. des Écoles Françaises d' Athène et de Rome, 39, 52) a guide of inestimable value for the first three centuries of the empire has been added by G. Lully (De Senatorum Romanorum Patria, Rome, 1918.) From Augustus to the Severi the number of provincial senators goes on increasing, and though the Italici formed always the largest group, most of the provinces were well represented (p. 251).

importance possessed also in the history of the Christian community by the same fact that the population of Rome, and therefore of the Christian community itself, comprised groups representing the various races and the various provinces of the empire. During the first two centuries the eastern element was preponderant, both in numbers and influence, in the Roman Christian community. Easterners had formed the bulk of the Roman Church from the beginning, and in the cosmopolitan environment of the capital Christianity had spread chiefly among that part of the population which by either birth or descent represented eastern races and traditions. At the same time the constant influx of eastern immigration continued to bring to Rome from the various Christian centres of the East individuals and groups which, while strengthening the ranks of the community, yet introduced into it the various peculiar practices and traditions developed by Christianity in the churches of Syria, Asia Minor, and Egypt. Very soon teachers of heresies and heads of schools representing special interpretations of the Christian tradition or new and striking messages to Christian spirituality flocked to Rome, with the result of introducing new divisions and provoking new conflicts.

About the end of the second century the Christian community of Rome was far from presenting the appearance of a strong organization destined to survive; on the contrary it seemed in process of complete disintegration. The main problem with which the Church of Rome was then confronted — a problem of the greatest importance on account of its far-reaching implications — was whether Christianity was to be a conglomeration of churches, schools, and sects, widely differing in doctrinal tenets and in liturgical practices but all coming under the general denomination of "the Christian Church," or whether it was to form a compact body of believers governed by the strict law of doctrinal unity and of practical uniformity. In other words the great problem of Christian unity came to be formulated in a striking way and to demand an immediate solution within the Christian community of Rome, which its narrow boundaries did not make less truly representative of the whole of Christianity.

The adoption of an inclusive policy of mutual toleration might not have appeared strange or impracticable to men living in an environment where syncretistic religious and philosophical views were predominant, and where the coëxistence and even the coördination of disparate religious conceptions seemed to satisfy both the masses and the thinkers in spite of all that could be and actually was illogical and inconsistent in such a situation. But on the other hand Christianity could not fail to apply to the dissidents within its own organization the same principle of intolerance and exclusion which it applied to all other religions. Its conception on the one hand,[7] inherited from Judaism, of a revealed religion and its sacramental doctrine and practice on the other, forbade Christianity to adopt the inconsistent and often merely external syncretism of the heathen religions.

Christianity was not only a religion of individual salvation through faith and sacraments. It had an ethical and spiritual content which in its realization could not fail to affect not merely the individual conscience but also the whole social and political life of human society. Christianity, therefore, had standards of belief and of conduct for the community, and as a consequence was bound to have an organization to formulate and to enforce these standards. Its claim to universality was more comprehensive and more real than that of the mystery-religions, which lacked an ethical teaching of their own, and which by virtue of their compromise with the exigencies of the religious-political principles of Rome could not, and did not, attempt to invade the special domain of the state religion. If Christianity had been a mere religion of individual salvation, nothing could have prevented its undergoing the same fate as the mystery-religions and being absorbed by the general syncretism of contemporary religious and philosophical thought. But Christianity was an organization, a Church, and the problem of its unity was identical with that of its uniqueness.

This problem of the unity of Christianity was thus by force of circumstances more urgently felt in Rome than elsewhere,

[7] G. F. Moore, 'The Rise of Normative Judaism,' *Harvard Theological Review*, 1925, pp. 27, 37 f.

and at the end of the second century had become the chief and vital problem of the Roman Church. The various shades of Christian thought and all the varieties of disciplinary and liturgical tradition which could be found in the various centres of Christian life were represented in Rome, and all of them were engaged in a deadly struggle to overcome one another and become the official doctrine or the official practice of the whole community. But the very fact of the variety and complexity of the principles involved in such a struggle obliged the Roman Church to turn for a solution not primarily to endless theological discussions and to philosophical elaborations, but rather to disciplinary measures. The problem of unity in Rome came to be considered primarily as a problem of organization; it was the simplest way, and the only practical one, of emergence from the impasse. Everything else came thus to be subordinated to the exigencies of the organization, and in the name of the rights of the organization all compromise with tendencies and doctrines which would have weakened its cohesion or diminished its sacramental power or attacked its hierarchical constitution was consistently refused.

But this situation, which at that period was responsible for all the troubles of the Roman Church, was also the instrumentality through which the path to leadership and supremacy was opened to the Roman community and to its bishops. The work of unification of the Christian church as a whole began within the circle of the Roman community, and it was energetically carried on and achieved there earlier than elsewhere, securing thus to the Roman Church an historical tradition to which appeal was made when the time came to claim universal validity for a new theological tradition of divine right to leadership and supremacy.

It has always been difficult to bring under one rule and to govern groups and bodies divergent in beliefs and practices when the governing power has no other resources than its own spiritual and moral authority. No wonder, therefore, that in the Roman community the monarchical form of the episcopate was somewhat slow in assuming a definite aspect and in becoming the primary factor of organization. The difficulties to be over-

9

come were greater than elsewhere; the struggle was harder and lasted longer.

The important Christian communities of the East, such as Antioch, Ephesus, Smyrna, and even Alexandria, appear to have reached a strong internal organization earlier than the community of Rome. The reason is obvious. In those centres, even in those which had a mixed population, gentile Christianity was represented by the local native element of the population. New-comers, either individuals or groups, were easily absorbed, or at least easily controlled, by the organization, which represented the authoritative local tradition of the Christian church. From the beginning the Christian communities of the East had more homogeneity in their membership and more unity in their organization than the Roman community. This and other reasons made possible in the East an early rise of the monarchical episcopate.

Moreover, in those centres hellenistic Christianity was at home; it had assumed the character of a local product, of a local elaboration, and could not be considered as a foreign importation. In Rome on the contrary, up to the middle of the second century, Christianity was still a foreign religion, and was so considered and dealt with by the government and by the Roman people. In a city which in spite of its cosmopolitan population and of the hellenistic and oriental infiltrations was still the representative of the Latin spirit and of the Latin traditions, Christianity was the religion of many groups of various foreign origins, using in their cult the Greek language and led by bishops who often were themselves of Eastern origin, or by teachers and theologians who had but recently come from Antioch, Asia Minor, or Egypt.

From the beginning hellenistic Christianity had laid stress upon both the doctrinal and the disciplinary factors of its religious life; teaching and organization went hand in hand as two inseparable parts of the same whole. But in spite of the emphasis put upon the organization, the hellenistic churches were soon affected by that peculiar hellenistic individualism which in the past had prevented the formation of a Greek empire from the city-states. They were also affected by the characteristic spiritual and intellectual curiosity of the race, so fond of analysis and of theories leading to discussion and disagreement, to quarrels and schisms. To an organization which claimed from the beginning a universal value, but which was still in the period of infancy and surrounded by mortal enemies, individualism and intellectual curiosity could not fail to become a serious danger. If Christianity had been left entirely under the control of the hellenistic spirit, it would undoubtedly have developed into numberless independent city-churches widely different in doctrinal tenets and in spiritual and religious content. In other words the hellenistic churches, in spite of the fact that each one of them had more internal homogeneity and a centralized government, would have been unable to solve the difficult problem of the juridical coördination of the churches, which alone could secure the unity of Christianity as a whole.

The struggle came first in Rome. There were heretics and dissidents in the Christian centres of the East, but on the one hand the existence of strongly centralized ecclesiastical governments in those communities made it more difficult for them to compete successfully with the traditional local authority; on the other hand the lure of Rome, and the knowledge of the great possibilities open there among the cosmopolitan population, were enough to persuade every leader of new movements, either doctrinal or practical, to move his headquarters to Rome and to make of the Roman community the chosen ground of active propaganda.

No doubt the governing body which in Rome represented the traditional authority did not remain altogether indifferent or passive to these invasions. But its power was questioned and its authority freely challenged by individuals and groups who claimed either a total or a partial autonomy, who urged for recognition, and when it was denied were ready to reject the claims of the bishop as the supreme head of the community. Moreover, this was not a meaningless conflict of idle thinkers or a sequel to the skirmishes of fanatical rhetoricians. It was, on the contrary, the crisis of growth of laborious Christian thought, which was trying to find its way in the task of absorbing all those elements of philosophical speculation which Christianity needed in order to present itself to the thinking classes as a consistent system of religious truth. At that stage, however, it was difficult to discern at the start all the possible implications of principles and theories; such a task could be accomplished only through a long period of development during which hesitations and mistakes were unavoidable. No wonder, therefore, that the policy of those who governed the Christian community of Rome during the first centuries was often uncertain and included hesitations and revisions. It was possible in Rome for schools and groups to prosper and to spread their peculiar doctrines almost unhindered by the representatives of the traditional authority to whom fell the enormous task of guiding, supervising, and controlling the vital and spontaneous outburst of intellectual elaboration of Christian beliefs into a Christian doctrine.

In spite of the difficulties and of the unavoidable hesitations, the process of eliminating doctrines which were essentially repugnant to the fundamental premises of the Christian system of salvation, and which were obviously in contrast with the teaching of the accepted body of apostolic literature, had to a certain extent been carried on in the Roman community. It had contributed to the formulation of a Symbol of faith which in its original simplicity sufficed to attain a certain fundamental unity of belief among those who were admitted to the baptismal initiation.[3] The two extreme groups which during the

[3] McGiffert, The Apostles' Creed, New York, 1905, has endeavored to prove that "the Old Roman Symbol arose as a protest against error" (p. 12), "and not as a positive statement of the Christian faith framed quite independently of existing errors and with a primarily evangelistic or missionary purpose" (p. 12, against the theory of Harnack and Kattenbusch). The evidence for his theory given by McGiffert (pp. 106–174) is very remarkable and for several points quite conclusive. There is no doubt that the inclusion of or the emphasis upon some of the articles of the symbol must have been suggested by reaction against heretical Marcionite teaching, but it does not seem entirely safe to conclude that the symbol was a mere protest and not a positive statement of the essentials of the Christian faith of the time, merely because certain omissions make it appear inadequate to supply a complete standard of orthodoxy. If the symbol was formulated not long after the middle of the second century, as McGiffert holds, it may be said that it contained everything which at that stage of doctrinal elaboration could be considered essential to the Christian profession of faith. To be sure, the Roman presbyters of the second century must have been aware that their creed was far from being an exhaustive summary of their beliefs, and have supplemented its deficiencies in their catechetical instruction; but it would be difficult to prove that in their apprehension the creed did not contain the essential points acceptance of which made

last decades of the second century stood as the great rivals of the traditional Roman Church, the Gnostics and the Marcionites, had been cut off from the communion of the Great Church. Their influence, however, was very strong, and their teaching appealed to people of culture and of vivid imagination. But besides these extreme formulations, there were to be found within the Roman community many teachers and groups who gave peculiar interpretations to one point or another of the common beliefs, or who denied one or another of the common traditions; upon these it was more difficult to pass judgment, but they all provoked discussions and animosities, bred divisions and conflicts, and so kept the whole community in a turmoil.

In addition there were groups not characterized by doctrinal divergences but by different traditions in matter of discipline and of liturgical practice. Such was for instance the group of the Asiatics and their followers who observed fast-days and celebrated Easter on a different date from the rest of the community.[9] The situation confronting a Roman bishop during the second half of the second century was a very serious one. Powerful groups which called themselves Christian, such as the Marcionites, were assuming the form of independent churches with their own ritual and their own hierarchy; other groups formed schools or didaskaleioi which attracted people of culture and claimed also alone to possess the Christian

a man a Christian, namely, God the Father and Creator; Jesus the Son of God; Jesus the man who really lived on earth and suffered death; Jesus the judge to come; the Spirit; and the resurrection of the flesh. That "Christ had brought a knowledge of God's will and truth, that he was the Saviour and that he had died for our sins or for us" (p. 121) were in a general way beliefs implicitly contained in the notions of Jesus as *God, Man,* and *Judge.* To describe these truths more explicitly would have required a theological formulation for which the time was not yet ripe. As De Faye remarks, "Les chrétiens [of the second century] ont des croyances bien arrêtées, mais ces croyances ne sont pas encore cristallisées en formules claires et précises. Ainsi ils sont tous monothéistes. Ils déclarent que le plus grand bienfait que leur a procuré la foi au Christ, c'est de savoir enfin qu'il n'y a qu'un seul Dieu, Créateur du ciel et de la terre. Ne leur demandez pas à ces chrétiens des précisions sur la nature du Christ ou sur son oeuvre rédemptrice" (Origène, I. Sa biographie et ses écrits, Paris, 1923, p. v).

⁹ The Easter controversy of the second century has been often discussed since the 18th century. See the bibliography up to 1906 in Hefele-Leclercq, Histoire des Conciles, I, p. 133, n. 1, and for the most recent publications, Krüger, *Harvard Theological Review,* January, 1921, pp. 348–349.

truth.[10] Within his own community, the bishop was hindered by doctrinal divergences, by conflicting liturgical practices, by personal rivalries and ambitions ready at any moment to give rise to new schism and to new independent groups. And beyond all this, was the hatred of the populace, the contempt of the learned classes, and the open persecution by the government.

Bishop Anicetus (154–166/7), who was a Syrian by origin and who may have been influenced by the strictly monarchical traditions of the episcopate of Antioch, tried to curb some of the groups and made an effort to introduce uniformity of liturgical practice. He called upon the Asiatic group of the Roman community to abandon their peculiar custom of fasting and of celebrating Easter on a different date. His demand was met with a refusal, and the Asiatics appealed for support to the churches of Asia Minor whose tradition they were following. The venerable bishop of Smyrna, Polycarp, according to the narrative of Irenaeus,

> went to Rome; there were between him and Anicetus other minor divergencies which were easily settled; but on this point they did not come to a breach. Anicetus could not persuade Polycarp . . . and Polycarp could not persuade Anicetus. . . . They remained in peace, and in the church Anicetus out of deference permitted Polycarp to celebrate the eucharist.

In other words, Anicetus gave up his attempt to impose the Roman custom on the Asiatics of his church.

The importance of this episode as described by Irenaeus and its far-reaching implications seem to me not to have been fully realized by historians, who have paid little attention to the presence of an Asiatic group in Rome and have considered this controversy as a direct quarrel between the bishop of Rome and the bishop of Smyrna. The following passage of Irenaeus,

[10] De Fàye (Origène, p. iv,) affirms that "jusqu'à la fin du IIe siècle la plus part des écoles gnostiques font encore partie de l'Église." This assumption is rather misleading, since at that time the Gnostic groups already formed separate bodies with their own ritual practices, and as such they were not part of the church, that is to say of the organization, though they still assumed to be within the circle of Christianity. It is true, however, that Gnosticism as a religion separated from Christianity only in the third century. See also E. Buonaiuti, Gnostic Fragments, 1924, pp. 1–4.

quoted by Eusebius, implies the existence of such a group in the Roman community:

> The presbyters before Soter who presided over the church which thou governest today, we mean Anicetus, Pius, Hyginus, Telesphorus, Xystus, neither kept [the Asiatic custom] themselves nor imposed [it] on those with them. Nevertheless, not observing [it] themselves, they maintained peace with those who came to them from the communities which observed [it]. But to observe [it] was more in contrast with those who did not observe [it]. None, however, was ever cast out on account of this peculiarity, but the presbyters before thee, though they did not observe [it], sent the eucharist to those from the communities who observed [it].[11]

It is obvious that in this passage of his letter to bishop Victor, Irenaeus wished to emphasize the tolerant attitude of his predecessors, who did not themselves observe the Asiatic custom but did not prevent others from doing so.[12]

Who were these other Christians whom the Roman bishops allowed to follow the Asiatic custom? "Those who came to Rome from the communities where that peculiar tradition was followed." The common interpretation given to these words of Irenaeus assumes that they were casual visitors from the churches of Asia Minor. But under that view the significant remark made by Irenaeus that "to observe the Asiatic custom was more in contrast with those who did not observe it," that is to say, that the different observance in the same place made the contrast more striking, would remain without justification. A casual visitor, or even a group of visitors, coming to Rome for a short time during the Easter celebration, could not be the cause of surprise and resentment in the Roman community, unless we also suppose that these groups of visitors were so large that, being accompanied by presbyters of their

[11] H. E., v. 24, 14.

[12] οὔτε αὐτοὶ ἐτήρησαν οὔτε τοῖς μετ' αὐτῶν ἐπέτρεπον, καὶ οὐδὲν ἔλαττον αὐτοὶ μὴ τηροῦντες εἰρήνευον τοῖς ἀπὸ τῶν παροικιῶν ἐν αἷς ἐτηρεῖτο, ἐρχομένοις πρὸς αὐτοὺς · καίτοι μᾶλλον ἐναντίον ἦν τὸ τηρεῖν τοῖς μὴ τηροῦσιν. καὶ οὐδέκοτε διὰ τὸ εἶδος τοῦτο ἀπεβλήθη ὁν τινες, ἀλλ' αὐτοὶ μὴ τηροῦντες οἱ πρὸ σοῦ πρεσβύτεροι τοῖς ἀπὸ τῶν παροικιῶν τηροῦσιν ἔπεμπον εὐχαρηστίαν. The first sentence leaves room for ambiguity. A different translation is offered: 'They did not observe it themselves and did not permit [to do so] those who were with them.' This seems to me unacceptable because it would mean that the Roman bishops did not allow any Christian in Rome to follow the Asiatic custom, while Irenaeus wishes to emphasize the opposite, namely, that they did permit this procedure.

own, they could hold a celebration apart. In other words, we must suppose a regular pilgrimage to Rome such as we may find today. Moreover, to satisfy this interpretation, these visits of large groups of Asiatics at Easter-tide must have been regularly repeated for half a century, since in this connection Irenaeus mentions all the bishops from Anicetus to Soter as having all kept peace with the supposed visitors. All this is obviously absurd.

But a clear confirmation of my assumption that the Asiatics were not casual visitors but a large group settled in Rome, probably in the early second century, may be found in the last sentence of the passage quoted above: "the presbyters before thee, though not observing the Asiatic custom, sent the eucharist to those from the communities who observed it." These words have puzzled all the commentators. The ancient interpretation that "the presbyters of Rome sent the eucharist to other parishes where the paschal festival was observed on the fourteenth of the month," may be summarily dismissed: there is no mention of such a custom and there were no Christian communities near Rome observing the Asiatic custom to whom the eucharist could be sent.[13] It remains to understand that the eucharist was sent to the supposed casual visitors. But, as McGiffert remarks, "it is difficult to understand why Irenaeus should speak of sending the eucharist to persons who observed the fourteenth, instead of merely mentioning the fact that the Roman Church communed with them. In the face of the difficulties on both sides it must be admitted that neither of the interpretations mentioned can be insisted upon."[14] Quite right; but all difficulty disappears if we admit that the eucharist was sent not to individual casual visitors but to a group of Asiatics settled in Rome who held the custom of their churches of origin, and who therefore had their liturgical celebration apart

[13] Valesius, quoted by McGiffert in his translation of Eusebius. McGiffert remarks: "It must be said that, so far as we are able to ascertain, only the Churches of Asia observed the fourteenth day at that early date, and it is difficult to imagine that the presbyters of Rome had been in the habit of sending the eucharist all the way from Rome to Asia Minor."

[14] Ibid., p. 244, n. 20.

on a different date from the rest. We know that it was an ancient custom in the Church of Rome that the bishop sent a fragment of the eucharistic bread consecrated by him to the presbyters who presided over the meetings in the various districts of the city. Of such a custom we have abundant evidence in the following centuries; it was the rite of the *fermentum* sent from the episcopal mass to the presbyters of the *tituli* to be mixed for their own consecration.[15]

This ancient custom might well have been established during the second century, and this passage of Irenaeus so interpreted would then be the oldest witness to its existence in the Church of Rome. This rite of the *fermentum*, according to the classical interpretation that obtained to the end, "was a symbol of the unity of the community and of the subordination of the presbyters to the bishop, *ut se a nostra communione separatos non judicent*." It must have been established in a period when it was necessary in the Roman Church to have an external sign of this unity, that is to say in a period in which the existence of so many groups claiming independence from the bishop could mislead simple believers and foster the ambitions of unscrupulous presbyters. The second half of the second century was exactly a time in which such a measure was most needed. When the monarchical rights of the bishop were challenged by the reluctant groups, the sending of the *fermentum* was, as it were, the sacramental expression of the unity of the community and of the subjection of all the groups to the bishop. That the eucharist was chosen for this purpose was in harmony with the Christian tradition as formulated by Ignatius: "Be careful to

---

[15] In the Liber Pontificalis it is said that Pope Melchiades "fecit ut oblationes consecratae per ecclesias ex consecratu episcopi dirigerentur, quod declaratur fermentum" (ed. Duchesne, I, p. 169). Pope Siricius (384–399) made this rule more specific (ibid., I, p. 216). The last mention of the fermentum is in the Epistle of Innocent I (401–417) to the bishop of Gubbio: "De fermento vero, quod die dominica per titulos mittimus, superflue nos consulere voluistis, cum omnes ecclesiae nostrae intra civitatem sint constitutae, quarum presbyteri, quia die ipsa propter plebem sibi creditam nobiscum convenire non possunt, idcirco fermentum a nobis confectum per acolytos accipiunt, ut se a nostra communione, maxime illa die, separatos non judicent" (Migne, Patr. Lat. XX, col. 556). Note the last sentence. On the 'fermentum' see Cabrol et Leclercq, Dictionnaire d'Archéologie chrétienne et de Liturgie, V, col. 1371.

use one eucharist, for there is one flesh of our Lord Jesus Christ, and one cup for union with his blood, one altar, as there is one bishop with the presbyters." [16]

But that the Asiatics in Rome were not casual visitors but formed a group within the Christian community is evident also from other sources than the narrative of Eusebius and the letter of Irenaeus to Victor. Eusebius mentions that in Victor's time a certain Blastus, a presbyter of the church, became the leader of a schismatic group in Rome and that against him the same Irenaeus wrote an epistle. But Eusebius does not specify the reason of Blastus's schism. Fortunately this is mentioned in another document, Pseudo-Tertullian, *Adversus omnes haereses*. This is found appended to Tertullian's treatise *De praescriptione*, and might be the so-called "Syntagma" of Hippolytus, or a summary of it. There we read that Blastus "wished to introduce Judaism in disguise; for he said that Easter ought not to be observed otherwise than according to the law of Moses on the fourteenth of the month." [17] These words dispel all doubt: the Asiatic group of Rome kept its peculiar tradition, and was tolerated by the Roman bishops who sent the eucharist to the Asiatic presbyters as they did to all other groups of the community; but Victor refused to follow his predecessors' example, and the Asiatics separated from his obedience and formed an independent church with Blastus as their bishop. This fully explains why Irenaeus not merely says that the Roman Church formerly communed with those who had come from the communities where the custom of the fourteenth was

[16] Philadel. 4. There are good reasons for thinking that the fermentum was established much earlier than the times of Melchiades. The duty to carry the eucharist was entrusted to the acolyti, who seem to have been a peculiar Roman institution for the purpose of taking the eucharist to those who were absent and, we add also, to the presbyters who presided at the various liturgical meetings of the scattered community. The institution of the acolyti belongs very likely to the second century, since about the middle of the third century they already formed a large body of minor officers in the Western Church. It has been surmised that the puzzling sentence in Victor's biography in the Liber Pontificalis: "Hic fecit sequentes cleros," followed by no other indication, might refer to the institution of the acolytes. Harnack concludes his remarks on this point: "So mag auch die Nachricht, dass unter Viktor die Akoluthen zuerst aufgetaucht sind, auf guter Überlieferung beruhen" (Die Mission, 4 ed. 1924, p. 863, note).

[17] Ed. Kroymann, CSEL. XXVII, 1906, p. 225.

18

observed, but mentions explicitly the fact that the bishop of Rome customarily sent the eucharist to their liturgical meetings.

The truth is, therefore, that the question of the Easter celebration was an internal problem of the Church of Rome. In the controversy between Polycarp and Anicetus it was not that the bishop of Rome assumed the right to interfere with matters affecting merely the churches of Asia; on the contrary it was Polycarp who, in order to defend the Asiatic tradition wherever it was observed, interfered with the government of the Roman Church and with the ordinances of its bishop.[18] If the Asiatic custom had not been habitually observed in Rome by a fraction of the local Christian community, there would have been no quarrel. Rome's own problems were too urgent for it to think of provoking the churches of Asia on this point of minor importance, if the liturgical divergence did not affect directly the Roman community. It was precisely the fact remarked by Irenaeus, that such a divergence was to be found within the narrow circle of the same church, that made it a serious question. Anicetus was right in attempting to introduce uniformity, for in a church rent by dissensions, and in which the rights of the monarchical episcopal power were daily challenged by obstinate opposition, a divergence of that kind

[18] The visit of Polycarp took place about the end of the year 154 or at the beginning of 155, a few months after the election of Anicetus and when Polycarp was more than eighty years old. There is no mention that Anicetus had summoned the churches of Asia to abandon their tradition: it would be very surprising if such a thing had happened at that time. The most natural explanation is that the Asiatics of Rome, to whom Anicetus's command had been given to desist from their Easter celebration on a different date, appealed to Polycarp, who was not only the bishop of one of the most important churches of their land of origin, but was also the oldest living representative of the apostolic tradition of the Asiatic churches. Polycarp thus came to Rome not to plead the cause of the Asiatic churches, whose tradition was not directly attacked, but on behalf of the Roman group, which was an offspring of the Asiatic churches, and whose condemnation would have affected indirectly the Asiatic tradition as a whole. It is not difficult to realize that in a period in which the system of relation between churches was based solely on the spirit of mutual love and had no juridical form, a bishop like Polycarp felt a sense of responsibility for the groups of his own people to be found in other communities than his own. If the right of interference in such cases had been recognized, it would have had far-reaching consequences. Anicetus's deferential attitude toward Polycarp formed a dangerous precedent, which, as we shall see, was effectively overcome by the different and energetic policy of Victor.

had become almost the symbol and tangible sign of the autonomy of a group, and gave to the presbyters who directed the group the character of independent and authoritative representatives of a tradition which was not the tradition of the Roman Church. The monarchical episcopate could not prevail in Rome unless the groups were abolished, and they could not be abolished unless the characteristics which secured their individuality were absorbed and lost in the law of uniformity.

But the coming of Polycarp to Rome led Anicetus to realize the serious implications of the step he was about to take. If the Asiatic custom was truly of apostolic origin, how could he forbid it in Rome? And if he forbade its observance in Rome, what about the churches of Asia? Could the same tradition be venerated in Asia and anathema in Rome? Anicetus recognized that while the question was an internal problem of the Roman Church, it was at the same time one which affected the church at large and could not be solved without a due consideration of the traditions and the feelings of other churches. And he did not dare to forbid the Asiatic custom, although it cost him the failure to enforce the law of the monarchical episcopate in his own community. This instance, of which we happen to know the details, is typical of the general situation; undoubtedly in many other cases of doctrinal or practical divergence the bishops of Rome found themselves confronted with similar alternatives. But their hesitations, though justified, were nevertheless gradually leading to the complete disintegration of the community. A reaction against this policy must soon have arisen in certain circles of the Roman Church; in a definite form it made its appearance in the last decades of the second century.

This reaction emerges to the light of history for the first time with a bishop of undoubted Latin stock and of Latin speech and training, Victor, a native of Roman Africa. It was at first merely a reaction against the local anarchy in the church, an attempt to impose a definite disciplinary rule and to enforce the rights of the hierarchy. Later, especially under Victor's successors Zephyrinus and Callistus, it assumed more openly the character of a strong reaction against what we should call the intellectualism of the learned groups of Eastern theologians and their philosophizing disciples. With Victor, who seems to have been himself a learned man, it was primarily a question of the rights of the monarchical bishop against the groups which claimed independence and autonomy while remaining in the membership of the church.

This reaction against the individualism of hellenistic Christianity, while it claimed to remain faithful to the doctrinal tradition, did not deny the validity of an intellectual elaboration, and at the same time, in the name of the disciplinary tradition, aimed at a further development of the local hierarchical system of church government and administration. It was Montanism that, claiming to represent a return to the original prophetic inspiration of early Christianity, implied a radical denial of both the legitimacy of the hierarchical system and the intellectualism of the theologians. The Roman Church under Victor advocated only the right to interpret tradition in the light of the practical needs and circumstances of the local Christian community.

Theology was not banished, but the principle was implicitly emphasized that Christianity was primarily not a theology but a saving faith and a Church in which unity and uniformity were necessary in order that it should be truly a universal instrument of salvation. In other words the aim was to check the development of opposing traditions of practice and also of unbridled theological passions by strengthening the hierarchical principle of government and by subordinating intellectual curiosity to the vital interests of the organization. On the one hand it was a return to the simple fundamental conception of Christianity as a way of salvation through faith and sacraments, but on the other it was a further step in the development of ecclesiastical polity by the adoption of the principle that the rights of the organization were above all local and group traditions, no matter how old and how sacred they might be.

Bishop Victor, with whom this program of government began to assume a concrete form, was undoubtedly a strong personality. His election to the episcopate, however, in a church which up to that time had been under the control of the hellenistic element of the community, suggests something more than mere chance or personal influence. It implies the presence in the community of a Latin group strong enough to hold the balance of power in the choice of the bishop. After all, by far the largest part of the Roman Christians were poor people of the humbler classes, little concerned with theological questions or with elaborate philosophical explanations of their simple faith. They looked upon the church as an instrument of salvation, a religious and social organization with practical purposes and with a definite program of spiritual and moral activities. They could see without difficulty that lack of unity in the church was the cause of many evils. It must have greatly affected even the charitable activities of the church and the work of assistance which had such vital importance in the life of the Christian community. The interests of the simple believers thus coincided with the interests of the monarchical episcopate, and their alliance was a decisive factor towards the solution of the crisis.

It is likely that Christianity early gained followers among the native population of Rome, but evidently for a long time they were too few to be of importance in the community. As early as the Flavian dynasty there is evidence that even certain members of the high Roman aristocracy embraced the Christian faith, and many more converts bearing famous names joined the church during the second century. But these were persons of culture; it was probably due to their hellenistic training that they had come to feel the value of Christianity, and they would find no difficulty in adapting themselves to the hellenistic character and traditions of the Roman Church. Undoubtedly the small Latin group must have grown; they must have had their special meetings for instruction and for liturgical celebrations in Latin. Passages from the Old and New Testament, with psalms, hymns, and prayers translated into Latin, must have been available for them and for the Christian propaganda among the Latin population of Rome.

About the middle of the second century the Latin group, belonging mostly to the poor and uneducated classes, already formed a considerable part of the Christian community. At least the Marcionites of Rome must have deemed the Latins an important element in the church, since pains were taken to translate into Latin the Marcionite Bible. Whether this was the first Latin translation of the sacred books, and whether and to what extent this translation affected the other Latin translations used in the West from the third century on, is a matter largely of conjecture. But the fact itself that such a translation was made in Rome shortly after the middle of the second century, shows that in their work of propaganda the Marcionites laid great weight on the conquest of the Latin element of the Roman population, as if they had surmised that the destiny of Roman Christianity was dependent upon the Latin race.[19]

We do not know how successful this propaganda was, but it must have been efficient enough to awaken the presbyters of the Roman Church to the necessity of counteracting the Marcionite missionary work among the Latins and thus led them to give more importance to the Latin element in the Christian community. Now there are good reasons to think that this Latin group of the Roman Church consisted not only of natives, but also, and probably in a larger measure, of African immigrants or of the descendants of African stock settled in Rome. Historians have neglected this fact, which seems to me of great importance, and yet the history of Rome at the end of the second century affords plenty of evidence that in that period the Africans played a part of primary importance in Roman

[19] A. Harnack, Marcion: Das Evangelium vom frenden Gott. Eine Monographie zur Geschichte der Grundlegung der katholischen Kirche (T. U. XLV), Leipzig, 1921. The evidence that the Marcionites had a Latin translation of their Bible is conclusive (pp. 47–54). It is derived from the passages quoted by Tertullian (Adv. Marcionem), which, as Harnack shows, were not Tertullian's own translations from the Greek Marcionite Bible, but were taken from an existing Marcionite Latin text. The fragments of this Marcionite Latin Bible and a comparison of them with the fragments of the Latin Bible of Novatian may be found in the recent book of A. D'Alès, Novatien, Étude sur la Théologie Romaine au milieu du III° siècle, Paris, 1925, pp. 79–82. This translation was probably made shortly after the middle of the second century, since, as D'Alès remarks, "la propagande marcionite battait son plain vers l'an 150 et il se pourrait que la Bible latine de Marcion ait été des lors creée à Rome comme instrument de cette propagande (idée lancée par Lietzmann, Der Römerbrief, p. 14, 15, 1919)" (p. 78 and note 1).

politics and also, it would seem, in the life of the Christian community.

The fact that in the year 193, when Septimius Severus, born of an equestrian family at Leptis in Roman Africa, was recognized as emperor, the Christian community of Rome was also governed by a bishop who was a native of the same Roman Africa, is highly suggestive. Needless to say, there is no direct connection between the two facts, but they bear witness to the importance then acquired by the African element in the life of the capital, and both facts affected more than is commonly recognized the future destinies of empire and of church.

Provincial emperors were not a new sight in Rome. Under the adoptive system Trajan and Marcus Aurelius, both from the Spanish province, as well as Antoninus himself, born at Lanuvium but of provincial stock, held the imperial authority with such success that their period marks the furthest point of Roman expansion. But in spite of their provincial origin the Antonines had assumed to represent the purest Roman political tradition. Under the new African emperor, on the contrary, the military monarchy overcame the last resistance offered by the ancient institutions.[19a]

It was not a mere chance that a provincial from an equestrian family of Roman Africa became emperor. Severus was not the first African to reach a prominent position in Rome. In the province conquered after a long and bloody struggle Roman colonization had created on the ruins of ancient Carthage a new centre of Latin spirit and Latin traditions. To be sure, the native Berbers were never truly romanized; a small number of them dwelling in the cities and in the Roman settlements were absorbed by the dominant element of the population, but the great bulk of Berbers, grouped in the mountains, preserved their laws, their customs, their religious traditions, and were very

[19a] Severus appears to have been very anxious to connect his family with the dynastic tradition of the Antonini. He assumed the titles: Divi Antonini Germanici Filius; Divi Pii Anton. Nepos; Divi Hadriani Pronepos; Divi Traiani Abnepos; Divi Nervae Adnepos. But this ideal dynastic connection, significant as it is, does not change the fact that his policy was a breach in the Antonine political tradition. On the significance of this attempt of Severus see Costa, Religione e politica nell'Impero Romano, Torino, 1923, pp. 11, 17ff.

little affected by Roman civilization. When therefore we speak of the Africans who represented the political and cultural life of that province, we must not forget that we are dealing with a population mostly of Roman descent, mixed in various degrees with the Punic element and affected by Punic institutions, especially those of a religious nature, but with only a slight infusion of Berber blood.

At the end of the second century there was in Rome a large African colony. Aside from the slaves and prisoners of war (mostly Berbers and Moors or members of other tribes which kept on attacking the Roman military posts even after the pacification of the province) and from the descendants of the prisoners of the Punic wars, the great majority of African immigrants in Rome either could trace their descent directly from Roman families or from officers and soldiers of the Roman army or were of Punic descent with admixture of Roman blood. Unlike all other foreigners they must have felt at home in the capital, since by language and family traditions they were not very different from the Romans of purely native descent.

Their feelings must have been much like those of the modern descendant of an English settler in Australia or Canada who establishes his residence in London. But in spite of this affinity, or perhaps on account of it, the Romans seem to have liked the African immigrants no better than those of other races. In high society they were considered intruders and made few friends. Among the common people the traditional characterization of the Africans as a treacherous race, unreliable, given to superstitious practices, a tradition which went back to the Punic wars and was probably strengthened during the war against Jugurtha, was very much alive and deeply rooted in the general consciousness. Evidently the Romans were bent on overlooking the blood-connection which linked the new African population to Rome, and ever saw in the African immigrants simply the descendants of the ancient Punic warriors who barely failed to conquer Rome.[20]

[20] The great African teacher of rhetoric, Cornelius Fronto, after having passed the greater part of his life in Rome and having received all the honors that a Roman could desire, including the consulate, complains in his letters that he had never found among

The presence in Rome of so many slaves of Punic descent and of the Berber race must have contributed not a little to the crystallization of public opinion as to the bad character of the Africans. In Rome they were crowded into the region between the Coelium and the Aventine next to the Subura, and the names of several vici of that district recall the African origin of the inhabitants.[21] The very fact that many Roman aristocratic families possessed large estates in the African province, and the close commercial and political relations of the capital with the chief source of the city's food-supply, accounts for the presence in Rome of a large group of immigrants from African cities and towns.[22] The service of the *annona*, especially after its reorganization by Commodus, contributed largely in bringing to

the Romans any sincere and warm friendship. "Simplicity, continence, truthfulness, honor are Roman virtues, but warmth of affection is not Roman, for there is nothing which, my whole life through, I have seen less of at Rome than a man unfeignedly φιλόστοργον. The reason why there is not even a word in our language for this virtue must, I imagine, be that in reality no one in Rome has any warm affection" (ad Verum, ii, 7, Loeb Class. Libr. II, p. 154). For the general opinion of the Romans about the Africans see a letter of Marcus Aurelius commending Ceionius Albinus from Hadrumetum, later a competitor of Severus for the empire, in which it is said: "Albino ex familia Ceionorum, Afro quidem homini sed non multa ex Afris habenti, duas cohortes alares regendas dedi." It was a title of honor to have little of the African character even in the eyes of a philosopher like Marcus Aurelius (Julii Capitolini, Clodius Albinus, p. x).

21 Through that district ran the famous Vicus Capitis Africae, where stood the well-known Paedagogium Caesaris, and also other vici whose names have a distinct African flavor, such as Vicus Stabuli Proconsulis, Vicus Syrtis, Vicus Byzacenus, and Vicus Capsensis. This list of names of Roman vici is found in the curious document known as the 'Appendix Probi', which has been often reprinted (Altfranzösische Übungsbuch von W. Foerster und E. Koschwitz, 3d. ed., 1907, pp. 226–234). It has been a subject of much discussion whether this list of vici was made in Carthage and is to be referred to a district of Carthage (G. Paris, Mélange Renier, 1867; Mélange Boissier, 1903, pp. 5–9; Sittl, 'Die Heimat d. Appendix Probi,' in Archiv f. latein. Lexicogr., 1889, p. 557) or, as is more commonly held, was made in a Roman school and refers to a Roman district (Ullman, Roman. Forsch., VII, 1891, p. 145; Foerster l. c.; Schanz, Gesch. d. Röm. Litt., III, 2, p. 444, 2d ed., 1913). The document is commonly assigned to the third century. The evidence, historical and archaeological, for the existence of the Vicus Capitis Africae in Rome between the Coelium and the Aventine is undeniable (C. Gatti, 'Del Caput Africae nella seconda regione di Roma', in Annali dell' Istituto di corr. arch., Rome, 1882, pp. 191–220).

22 On the possessions of Roman families in Africa see the remarkable work of J. Mesnage, L'Évangélisation de l'Afrique, Part que certaines familles Romano-Africaines y ont prise, Paris, 1914.

Rome African settlers or sojourners such as, for instance, the mariners of the annonarian navy, who during the winter lived in Ostia and Rome waiting for the reopening of the traffic in the spring. The surprising number of *stationes naviculariorum* for African sailors found in Ostia, is witness of the numbers and importance of this part of the African population in or near the capital.[23]

But the most remarkable and interesting group of African immigrants was that of professional men and of members of wealthy families. For the scions of the African aristocratic families, who so often traced back their origin to famous Roman names, Rome was the place of higher education and of training for a public career. The African branches of the Caecilii, the Caeionii, the Valerii, and as well the sons of wealthy families of African origin, following their example, could not consider an education completed without an experience of life in the capital. Still more urgent must have been the call of Rome to those who cherished political ambitions, not restricted to the provincial *cursus honorum*, but with a broader outlook on the empire at large. From the beginning of the second century the influence of the Africans in the public life of Rome began to grow, and later under the Antonines it received a great impulse. Numbers of Africans are then found holding prominent positions in the army and magistracies and in the literary circles of the capital. Under Trajan we find no less than five Africans sitting in the Roman Senate, and the number increased to eleven under Antoninus Pius.[24] From the letters of Fronto, an African native of Cirta, the greatest rhetorician of his time and the teacher of Marcus Aurelius, we learn that both in the Curia and in the Palace many Africans, especially natives of Cirta, occupied positions of importance.[25] But the summit of African influence was reached under Severus, and it is remarkable that one of the competitors of Severus for the imperial

---

[23] P. Cagnat, L'Annone d'Afrique (Mémoires de l'Acad. d'Inscrip. et Belles Lettres, XL, 1915, pp. 247 f.) On the *stationes* of the *navicularii Africani* in Ostia see Calza, 'Le Stazioni,' etc., in Bull. Com. Roma, 1913, pp. 178 f.; and description of new discoveries in Notizie degli Seavi, 1916, pp. 326 f.; 1920, p. 166.

[24] G. Lully, pp. 243–249.   [25] Fronto, Loeb Class. Library, II, p. 292.

succession, and one to be greatly feared, was another African, Clodius Albinus, legate of Britain.[26] That among the African immigrants in Rome there were many Christians would be naturally surmised, and is proved by archaeological and historical evidence. When the church of Africa comes into the light in the last decades of the second century, it is already Latin in language and liturgy, though Greek influences were not lacking in the Christian community of Carthage. But in spite of its probable Eastern origin, the church of Africa shows the influence of the peculiar character of the Latin and Punic population among which it was established, through the presence both in its teaching and its liturgy of a tradition of its own, and it acquired a marked individuality. The African church was a Latin church when the Church of Rome was still hellenistic and Greek-speaking.[27]

Gnosticism did not find a favorable ground, and never gained a foothold, in the church of Africa: the African Christians did not assume that Christianity was to solve at once the

[26] Aelius Spartianus, the biographer of Severus, remarks that Septimius, in rebuilding the great monument in Rome called in his honor the Septizonium, "had no other thought than that his building should strike the eyes of those who came from Africa to Rome" (xxiv, p. 3). On the special care that Septimius took of the African provinces, and on the enthusiasm of the Africans for Severus, see Leclercq, L'Afrique chrétienne, I, p. 26 and Platnauer, pp. 299 ff.

[27] The origins of the African church are unknown. On the much debated question of its early Eastern or Roman connections see Monceaux, Histoire littéraire de l'Afrique chrétienne, I, Paris, 1901, pp. 1–28; Leclercq, L'Afrique chrétienne. I, pp. 31–68 (Paris, 1904); and the article 'Afrique' by the same in DACL. I, cols. 576 ff.; Mesnage, Le Christianisme en Afrique, Paris, 1914, pp. 1–79 (in favor of the apostolicity of the African church); Lejay, Les origines de l'Église d'Afrique, Liège, 1908 (Mélanges Kurth). The presence of Greek elements and the use of the Greek language in the early Christian community of Carthage is not necessarily an evidence of the Eastern origin of that church, since the Church of Rome at that time also consisted chiefly of Greek-speaking groups. More weight is to be found in the fact of the presence in the African liturgy of traditions which connect it directly with the churches of Asia (Monceaux, I, p. 7; Duchesne, Origines du Culte chrétien, pp. 220–222). On the complicated liturgical question see D. Cabrol, 'Afrique, Liturgie' in DACL. I, cols. 591 f. and Thibaut, La Liturgie romaine. Paris, 1924. After all it seems to me that the conclusion of Monceaux is still the most satisfactory, that Christianity was probably introduced into Africa from Asia Minor, but spread in the interior through the missionary work of the Roman Church (I, p. 8). As for the hellenistic character of the early African church, we may accept the general statement of Leclercq: "L'Afrique fut témoin d'un essai d'hellénisme; il dura peu et il n'en resta rien" (L'Afrique chrétienne, I, p. 91).

great problems of contemporary thought, nor had they the tendency to consider the church as a school for philosophical learning. Their interest was in the ethical and juridical content of revelation and redemption, rather than in their metaphysical aspect and implications. Another but no less significant fact is the slight importance given by the African Christians to the apocryphal writings. When we realize that in the Eastern churches and those which grew up under Eastern influence the apocryphal literature gave rise to authorized popular traditions which through the centuries found expression in peculiar forms of doctrine and of religious practice, we can see how the absence of this important element among the Africans concurred with the absence of Gnostic influences to imprint upon African Christianity a notably practical character in contrast with the doctrinal preposessions of the hellenistic churches.[28]

Very early the church of Africa came to possess a Latin translation of the Bible of its own and also Latin translations of other Christian writings such as the Shepherd of Hermas and the Epistle of Clement.[29] It seems therefore that there were close relations between the Christian community of Rome and those of Africa, and the archaeologists have even found traces of undeniable Roman influence in the oldest African cemeteries. But about the end of the second century it would seem that African Christianity was in its turn influencing the Roman community and contributing largely to the new development of the Roman Church.

It is true that the archaeological evidence of the presence of large groups of African Christians in Rome belongs to the third century,[30] and that to this later period is limited the large docu-

[28] E.Buonaiuti, Il Cristianesimo nell'Africa Romana, in Saggi sul Cristianesimo primitivo, Città di Castello, 1923, pp. 357–379.

[29] Monceaux, Hist. Litt. de l'Afrique chrét., I, pp. 97–173: Hans von Soden, Das lateinische Neue Testament in Afrika zur Zeit Cyprians (T. U., XXIII), Leipzig, 1909; Harnack, Geschichte der Altchristlichen Literatur, II, pp. 881 ff.; Schanz, Geschichte d. römischen Litteratur, III, 3rd ed., 1922, with complete bibliography, pp. 441–458.

[30] O. Marucchi in his description of the Catacomb of Commodilla (NBAC. 1904, pp. 41–160) gives all the inscriptions with African names found in that cemetery. See also his preface to Mesnage, L'Évangélisation de l'Afrique, p. vi: "Une partie du cimetière de Commodilla a été reservée à la sépulture des Africains, qui très probablement demeuraient dans les environs de la voie d'Ostie." On the paintings of the Ostrianum

mentary evidence of mutual influences between the Church of Rome and the churches of Carthage: but the events of the third century must have been a further development of a situation already in existence at the end of the second century. The process, for instance, through which so many formulae and traditions of the African liturgy appear to have been early in-troduced into the Latin liturgy of Rome must be referred to the period in the last decades of the second century when the Latin group in Rome began to acquire importance. The large group of African Christians in Rome was the natural channel through which African traditions were introduced there, and to this group, allied to the native Latin group of the community, is due the beginning of the latinization of the Roman Church.[31]

The election of Victor is itself significant of the numerical strength of the Africans and of the importance they had ac-quired in the community. We know nothing about Victor pre-vious to his election to the episcopate, except that he was an African. Possibly he had come to Rome as a presbyter for the spiritual assistance of the African group. Presbyters and dea-cons who emigrated to foreign cities were not infrequent even in that early period. In the time of Cyprian it is clear from his epistles that such occurrences were common.[32]

representing scenes from the Annona Africae see DACL. I, 1704, art. 'Amphore,' and I, 2267–2279, art. 'Annone,' by Leclercq. About the African Christians in Rome, Mes-nage (Le Christianisme en Afrique, Paris, 1914) has written a few rather poetical pages, with several questionable assumptions, as for instance, that the " castra pere-grina " were " sans doute, la caserne des soldats Africains de passage dans la capitale " (p. 86), or that Callistus was a deacon of Victor (p. 87). But his remark: " C'est Rome et ses Catacombes qu'il faut interroger pour avoir une idée de la puissante vitalité de l'Église d'Afrique à la fin du II° siècle et au commencement du III° " (p. 85) presents in a few striking words the true situation.

[31] Duchesne, Origines du culte chrétien, 2nd ed., p. 83; DACL. I, cols. 591 f., art. 'Afrique, Liturgie,' by Cabrol, cols. 658 ff.; art. 'Afrique, Archéologie,' by Leclercq; Dict. d'Hist. et Geogr. chrét., I, art. 'Afrique,' by Audollent.

[32] That Victor was an African seems beyond doubt, though several indications found in the Liber Pontificalis concerning the land of origin of the early bishops of Rome are open to question or even entirely wrong. See: Harnack, Die Mission, 4th ed. Exk. I, 'Die Herkunft der ersten Päpste,' pp. 817–832, and for Victor p. 826. The earliest mention of an African Martyr in Italy is that of Caesarius, deacon in Terracina under Nero. That he was an African is affirmed by his ' Acta ' of the late fifth or sixth century. Probably a mere invention of the writer. The supposed emigration of saints from Africa to Italy was a favorite theme of the sixth century hagiographers: F. Lan-

Victor's advent to the episcopal chair secured a more considerable place for the Latin language in the Roman liturgy, since presumably with him Latin became the language in which the head of the community officiated. To be sure the other groups of Oriental origin continued to use their Greek liturgical language and later there were bishops of Greek origin who may have used it again, but for the first time the Latin language had come out from the inconspicuous place which it held up to that time, and had made a definite step toward becoming the official language of the Roman Church. In his polemical treatises also Victor used the Latin language, a bad Latin, hints Jerome, who had read his works, probably as bad as the Latin of Septimius, but it must have been a very energetic Latin if Victor wrote with the same determination with which he administered the Roman Church.[33]

It will not be useless to remark that this establishment of the Latin language in the Roman Church coincided with a certain tendency in some Roman circles of the time to react against the process of hellenization of Roman literature, which had already gone too far. Such a reaction began to be felt even in the time of that most hellenistically inclined emperor Hadrian, who in reorganizing the imperial chancery separated the Latin secretarial office from the Greek and made of it a special department. But the reaction assumed a more definite form later, when Fronto and his circle, as we are told by his friend Aulus Gellius, undertook the restoration of the Latin language.[34] And it is remarkable that Fronto, the champion of this restoration, a purist not free from pedantry, a teacher who used to inflict

zoni, Le origini delle diocesi antiche d'Italia. Rome, 1923, p. 106 and Appendix p. 607–652.

[33] De viris illustribus, 34; Chron. ann. 193: "Victor cuius mediocria de religione extant volumina"; Schanz, III, 3rd ed., 1922, p. 272. On the attribution to Victor of De aleatoribus, see Monceaux, I, p. 54; Bardenhewer, Geschichte der altkirchlichen Literatur, II, 2nd ed., 1914, p. 497, and Schanz, l. c., p. 376.

[34] Aul. Gellius, ii. 26; xiii. 28; xix. 8–13. On Fronto's characteristics see Schanz, l. c., III, pp. 88–100. His 'elocutio novella' was to consist "partly of the good old Latin words which had died out in the days of classicism, and partly of new words which were in use in the language of common life but were excluded from literature" (D. Brook, Fronto and His Age, Cambridge, 1911, p. 104). See also A. Beltrami, Le tendeuze letterarie negli scritti di Frontone, Rome, 1907.

punishment on his pupil Marcus Aurelius because the boy preferred to write in Greek rather than in Latin,[35] this man whom
his contemporaries called unique in his knowledge of the Latin
language, was, as we have already noticed, an African and, far
from being ashamed of that, used to call himself a Libyan of the
Libyans. The circumstance that Fronto, the leader in this literary movement, and Victor, the first Roman bishop to use Latin
as the official language of the church, were both Africans, is
again a striking coincidence.

As already observed, Victor appears as the authoritative representative of the reaction against the hellenistic spirit and the
policy of the Eastern groups which up to that time had controlled the Roman Church.   With him the latinization of the
Roman Church received a great impulse and the Western
Church, not as a mere geographical expression but as a new
powerful factor in the development of Christianity, emerges into
the light of history. A man like Victor, who though he had theological culture [36] is more conspicuous for his practical Roman
mind, was naturally led to consider the church primarily as an
organization and not as a theology. He was bound to give more
weight to the vital interests of the institution of which he was
the leader and guardian than to the sentimental value of more
or less authoritative traditions.

The episode of his conflict with the Asiatics is very suggestive. Whereas Anicetus, about the middle of the century, had
not dared to condemn the Asiatic group of Rome after Polycarp
had persuaded him that the Asiatic tradition of the celebration
of Easter was of apostolic origin, Victor on the contrary, less
than thirty years later, was not deterred by the argument of
apostolicity and by the resolute language and defiant attitude of
Polycrates and the other Asiatic bishops, and did not hesitate to
separate them from his communion, and with them the Asiatics

[35] Marcus Aurelius to Fronto: "Tune es qui me nuper concastigaras quorsum
graece scriberem?" (Loeb Class. Library, Fronto, i, p. 18).
[36] It is known that Victor wrote treatises or epistles on doctrinal topics. Hippolytus, who according to the suggestion of De Rossi (Bullettino di archeologia cristiana,
1866, p. 13) had probably been a deacon or official of the Roman Church under Victor,
speaks very respectfully of him.

of the Roman group. Unlike Anicetus, Victor was confronted from the beginning with the problem as a whole and not only in relation to the Asiatics of his community. The necessity laid upon him was but the consequence of Anicetus's concession to Polycarp thirty years before. In their compromise both of the two traditions, Asiatic and Roman, had been implicitly recognized as lawful and to be freely observed, the one in Asia and by Asiatics in Rome, the other by those churches which followed the Roman custom. Any attempt on the part of Victor to oblige the Asiatics of Rome to give up their tradition was sure to meet with their legitimate resistance, in the name of that compromise to maintain the status quo. It was evident that the question could not be reopened now without dealing directly with the churches of Asia. This explains the wise tactics of Victor in urging the bishops not merely of Asia but of other provinces to call synods and to inform him as to what was the tradition followed in their churches. Victor, foreseeing the resistance of the Asiatics both of Rome and of Asia, wished to be sure that the majority of the Christian churches were on his side, and the referendum taken at his request was to be the justification of his firm decision to deny to his opponents communion with the Roman Church.[37]

[37] Eusebius (H. E., v. 23) says that synods were held in Rome, in Palestine, Pontus, Corinth, Osroene, and "in other places," and that all of them pronounced in favor of the Roman tradition. The fact that a synod of bishops was gathered in Rome at this time suggests that the Christian communities of Italy had begun to be organized under the episcopal régime. In the almost total absence of trustworthy historical evidence on the origin of the early Italian bishoprics, authoritative scholars like Duchesne (Histoire ancienne de l'église, I, pp. 253 ff. and 524–526) and F. Savio ('Alcune considerazioni sulla prima diffusione del Christianesimo in Italia,' in Rivista di Scienze Storiche, 1914, pp. 108 ff.) have conjectured that during the first and in part of the second century, the Christian communities around Rome and even of Southern Italy had no bishops of their own, but were governed by the bishop of Rome through both resident and visiting presbyters and deacons. A parallel is found in the bishop of Alexandria, who for a long time was the only bishop of Egypt. F. Lanzoni (Le origini delle diocesi antiche d'Italia, Rome, 1923, pp. 595 ff.) agrees with Duchesne and Savio, but remarks that such a situation had come to an end at the time of Victor. (See remarks by A. Harnack, Die Mission und Ausbreitung d. Christentums. 4 ed. 1924, p. 866–872.)

It is possible, however, that bishoprics were established in Southern Italy at an early date under the influence of Eastern missionaries, and that the bishops of the Roman synod under Victor were from those regions. But it is significant that the effec-

It was a bold stroke, which inspired much fear in many pious souls and much criticism even among those who were in accord with the Church of Rome. Warnings came from various sides, and especially from Irenaeus, who then wrote the letter to Victor quoted above, recalling the respect due to the old compromise between Anicetus and Polycarp. But for Victor it was a matter of vital importance; the root of the question was always the internal problem of his own church, which could be solved only by enforcing the law of unity and uniformity in the whole Roman Christian community. It was only in this way that he could secure the recognition of his episcopal authority as the supreme law of his own church, and restore peace and order among those entrusted to his pastoral care.

As we mentioned above, the Asiatics of Rome rebelled, and formed an independent sect with Blastus as their leader. The churches of Asia kept their tradition; but how long they remained away from communion with Rome we do not know. Probably not very long, since on the one hand Victor could not fail to be impressed by the unfavorable reaction of many churches against his rash measure, and on the other hand the rebellion of the Asiatics of Rome settled the matter so far as his own community was directly concerned. A small group of that kind could not long survive after its secession from the local church.

The unfavorable reaction of the churches, of which Irenaeus's letter is witness, was evidently caused by the fact that

tive episcopal organization of Italy begins about the end of the second century, and it is found well advanced about the middle of the third. Northern Italy does not offer any evidence of a Christian penetration up to that time, since, as Lanzoni has conclusively shown, the two most ancient sees north of Rome, Milan and Ravenna, were established not earlier than the late second century (p. 585). It seems, therefore, that the regions of Italy, which, with exception of a few maritime and commercial centres, were but little or not at all affected by Hellenism, began to be evangelized with a certain success at the same time that the Roman Church itself was undergoing the process of latinization. The episcopate of Victor would then mark also the turning-point in the missionary work of the Roman Church among the Latin populations of Italy. Was the Roman synod gathered by Victor an occasion for awakening his interest in such a work? Did Victor take definite steps in this direction? There is no way of knowing, but the suggestion in favor of such an hypothesis would throw light on the importance of Victor's episcopate, which has generally been overlooked by the historians except for a few remarks by Langen, in his Geschichte der römischen Kirche, I, Bonn, 1881, pp. 179 ff.

Victor's policy in this controversy represented a striking innovation in the attitude of organized Christianity towards tradition in general. It seems as if the same spirit which had led the
new Roman juridical school to oppose old-fashioned formalism
in the interpretation of legal tradition, was at work in the Roman Church, and as if the son of Roman Africa who now occupied the episcopal chair had a different idea of the value of
the so-called apostolic tradition from that of his Greek and
Oriental predecessors. When he dared to ban a tradition
which went back to apostolic times, but which had become
a stumbling block to the unification and the peace of his
community and to the triumph of the episcopal supremacy,
Victor formulated implicitly the doctrine that tradition was
not to be a millstone around the neck of a living institution,
but was to be subordinated to the vital exigencies of Christian
discipline, nay, was to be considered as one and identical with
the institution itself, moving and developing with it according
to the growing needs of a healthy organism.

This came to be precisely the main difference between the
hellenistic Christian tendency and the new Latin Christian
policy; the former conceived of tradition as something eternal,
having a divine value in itself, unchangeable even in its smallest
details, to be kept under any circumstances, and above all historical exigencies and all human judgments; the latter, on the
contrary, looked at tradition rather as of relative validity, and
reserved to the controlling power the right to modify and to re-
interpret it in the light of new events and of the new circumstances created by the practical situation and urgent needs of
the organization. This was the beginning of that historical
process which in time led the Roman Church to identify Christian tradition with its own doctrine and its own organization.

It was the adoption of this program and the growing consciousness of its implications that made of the Church of Rome
a Latin church, — not so much through a gradual change in its
liturgical language and in the formulae of its official correspondence as by the change in the general direction of its religious and ecclesiastical policy. Such a change could not fail
to provoke a rapid development of a definite system of interchurch relations and to secure a higher value for the function

of the Roman hierarchy in the whole church. It implied also the working out of a more definite system of relations between the church and the world, based not on the heroic standard of morality which had been the ideal of early Christianity kindled by the apocalyptic hope, but on a more sympathetic understanding of human weaknesses and human possibilities. If the church was to be an instrument of salvation for the whole world, it could not insist on offering as a common standard of morality an ideal that could be reached only by few; the church had to formulate rules of conduct which could be really observed by the average man. If Christianity was to become truly the universal religion, it needed a sounder basis than conflicting traditions, prophetic enthusiasm, and apocalyptic visions.

This new program of the church, which was gradually formulated as a result of trying experiences, especially in the large communities such as Rome, appears already implicitly contained in the attitude of Victor towards tradition and still more clearly in the various activities of his episcopal administration. It was carried on and developed to its logical conclusion by his successors: by Callistus, who took a definite stand against the irreconcilable rigoristic interpreters of the disciplinary tradition of the church; by Cornelius, who sanctioned the principle of indulgence toward the *lapsi* against the narrow puritanism of the Novatians; by the Roman bishops, who stood for the validity of baptism administered by heretics. The opposite tradition on sacramental validity, propounded by Cyprian of Carthage and by numbers of Eastern bishops, was probably more in harmony with the spirit of Christian teaching and its theoretical implications, but it would have been fatal to the organization and to the hierarchical government in its unavoidable practical consequences. This was enough to make the governing power of the Church of Rome take sides against it and adopt, defend, and impose with all its might the opposite principle.

Historians have called attention to the far-reaching interaction between ethics and eschatology in the first Christian centuries. Christian morality became more elevated and more heroic, the more closely it was linked to the intense expectation of the impending parousia.[38] But about the beginning of the third century the great apocalyptic dreams had lost much of their impressiveness for the growing Christian masses, and in spite of prophetic outbursts and sporadic revivals, the need of reducing the Gospel teaching of renunciation to the formulas of a religion capable of adapting itself to circumstances and making compromises with them was strongly felt in both the East and the West. And especially was it felt in the great Christian centres where the bishops found themselves confronted with the impossibility of imposing the ideal program of Christianity upon large and growing communities. That it frankly admitted this necessity and acted accordingly with official authority was the merit of the Church of Rome, where from the time of Victor the new policy gradually assumed a definite shape.[39]

It is thus no exaggeration to say that the episcopate of Victor marks a turning-point in the history of the Church of Rome. With a truly Roman insight Victor realized that the worst policy was to permit the equivocal situation of uncertainty as to doctrine and practice in the community to continue unaltered, so that in the end Christians themselves would have been puzzled to know who were the real Christians. Fully aware that the avowedly heretical groups, such as Gnostics and Marcionites, were outside the reach of his authority, Victor concentrated his efforts upon establishing a closer union among the other groups partly by assimilation, partly by the elimination

[38] E. Buonaiuti, 'The Ethics and Eschatology of Methodius of Olympus,' *Harvard Theological Review*, July, 1921, p. 264.

[39] Needless to say, this contrast between the spirit of renunciation of the early Christian tradition and the practical exigencies of the ecclesiastical organization was not peculiar to Rome. It was felt everywhere in the church, and everywhere long produced disturbing movements. It was at the root of Montanism in Asia. The hypothesis of Calder ('Philadelphia and Montanism,' Bulletin of the John Rylands Library, Manchester, 1923, pp. 309-354) of the existence in Asia Minor, from the time when the Apocalypse was written, of two antagonistic missionary schools, one in the Northern provinces and spreading along the valley of the Maeander river, which emphasized the apocalyptic hope, and urged an austere morality and an uncompromising attitude toward the world, the other centring in Philadelphia, with a milder interpretation of the ethics of the Gospel, is little more than a suggestion, but it would leave room for a sufficient period of incubation to account for the sudden rise of Montanism about the middle of the second century.

238 HARVARD THEOLOGICAL REVIEW

of those who, whether on doctrinal grounds or in practical matters, refused to be absorbed by the law of uniformity. As a consequence of this resolute policy, new schisms were to be expected, but at least the church and its bishop would dissipate
all misunderstanding and make known exactly where they
stood.

The stern measures against the Asiatics were only the first
step in this work of reorganizing the Roman Church. A more
serious task was that of bringing order and unity into the doctrinal teaching of the community. The old Roman symbol
which was in use at least from the middle of the second century
shows that the official teaching of the Roman Church imposed
the belief in God, Father omnipotent; in Jesus Christ, Son of
God, born of the Virgin Mary, crucified under Pilate, risen from
the dead, sitting at the right of the Father, to come again as
judge; and finally the belief in the Holy Ghost, and in the resurrection of the flesh. But did the Roman Church teach any
official doctrine concerning the crucial problem of the specific
character of Jesus Christ's divine sonship? There is no evidence
of any official teaching on this point: but there is plenty of evidence of the existence in the community of the various and opposite solutions which had been formulated up to that time.
Modern historians have laid great stress on the important point
that there was a fundamental divergence between the simple
belief of the popular Christian class and the new philosophical
elaborations of the theologians. The former represented the
primitive naïve juxtaposition of belief in Christ, the Saviour
God of Christianity, and belief in the God of Israel, inherited
from the Jewish tradition; the latter was the learned product
of the contamination of the Christian tradition with the philosophical thought of the times in the attempt to bring Christianity into a larger setting and to give to it universal significance.[40]

[40] On this topic a learned article has recently been published by J. Lebreton ('Le
désaccord de la foi populaire et de la théologie savante dans l'Église chrétienne du IIIᵉ
siècle,' Revue d'Histoire Ecclésiastique, Louvain, 1923, pp. 481–506 and following
number) in which are collected and analyzed important passages of third-century
writers. Lebreton emphasizes the difference between the learned groups, which claimed
to be the best champions of Christianity and complained of being misunderstood and
suspected by the unlearned, and the popular groups led often by presbyters and bishops

But the rank and file of Christians remained more or less indifferent to the philosophical elaboration. To them Jesus Christ was the Saviour God, to Him they addressed their prayers and on Him centred their hope. God the Father, whose name they repeated in the creed, was little more than an abstraction which assumed a religious value only in so far it could be and was connected with Christ.

The traditional phrase 'Jesus Christ Son of God,' which originally derived its religious value from its moral content and implications, lent itself to concrete, mythological interpretation and to abstract, metaphysical elaboration; it was but natural that the former should appeal to the unlettered masses, and the latter to the thinkers and to those of philosophical training. A vague form of adoptionism seems to have been cur-

who considered all philosophical speculation foreign to Christianity and dangerous to faith. But besides these two classes, there were, remarks Lebreton, "des esprits supérieurs, âmes saintes, intelligences droites et fortes, qui ne se laissent ni éblouir ni effrayer." Such were Irenaeus, Cyprian, and the great Roman bishops Fabian and Dionysius; they were the real representative of the true tradition (p. 491). But the most radical attempt to make of this distinction the main characteristic of the doctrinal situation in the early centuries and the key to the explanation of their peculiar forms of doctrinal development is the recent book of A. C. McGiffert, The God of the Early Christians, New York, 1924. According to Professor McGiffert the problem, "how to explain the addition of the worship of Christ to the worship of God," to which historians have hitherto confined themselves, is one-sided. Another problem equally pressing is, "how to explain the addition of the worship of God to the worship of Christ" (pp. 63-64). This would imply the existence of considerable sections of Christians who recognized only Jesus Christ as their God, excluding or ignoring the God of Israel inherited by Christianity. Modalism would in the last analysis represent the reaction of this purely gentile Christianity against all attempts to make of Christ a subordinate God. Their identification of the Father and the Son, suggested as it was by practical and not speculative reasons, aimed only to safeguard the uniqueness of the God Christ. The system however was philosophically unsound, and could not overcome the learned theology of the Logos (p. 108). Though it cannot be said that there is any definite evidence of the existence of such a distinct purely gentile Christianity, it is undeniable that in the consciousness of large popular Christian groups Christ was the real object of piety; yet is it necessary to assume that they altogether ignored God the Father, even if in their worship the thought of Him had but little value? The confusion in applying the term God both to the God of Israel and to Christ found in certain primitive writings would suggest the juxtaposition of the two conceptions correlated by the idea of the Sonship, rather than the denial of one of them. The theory of Professor McGiffert is however very suggestive, and with certain limitations may be adopted as a good explanation of various otherwise obscure problems of early doctrinal development.

rent among the Christians of Rome in the middle of the second century; but thereafter modalistic views, which afforded a solution easily accessible even to simple minds, and had the advantage of preserving unimpaired the absolute deity of Christ, seem to have made a strong bid for popularity. It was remarked above that practical reasons, urgent practical motives, due to the presence of so many conflicting groups in the community, had brought about a coincidence of interests and a coöperation of the monarchical bishops and the simple believers. Now did this alliance affect also the doctrinal attitude of the Roman bishops, who refused to be identified with any of the learned schools not only because of the uncertain state of the doctrines themselves, but also out of practical motives which made it inadvisable to disturb the simple faith of the crowd? Very likely.

But such an attitude could not last for ever: the process by which faith had to become a doctrine could not be stopped, and the necessity of taking sides was becoming more and more urgent. From this point of view the episcopate of Victor has greater importance than is commonly thought. At the time of his election doctrinal confusion was at its worst. The doctrine of the Logos-Christ derived great advantage from so authoritative a tradition as that of the Gospel of John; but on the other hand it was subject to the disadvantage of having been misused by Gnostics and Marcionites, whose appropriation of that doctrine could not fail to cast a shadow of suspicion on the whole terminology which had to be used in any further elaboration of it. Justin Martyr had introduced a teaching about the Logos which in the hands of his disciples and especially of Tatian seems to have assumed a Gnostic quality; at least Irenaeus affirms that Tatian held a theory of aeons and their succession similar to that of Valentinus. But in spite of all these drawbacks the Logos doctrine had strong roots in the ecclesiastical Roman tradition and was very likely the doctrine held by Victor himself. Hippolytus's respectful language in mentioning Victor, and the fact that the learned clergy of Carthage as represented by Tertullian adopted this view of the 'oeconomia' of the deity, make this probable. A tradition current among certain Roman adoptionists of the third century affirmed that

Victor, as well as some of his predecessors, professed an adoptionist doctrine; but this assumption, as the anonymous writer quoted by Eusebius remarks, seems to have had no foundation, in view of Victor's condemnation of the adoptionism of the Theodotians.[41]

Very likely the teaching of Victor on this point was not different from that of Irenaeus. The two men were in close relation and it was Irenaeus who called Victor's attention to the errors of Florinus and asked for the condemnation of the latter which Victor did not hesitate to pronounce. Like Irenaeus, Victor must have confined himself to mere doctrinal statements and abstained from any personal speculative contribution. The Son was God, truly God, begotten by the Father, and then united to human nature by a 'commistio' of a mysterious character. Like Irenaeus, Victor must have had a great dislike for those thinkers who pretended to explain the generation of the Logos 'quasi ipsi obstetricaverint,' and of whom it was charitable to say:

It is better and more profitable to belong to the simple and unlettered class, and by means of love to attain nearness to God, than by imagining ourselves learned and skilful to be found with those blaspheming God. . . . It is better . . . that one should search after no other knowledge except that of Jesus Christ, the Son of God who was crucified for us, than that by subtle questions and hair-splitting expressions he should fall into impiety.[42]

At least this would be the mental attitude suggested by Victor's policy in dealing with the doctrinal movements of his time. Florinus, a presbyter who had been a disciple of Polycarp of Smyrna, and who in a long period of residence at Rome had acquired there influence and authority, began to teach a Logos doctrine which aroused the suspicions of many. It even reached the ears of Irenaeus, who took a great interest in the refutation of his former friend, writing letters and dissertations against Florinus, and urged the bishop to take severe measures against the spread of his doctrines. It is probable, as has been suggested, that Florinus was but the continuator of the school which went back to Tatian and Justin; as in the case of Tatian,

[41] H. E., v. 28.
[42] Adv. Haer. ii. 28; ii. 26.

41

Irenaeus accuses him of holding Valentinian theories. Whatever the fact as to this may have been, Victor condemned Florinus, but the obstinate presbyter refused to submit and organized a sect of his own, which, however, gained no considerable following and soon disappeared.[43]

At the same time another problem came into prominence. The vague and indefinite tendencies of the simple Christians who, though they had no interest in theology, yet under the stress of the monotheistic profession of faith of their symbol instinctively tried to overcome the apparent dualism of God Christ and God the Father either by a naïve conception of a divine adoption of mythological character, or by the assumption of an identity of the two by analogy with the many plurinominal deities of the pagan cults, began to emerge from the

[43] Eusebius, H. E., v. 15; 20; 28. In what the novelty of Florinus's teaching consisted is difficult to say. The titles of Irenaeus's treatises against him mentioned by Eusebius would suggest specific Gnostic doctrines. Among the Syrian fragments of Irenaeus is one which purports to be part of a letter written by Irenaeus to Victor about Florinus, "a follower of Valentinus and author of an abominable book." From this letter it appears that it was Irenaeus who called Victor's attention to the heretical character of Florinus's teaching: "Nunc autem, quia forte vos lateant libri eorum qui etiam ad nos usque pervenerunt, notum facio vobis ut pro vestra dignitate ejiciatis e medio scripta illa, opprobrium quidem afferentia in vos, quia scriptor jactaverit se unum esse e vobis" (Harvey's ed., Cambridge, 1857, II, p. 457). The connection of Florinus's teaching with the tradition which went back to Tatian and through Tatian to Justin Martyr, has been suggested by K. Karsen ('Irenaeus von Lyon und der römische Presbyter Florinus', Der Katholik, 1910, II, pp. 40–50; 88–105), who attempted to identify Florinus with Florens Tertullian of Carthage. This identification was strongly opposed by H. Kock ('Tertullian und der römische Presbyter Florinus', Zeitschrift für die neutestamentliche Wissenschaft, 1912, pp. 59–83), to whom Larsten replied with a further article ('Zur Kontroverse über den angeblichen Ketzer Florinus's, ibid., pp. 133–156). Kock's view, however, has been rejected on good grounds by A. Baumstark ('Die Lehre des römischen Presbyter Florinus', ibid., pp. 306–319), who called attention to the exposition of Florinus's Gnostic teaching found in the 'Kitab al unvan,' an historical compilation of the Melkite chronicler Agapios, bishop of Hierapolis–Minbii in the tenth century (Patrologia Orientalis, tom. V, fasc. 4; VII, 4; VIII, 3. (The passage concerning Florinus is in VII, pp. 516–517, translation by Vasiliev.) By the passage of Agapios, the Gnostic character of Florinus's teaching and the impossibility of identifying him with Tertullian is strongly confirmed. But even if Karsten's assumption that Florinus's Valentinianism was a mere exaggeration of Irenaeus be rejected, his suggestion that the Logos doctrine of the school started by Justin and continued by Tatian played a part in the doctrinal controversies of Rome at that period is very valuable. Florinus may well have represented that tradition, even if in his Valentinian sympathies he went a step further than Tatian.

vagueness of mere popular unauthoritative explanations and to assume in the hands of new theologians the form and character of a doctrinal synthesis claiming philosophical and traditional value. Adoptionism and Modalism, as they appear in the late second century and at the beginning of the third, were the product of theological speculation; such were the Adoptionist system of the Theodotians, and shortly afterwards the Patripassianism of Praxeas, and finally the systematic Modalism of Sabellius. This was a new and serious complication, which could not fail to affect profoundly the policy of the bishop. On the one hand it must have increased Victor's hostility to the wave of intellectualism which was now reaching even the lower strata of the Christian population, and on the other it must have made it necessary to face more directly the doctrinal problem. The Theodotians were condemned, and they too refused to submit. But unlike Florinus, Theodotus seems to have had a large following, and the church organized by him became and remained for some time a serious competitor with that of the bishops.[44]

The history of Modalism belongs to the following period and to the episcopates of Zephyrinus and Callistus: it seems to me, however, that from the point of view of the doctrinal orientation of the Roman Church, the thirty years from Victor to the death of Callistus are to be considered as forming a definite period, which taken as a whole marks the end of the long doctrinal uncertainty and cleared the way for the ecclesiastical doctrine of the Logos to become the official doctrine of the Roman Church. Victor, by condemning the philosophical su-

[44] Eusebius, H. E., v. 28. The teaching of the Adoptionist schismatic group established by Theodotus the currier was developed further by Theodotus the banker and finally by the school of Artemon. It seems that gradually the Adoptionist church of Rome became a circle of literary and learned men who not only ascribed great importance to philosophy and science, but occupied themselves with biblical studies, especially in restoring the text to supposed primitive correctness, and in grammatical and literal exegesis. The fact, however, of their choice of the ignorant confessor Natalis as their bishop at the beginning of the episcopate of Zephyrinus would suggest that this great interest in learning was not characteristic of the first Theodotian group, but a later development. It is more probable that at the beginning the group was formed of popular elements under the leadership of the new theologians.

perstructure of Florinus, which led at least to compromise
with Gnosticism, and by refusing to yield to the popular pressure in favor of the new theological formulations of the Theodotians, opened the way towards that complete elimination of
early christologies which was achieved by Callistus's final condemnation of Sabellius. Zephyrinus and Callistus, in spite of
their hesitations and inconsistencies, if we accept Hippolytus's
insinuations, are after all the continuators of Victor's policy.
The words attributed by Hippolytus to Zephyrinus, when put
in relation to the general situation of the doctrinal conflict of
the Roman Church at the beginning of the third century, are
not so naïve as is commonly thought. They undoubtedly show
a state of theological hesitation, but they also show progress towards a solution. On the one hand he would affirm: "I know
only one God Jesus Christ and beyond him none other who was
born and who suffered"; and on the other hand he would protest: "It was not the Father who died, but the Son." [45] If
these words mean anything at all they suggest the firm ecclesiastical tradition of Jesus Christ God and Son of God, a mere
neutral statement of faith; but at the same time they show an
advance toward a solution by denying altogether the personal
identification of the suffering Son with the Father. The repu-
diation of Modalism and of Sabellius was but the logical outcome of this whole process of orientation begun by Victor, followed even by the ignorant Zephyrinus, and finally completed
by Callistus.

But the troubles of Victor were not over; still further com-
plications came from another side and this time on a different
ground. Another group which was then acquiring importance
in the Roman community was that of the Montanists. The
history of early Montanism in Rome is very obscure, and has
given room for the most diverse theories among modern historians.[46] What seems probable is that the movement reached

[45] Philosophumena, ix. 11, ed. P. Wendland, 1916, p. 246.

[46] The most comprehensive work on Montanism is still Labriolle, La Crise Mon-
taniste, Paris, 1913, and his collection of the sources, Les sources de l'histoire du Montanisme, Paris, 1913, which have superseded both the previous study and the collection
of sources of Bonwetsch (1881). A full bibliography up to 1913, is to be found in La

Rome during the first years of the episcopate of Victor's predecessor Eleutherus (174/5–189); it was not proscribed by the bishop; although there was some opposition, as is suggested by the letter of the Gallican martyrs to Eleutherus. But some time afterward a Roman bishop, as we are told by Tertullian, who does not mention his name, had decided to recognize the authenticity of the prophetic inspiration of the Montanists and had prepared and even signed letters in their favor addressed to the churches of Asia. At that moment, however, a certain Praxeas arrived from Asia and succeeded in persuading the bishop to withdraw his approval.[47]

There is good reason to think that this bishop was Victor.[48] As a matter of fact Montanism at that period in Rome could

Crise, pp. vii–xx. Among recent publications the most remarkable are Faggiotto, L'Eresia dei Frigi, Fonti e Frammenti, Rome, 1924, and Tertulliano e la Nuova Profezia, Rome, 1924. Faggiotto subjects the sources to a new and painstaking revision, and draws from them conclusions which are in many ways different from those of Labriolle. Above all Faggiotto seems convinced that ascetic tendencies and practices did not have in the early period of the movement the importance commonly attributed to them, and that these became characteristic of Montanism only later. It was in the beginning a mere revival of prophetism based on a vivid apocalyptic expectation, and did not teach any heretical doctrines, nor take an antagonistic attitude towards the church organization. As a consequence, Faggiotto emphasizes the distinction between the first period of the New Prophecy and the second period of the Heresy of the Phrygians. Among the questions of detail concerning the sources, Faggiotto, as it seems, has solved the problem of the enigmatic Miltiades mentioned by Eusebius (H. E., v. 16), and against the common opinion, which sees in Miltiades one of the new prophets, makes of him a writer against Montanism to be identified with Miltiades the apologist (L'Eresia dei Frigi, pp. 25–35).

[47] Tertullian, Adv. Praxeam 1: "Nam idem tunc episcopum Romanum agnoscentem iam prophetias Montani, Priscae, Maximillae, et ex ea agnitione pacem ecclesiis Asiae et Phrygiae inferentem, falsa de ipsis prophetis et ecclesiis eorum adseverando et praedecessorum eius auctoritatem defendendo, coegit et litteras pacis revocare iam emissas et a proposito recipiendorum charismatum concessare." The interpretation of this passage has provoked endless discussions. A detailed analysis of the various opinions is to be found in Labriolle, La Crise, pp. 257–275.

[48] Eleutherus is the choice of Schwegler, Ritschl, A. Réville, Lipsius, Bonwetsch, Duchesne; Victor is preferred by Langen, Hilgelfeld, Zahn, Voigt, Monceaux, Preuschen, Esser, Faggiotto; Labriolle proposes Zephyrinus. Leclercq simplifies the question by suggesting three successive episcopal edicts in Rome concerning the Montanists: one by Eleutherus "provoked by the letter of the confessors of Lyons (Eus. H. E., v. 3); a second by Victor provoked by the intervention of Praxeas mentioned by Tertullian; and a third by Zephyrinus provoked by the issue of the debates between Proclus and Gaius (H. E., ii. 25; iii. 28; vi. 29)" (Hist. d. Conciles, I, p. 133, note). As a matter of fact, what complicates this whole question is Tertullian's affirmation that Praxeas

not be called a heresy: it did not attack any specific Christian doctrine, and it professed complete adherence to the body of traditional Christian teaching. As a reaction against the intellectualism of the theologians who caused so much trouble to the Roman community, Montanism would have caused no ill feelings in the ranks of that large party which had no interest in theological quarrels and was opposed to the spirit of doctrinal controversies. At the same time the austerity of the new prophets, in that period apparently beyond suspicion, could not fail to make a favorable impression on the pious element of the community. On the other hand, the individualistic spirit inseparable from a prophetical régime was a menace to the rights of the hierarchy, and if perceived could not but repel a man like Victor, whose program aimed above all at the restoration of Christian unity in his church by strengthening the hierarchical principle of authority and government.[49]

"coegit" the Roman bishop "praedecessorum eius auctoritatem defendendo." These words are interpreted as meaning that at least two of the predecessors of the bishop had already passed an unfavorable judgment on the new prophecy. If therefore Victor was the bishop in question, it would follow that Soter and Eleutherus had condemned Montanism. This assumption seems to receive confirmation from the passage of the 'Liber Praedestinatus' which says that Soter wrote a treatise, or a letter, against the Cataphrygians (i. 26). But the Praedestinatus, a compilation of the late fifth century, has been shown to be entirely untrustworthy on all kinds of historical information, and strong chronological reasons make it impossible for Soter to have taken any part in this controversy. It seems that Montanism did not reach Rome and was not discussed there before the year 177 under Eleutherus (Faggiotto, La Diaspora, pp. 39–40). That Eleutherus was concerned with the question is undeniable, since to him among others the confessors of Lyons sent their appeal for the peace of the church. But that Eleutherus issued a definite condemnation of Montanism is unlikely. If such had been the case, there would have been no need for his successor to pass a new judgment; the hesitation and still more the approval of Victor would be a puzzle. We must admit that an explicit condemnation of Montanism on the part of Rome had not occurred when Praxeas urged the bishop to withdraw his letter of approval of the new prophecy. That being so, what is the value of Tertullian's obscure statement? It seems to me that in view of these difficulties it is impossible to assign to it a specific meaning, or to see in it a direct reference to the Montanist problem. It remains to interpret it in a general way, and to assume that Praxeas urged the Roman bishop not to depart from the policy of his predecessors, who had always been opposed to the introduction of novelties in the church.

[49] It is well to keep in mind the wise remark of P. Batiffol: "L'épiscopat ne prenait pas ombrage de la persistance des charismes prophétiques. Comme au temps de Saint Paul, on jugeait le prophète d'abord à sa sainteté, et tout autant à sa soumission à la hiérarchie. Le montanisme ne proclamait aucune nouveauté, quand il disait: Il faut

It is probable, however, that up to that time Montanism in Rome had not taken an attitude antagonistic to the hierarchy, for it was seeking the latter's approval. One can easily understand the hesitation of Victor on this account. If the narrative of Tertullian is trustworthy and refers to Victor, this hesitation was at first overcome, and a decision reached in favor of Montanism. This fits well with Victor's policy, which had set out to clear the field of all equivocations and ambiguities. It is possible also that the attitude of the Asiatic bishops who had refused to accept Victor's decision on the celebration of Easter, and from whom he had withdrawn communion, may have affected Victor's feelings in the matter, since they were exactly the bishops who now condemned Montanism and called upon other bishops in the church to condemn it. On the one hand, the lack of peremptory reasons, either doctrinal or disciplinary, for the condemnation of the Roman Montanists, and on the other, the necessity of establishing a definite policy, together with feelings of irritation against the Asiatic bishops, would fully explain the fact that Victor was brought to recognize the legitimacy of the new prophecy.[50]

But in Asia Montanism had already assumed the character of an anti-hierarchical movement, and had developed the prac-

recevoir les charismes et qu'il y ait des charismes dans l'Église. (Epiph., Haer., 48, 2.) La nouveauté du montanisme fut de vouloir imposer ses révélations particulières comme un supplément au dépôt de la foi, et de vouloir les accrediter par des extases suspectes et des convulsions" (L'Église naissante, 9th ed., 1922, p. 264). But even so, "La décision à prendre était complexe: il fallait sauvegarder le principe de l'action surnaturelle de l'Esprit, et en même temps le définir" (ibid., p. 266).

[50] Labriolle remarks on this point: "C'est bien gratuitement que l'on suppose chez Victor cette étrange disposition, aussi peu charitable que possible, qui l'aurait induit à susciter à l'épiscopat d'Asie des difficultés très graves pour le plaisir d'exercer sa vengeance contre lui, et pour le punir de ses résistances dans la question pascale. On prête à ce caractère obstiné et violent des procédés mesquins qui ne lui vont guère" (La Crise, p. 273). To put the question in this way is to misunderstand the situation. It was not a petty vengeance, but rather a question of principle which involved the right of each bishop to pass judgment on controversies affecting his own church, according to the local situation and not according to the exigencies of other churches. The bishops of Asia, in the name of their local autonomy and their local needs, had refused to coöperate with Victor for the pacification of his own community in the Easter question; it was natural that in the question of Montanism Victor should adopt the same policy with reference to the local situation in Rome, which made him feel an approval of the new prophecy to be desirable.

tical implications of the prophetic claim, degenerating into a spiritual and ecclesiastical anarchy. Praxeas, coming thence, opened the eyes of Victor to the serious consequences of an official recognition of the movement. The letters ready to be sent were withdrawn and judgment was held in suspense.

Recognition was not granted, but no condemnation was pronounced. This episode of the Montanists must have taken place about the end of Victor's episcopate and is no less instructive than his quarrel with the Asiatics on the question of Easter. It presents another side of the same conflict concerning interchurch relations, and throws still more light on Victor's conception of his episcopal authority and of the responsibilities of his office. Montanism had early provoked in Asia the resistance of the hierarchy: the episcopate of the province was rightly concerned at seeing the movement degenerate into a fanatical outburst and at hearing the claims of the new prophets who assumed the right to represent the Paraclete and to be above all hierarchical authority. They condemned these extravagant claims and initiated a vigorous campaign against the Phrygian prophets.

Was the verdict of the Asiatic bishops to be accepted without discussion by bishops elsewhere in whose communities Montanist groups had been formed? Was the judgment of his Eastern colleagues binding on the bishop of the Christian community of Rome? It was fundamentally the same question of principle that had provoked the clash between Victor and the Asiatic bishops over the date of Easter; but this time the situation was inverted, the condemnation came from Asia. There is no statement that the bishops of Asia had sent a request to Victor or to the Roman bishop to follow their example and condemn Montanism, but even so, why did not the head of the Christian community of Rome feel the duty of joining those bishops in the condemnation of Montanism? [51]

[51] It is commonly surmised that the Montanists of Asia had asked for the intervention of the bishop of Rome ("Il dut y avoir, de la part des Montanistes, un nouvel effort pour se faire reconnaître à Rome, car pour quoi le pape aurait-il pris l'initiative d'un tel acte?" Labriolle, La Crise, p. 260), and that their appeal to Rome shows that the consciousness of the superior authority of the Roman bishop was already present in the

The first and obvious reason is the fact that Montanism had not everywhere taken the same extreme character as in the land of its birth; in Rome it was still a mild prophetic revival, stressing more the principle of ascetic conduct and the apocalyptic hope but remaining faithful both to the traditional doctrine and to the organization. Moreover, while in Asia entire communities had turned Montanists, and the whole Asiatic church was in a turmoil, in Rome the group was small and did not need at that moment to be taken very seriously, especially by a bishop who was confronted with more urgent problems and much more dangerous movements and schisms. To be sure, Victor's ignorance of the real situation in Asia must be taken into account in explaining his first and favorable decision, in the same way that Praxeas's report explains the withdrawal of the recognition; but that does not explain the fact that Victor did not feel in duty bound to go further and join the Asiatic bishops in the condemnation of Montanism.

Here again we find at bottom the same reasons which had prompted Victor's aggressive attitude in the question of Easter. Montanism transplanted to Rome had become an internal problem of the Church of Rome, to be solved by the bishop of the Roman community. And since in Rome it appeared harmless and rather helpful in raising the standard of morals and counteracting the propaganda of Gnostics and heretics, it could be approved. This approval, suggested by local reasons, would

whole church. "Notez, avec M. Harnack, qu'il ne s'agissait pas là de Montanistes romains, mais que les Montanistes de Phrygie et d'Asie étaient visiblement en instance pour se faire reconnaître, eux et le principe de la nouvelle prophétie: le jugement de Rome leur importait donc!" (Batiffol, L'Église naissante, p. 267). It is very likely that the Montanists of Asia were doing their best to enlist the support not only of the Roman Church, but also of the bishops of the communities where Montanism had found followers. But to see in this a manifestation of definite principles affecting the hierarchical government of the church as a whole, is a rather far-fetched conclusion. No less arbitrary is it to exclude from the controversy the Montanists of Rome and to assume that those of Asia were the only ones concerned in the decisions of the Roman bishop. The approval of the Roman bishop, communicated in the prepared but not yet delivered letter, concerned Montanism as a whole; it was an approval of the new prophecy as represented by the Roman groups as well as by the other groups everywhere. It is therefore natural to surmise that the Roman Montanists, both in their own interest and in the interest of their Asiatic brethren, urged the bishop of Rome to make known his approval in the hope of overcoming the opposition of the bishops of Asia.

again affect the church at large as had been the case with Victor's decision on the celebration of Easter; wherefore letters for expedition to the churches of Asia were prepared and signed. A new clash between Rome and the East was imminent. Praxeas's timely arrival prevented a serious mistake on the part of the Roman bishop, but did not bring about the condemnation of Montanism. Victor's policy was short-sighted, since even in Rome the new prophetism could not fail to develop into a movement against the hierarchy; but it shows the spirit of independence of the Roman bishop, the consciousness of his right to pass judgment on questions concerning his own community from the point of view of the interests and the situation of his own church even against the judgment of other churches, and his unwillingness to accept the judgments of other bishops when not justified in his eyes by the situation which he found in his own church.

In any case there is no doubt that practical reasons of much weight at the moment must have suggested Victor's attitude towards Montanism. As a matter of fact, at the end of his episcopate Victor could not flatter himself that he had succeeded in his attempt to unify the Roman community and firmly establish his authority as a monarchical bishop. After several years of remarkable efforts to destroy the groups which refused to follow the directions and laws of his episcopal government, Victor had the bitter disappointment of seeing three more groups of rebels raise their head before his eyes and as a consequence of his own policy: the group of those who followed the Asiatic custom in the celebration of Easter with their own bishop Blastus; the group of the Theodotians, who a few years later appear with a bishop of their own, the confessor Natalis; and the group of Florinus. When we add to these probably two groups of Marcionites and three or four more groups of Gnostics, it is evident that about the end of his episcopate, Victor saw in Rome some ten Christian bishops, or heads of independent groups and schools, all claiming to represent exclusively the true Christian tradition. The hesitation of Victor in the question of the Montanists may be easily understood: it must have seemed a rash and unwise policy to provoke by a hasty condemnation the formation of still another group of rebels, while there was not as yet sufficient reason to repudiate them so far as the community of Rome was concerned.[52]

If Victor's policy were to be judged by the immediate results of his various condemnations of heretics, we should say that it was a failure. But though it may have appeared so to Victor himself and to his contemporaries, the historian of today, looking at those events in the light of the later development of pontifical authority in the church, must conclude that it was on the contrary a definite step toward the unification of the community. The exclusion of all the elements which could not be assimilated, even if it temporarily reduced the numerical strength of those who gathered around Victor, yet in the long run was a great benefit; by clearly defining the issues their exclusion added to the vitality of the institution.

Moreover, all these heretical sects that had gained a foothold in Rome were conducting a work of propaganda in many other churches, East and West. In their attempt to conquer the churches of the provinces, they carried the mark of disapproval impressed upon them by the Roman bishops. The communities where new branches of heretical churches were seeking to spread, could not be ignorant that the cause of the dissenters was already lost, and that they had been rejected by such an important and authoritative church as that of Rome. The heretics themselves thus became unwillingly the instrument of the rapid growth and expansion of the authority of the Roman Church. The remote historical origin of that extremely im-

---

[52] The hesitation of Victor may receive some further light by comparing it with the attitude of Irenaeus toward Montanism. Irenaeus was the man who as a presbyter of the Church of Lyons brought to Rome the letter of the Gallican martyrs to Eleutherus, a touching appeal for the peace of the church and, as it seems, a warning against a hasty condemnation of the new prophecy. In his 'Adversus Haereses' Irenaeus does not mention the Montanists, although in one passage he indirectly refers to the false prophets who deny that the church possesses the prophetic charismata (iii. 11, 9). Evidently what Irenaeus condemned was the claim, made by some fanatics of the new prophecy, to the sole possession of the Paraclete; but at the time when he wrote, that is to say under Eleutherus in Rome, he had no reason to condemn the whole movement or to consider it as a heresy or even a schism. A few years later under Victor the situation in Rome must have been still the same, and his attitude would not have been very different from that of Irenaeus.

portant institution of Christianity, the Roman primacy, is to be found in this peculiar situation of the Christian community of the capital. It is not historically exact to say that the Roman bishops assumed from the beginning the right to interfere with matters concerning other churches and to dictate laws and regulations. Such a view is inconsistent with the known facts pointing to a period of development of the monarchical episcopate even in Rome itself, and with the existence of theories about the nature of episcopal authority which found an eloquent exponent in Cyprian, when the Roman bishops had already gone some way on the path which was to lead them to supremacy.

The fact was that the many problems which concerned so many churches were at the same time problems of the Roman community. When, therefore, the Roman bishops sought a solution of them, in order to safeguard the organization and unity of their own church, and excluded the dissidents from their communion, these solutions and these condemnations created a precedent which could not be ignored or challenged by other bishops or churches without arousing the resentment and resistance of Rome. The Roman bishops were bound to uphold in the whole church their decisions taken originally under the pressure of local needs and circumstances, and to make them prevail in other churches, where the same heretics and dissidents had organized, or came to organize, new groups and heretical churches. So it came that the authority of the Roman bishop had to be reckoned with in the church at large even before any theory had been advanced to clothe it with a divine right. And, as we have seen, it was under Victor that this process of expansion of Roman influence began to assume a definite form and to give rise to a tradition which was destined to play a part of capital importance in the history of Christianity.[53]

[53] The famous passage of Irenaeus: "Ad hanc enim ecclesiam [Rome] propter potentiorem principalitatem necesse est omnem convenire ecclesiam, hoc est eos qui sunt undique fideles, in qua semper ab his qui sunt undique conservata est ea quae est ab apostolis traditio" (iii. 3), which has been the subject of so many discussions and interpretations, might take on a more definite value if understood in the light of the situation in Rome about the end of the second century, as we have tried to describe it.

In spite of the internal conflicts which we have mentioned, the ten years of Victor's episcopate were a period of intense and very successful Christian propaganda among the population of Rome. Under Commodus Christianity was little disturbed, and according to the well-known words of Eusebius, "the doctrine of salvation led at that time the souls of men of all races to the pious religion of the Lord of the universe, so that even then many Romans well distinguished for their wealth and their high birth went towards salvation with all their household and their relatives." [54] After making allowance for some exaggeration as to the numbers of those converts, there is no reason to doubt that Eusebius's statement is substantially true. As a matter of fact, archaeological evidence shows conclusively that several members of famous Roman families were converted to Christianity during the latter part of the second century.[55]

There is no evidence that men of the old or new senatorial nobility embraced Christianity in any considerable number before the time of Constantine, but during the whole second

Undoubtedly the phraseology is strange, but when we reflect that what we have is a translation, the repetion of 'undique' in an awkward clause is not necessarily the sign of a scribal error, as Dom Morin has suggested. It seems to me that the clause 'ab his qui sunt undique' might well be understood as referring to the composite character of the Roman community, where so many various groups represented the various traditions of Christianity which, according to Irenaeus, fundamentally agreed (Adv. Haer. i. 10, 2). The preceding clause, 'hoc est eos qui sunt undique fideles,' is an explanation of the meaning of the term 'omnem ecclesiam' and though 'undique' might have been improperly used for 'ubique,' there can be little doubt that it means 'the faithful who are in all the Christian communities.' The general sense would then be: 'with the Church of Rome must agree every church, that is to say all the faithful from every community, because in the Church of Rome by those who have gone there from all communities the apostolic tradition has always been kept unchanged.' The 'potentior principalitas' of the Roman Church could then be understood as referring not only to its priority in time, but also to its being the representative not of a single local tradition but of the tradition of the whole church, on account of the composite character of the Roman community. See Batiffol, L'Église naissante, pp. 250–252, and Le Catholicisme de Saint Augustine, 1920, p. 102, in which he revises his earlier opinion on the meaning of 'principalis,' found in a similar phrase ('ecclesia principalis') of Cyprian and usually interpreted as that of Irenaeus. On this point see A. D'Alès, La Théologie de Saint Cyprien, Paris, 1922, pp. 389–395.

[54] H. E., v. 21.

[55] A complete account of the discoveries of De Rossi and of subsequent archaeological discoveries throwing light on the Christian aristocratic families of Rome is presented by Dom Leclercq in art. 'Aristocratiques (Classes)' DACL. I, 2845–2886.

century conversions of aristocratic ladies were numerous. Their membership in the church was eagerly sought in particular because of the assistance they could offer to the poor and in securing burial places for the dead of the community.[56] In the time of Commodus Victor succeeded even in gaining the support of influential members of the imperial circle, and especially of Marcia the emperor's concubine. Through her good offices he obtained the release of the Christians who under Marcus Aurelius had been condemned to the mines of Sardinia.

An elder of the Church, Hyacinthus, who seems to have been in some way personally related to Marcia, was sent to the island with an imperial order of release for the prisoners, of whom a list had been prepared by Victor. He brought back the confessors to Rome, and among them Callistus, a former slave and future bishop of Rome. Hippolytus affirms that Callistus's name was not on the list, because he had been condemned for common crimes, and that Hyacinthus took pity on him and secured his release from the governor of Sardinia on the authority of his own connection with Marcia.[57] This episode is very significant. It shows that Marcia's name could be used successfully by Christians in persuading a Roman officer to disregard the regulations of his office for the benefit of members of the Christian community. And it may throw an indirect light upon another and more complicated problem which belongs to the history of Victor's episcopate.

There are valid reasons for believing that Victor was the first Roman bishop to adopt a new policy in the administration of the Christian cemeteries. Up to that time the Christians had secured for their use the private cemeteries of wealthy families of their community. These, even when used by the Christians, remained the private property of those families, and did not belong to the community, since a proscribed religion or association could not acquire property or enjoy any of the rights granted to the religious or funerary corporations recognized by

[56] Celsus had already made this remark (Origen, Contra Celsum, iii. 44, 55), and Hippolytus says the same thing against the Callistians (Philos. ix. 12).
[57] Philos. ix. 12. On the assumed Christian profession of Marcia, see DACL. I, 2860–2863.

the law. About this time, however, it seems that the Church of Rome finally succeeded in acquiring legal possession of a cemetery on the Appian Way, still known under the name of the Catacomb of Callistus.[58]

For a long time the tradition prevailed that Callistus was the original founder of this catacomb, but archaeological discoveries and the studies of the famous J. B. De Rossi led to the conclusion that the cemetery was already in existence before Callistus, that it was Bishop Zephyrinus who acquired the property for the church and entrusted its administration and its development to Callistus, then a deacon. The name of Callistus was appropriately given to the catacomb, since extensive works under his care, first as superintendent, and then as bishop after Zephyrinus's death, caused it to become the greatest Christian cemetery of Rome.[59] Of this enlargement by Callistus there is no doubt, but that the cemetery was acquired for the church by Callistus, or indeed by Zephyrinus, seems to me a theory lacking sufficient evidence.

The contentions on which rests the claim in behalf of Callistus and Zephyrinus, as stated by De Rossi and the archaeologists who follow his theory, may be summarized as follows: 1. The occasion which made it possible for the Church of

[58] The historical evidence that about the middle of the third century the Church of Rome had for a long time been in legal possession of cemeteries was gathered and analyzed by De Rossi (Roma Sotterranea, i, pp. 101 ff.). J. P. Kirsch ('Die christliche Cultusgebäude in der vorkonstantinischen Zeit,' in Festschrift d. deutschen Campo Santo in Rom, Freiburg, 1897, pp. 6-20) collected numbers of texts giving evidence that about the end of the second century or the beginning of the third the Christians had special meeting-places for their religious cult and that these places, even in the eyes of the government, belonged to the Christian communities. But how was it possible for a persecuted religion to enjoy the right of possession of cemeteries and meeting-places is difficult to explain. Tillemont was the first to suppose that in the period of Severus Alexander (222-235), who is described by his biographer Lampridius as very sympathetic to the Christians, the church obtained a certain legal recognition. With better reasons De Rossi was led to set the date earlier, and pointed to the period of Septimius Severus as the one most likely to have offered to the church the opportunity to act as a legal corporation.

[59] Roma Sott., II. The whole second volume of this monumental work consists of a detailed description and history of the Catacombs of Callistus. For all subsequent discoveries and studies see the collections of the Bullettino and of the Nuovo Bullettino di archeologia cristiana, Rome, 1863-1923, and the monograph of Leclercq, DACL. II, 1665-1774.

Rome to acquire a legal title of possession of the cemetery is to be found in the edict of Severus confirming and extending to the provinces of the empire the privileges granted to the funerary associations. The date of this rescript falls within the episcopate of Zephyrinus.

2. Under Zephyrinus the Christians in Rome formed funerary associations, such as were allowed by the law, and thus obtained recognition of their property-right over the cemetery.

3. Under Zephyrinus the ancient Vatican cemetery, where all his predecessors were buried, was closed and a new *crypta papalis* built in the catacomb of Callistus; and there Zephyrinus himself was laid to rest at his death.

4. For a time the catacomb was called 'the cemetery of Zephyrinus' in memory of its real founder, and only later was his name superseded by that of Callistus.

These assumptions seem to me far from exact and conclusive, and I think that stronger arguments may be brought in favor of the theory that the acquisition of the new property in the name of the church took place in the episcopate of Victor. First of all, it is not exact to say that Severus's rescript in favor of the *collegia tenuiorum* falls within Zephyrinus's episcopate. As De Rossi himself remarks, the rescript was issued in the name of Septimius Severus alone, not under the joint names of Septimius and Caracalla. Now there is no doubt, according to recent historical investigations, that Caracalla was raised to the position of caesar and imperator designatus in 196, and that rescripts under both names are found as early as 197. The rescript for the funerary associations must therefore have been issued between 192, the year of Septimius's accession, and 196, the year of the proclamation of Caracalla, that is to say, it falls within the episcopate of Victor, which lasted until 198/9.[60]

[60] Caracalla became caesar in 196 after the last surrender of Niger's party and at the beginning of the new war against Albinus. Spartianus's statement is confirmed by numismatic evidence. It was at the time when Caracalla was made caesar and imperator designatus that he assumed also the name of Antoninus, and not in 198 as Lampridius says. This is also confirmed by numismatic evidence (Platnauer, pp. 103, 124, n. 3; Hasebroek pp. 86–90; De Ruggero, Dizion. Epigr. II, p. 197). The two earlier rescripts in which Caracalla appears as joint ruler with Septimius are dated in the Digest, January 1, 196 (Cod. Just., ix. 41, 1), and June 30, 196 (iv. 19, 1). Since, however,

But even if it be granted that the rescript of Severus might have come too late to be used by Victor, to explain through it the change in the policy of cemeterial administration of the church is to exaggerate the importance of the rescript, as if it had introduced new legislation. It did not; it simply confirmed privileges already in existence. The text still to be found in the Digest says: *"divus quoque Severus praescripsit,"* which proves, as Waltzing remarks, that similar rescripts had before been published.[61] As a matter of fact, the great period of development of the *collegia tenuiorum* began with Marcus Aurelius and continued to the Severi, under whom they spread also through Italy and the western provinces. In the East they remained unknown; in the West their number decreased during the third century, to disappear entirely in the fourth. It would, therefore, have been as possible and easy for Victor to organize a Christian funerary association in Rome before the publication of Severus's rescript as for Zephyrinus to do so after it.

But after all, the value of this rescript in relation to the acquisition of the cemetery by the church depends upon the assumption that the Roman Christian community formed funerary associations and were registered in the books of the praefectura urbana as *collegia tenuiorum* thus evading the laws against Christian religious associations. Now this is very far from being certain; the circumstantial evidence gathered by De Rossi is altogether weak, and no further light has been thrown on this point by any of the important archaeological discoveries made since his death. His theory, at first adopted with enthusiasm by historians, has been almost completely demolished by the attacks of authoritative scholars and archaeologists, and the prevalent theory now is that formulated by Duchesne that under Commodus the Christian community of Rome was tolerated, obtained a certain recognition, and was allowed to acquire property, not by use of the legal fiction of a

---

Caracalla was saluted caesar only in September of 196, both dates are wrong and must be shifted to the following year (Platnauer, p. 103, n. 3). At any rate the rescript of the collegia tenuiora must have been published at least three years before Victor's death.

[61] Étude historique sur les corporations professionnelles des Romains, I, pp. 141–153, and art. 'Collegia,' in DACL. III, 2112–2113.

funerary association but as a church, that is to say as a religious association.[62]

But whether the Christians formed funerary associations or not, it is obvious that the acquisition of property in the name of a Christian association could happen only in a period of great tolerance and of a friendly attitude of the government toward the Christians. Even De Rossi himself and his staunchest followers, such as Dom Leclercq, admit that the subterfuge of being registered as funerary associations could not deceive the government, and that the permit was granted by the Roman officers in full knowledge that it was asked by the Christian community and for the purpose of providing a burial ground for Christians.[63]

Now in the whole history of the last quarter of the second century and the first decades of the third the only period in which such a thing may reasonably be supposed to have taken place is that of the last years of Commodus and the first years of Severus, roughly the decade from 186 to 196, which falls chiefly within the episcopate of Victor. The martyrdom of Apollonius in 183–185 marks the last case known with certainty of a death penalty upon a confessed Christian inflicted in Rome under Commodus,[64] and at the other extreme the

[62] Duchesne (Histoire ancienne de l'Église, I, pp. 381–387, and in earlier publications) and Schulze (De christianorum veterum rebus sepulcralibus, Gotha, 1879) were the first seriously to attack De Rossi's theory, which is also rejected by such authoritative scholars in the field of early Christian history as Batiffol, Harnack, Sohm, and Kirsch. One of the most competent writers on the subject of the Roman collegia, Waltzing, has also rejected it. The theory of De Rossi, however, is still followed by many Roman archaeologists and by Dom Leclercq. A detailed exposition and discussion of the two theories with reference to the sources and complete bibliography is found in DACL., articles 'Agape,' 'Area,' 'Calliste,' 'Catacombes' by Leclercq, and article 'Collegia' by Waltzing.

[63] Waltzing, after having remarked: "De Rossi ne soutient pas seulement que le gouvernement laissait se commettre une fraude légale, mais qu'il y prêtait lui-même les mains, qu'il était de connivence avec les contravenants, puisqu' il leur reconnaissait formellement les privilèges des collèges funéraires," concludes that to simplify the juridical question it is better to assume outright that the government "fermait les yeux sur un catégorie d'associations religieuses sans leur conférer aucun droit, et il leur permettait de vivre sous le régime du droit commun, comme à beaucoup d'associations religieuses, professionnelles et autres" (DACL. III, 2115–2116).

[64] After the discovery of the Greek and of the Armenian text of the Acta Apollonii the fact of his martyrdom in Rome under Commodus is commonly admitted. Not,

persecution of the Christians of Carthage in 197 marks the beginning of the hostile policy of Severus against the church.[65] If there was a period in which the Roman magistrates could and would ignore the usual procedure against the Christians, and deal with their associations, either under an assumed funerary character or otherwise, as if they were not banned by the law, it was the period of Victor, the same period in which the bishop was able to obtain the release of Christian prisoners and in which Hyacinthus, by merely pronouncing the name of Marcia, could persuade the Roman governor of Sardinia to free a state prisoner without any superior authorization.

It is altogether unlikely that the same attitude could have been taken by the Roman magistrates in the time of Zephyrinus. Plautianus, who governed Rome in the absence of Severus, was avowedly an enemy of Christianity, and after the publication of the edict of 201, by which Severus tried to check Christian propaganda altogether, the persecution assumed a more and more severe character. The next period of respite came with the reign of Severus Alexander,[66] but at that time the cemetery of Callistus was already developed and had been a possession of the church for several years.

And now let us turn to the more important question of the archaeological evidence. Of the three large *areae* which form the great catacombs of Callistus only the first goes back to that period and is properly called by his name. The long and painstaking studies of J. B. De Rossi and his brother Michael De Rossi led by sound reasoning to the conclusion that the first *area* of the cemetery, established on a *praedium* belonging originally to the family of the Caecilii, underwent before the time of Callistus three successive stages of enlargement. The

however, the legend that Apollonius was a senator and that his trial took place before the Senate. A full account of the complicated problem of Apollonius's trial is given in DACL. art. 'Droit persecuteur,' IV, 1633–1648; bibliography, ibid., Nos. 4–14).

[65] Tertullian, Apologeticus, 1, 7.

[66] The searching criticism of K. Bihlmeyer (Die syrischen Kaiser zu Rom und das Christentum, 1916) on Lampridius's biography of Alexander has greatly reduced the value of this witness to the friendly attitude of the emperor toward Christianity and to the assumed Christian influences upon his religious thinking, so much emphasized by many historians, as for instance by P. Allard, Histoire des Persécutions, II, pp. 183–205.

first was coincident with the foundation of the hypogeum of the Caecilii, and may go back to the time of Marcus Aurelius. The second series of works took place undoubtedly under Commodus, and many Christians were then buried there. But the need for still more space was urgent, and during the last years of Commodus or the first years of Severus a deep staircase was built in order to dig new galleries at a lower level; the ground, however, proved too friable and the plan was abandoned.[67] Later, when Callistus assumed the control of the cemetery, he continued the work in another direction and carried out a more important series of extensive works in this third section of the first *area* of the catacombs.

It is therefore undeniable that the hypogeum of the Caecilii began to be used extensively as a Christian cemetery under the episcopate of Victor. The names and trade-marks on the bricks used in the construction of the staircase which closes the second stage of works of the catacomb afford conclusive evidence that they belong to the period of Victor. De Rossi affirms emphatically that this evidence "is so eloquent that all doubts on this point must be set aside."[68] Dom Leclercq states still more explicitly: "The chronology of the trade-marks of the bricks does not permit in any way the assignment of these early works to the time when Callistus was superintendent of the catacomb. When he took office he found already a great number of tombs there in the galleries."[69]

But in spite of the undeniable fact that the place was already a considerable Christian cemetery under Victor, archaeologists and historians, following De Rossi, have agreed that it became

[67] Roma Sott., II, pp. 240–244.

[68] Ibid., p. 244. The bricks used in the corridor leading to the staircase and in the staircase itself all have the trade-mark of two fishes and the inscription, 'Opus doliare ex praediis domini nostri et figulinis novis.' This trade-mark is well known to archaeologists; it belonged to the imperial brick-factories of the time of Marcus Aurelius and Commodus. "The constant uniformity of the bricks used in a construction is an evident proof," says De Rossi, "that they were new bricks coming from the factories and form a sure index of the date of the construction." When old material was used, we commonly find a mixture of bricks belonging to various periods and to different factories. The staircase, therefore, was built either during the last years of Commodus or shortly after his death (ibid., p. 241).

[69] DACL. II, 1696.

a property of the church only under Zephyrinus, when Callistus was put in charge of it. The theory of De Rossi is that the hypogeum of the Caecilii was started, or at least began to be used by Christians, when the martyr Caecilia, a member of that illustrious family executed under Marcus Aurelius, was buried there. Following the Christian custom many Christians obtained permission to be laid to rest near the relics of the martyr, and thus the cemetery developed in the same manner as all other early Christian catacombs established in the burial grounds of private families.[70] Later, as we have said, it is supposed that under Zephyrinus the Christians formed a special funerary *collegium* of which the deacon Callistus was officially the syndic, and took possession of the cemetery as a corporation recognized by law.

Unfortunately this theory of the great Roman archaeologist is based on very doubtful evidence. His learned effort to prove that Caecilia's martyrdom took place under Marcus Aurelius falls short of being conclusive. Her Acts are a late forgery; the chronological and historical indications contained in them are obviously erroneous. As a matter of fact, at the present stage of hagiographical studies, there is so large a variety of opinions about the time of Caecilia's martyrdom as to cover the whole range of Roman history from Marcus Aurelius to Julian the Apostate. The date which seems more probable is that of Diocletian's persecution.[71] The martyr Caecilia, then, had nothing to do with the beginning of the catacombs of Callistus. The only positive conclusions of De Rossi on this early period of the history of the catacomb are (1) that it was established on the property of the Caecilii, and (2) that it was used as a Christian cemetery under Victor, even if it did not as yet contain the tomb of the famous martyr. Why then must this passage of the right of property from the family of the Caecilii to the church be assigned to the time of Zephyrinus and not to the time of Victor?

[70] Roma Sott. II, Introd. chap. 2, pp. xxii–xliii, 113–161, 361–365.
[71] DACL. II, 1691, n. 1; 2712–2738.

The sources of information on this event so far available are as follows. (1) The narrative of Hippolytus in the Philosophumena. (2) The indications of the Liber Pontificalis. (3) The archaeological evidence of the so-called *crypta papalis* of the Catacomb of Callistus. The narrative of Hippolytus contains only the statement: "After Victor's death, Zephyrinus, . . . sending for Callistus from Antium, set him over the cemetery." [72] De Rossi remarked that the fact that Hippolytus calls the place merely 'the cemetery' without any further qualification is significant. There were many Christian cemeteries called by the names of their early proprietors or by those of famous persons and martyrs buried in them; if this one is called simply 'the cemetery,' in the singular, that means that it was the only one which belonged to the church and so was differentiated from all others. It is, however, probable, De Rossi suggests, that the cemetery was already called the cemetery of Callistus, and that Hippolytus, who hated Callistus's memory, purposely omitted to call it by his opponent's name.[73]

It seems to me that if this laconic mention of the fact can prove anything, it is that the cemetery was already the property of the church when Callistus was entrusted with its management. The three parts of the sentence, 'after Victor's death,' 'sent for Callistus from Antium,' 'set him over the cemetery,' are related as consecutive stages of the act by which Callistus coming from Antium took charge of the cemetery. 'The cemetery,' then, was the name by which it was called at

[72] Philos. ix. 12 (ed. Wendland, p. 248). The whole passage reads as follows: "After [Victor's] falling asleep, Zephyrinus having selected [Callistus] as assistant in the government [reformation?] of the clergy, honored him to his own detriment, and calling him back from Antium set him over the cemetery."

[73] Roma Sott., I, p. 197; II, p. 370; Bull. arch. crist., 1867, pp. 8–12. Dom Leclercq (DACL. II, 1693) comments on the passage from Hippolytus as follows: "A la fin du II⁰ siècle il ne peut venir à l'esprit de personne de supposer que la communauté chrétienne de Rome ne possédait qu'un seul cimetière, en ce cas, pourquoi ne pas dire que Calliste fut préposé à la direction d'un cimetière, ou de l'un des cimetières?" The logical answer to this question seems to be that the term 'the cemetery' was used without qualification because it belonged already to the community when Callistus assumed its management. But on the contrary, the answer of Leclercq is that at that time it did not belong to the community, but was acquired later by Callistus. Then what becomes of the value of the evidence?

that time, since the name of Callistus was added only much later, after the many years of his administration. Granted that the phrase 'the cemetery' has the meaning attributed to it by De Rossi, it is logical to assume that the catacomb was already the property of the church at Victor's death, at the time of the event mentioned by Hippolytus in connection with which he uses the significant absolute term 'the cemetery.' But whatever the fact might have been, this passage of Hippolytus cannot be construed as meaning or implying that the cemetery became a church property under Zephyrinus and by the act of Callistus.

The Liber Pontificalis has this brief note about Callistus: *"Qui fecit alium cymiterium via Appia, ubi multi sacerdotes et martyres requiescunt, qui appellatur usque in hodierno die cymiterium Callisti."* [74] Since it is beyond doubt that Callistus was not the founder of the cemetery, this passage only shows that in time a tradition arose which wrongly attributed to him the establishment of the catacombs bearing his name; and it throws no light on the problem. More important is the passage which says of Zephyrinus: *"sepultus est in cymiterio suo iuxta cymiterium Callisti via Appia."* [75] This passage is puzzling; it seems to imply that there was a cemetery near to but different from that of Callistus and called the cemetery of Zephyrinus. If there were definite evidence that the cemetery of Callistus was once called the cemetery of Zephyrinus, it would be a valuable argument in support of the opinion that Zephyrinus has something to do with the acquisition of the cemetery. But the passage quoted above is far from affording this evidence; it would prove on the contrary that the so-called cemetery of Zephyrinus was not the cemetery of Callistus. To overcome this difficulty an ingenious theory was formulated by De Rossi.

According to his conclusions, Zephyrinus was first buried in a special chamber of the catacombs of Callistus, a new chamber set aside for the burial of the bishops, but later, after 258, his body was removed from there to make room for the relics of the martyr bishop Xystus II, who was for a long time the object

[74] Ed. Duchesne, I, p. 141.
[75] Ibid., p. 139.

of a special cult in the *crypta papalis* of the catacomb. Zephyrinus's body was then transferred to a tomb in the open cemetery outside the catacomb, but very near to the stairs of its entrance. It remained there probably until the ninth century. The author of the biography of the Liber Pontificalis was ignorant of this translation of Zephyrinus's relics, and thus, while he kept the ancient topographical indication found in the records, "*sepultus est in cymiterio suo*," on the other hand, since he knew that the tomb was outside the catacomb, he added a further indication "*juxta cymiterium Callisti.*" If he had known better, he would have said: '*in cymiterio suo, et secundo iuxta cymiterium Callisti.*' This would have afforded the evidence that the catacomb, or at least a part of it, was once called *cymiterium Zephyrini.*[76]

With all due respect to the great De Rossi, it seems to me that even granted the possibility of a removal of Zephyrinus's body from one place to another, the conclusion that the phrase *cymiterio suo* is to be referred to the catacomb of Callistus is unwarranted by the fact that there is no other mention whatever that Zephyrinus was ever buried there or that his name was ever given to the catacomb. The natural explanation of the words *cymiterio suo* is either that the upper cemetery was called by the name of Zephyrinus because he was the most conspicuous person buried there, or that they are to be taken only in the general sense, 'in a place of his own,' as distinct from the *crypta papalis* in which were laid to rest several of his successors. But this question is closely connected with the more general problem of the archaeological evidence concerning the *crypta papalis.*

It seems to me that the real reason which has led archaeologists and historians to discard Victor's name as the founder

---

[76] Roma Sott., II, pp. 4-13, 50-51. De Rossi himself, however, presents his theory as a mere hypothesis: "If in the most conspicuous place of the papal sepulchral chamber was laid, as is credible, a pope, I do not see to whom to assign that place better than to Zephyrinus. Perhaps Xystus III decided later to give that place to his famous predecessor Xystus II, and this might have caused the translation of Zephyrinus to the upper chapel. But it is certain that Xystus III in the catalogue put within the crypta made no mention of Zephyrinus." In his later pages, however, De Rossi treats the fact of Zephyrinus's first burial in the crypta as quite certain, and builds on it the whole theory of the crypta papalis.

of the cemetery is the striking fact that at Zephyrinus's death the ancient custom of burying the bishops in the ancient Vatican cemetery near the tomb of Peter was discontinued. The abandonment of this custom is very surprising, for the churches at that time attached great importance not only to the possession of a list of their bishops but also to the assemblage of their tombs in the same place as alike constituting eloquent evidence of legitimate succession and unbroken doctrinal tradition from the early apostles. We do not know the reason which decided or obliged Callistus to assign to Zephyrinus a resting-place far from his predecessors.[77] Had the Vatican cemetery become incapable of further use? Had it become dangerous for political reasons? Had it fallen under the control of some dissident group? Was this innovation caused by the works executed in the Vatican by Elagabalus to fit the place for special spectacles and games? Had any of these reasons any connection with a possible transfer of Peter's body from the Vatican to the place known as 'ad Catacumbas' on the Appian Way, not far distant from the cemetery of Callistus?[78] There is no way of finding a definite answer to these questions, but undoubtedly the breach in the old tradition took place in this period.

Was either Zephyrinus or Callistus the founder of the *crypta papalis*? Definite historical evidence is lacking. As we have seen, that Zephyrinus was buried there is a mere supposition, while Callistus was not laid to rest in the cemetery which had been the object of so much care during his twenty-five years' ecclesiastical activity, but in the cemetery of Calepodius on the

[77] Roma Sott., II, pp. 4–97; DACL. II, 1665, n. 1.

[78] Any connection between the two events is energetically rejected by De Rossi. The question of the transfer of Peter's and Paul's relics to the place 'Ad Catacumbas' on the Appian Way, has been discussed afresh after the new excavations of recent years in the Basilica of St. Sebastian ad Catacumbas. See bibliography on this question in my article, 'The Tombs of the Apostles ad Catacumbas,' *Harvard Theological Review*, 1921, p. 87, and Lietzmann's article on the same question in the number for April, 1923. For the new excavations of 1921–23, see O. Marucchi in Nuovo Bull. arch. cris., 1921, pp. 3–14; and 1923, pp. 3–27. The further evidence found in these excavations continues to make probable the theory that the transfer really took place, but a definite and final proof is still lacking, and the question of the date still presents serious difficulties. See K. Erbes, 'Die geschichtlichen Verhältnisse der Apostelgräber in Rom,' Zeitschrift für Kirchengeschichte, 1924, pp. 38–92.

Aurelian Way.[79] Very doubtful is also the case of his successor Urbanus.[80] The first Roman bishop whose tomb was undoubtedly in the crypta was Antheros († 236); a few years later the body of his predecessor Pontianus, brought back from Sardinia, was also buried there. So far the historical evidence. The archaeological evidence would seem more conclusive. The absence of arcosolia in the original cubicles of the crypta has led De Rossi to the conclusion that it was built in the time of Zephyrinus, or at least before the construction of the second and third *areae* of the catacomb. This is possible, though the period in which this archaic form of the cubicles gave way to the more elaborate form of the arcosolia cannot be determined with

[79] This fact that Callistus was not buried in his catacomb nor in the crypta papalis, which is supposed to have been already in existence and inaugurated by the tomb of Zephyrinus, has puzzled the archaeologists and historians, who have seen in it "une étrange bizarrerie du sort" (Leclercq, DACL. II, 1660). An explanation was sought in the apocryphal Acta Callixti, in which it is said that Callistus by order of the Emperor Alexander Severus was stoned to death, thrown in a pit, and then buried by the Christians in the cemetery of Calepodius. Tillemont (Mémoires, III, p. 251) suggested that the unusual way in which Callistus was put to death suits better an irregular execution by a mob than a regular trial. De Rossi accepted this suggestion. Duchesne formulated in a more definite way the theory that Callistus was killed by an angry mob, which "détournant les fidèles de Rome de tenter le passage du Tibre et de s'aventurer sur la voie Appienne, les força de s'échapper avec le corps de leur évêque, par la porte la plus voisine du théâtre de sa mort" (Lib. Pont., I, p. xliii). The explanation is ingenious, but is only an hypothesis based on the acceptance of one part of the apocryphal acts and the rejection of the rest.

[80] The question of Urbanus's resting-place is one of the most complicated in Christian archaeology. The Liber Pontificalis and the ancient martyrologies said: "Urbanus sepultus est in cymiterio Praetextati," but the apocryphal Acta S. Caeciliae and some manuscripts of the Martyrologium Hieronymianum said: "in coemeterio Callisti." It seems that in the list of interments in the crypta papalis which Xystus III caused to be inscribed on a tablet in the crypta, the name of Urbanus did not appear (DACL. II, 1730). The hypothesis of two Urbani, one the bishop of Rome and the other a bishop of some other city who died in Rome on a visit, and of a confusion between them was formulated by De Rossi (Roma Sott., II, pp. 52–54). The discovery of a slab in the crypta papalis with the name of Urbanus seems to confirm the statement that the bishop of Rome was buried there. It must be noticed, however, that the name is engraved not on the face of the slab but on one side, and the inscription itself shows a peculiar form of the letter A. De Rossi thinks that these peculiarities confirm the archaic character of the slabs. Others on the contrary think that they show a later period (Wilpert, Die Papstgräber und die Caeciliengruft, Freiburg, 1909, p. 17). Authoritative scholars still think that Urbanus was buried in the cemetery of Praetextatus, and that the Urbanus lying in St. Callistus was a later bishop from some other city (Kirsch, Cath. Encycl., XV, p. 269).

precision, and its chronological limits may be stretched several years without much difficulty.

But all this granted, do we find in it any evidence that bears upon the attribution to Zephyrinus and Callistus of the acquisition of the cemetery in the name of the church? None whatever. There is no necessary connection between the two facts, the abandonment of the Vatican cemetery and the acquisition in the name of the church of the cemetery of Callistus. The former was abandoned for serious and impellent reasons unknown to us; the latter was chosen as a new place for the episcopal burials because, belonging to the church, it was a safer place than any other. But that does not prove that the cemetery was secured to the church by Zephyrinus and not by Victor.

What still remains beyond doubt is only the fact that the first works of enlargement and adaptation of the cemetery for the use of a community took place under Victor; and in a question enveloped in so much obscurity this single piece of incontrovertible evidence ought to have a higher value than any learned hypotheses. Now is it probable that Victor undertook the development of the hypogeum of the Caecilii while still, at least in the eyes of the law, the private property of that family, and without having secured direct possession of it? The analysis of the circumstances and of the general situation of the Roman Christian community during the years of Victor's episcopate confirms, if I am right, the conclusions of the archaeological evidence in his favor.

The motives which impelled the Roman Church to adopt a new cemeterial policy are obvious, and were well summarized by Dom Leclercq on the lines traced by De Rossi. The community had grown to such an extent that the ancient small cemeteries owned by private families were insufficient. It was necessary to enlarge them by digging new galleries and sepulchral chambers, and it could not be expected that the owners would themselves undertake such extensive works of construction and the upkeep of such large places. On the other hand, it would have involved great risk for the ecclesiastical administration to take upon itself such an enterprise without possessing a legal title to the cemeteries, since it was always possible that by right of inheritance they might fall into the hands of pagan members of the families concerned, be again used as burial places for heathen, and be lost to the church.[81]

If these were the reasons which made it urgent for the church to find a new solution of the cemeterial problem, we must say that they are suited to the time of Victor's episcopate. We have already mentioned that the extraordinary growth of the Christian community of Rome took place during the period of peace and tolerance in the reign of Commodus and the first years of Severus. The passage of Eusebius quoted above also states that at that time many members of the aristocracy of Rome were gained for the Christian faith. Thus we find present both the urgent need of the growing community and large possibilities of obtaining the necessary *praedium* for a new cemetery, through increase in the number of wealthy Christian families. If about the year 200 it would have been attended with risk for Zephyrinus and Callistus to undertake extensive works in the catacomb without having first acquired a right of property in the name of the church, would it have been less dangerous for Victor to do the same thing in the year 190? And since there is no doubt that extensive works were carried on in the cemetery under Victor, it is natural to infer that the hypogeum of the Caecilii had already passed under the full control of the Roman bishop.

But there is another reason which has been overlooked by historians, and which, it seems to me, must have played an important part in the adoption of a new program of cemeterial development. The Christian cemeteries, not being the legal property of the church were not under the absolute control of the central government of the bishop. Obviously, in a community divided into so many conflicting groups as was the Roman Church at the end of the second century, a private cemetery was exposed not only to the danger of falling eventually into the hands of a heathen family, but also to that of coming under the control of a dissident group with which the legal owner of the cemetery might have sympathized. And such a danger must have been the more acute that some of the

[81] DACL. II, 2425.

groups, by reason of their philosophical teaching and hellenistic culture, could not fail to attract the favor of Christian members of the upper classes.

The situation must have been serious for a bishop like Victor, who found himself confronted with eight or ten leaders of independent groups all claiming to be the legitimate rulers of the Christian community and the representatives of true Christian tradition. To see any one of the ancient and venerable cemeteries fall into the hands of an heretical group would have been a great misfortune for the Roman bishop. Not only by such an event were the sacred places, where martyrs and confessors were resting in peace, in a way desecrated by the presence of the tombs of heretics, but it would become impossible for the bishop to use the place for the burial of the faithful of his following. For the existence of cemeteries of heretics separate from those of other Christians there is plenty of historical and archaeological evidence from the third century.[82] But it is plain that even in the second century the heretical and dissident groups must have been confronted with the problem of providing a burial ground for their followers. The need would arise whenever a group was excluded from the communion of the church. It had either to find wealthy members willing to provide new burial grounds for their community, or to gain to its side some family which had already given to the Christians the use of their pri-

[82] In the third century cemeteries of heretics must have been very numerous. The Novatianists had their own (De Rossi, Bull. arch. cris., 1863, p. 20); the followers of Hippolytus had also their own catacomb, and there his body was buried after it was brought back from Sardinia (Marucchi, Éléments d'archéologie chrét., I, 337; II, 296). The Sabellians had a cemetery in which originally stood the well-known inscription: "Qui et Filius diceris et Pater inveniris" (De Rossi, Bull., 1866, p. 95). De Rossi, however, thinks that it belongs to the fourth century. In 1903 a small cemetery was discovered on the Via Latina which probably belonged to a group of Valentinians and in which probably was originally placed the famous Gnostic inscription for a woman (CIG. IV, 9595a; Marucchi, Nuovo Bull., 1903, pp. 301–314). In 1910 another hypogeum was discovered on the same Via Latina, which is known as the sepulchre of Trebius Justus (Kanzler, Nuovo Bull., 1911, pp. 201–207). From the paintings and the decorations Marucchi concluded that this also belonged to a Gnostic group (Nuovo Bull., 1911, pp. 209–235). On the cemeteries of the heretics in general and their characteristics see De Rossi, Roma Sott., I, pp. 108–109; Marucchi, N. Bull., 1903, p. 304; Leclercq, DACL. II, 2383.

vate cemetery. It seems that both possibilities were exploited by the heretics and dissidents.

Of the former solution a new evidence has recently come to light in the hypogeum of the Viale Manzoni discovered in 1919.[83] The oldest part of this catacomb is assigned on sound archaeological grounds to the late second century, and an inscription mentioning the "*Liberti Aurelii*" shows that the place originally belonged to some branch of the gens Aurelia. There is no doubt that the development of this catacomb went through the same stages as all other Christian cemeteries of ancient Rome: "to a small and well-decorated funeral chamber belonging to a private family gradually several simple and bare galleries were added for the use of a community." [84] From the subject and the symbolism of the paintings archaeologists have agreed that this catacomb must have been used by a Christian heretical group, probably a group of Valentinian Gnostics.[85]

More difficult is it to find evidence of the other practical solution of the heretics' problem, that is to say, of the eventual and temporary control of one or another of the ancient Christian cemeteries by some heretical or dissident group. The reasons are obvious. First of all, some of those groups were not heretical but only dissident in the matter of discipline, as was the case with the Asiatics; their funerary symbols and formulae were the same simple generic symbols and the same laconic phrases used by all the Christians. Even the burial places of the heretics rarely betray their heretical character through any peculiar phrase in the inscriptions. Furthermore, in cases in which the heretics during their temporary control of a cata-

[83] G. Bendinelli, 'Ipogeo con pitture scoperto presso il Viale Manzoni,' Notizie degli Scavi, 1920, pp. 123–141; and 'Nuove scoperte,' ibid., 1921, pp. 230–234.

[84] Ibid., 1920, p. 140.

[85] O. Marucchi, Nuovo Bull., 1921, pp. 44–47, 83–93; Grossi-Gondi, Civiltà Cattolica, Rome, 1921, pp. 2, 127; G. de Jerphanion, 'Les dernières découvertes dans la Rome souterraine, in Les Études, 5 Avril 1922, pp. 59–80. In his second article Marucchi very ingeniously interprets the paintings of this hypogeum as representing scenes from the book of Job, which, as is known from Clement of Alexandria (Stromata, iv. 12), was used by some Gnostics and especially by Basilides in their effort to solve the obscure problem of evil (Buonaiuti, Gnosticismo, p. 164). His theory has not been accepted by all (Wilpert, Jerphanion), but all agree that this cemetery belonged to heretics, and that it was established in the late second century.

comb used symbols or caused scenes to be painted which could hurt the feelings of orthodox believers, these evidences of their passage were entirely destroyed as soon as the Great Church entered again into possession of the place. For the third century historical evidence is not lacking of heretical attempts to get possession of Christian cemeteries; [86] it is likely that similar attempts were also made in the second half of the second century, when the cemeterial administration of the church was still on a more uncertain and weaker basis than after the episcopate of Victor.

In view of the general situation of the Christian community it is obvious that during the last decades of the second century the many divisions and conflicts of the various Roman groups must have created an acute problem concerning the Christian cemeteries. And such a problem must have been more urgent and more vital for the large community of which Victor was the recognized and obeyed leader than for many other groups. The dissident and heretical groups were smaller, and their needs were limited: moreover, many of them through their philosophical and mystical theories, which attracted persons of culture, had in their ranks far more members of better social condition than were found in the large humble crowds gathered around Victor. The propaganda of the conflicting groups in the effort to gain followers from the ranks of their competitors was undoubtedly very active and in many cases even unscrupulous, as we find for instance a few years later in the conflict between Hippolytus and Callistus. The possession of a cemetery must have been a great advantage and a good instrument for efficient propaganda.

To the Christians of the poorer classes, as to everyone else at that time, it was of primary concern to secure through a religious affiliation a decent funeral and a burial place after death. It was the common aspiration of all the humble people crowded

---

[86] Of the Novatianists it is said that they stole from the cemetery on the Via Salaria the body of St. Silanus and concealed it in their catacomb (De Rossi, Bull., 1863, p. 20). Under the Emperor Maximus two Tertullianists who settled in Rome from Africa were granted a permit to build a 'collegium extra muros urbis,' and they came by force into possession of the tomb of the martyrs Processus and Martinianus, but after the fall of Maximus they were expelled from the place (DACL. II, 2383).

in the capital; the *collegia tenuiorum* were multiplying under the protection of the law, so that there was no group of men belonging to the same trade or profession, or devotees of the same deity, or even united as freedmen and slaves of the same large household, who did not form a collegium in order to escape after death the horrors that the popular tradition assigned to the dead whose bodies lacked funeral honors. The Christian propaganda among the common people of Rome could not ignore this important point, the more so that the Christian belief in the resurrection of the flesh added still more valid reasons for the traditional care of the dead. Nor could this point be ignored by the various Christian groups in their mutual conflicts.

The great bulk of Victor's followers were poor people, and among them, as we have already noticed, were numbers of Africans and Latins. Probably these could not be easily gained by the philosophical theories of the Gnostics, or even by the austerities of the Marcionites, but they might easily be attracted by the promise of the same advantages that the heathen secured through their *collegia tenuiorum*, unless the Great Church could make provision to satisfy this need. The possession of a cemetery which could be developed on a large scale, and on which the bishop could at any time enforce his right of ownership without interference by families or by hostile groups, must have appeared to Victor as necessary and also as a valuable means of keeping the multitudes of his following together.

At this point the obvious suggestion arises that the African origin of Victor, and the large number of African Christians which were to be found in his community, might throw some light on this problem of the acquisition of the hypogeum of the Caecilii for a Christian cemetery. As a matter of fact it seems that the Christian community of Carthage came into possession of the *areae* used as Christian cemeteries either earlier than the Church of Rome or at latest at the same time. The famous passage of the 39th chapter of Tertullian's 'Apologeticus,' in which the characters of the Christian association are described, is the *locus classicus* of De Rossi's argument for his theory that the Christians formed *collegia funeraticia*, and possessed the cemeteries in that capacity. The 'Apologeticus' was undoubtedly written during the last months of 197, when Victor was still alive. And since Tertullian speaks of the Christian organization as of something which was not new but already traditional, that would suggest that in Africa the Christian *collegia tenuiorum*, if they ever existed, must have been organized earlier than in Rome.[87]

The objections, however, against such an interpretation of the passage from Tertullian are strong, and the whole theory of the Christian collegia rests on doubtful evidence. But that the Christians in Carthage formed an association with special laws, some of which were very similar to those adopted by the funerary associations of the heathen, is admitted; the divergence is only on the question whether they appeared in the eyes of the law as *collegia funeraticia* and as such were recognized by the government, or whether they were simply religious associations which, though forbidden by the law, were left undisturbed, as was often the case with all kinds of illicit associations in periods of tolerance or indifference on the part of the government.

But either as a funerary association or a tolerated religious association, the community of Carthage seems to have possessed the *areae* in its own name. There is no direct evidence for this in the 'Apologeticus,' but such evidence is found in another writing of Tertullian, the epistle 'Ad Scapulam,' written about 212. That the Christians of Carthage could have acquired the property of the *areae* during this interval between 197 and 212 is difficult to admit, since it was a period of persecution, and the violence of the populace against the Christians was such that the Roman governors did not dare even to punish the open violation of the sacred laws which forbade the desecration of cemeteries, irrespective of their owners. The possession of the *areae* by the Christian corporation of Carthage must therefore go

[87] De Rossi agrees that the appearance of cemeteries owned by the Christian communities is simultaneous in Rome and in Africa. But he naturally assigns them to the period of Zephyrinus: "The first signs of cemeteries belonging to the corporation of the Christians and openly administered in the name of the corporation appear in Rome and in Africa under Zephyrinus" (Roma Sott., II, p. 370). Since, however, his main argument for the existence of such corporations is based on the 39th chapter of the Apologeticus of Tertullian, which was written in 197 before Zephyrinus became bishop, his statement involves a contradiction.

back to the period of Commodus. Was it then the example of the church of his native Africa that persuaded Victor to adopt in Rome the same system which had been successfully carried through in Carthage? Or was it Victor himself who, grasping the opportunity of the indifference of Commodus and the protection of Marcia, first attempted in Rome this radical and much needed provision for the cemeterial administration, and at the same time suggested to his compatriots of Carthage to adopt the same system? Either alternative may be accepted. But the simultaneous establishment of the new system both in Rome and in Carthage through the initiative of Victor, made possible by the temporary peace of the church and easily explained by the close connection between Rome and Carthage and the presence in Rome of a large group of African Christians and a bishop of African origin, seems to be the most satisfactory view of the origin of corporate property in the Christian church.[88]

The last two years of Victor's episcopate were saddened by the outbreak of new persecutions. While Septimius Severus was

[88] It is interesting to notice that the family of the Caecilii, which granted to Victor the property of their hypogeum on the Appian Way, was one of those families which had branches in Africa. The Caecilii of Cirta were among the most illustrious aristocratic families of Roman Africa. It is true, however, that there is no evidence that Christianity was embraced by any of them before the third century (F. Mesnage, L'Évangélisation de l'Afrique, p. 69). In the Octavius of Minucius Felix the pagan opponent is an African Caecilius. F. Mesnage has studied in his work the question of the possible influence of the aristocratic Roman-African families in the development of the African church. More than thirty African bishoprics of the third and fourth centuries were established in places called by the names of those families and belonging to their domain (pp. 1–4). There are traces, however, that Christian members of African aristocratic families may have played a part in the Christian propaganda in Rome. The inscription of Petilius dictated by one Fronto in the catacombs of Callistus (De Rossi, Roma Sott., II, p. 116; Mesnage, pp. 65–68) may offer some suggestions. But the material is here very scanty, and we are too much inclined to speak of Roman influence on Africa rather than vice versa. Thus Dom Leclercq remarks: "Il n'est pas douteux que sa [Victor's] présence à Rome n'ait exercé une influence considérable et définitive sur l'Église d'Afrique. Ce pape latin sut tourner ses compatriotes africains vers le génie latin et la langue latine" (Afrique chrétienne, I, p. 93). Without denying the possible influence of Victor on the African church it seems, however, more proper to say that this African Latin pope first turned the hellenistic church of Rome towards the Latin genius and the Latin language.

engaged in the Parthian war, the African Plautianus, who controlled the government in Rome and had no sympathy for the Christians, put an end to the period of benevolent tolerance towards the church. The news of the bloody events and antichristian riots at Carthage of the year 197 must have dispelled all doubts in Victor's mind as to the hostile policy of the African Roman emperor and of his powerful African lieutenant Plautianus. We like to think that Tertullian's 'Apologeticus,' which must have reached Rome in the early months of 198, filled Victor's heart with hope at a moment when the future appeared so dark for the Christian cause. From his native Africa had come this eloquent defence of the Christian faith and this persuasive exhortation to Christians to cling faithfully to the truth and to the ideals of the church.

That Victor died a martyr is affirmed by pious legends only; it is unlikely, since the persecution in Rome appears to have begun a little later under Zephyrinus, and no trace of the assumed martyrdom of Victor is found in any trustworthy tradition. When he died in 198/9 the situation of the Christian community of Rome was still made difficult by internal conflicts; the problems which he had set himself to solve were still harassing the Great Church. But Victor's determined policy had shown the way; he had effected the final triumph of the monarchical episcopate in the community and had reorganized on a sounder basis the system of ecclesiastical administration. His greatest contribution to the future of the Roman Church, however, lay in his daring to confront in a resolute fashion the problem of the relations among the churches, and in his intimation to the other churches that the authority of the Roman bishop was to be reckoned with in all questions affecting either the doctrinal or the disciplinary tradition of Christianity, since most such questions affected directly the Roman community.

The process of latinization of the Roman Church, so well started at the end of the second century, went on, gradually overcoming all resistance. By the middle of the third century, the time when Christianity in Rome was but a foreign religion had wholly passed. The Latin element had gained full control of the Roman Church. As we have seen, this movement for the latinization of the church received a great impulse from the African element in Rome. The traditional idea which traces the development of the church as a double line from the East to Rome and from Rome to the East, considering Carthage as a mere appendage of Rome, must be modified in so far it applies to this period. Whatever may have been the Roman contribution to the early expansion of Christianity in Africa, the situation during the last quarter of the second century was certainly changed. Rome was the recipient of influences both from the East and from Africa. The history of the relations between Rome and Carthage in the time of Cyprian, the attitude, at times patronizing and even defiant, that the latter assumed toward the Roman bishops, the eagerness with which the clergy of each city and the conflicting parties in each sought support in the other, all this would find a psychological explanation in the tradition established when the Africans in Rome played an important part in the latinization of the Roman Church.

But Rome was not merely passive; the function of Christian Rome, the great laboratory of Christianity, was to receive from all sides the various constructive and conflicting elements of both thought and institutions, to eliminate all that was not assimilable or not practical in them, to interpenetrate them with its own spirit, and finally to mould all these elements into a consistent whole within the framework of a strong organization. As we noticed above, African Christianity, in striking contrast with the hellenistic churches, shows from the beginning little or no interest in merely speculative problems; emphasis was primarily, if not entirely, concentrated on moral issues and on disciplinary and sacramental implications. If Christianity had been left in the hands of the Africans, this tendency would probably have prevented the development of a well-balanced system of doctrine and in so far as concerned the organization, it would have been unable to go beyond the narrow limits of an archaic ecclesiology. The motto of Tertullian, "*ne ultra regulam*," remarks De Faye, "could never become the flag of the thinkers of Greek origin, readers of Plato and eager to conquer for their faith philosophy itself." On the other hand, the same motto could not have become the flag of the Roman

Church until '*regula*' was understood as meaning tradition in general, or even the obstinate and uncompromising rigorism of Tertullian himself — two conceptions incapable of appealing to the far-seeing Roman mind. *Ne ultra regulam* became the motto of the Roman Church only when Rome identified itself with '*regula*.'

The logical development of African Christianity could but lead to the colorless theology of Cyprian, to his narrow interpretation of sacramental validity, and to his inconsistent ideal of church government, by which he thought it possible to secure both unity and uniformity under the system of episcopal oligarchy. It would have led, as it did, to the paradoxical ecclesiology of the Donatists, and made of Christianity the heritage of a fanatical religious clan. But the same comprehensive and well-balanced Roman spirit which in the Christian community of Rome checked the disintegrating individualism and the unbridled intellectualism of hellenistic Christianity, which would have dissolved the church into the thin air of a vague theology, checked also the spiritual provincialism of the Africans, which would have reduced the church from its universal character and aspirations to a fanatical congregation of beggars.

The historical problem of Christian unity during the first centuries thus receives a great light from the history of the Roman Church. The composite character of the Roman community and the consequent conflicts led that church to adopt a policy which, while aimed primarily at securing unity and order in its internal organization, was at the same time laying the foundations of a new system of hierarchical government for the whole church.

THE NORM OF FAITH IN THE PATRISTIC AGE

JOSEPH F. MITROS, S.J.

Fordham University

CHRISTIANITY IS a revealed religion. It was born as a response of faith of a small group of people to Jesus Christ, a man mighty in word and deed. He called Himself Son of Man and Son of God. His followers recognized in Him the promised Messiah of the Old Testament and later on discovered the God-become-man. Jesus Christ was, in the belief of His disciples, the fulfilment of the promises given by Yahweh in the Old Dispensation and the realization and center of God's self-revelation in the New. The faith of the followers of Christ was their response to the call of the self-revealing God in and through Christ. The revelation called for a total self-commitment and that total surrender was their faith. What was the model, the criterion, the norm of faith? It was Christ Himself as the self-revelation of God. The Letter to the Hebrews tersely describes the revelation of God and the role of Christ in it: "At various times in the past and in various different ways God spoke to our ancestors through the prophets; but in our own time, the last days, He has spoken to us through His Son, the Son that He has appointed to inherit everything and through whom He made everything there is. He is the radiant light of God's glory and the perfect copy of His nature, sustaining the universe by His powerful command."[1] In similar vein the primitive tradition, recorded by Matthew, puts on the lips of Jesus the following words: "Everything has been entrusted to me by my Father; and no one knows the Son except the Father, as no one knows the Father except the Son and those to whom the Son chooses to reveal Him."[2] These texts describe the kind of revelation which modern scholars call "propositional." God also revealed Himself through and in the person of Christ and His mighty deeds. Modern scholars call it "activist" revelation. The New Testament contains several references to this self-revelation of God. Christ is the epiphany of God: "Who sees Him, sees God."[3] In Him "God's grace has been revealed,"[4] in Him "the kindness and love of God our Saviour for mankind were revealed."[5] The mighty deeds wrought by

---

[1] Heb 1:1–3. [2] Mt 11:27. [3] Jn 1:14, 18; 14:9
[4] Tit 2:11. [5] Tit 3:4.

444

Christ attest to His mission conferred on Him by His Father: "The works my Father has given me to carry out, these same works of mine testify that the Father has sent me."[6] Jesus stresses the same on the occasion of the resuscitation of Lazarus: "for the sake of all these who stand around me, so that they may believe it was you who sent me."[7]

The revelation brought by Christ was the consummation of God's revelatory activity. It came to an end. His life was stopped and His words were silenced by the tragic event of His death. The work had to be continued by His disciples. Whatever they had learned from Jesus, whatever they had known about Him, whatever they had seen in Him, they taught and preached to others and realized it in practice and worship. They worked to be sure that all they had received would be handed down to posterity. The transmission of teaching and practice became the first tradition, the apostolic tradition. It was passed on to the churches orally and in writing. A part of that tradition was the Scriptures of the Old Testament, recognized by Christ Himself as speaking of Him and as containing eternal life. The apostles themselves interpreted these Scriptures as speaking of, leading to, and fulfilled in, Christ. In brief, they interpreted Scripture Christocentrically. Till the middle of the second century the books of the Old Testament alone remained the Word of God. It is true that side by side with the sacred books of the Old Dispensation there grew steadily the body of apostolic writings, revered because of their apostolic origin. However, they acquired the character of the Word of God only in the latter half of the second century. Towards the end of this century a list of canonical books was composed. Meanwhile, a group of intellectualistically-minded Gnostics began to challenge the whole of the Old Testament and some books of the New. They refused to accept them as the work of the good God, the Father of Jesus Christ. In their stead they claimed to be able to produce secret traditions (gnosis) that allegedly had come directly from Jesus through some apostles or other contact men. The Fathers of this period, such as Irenaeus and Tertullian, in order to counteract the Gnostic propaganda, appealed to public tradition handed down, preserved, and explained by the churches presided over by the bishops, legitimate successors to the apostles. They saw that tradition, in contrast with Scripture, condensed in the so-called "rule of faith" or "the canon of the truth." In addition to this

[6] Jn 5:36.   [7] Jn 11:42.

oral tradition they knew still another kind of tradition, the apostolic tradition as the totality of the teaching of the apostles transmitted to the churches both in writing and orally. This concept of tradition will be retained by the Fathers of the following centuries. Meanwhile, after the danger of Gnosticism, stressing the importance of a secret tradition, had passed, the Fathers began to appeal to Scripture more and more. Parallel with this development, the concept of a purely oral tradition emerged with Tertullian and was taken up by several Fathers of the succeeding centuries.

The Scriptures were always for the Fathers a supreme and total wisdom, since they contained the Word of God. As to the origin of these Scriptures, only a few Fathers ventured to rationalize. All of them recognized that the sacred books were inspired by God, but they did not agree as to the way of inspiration. Some viewed the inspiration as a species of possession of the sacred writer by the Spirit of God, denying any contribution to the composition of Scripture by the human authors; still others thought that human writers co-operated effectively in the creation of the record of revelation, leaving on it the imprint of their personal education, style, and culture.

Another important problem concerning Scripture was its interpretation. Here two distinct schools of thought arose, each springing up from its own ground of philosophical and theological tradition: the school of Alexandria and the school of Antioch. The former school developed on the philosophical premises of Platonism and Neoplatonism under the influence of the Jewish Midrash and Alexandrian allegorical interpretation of the Bible. The latter school grew rather on the Aristotelian system of philosophy and under the influence of a literal exegesis of Scripture (particularly concerning the so-called messianic prophecies) practiced in some Jewish circles in Palestine.

According to Plato and his followers, a man may experience several kinds of perception of things: he may have an opinion concerning the changing and fleeting world of senses or he may have a true knowledge of the ideal world of ideas (to mention only two pertinent kinds of cognition). Since the ideal world, according to Plato, is not subject to our direct contemplation while we are still imprisoned in the body, our knowledge of it must be a reminiscence of that knowledge which we acquired while dwelling in the sphere of ideas. The school of Alexandria appropriated the metaphysics, epistemology, and psychology of

Plato to find a solution to several theological problems. One was the interpretation of the Bible. Scripture was, for all the Fathers, the Word of God that had assumed the form of human language. Thus the invisible and incomprehensible world became a visible and palpable reality. However, this visible and accessible reality is only a shadow of the invisible true divine reality. How can we know this divine world of ideas? Only by means of spiritual, allegorical interpretation of the shadows of Scripture's literal sense. The literal sense is only a symbol and allegory of the world of God. Here one is reminded of the Platonic allegory of the cave. The Platonic concept was combined here with the Christian idea of Christ: the Word of God become man was reflected in Scripture as the Word of God become human word. The allegorical interpretation of the Bible by Philo was a singular source and encouragement for the school of Alexandria in using this kind of exegesis. The Christology of Alexandria, in which the humanity of Christ tended to be absorbed by the divine Word, seems to be another clue to the disappearance of the human word of Scripture in the divine meaning of allegory.

The school of Antioch had a different background for developing the literal interpretation of Scripture: the Aristotelian epistemology, the metaphysics and psychology of knowledge, and the literal interpretation of the Bible within Palestinian Judaism. According to Aristotle, we get to know the reality of the surrounding world by a concurrence of this very reality and our cognitive faculties. Our knowledge reaches the reality itself. The Christology of this school was another factor contributing to emphasis on the literal sense, that is, on the human aspect of the Word of God. Antiochene Christology always showed a tendency to stress the humanity of Christ at the expense of its union with the divinity, to underscore the importance of our Lord as the model to be imitated by man in his pursuit of Christian perfection. In the interpretation of Scripture, its human aspect, i.e., the literal sense, was brought out.

On one point both schools agreed: both accepted the typical sense of Scripture, which saw in the realities, events, and personalities of the Old Testament types, figures, and foreshadowings of Christ, of His life and activities. But even here the school of Antioch proceeded more cautiously by limiting the number of instances of typology.

Before returning to the main topic of our investigation, the norm of faith, we can say that for the Fathers God Himself was the ultimate source of salvation and norm of revelation. But to most of them God is absolutely transcendent, incomprehensible, and incommunicable. God has accomplished all the work of salvation and revelation through His Son Jesus Christ. Thus, for all practical purposes, Christ was the source and norm of faith for the Fathers. Christ was for them the supreme Teacher, Truth, Light, Way, and Lawgiver, and His revelation was the supreme wisdom, the Word of God, the good news, divine tradition, the gospel. Christ committed His gospel to the apostles as His eyewitnesses, and the apostles in their turn handed it down to the churches they had founded, orally and in writing, that is, in Scripture and tradition. Scripture and tradition became in their turn the norm of faith for the Church, but in unequal measure. Scripture was to the Fathers the supreme and ultimate norm, but to be interpreted in the light of tradition by the Church, which is the home of the Holy Spirit.

The problem to be discussed in the present essay against the general background sketched above is the norm of faith, or Scripture and tradition, as they are, according to the Fathers, guarded, preserved, interpreted, and handed down in the Church and by the Church.

The patristic era from the end of apostolic times to the end of its golden age can be divided into several periods due to the attitude of the Fathers towards the media of preservation, transmission, and interpretation of the gospel. The first period covers the Apostolic Fathers and the Apologists to the middle of the second century. The second period deals with the latter half of the second century, comprising Irenaeus and Tertullian. The third comprehends the third and succeeding centuries.

APOSTOLIC FATHERS AND APOLOGISTS

According to the Apostolic Fathers and the Apologists (all of them active roughly in the earlier part of the second century), Jesus Christ, the Word of God, the Truth and Light, is the Teacher of men, and His revelation or gospel is the source of the Church's teaching and the basis of her faith. What are the media through which the Church receives the gospel? The Fathers in question answer that Christians receive the gospel of Christ from the prophets, who announced Him in advance, and from the apostles, to whom He entrusted His gospel and whom He sent to preach it. Practically, it meant that the Old Testament, accepted by these Fathers as the Word of God and consequently as the norm of faith, was interpreted by them as a Christian book, speaking about Christ and preparing for Him. Furthermore, it meant that the teaching of the apostles, in whatever way it might have been transmitted, constituted another source and norm for the Church's teaching and another authority for her faith. As to the written record of apostolic teaching, the main body of the apostolic writings was completed by the end of the first century. Although it was elevated to the status of the Word of God only by the middle of the second century, it enjoyed an extraordinary respect among the Fathers as the "memoirs" and "letters" of the apostles, the eyewitnesses of Christ, commissioned by Him. Besides the writings of the apostles, there existed other media through which the teaching of Christ's disciples was transmitted, particularly the kerygmatic and catechetical instructions and the liturgy. Thus the whole body of doctrines and beliefs comprising the Christocentrically interpreted Old Testament and the writings of the apostles, the kerygmatic, catechetical, and liturgical doctrinal elements of the Christian message, constituted the apostolic deposit or gospel. The term "tradition" (*paradosis*) as designating this apostolic deposit was not used during this period of patristics. It must be added that already in this period of Christian history there had emerged a conviction among the Fathers that the Church's ministers, particularly the bishops, were the divinely appointed successors of the apostles, commissioned by them to preach, preserve, and hand down the gospel.

Clement of Rome opens the first period. He outlines briefly the process of revelation as it comes from God through Christ to the apostles. The apostles are messengers of Christ and ultimately of God Himself. It is through the apostolic preaching that the message of the gospel reaches men:

The apostles are sent to us as messengers of the good news through the Lord Jesus Christ. Now Christ comes from God, and the apostles come from Christ: these two points proceed in perfect order from the will of God. Strengthened with the instruction of our Lord Jesus Christ and fully convinced by His resurrection, the apostles, strengthened by the Word of God, went out, with the assurance of the Holy Spirit, to announce the good news, the approach of the kingdom of God.[8]

Ignatius of Antioch expresses similar ideas when he encourages his

[8] *1 Clement* 42, 1–3 (quoted by R. Latourelle, *Theology of Revelation* [Staten Island, N.Y., 1966] p. 87).

readers to abide in the "teaching of our Lord and the apostles"[9] and to remain "inseparable from Jesus Christ our God and the bishop and the precepts of the apostles."[10] In another letter he expresses his trust "in the gospel as in the flesh of Jesus Christ, and in the apostles as the presbytery of the Church. And we also love the prophets, for they too announced the gospel, they hoped in Jesus Christ and waited for Him; believing in Him, they have been saved; and abiding in the unity of Jesus Christ, they are saints worthy of love and admiration, they have received the testimony of Jesus Christ, and have been admitted in the gospel of our common hope."[11] Polycarp encourages the Philippians to serve our Lord "according as He has commanded, just like the apostles who have preached the gospel to us and the prophets who have announced the coming of the Saviour."[12]

According to Justin Martyr, the prophets announced Christ and His mystery.[13] They announced what they "heard and saw, filled with the Holy Spirit. It is not in terms of human reasoning that they spoke: far beyond all human reasoning, they were worthy witnesses of the truth."[14] For Theophilus, "the prophets have been taught by God, have been acting as His organs and communicating to men His holy will."[15] God has given mankind "a holy law and holy commandments."[16]

The above-mentioned Fathers appealed to the Old Testament because they viewed it as a Christian book and interpreted it spiritually or allegorically: "The Scriptures are much more ours than yours," wrote Justin while addressing the Jew Trypho; "for we let ourselves be persuaded by them, while you read them without grasping their true import."[17] In another text he writes again: "How could we believe that a crucified man is the first-born of the ingenerate God, and that He will judge the whole human race, were it not that we have found testimony borne prior to His coming as man, and that we have seen that testimony exactly fulfilled?"[18] In similar vein Barnabas wrote saying that the law was not meant for Jews but for Christians: "Moses received it when he was a servant, but the Lord Himself gave it to us

[9] *Magn.* 13, 1.   [10] *Trall.* 7, 1.   [11] *Philad.* 5, 1–2 (Latourelle, p. 88).
[12] *Philipp.* 6, 3 (Latourelle, p. 87).   [13] *Dial.* 14, 8; 24, 2.
[14] *Dial.* 7, 1–2 (Latourelle, p. 91).   [15] *Ad Autol.* 2, 14; 2, 33.   [16] *Ad Autol.* 2, 27.
[17] *Dial.* 29 (quoted by J. N. D. Kelly, *Early Christian Doctrines* [London, 1960] p. 66).
[18] *Apol.* 1, 53 (Kelly, p. 66).

as the people of inheritance, by suffering for our sake."[19] He was convinced that the Jews misunderstood the law because they interpreted it literally, misled by an evil angel. The right interpretation of the Old Testament must be genuinely spiritual, and by a spiritual exegesis he meant an allegorical explanation of every sentence and every word of Scripture.[20] To give only a sample of his allegorizing method, the number 318 of Abraham's servants means Jesus and His crucifixion, since the Greek letters IH stand for 18 and point to IHSOUS (Jesus), and Greek T stands for 300 and points to the cross.[21] This is also true of Justin Martyr, who often interprets the Old Testament texts allegorically, e.g., Is 9:6: "And the government will be upon His shoulder" signifies the crucifixion of Christ.[22] Some Apologists such as Aristides[23] and Tatian[24] oppose allegory but calmly use it themselves.

When the Fathers of this period speak of Scripture, they mean the Old Testament Scriptures. However, they already are acquainted with the apostolic writings, which they mention with great respect. Ignatius speaks of the gospel as enjoying the same authority as the prophets.[25] Barnabas and Justin introduce their quotations from the New Testament with the formula "It is written."[26] According to Justin, the "memoirs" of the apostles (Gospels) are read during the Eucharistic Sunday celebration along with the prophets.[27]

Already in this time there emerges the conviction that the ministers of the Church have the divinely appointed mission to guard and preach the gospel. This is particularly apparent in the text of *1 Clement* quoted partially above:

The apostles preached to us the gospel received from Jesus Christ, and Jesus Christ was God's ambassador. Christ, in other words, comes with a message from God, and the apostles with a message from Christ. Both of these arrangements, therefore, originate from the will of God. . . . From land to land, accordingly, and from city to city they preached, and from the earliest converts appointed men whom they had tested by the Spirit to act as bishops and deacons for the future believers.[28]

---

[19] *Barnabas* 14, 4 (J. Quasten, *Patrology* 1 [Utrecht, 1950] p. 86).
[20] *Barnabas* 1–17; see particularly chap. 9.   [21] *Barnabas* 9.   [22] *Apol.* 1, 32.
[23] *Arist.* 13, 7.   [24] *Adv. Graec.* 21.   [25] *Smyrn.* 5, 1; 7, 2.
[26] *Barn.* 4, 14; *Dial.* 49, 5.   [27] *Apol.* 2, 67.
[28] *1 Clement* 42 (Quasten 1, 45 f.).

Ignatius, too, sees in the office of the ministers of the Church the embodiment of the authority of God:

I exhort you to strive to do all things in harmony with God: the bishop is to preside in the place of God, while the presbyters are to function as the council of the apostles, and the deacons, who are most dear to me, are entrusted with the ministry of Jesus Christ.[29]

The bishop, "who embodies the authority of God the Father . . . the Father of Jesus Christ, the bishop of all men,"[30] is the teacher of the faithful and as such protects them against error and heresy.[31] In similar vein 2 Clement inculcates obedience to the presbyters, whose task is to preach the faith that comes from Christ.[32]

In conclusion one can say that, according to the Fathers of the first period, the gospel or the teaching of the apostles constituted the source of the Church's preaching and practice and the basis of her faith. The content of that gospel was made up of the Old Testament Scriptures interpreted Christocentrically, the writings of the apostles, and the teaching, preaching, and liturgical practice of the Church. The ministers of the Church are believed to have a divinely given mission to explain and propagate the gospel.

IRENAEUS AND TERTULLIAN

For Irenaeus and Tertullian, too, Jesus Christ, the Word of God, was the Teacher and the Truth through whom God had revealed Himself and His plans of salvation. This original revelation or gospel was entrusted by Christ to the apostles, and the apostles in their turn handed it down to the churches they had founded. Irenaeus and Tertullian called this original message or the teaching of the apostles "tradition" or "apostolic tradition," designating thereby the whole body of doctrines and beliefs regardless of the way in which they might have been transmitted. This usage of the term became classic in the succeeding centuries. They also used the term "tradition" in a restricted and new sense, meaning by it the unwritten beliefs and doctrines in contrast with the Scriptures. This unwritten or oral tradition practically coincided for Irenaeus with his "canon of the truth," and for Tertullian with the "rule of faith." The canon of truth or the rule of

[29] Magn. 6, 1 (Quasten 1, 67); Magn. 3, 1.   [30] Magn. 3, 1.
[31] Trall. 6; Phil. 3.   [32] 2 Clement 17.

faith meant for both the pattern of Christian teaching or the summary of Christian doctrines and beliefs, constant in content and varying in wording, believed to be of apostolic origin. Against the Gnostic appeal to a secret tradition, Irenaeus and Tertullian emphasized the importance of this public oral tradition, whose authenticity and apostolicity were guaranteed by the apostolic succession of bishops, to whose care the gospel was entrusted, and by the presence of the Holy Spirit in the Church. They also held that the whole of revelation was to be found in the Scriptures, that is, in the Old Testament and in the apostolic writings: the fourfold Gospel and the letters of the apostles, which were elevated to the status of the Word of God by the middle of the second century. Thus, in the view of Irenaeus and Tertullian, Scripture and tradition were rather two modes of transmission of the same original revelation and apostolic tradition (different in form, coextensive in content). In addition to this view, both firmly insisted that the Church alone was entitled to interpret the Scriptures, since she was in possession of the original and unadulterated tradition set out in the clear and unambiguous form of the rule of faith or truth. It must be added that Tertullian introduced still another use of the term "tradition," to designate the long-standing customs, practices, and rites presumably emanating from the apostles.

Irenaeus

In his usual lapidary formula Irenaeus outlines the history of revelation: "Such is the preaching of the truth: the prophets have announced it, Christ has established it, the apostles have transmitted it, everywhere the Church presents it to her children."[33] The Old Testament announced Christ, His life and passion, in figures and images only;[34] the apostles received the power to preach the gospel as eyewitnesses sent by Christ their Teacher:

The Teacher of all things has given His apostles the power to preach the gospel. It is through them that we know the truth, that is, the teaching of the Son of God. ... This gospel they first of all preached. Then, through the will of God, they handed it down in the Scriptures, so that it became the basis and support of our faith.[35]

[33] *Demonstr.* 98 (quoted by T. Camelot, "Tradition," in *Vatican II* [Washington, D.C., 1963] p. 186).
[34] *Adv. haer.* 4, 33, 10–14.   [35] *Adv. haer.* 3, 1, 1 (Latourelle, p. 103).

Irenaeus was the first to call the preaching of the apostles or the gospel "tradition." Speaking of the faith received from the apostles and preached everywhere in the Church, Irenaeus names it "tradition," without implying any contrast between Scripture and tradition.[36] In another text he designates it "apostolic tradition": "Anyone who wishes to discern the truth may see in every church in the whole world the apostolic tradition clear and manifest."[37]

How was the original gospel or apostolic tradition handed down to posterity? Irenaeus answers: by preaching and in writing.[38] Against the contemporary Gnostics, who claimed to possess access to a secret extrascriptural tradition, Irenaeus insisted on the importance of public oral tradition preached and transmitted in the churches founded by the apostles and commissioned by them to preach the gospel. Time and time again he repeats the term "tradition" to signify the oral preaching of the Church.[39] He could point to many barbarian tribes that received their faith without Scripture by following the original oral tradition:[40] "Why, he wrote, even if the apostles had not left the Scriptures to us, would it not be right to follow the pattern of tradition which they handed down to those to whom they entrusted the churches?"[41] Practically, the oral tradition of Irenaeus coincided with his "canon of the truth," a summary of the main articles of faith coming from the apostles. We find a detailed description of the canon as tradition in the following text:

The true knowledge, the teaching of the apostles, and the primitive structure of the Church throughout all the world, and the nature of the body of Christ according to the succession of the bishops to whom they entrusted the Church which is in every place; this teaching has come down to us, having been preserved without any use of forged writings, by being handled in its complete fullness, neither receiving addition nor suffering curtailment; and reading without falsification, and honest and steady exposition of the Scriptures without either danger or blasphemy; and the special gift of love which is more precious than knowledge, and, further, more glorious than prophecy, and also superior to all the other sacred gifts.[42]

The canon of the truth or the rule of faith most probably developed

[36] *Adv. haer.* 1, 10, 1-2. [37] *Adv. haer.* 3, 3, 1. [38] *Adv. haer.* 3, 1, 1.
[39] *Adv. haer.* 3, 2-5. [40] *Adv. haer.* 5, praef.; 3, 2-5.
[41] *Adv. haer.* 3, 4, 1 (quoted by R. P. C. Hanson, *Tradition in the Early Church* [London, 1962] p. 94).
[42] *Adv. haer.* 4, 53, 2 (Hanson, p. 95).

from the apostolic kerygma and it prepared material for the future Apostles' Creed. Irenaeus sums it up as follows:

All teach one and the same God as Father and believe the same economy of the incarnation of the Son of God and know the same gift of the Spirit and take to heart the same commandments and preserve the same shape of that ordinance which is towards the Church and wait for the same coming of the Lord and uphold the same salvation of the whole man, that is, of soul and body.[43]

The authenticity or apostolicity of this tradition was guaranteed, according to Irenaeus, by the unbroken succession of bishops to the apostolically founded churches,[44] by the presence of the Holy Spirit in the Church,[45] and by "an infallible charism of truth" the bishops have received from God.[46] Irenaeus is also convinced that besides the oral transmission of the original gospel, the apostolic tradition has been conveyed to the Church in Scripture: "This gospel they [the Apostles] first preached. Then, through the will of God, they handed it down in the Scriptures, so that it became the basis and support of our faith."[47] Irenaeus knew very well that the Gnostics claimed to know secret traditions allegedly coming from the apostles, and by appealing to those traditions they twisted the Scriptures. For this reason he insisted so much on the right interpretation of Scripture. As he saw it, only the apostolically constituted Church had the prerogative of explaining the Scriptures, since she alone was in possession of the original apostolic tradition clearly set out in the rule of faith.[48]

If we ask what served for Irenaeus as the norm of the Church's teaching and the basis of her faith, the answer would be: both Scripture and tradition. Scripture is "the basis and support of our faith," and the tradition is substantially identical with the canon of the (apostolic) truth. Which of them is the superior or the ultimate norm? He never asked this question (as a matter of fact, no Father ever asked it); understandably, then, he never gave a direct and explicit answer to it. Indirectly, however, he seems to have used the Scriptures as the last court of appeal. As we have seen, he calls Scripture the foundation of Christian faith, defends orthodoxy by appealing to Holy Writ,[49] and views even the canon of the truth as a condensation of Scripture.[50]

[43] Adv. haer. 5, 20, 1 (Hanson, p. 96).   [44] Adv. haer. 4, 53, 2; 3, 3, 3.
[45] Adv. haer. 3, 24, 1.   [46] Adv. haer. 4, 26, 2.
[47] Adv. haer. 3, 1, 1 (Latourelle, p. 103).   [48] Adv. haer. 1, 8, 1; 4, 26, 5; 5, 20, 2.
[49] Adv. haer. 2, 35, 4; 3, 5, 1; 4, praef. 1; 5, praef.; 3, praef.   [50] Adv. haer. 1, 9, 4.

Tertullian

Tertullian substantially re-echoes the views of Irenaeus concerning the norm of the Church's faith and teaching. Christ taught the apostles, and the apostles "have faithfully passed on to the nations the doctrine received from Christ."[51] Tertullian terms this doctrine or gospel[52] the "apostolic" or "Catholic tradition," without contrasting it with Scripture.[53] This gospel "obviously contains whatever the churches received from the apostles, the apostles from Christ, and Christ from God."[54] How was this tradition transmitted? The apostles handed down the apostolic tradition to the churches "they founded in person, and they themselves instructed, both with their living voice, as we say, and later through letters."[55] Thus Scripture and (oral) tradition are brought out again as two vehicles of the original revelation or gospel. Against the Gnostic secret extrascriptural tradition, he underscores the Church's public tradition.[56] In the public oral tradition of the apostolically founded churches and in their unanimity Tertullian saw the guarantee for the authenticity of the transmission of the original apostolic tradition.[57] Like Irenaeus, he identified the oral tradition with the rule of faith, which was for him the intrinsic pattern of the original revelation, an advanced form of the apostolic Christologico-Trinitarian kerygma.[58]

The other vehicle of the apostolic tradition, for Tertullian, was Scripture. His insistence on the absolute authority of the Scriptures can hardly be exaggerated.[59] However, Scripture for him too must be interpreted in the Church and by the Church, which has the key to its exegesis in the form of the original apostolic testimony, i.e., the rule of faith.[60]

For the first time in the patristic age, Tertullian introduced the concept of purely oral traditions which concerned rather religious customs, rites, and practices.[61]

---

[51] *De praescr.* 6, 4.   [52] *De praescr.* 44, 9.
[53] *C. Marcionem* 4, 5; 5, 19; *De monog.* 2.
[54] *De praescr.* 21, 4; 20, 4–8; 37, 1 (Latourelle, p. 134).
[55] *De praescr.* 21, 3 (Latourelle, *loc. cit.*).
[56] *Apologet.* 47, 10; *C. Marcionem* 1, 1, 6; 3, 1, 2; *Adv. Hermog.* 1, 1; *De carn. Chr.* 2, 3, 5.
[57] *De praescr.* 21; 28; 32; *C. Marcionem* 4, 5.
[58] *Adv. Prax.* 2; *De praescr.* 13, 1–6; *De virg. vel.* 1, 3.
[59] *De carn. Chr.* 6; 3; *Adv. Prax.* 29; *Adv. Hermog.* 22.
[60] *De praescr.* 19; 20; 31.   [61] *De corona* 3.

Thus Scripture and tradition appear to Tertullian the norms of teaching and faith. It is very difficult to determine which of them was the ultimate norm for him.[62]

In conclusion, we can say that Scripture, tradition, and Church constituted for Irenaeus and Tertullian the three most intimately connected factors. Scripture is the norm of the Church's teaching and faith, but interpreted by the Church in the light of apostolic tradition.

THIRD CENTURY AND GOLDEN AGE

The position of Irenaeus and Tertullian concerning the apostolic tradition as containing the whole of Christian revelation and the acceptance of Scripture and (oral) tradition as the two coextensive modes or forms of the transmission of that revelation or gospel remained classic in the third and succeeding centuries. It is self-evident that Jesus Christ was always viewed as the source of revelation, and His gospel entrusted to the apostles continued to be the supreme authority of teaching and faith. In the concrete, Scripture and tradition, those two complementary authorities identical in content and different in form, constituted the basis of the Church's teaching and faith. Both enjoyed equal respect due to their apostolic origin. Scripture was always considered by the Fathers of this period as a supreme wisdom, containing all truth necessary for salvation and, from the point of view of its content, totally sufficient. All theological activity of the Fathers of this era concentrated on the exegesis of Holy Writ and every theological proof had to be founded on Scripture. The oral-tradition concept of Irenaeus and Tertullian was retained by Clement of Alexandria and Origen in their "rule of faith" or "ecclesiastical canon." In the following centuries, however, the concept of oral tradition was expanded. It assumed a new meaning, to designate the totality of ecclesiastical life, such as the liturgy, the Apostles' Creed, the catechetical instructions, the decisions of synods and councils, the teaching of the Fathers—all this believed either as emanating from the teaching of the apostles or as clarifying their testimony. The Fathers of this period continued to dwell on the idea of purely oral traditions which concerned mainly religious customs and rites, without making any significant contribution. If the Fathers always viewed Scripture as a supreme wisdom and all-sufficient, they also always

[62] See *De praescr.* 14, 3, 4.

91

insisted that Scripture had to be interpreted in the Church and by the Church, since it was always assisted by the Holy Spirit and had at its disposal the living apostolic tradition supplying the rule of faith as an apt instrument of interpretation. Scripture, tradition, and Church invariably appeared in the view of these Fathers as most intimately associated with one another. The question of superiority or priority of any of these authorities over the others never arose; consequently it was never answered or solved. The greatest concern of the Fathers in this period was the integrity of the apostolic tradition. It was the task of the Church to preserve, explain, and hand down that tradition without adding anything to it or subtracting from it. As to the oral tradition, the Fathers tried rather to prove its tenets from Scripture. Meanwhile the importance of the Roman Church as a custodian and mouthpiece of the apostolic tradition grew steadily. The appeal to the testimony of the Fathers of previous centuries increased considerably from the fourth century on. It would be a mistake, however, to view the teaching of the Fathers as a distinct norm of faith: their testimony was looked upon rather as an interpretation of the apostolic tradition than anything else.

Entrusted by Christ to the apostles and handed down to the churches, the original revelation remained for the Fathers of the period under consideration simply the apostolic tradition. Cyprian has in mind this kind of tradition when he speaks of a tradition which concerns "the gospel and apostolic tradition," which "proceeds from the authority of the Lord and the gospel, from the precepts and the letters of the apostles."[63] Origen seems to speak of the same tradition in the following text:

Since the teaching of the Church, transmitted from the apostles according to the order of succession, has been preserved in the churches up to the present time, one should accept as truth only what does not depart at all from the ecclesiastical and apostolic tradition.[64]

Gregory of Nyssa writes in similar vein of the original apostolic tradition: "We have, as a more than sufficient guarantee of the truth of our teaching, tradition, that is, the truth which has come down to us

[63] *Ep.* 74, 2 (Latourelle, p. 138); see *Ep.* 63, 19, in which text he calls the teaching of Christ "the tradition of the Lord."

[64] *De princ.* 1, praef. 2 (Camelot, p. 188); cf. *Comm. in. Matt.*, serm. 46.

by succession from the apostles, as an inheritance."[65] Athanasius likewise expresses his views clearly: "Let us see in the same way, over and above the tradition that goes back to the beginning, the teaching and faith of the Catholic Church, which the Lord has bestowed on us, which the apostles have proclaimed, which the Fathers have maintained."[66]

The Fathers of this period took it for granted that the apostolic tradition was to be found in Scripture and the living tradition of the Church. A few examples will illustrate the statement. Cyprian writes of "the gospel and the apostolic tradition" as the vehicles of apostolic tradition.[67] According to Basil, the "necessary and salutary doctrine" of revelation is to be found in Scripture[68] and in oral tradition.[69] Similarly, Gregory of Nazianzus,[70] Epiphanius,[71] and Chrysostom[72] bring out the distinction between oral tradition and Scripture. Vincent of Lerins sums up the classic position of the period when he writes: "Take to yourself a double protection: first, the authority of the divine law, and then, the tradition of the Catholic Church."[73]

Scripture is a supreme wisdom for the Fathers. They explain it, comment on it, appeal to it. It is the source and norm of Christian teaching and faith and the criterion of dogma.[74] As far as its content is concerned, it is all-sufficient and more than sufficient. It contains all truth necessary for salvation. Innumerable examples have been collected by historians in support of the patristic view concerning the sufficiency of Scripture. For Tertullian, a doctrine is false if Scripture does not mention it.[75] Irenaeus describes the Gospels as "the pillars of the Church,"[76] as divine and perfect, since they communicate the Word of God and His Spirit.[77] Clement of Alexandria and Origen emphasize the absolute authority of Scripture. Clement tries to build a Christian gnosis on it. Origen knows two incorporations of the Word:

[65] C. Eunom. 4 (Y. Congar, Tradition and Traditions [New York, 1967] p. 43).
[66] Ep. ad Serap. 28 (Congar, p. 43).   [67] Ep. 74, 2.
[68] De Spir. S. 4, 32, 77; 10, 32, 11–113.   [69] De Spir. S. 27, 32, 188, 193.
[70] Ep. 101.   [71] Haer. 61, 6.   [72] In 2 Thess. hom. 4, 2.
[73] Common. 2 (Congar, p. 44).
[74] Cf. Clement, Strom. 7, 16, 93; Origen, De princ. 1, praef. 10; 3, 6, 6; 2, 5, 3; C. Cels. 3, 15.
[75] Adv. Hermog. 22; De carn. Chr. 6; Adv. Prax. 29; De praescr. 38, 1–2; De anima 1; C. Marcionem 3, 17.
[76] Adv. haer. 3, 11, 11.   [77] Adv. haer. 2, 41, 1.

the Incarnation and Scripture.[78] Athanasius insists that "the holy and inspired Scriptures are fully sufficient for the proclamation of the truth."[79] Cyril of Jerusalem writes on the same subject: "The certitude of our faith does not depend on reasoning based on whim, but on the teaching drawn from the Scriptures."[80] John Chrysostom insists: "Await no other master; you possess the Word of God, and no instruction compares with that."[81] "Everything in the divine Scriptures is clear and straightforward; they inform us about all that is necessary."[82] Jerome is the most explicit: "Ignorance of Scripture is ignorance of Christ."[83] Theophilus of Alexandria is not less outspoken: "It would be acting according to demoniac inspiration to follow the thinking of the human mind and to think that there could be anything divine apart from the authority of the Scriptures."[84] Cyril of Alexandria comments: "Not all that the Lord did was written down, but only what was deemed sufficient, either from the point of view of morals, or from the point of view of dogmas, in order that we might come, adorned with good works and virtues, to the heavenly city, and be reunited to the Church of the First-Born. How can we prove and certify as true something which Scripture does not attest?"[85] Augustine insists that "in open teaching of Scripture one finds all that concerns faith and moral conduct, that is, hope and charity."[86] Finally Vincent of Lerins: "Fortify our own belief in two ways: first, by the authority of the divine law, and then, by the tradition of the Catholic Church. . . . For the canon of Scripture is complete, and sufficient of itself for everything, and more than sufficient . . . . "[87]

The concept of (oral) tradition in this period at first reflected the views of Irenaeus and Tertullian; later on it was expanded to comprise not only the rule of faith but also the liturgy, the Apostles' Creed, the decisions of synods and general councils, the teaching of the Fathers— all this believed to reflect the teaching of the apostles. Clement of Alexandria and Origen defended the views of the preceding period by accepting and identifying the oral tradition either with the "ecclesiastical canon"[88] or with the "ecclesiastical preaching"[89] comprising the

---

[78] *In Jer.* hom. 9, 1; 21, 2; *Jo.* 2, 1–9; *In Lev.* 5   [79] *C. gent.* 1.   [80] *Catech.* 4, 17.
[81] *In ep. ad Col.* 9, 1.   [82] *In ep. 2 Thess.* 3, 4; *In ep. 2 Cor.* 13, 4.
[83] *In Is.* prol.   [84] *Inter op. Hier. Ep.* 96, 6.   [85] *In Jo.* 12.   [86] *De doctr. chr.* 2, 9, 14.
[87] *Common.* 2 (J. R. Willis, *The Teaching of the Church Fathers* [New York, 1966] p. 119).
See the texts on the sufficiency of Scripture collected in Congar, pp. 107–11.
[88] Clement, *Strom.* 6, 7, 61; 6, 8, 68.   [89] Origen, *De princ.* 3, 1, 1; 4, 2, 2.

totality of Christian faith as contrasted with Scripture. Both accepted also some form of Christian secret tradition supposedly coming from the apostles. Clement seems to have confused it with his canon of faith.[90] Origen most likely identified it with his esoteric interpretation of the Bible.[91]

Meanwhile the concept of oral tradition was expanded. First, the liturgy of the Church, embracing the catechetical instructions, baptismal as well as Eucharistic rites, began to enjoy the designation of "apostolic tradition," as is apparent from the title given to a collection of religious services by Hippolytus. Second, the rule of faith of the second century gradually developed—in connection with the baptismal confession of faith—into baptismal creeds, those short summaries of the main articles of faith sanctioned by the Church.[92] The title "Symbol of the Apostles" or the "Apostles' Creed" and the legend ascribing it to the apostles themselves point to the conviction of the Church that the Creed originated with the apostles.[93] Basil seems to have expressed the reason behind this attitude of the Church when he said that the apostolic tradition had been transmitted in the mysteries as well as in Scripture.[94] Third, appeals to the decisions of synods and councils and to the testimony of individual Fathers as interpreting and clarifying the teaching of the apostles became more and more frequent. Special dossiers of authorities were compiled. To cite only a few examples, Origen,[95] Eusebius of Caesarea,[96] Athanasius,[97] Gregory of Nazianzus,[98] Cyril of Alexandria,[99] and Theodoret[100] in defense of their views appealed to orthodox Fathers and particularly to the Council of Nicaea, which enjoyed an unimpeachable authority. The appeal to the Fathers developed later on into the so-called argument from tradition. However important the appeal might have appeared in the eyes of the Fathers, it would be wrong to draw from this appeal a hasty conclusion that the authority of the Fathers constituted a distinct and independent norm and criterion of teaching and faith. Those who appealed to the

---

[90] *Strom.* 6, 7, 61; 6, 15, 131.
[91] *C. Cels.* 1, 7; *In Jos.* 23, 4; *Comm. in Matt.* 10, 6.
[92] Hanson, *Tradition in the Early Church*, chap. 2.
[93] Cf. Ambrose, *Ep.* 42, 5; Cyril of Jerusalem, *Cat.* 5, 12; Augustine, *Serm. ad cat.* 1; *Serm.* 212, 2; Cassian, *De inc.* 6, 3; Leo, *Serm.* 96, 1; *Ep.* 45, 2.
[94] *De Spir. S.* 26; 28; 66; 67. [95] *In Num.* hom. 22, 2. [96] *Ep. ad Caes.* 2.
[97] *De decr. Nic. syn.* 27; *Ad Afr.* 1; *Ad Serap.* 1, 28. [98] *C. Eunom.* 4.
[99] *In John ev.* 4, 11; *Adv. Nest.* 4, 2. [100] *Ep.* 89; *Ep.* 151.

Fathers were themselves anxious to admit that they did so only because they saw in them interpreters and transmitters of the teaching of Christ and the apostles.[101] Theodoret explains the position of them all when he writes while defending the orthodox faith transmitted "not only by the apostles and prophets, but also by those who interpreted their writings—Ignatius, Eustathius, Athanasius, Basil, Gregory, John, and other luminaries of the world, and also by the holy Fathers who before these assembled at Nicaea."[102] Theodoret expressed his own opinion candidly: "I yield obedience to the Holy Scriptures alone."[103] Cyril, too, ultimately appealed to "the tradition of the apostles and evangelists . . . and the bearing of divinely inspired Scripture as a whole."[104]

Thus the idea of tradition, although expanded in the present period, was believed to be based on the teaching of the apostles transmitted through various media in the Church.

What was the relationship of Scripture, tradition, and Church in the opinion of the Fathers under discussion? While dealing with Irenaeus and Tertullian, we saw that these three factors appeared to them as inseparable from one another. Scripture was a supreme wisdom and the norm of faith, but only the Church was divinely empowered to interpret it in the light of the apostolic tradition. We find almost the same situation in the present era. The ancient conviction that only the Church, enjoying the assistance of the Holy Spirit and being in possession of the apostolic tradition, is the divinely empowered interpreter of Scripture persisted also in the time under consideration.[105] The true faith and the authentic interpretation of the Bible are to be found only in the churches founded by the apostles and in the light of the apostolic tradition. Clement of Alexandria was convinced that the true interpretation of Scripture belonged exclusively to the Church as her apostolic heirloom,[106] since her pastors are our masters preserving the true apostolic tradition: "Those masters who preserve the true tradition of the glorious teaching derived in a straight line from the holy apostles Peter, James, John, and Paul, transmitted from father to son . . . have come down even to us, by God's grace, to plant in us

---

[101] Hilary: *Fragm. hist.* 7, 3; Cyril of Alexandria, *De recta fide ad reg.* 3.
[102] *Ep.* 89 (quoted by Kelly, *Early Christian Doctrines*, p. 49).
[103] *Eranistes* 1.   [104] *De recta fide ad reg.* 2 (Kelly, p. 49).
[105] Irenaeus, *Adv. haer.* 3, 24, 1; Tertullian, *De praescr.* 19.   [106] *Strom.* 7, 16, 103.

these glorious seeds of their forebears and of the apostles."[107] He also sees in the rule of faith the authentic instrument of interpretation: "Everything comes intelligible for those who preserve the interpretation that the Lord has given of Scripture, by accepting it in accordance with the ecclesiastical rule, a rule which is the unison and symphony of the law and the prophets with the Testament transmitted when the Lord came."[108] Origen, too, warns not to abandon the ecclesiastical tradition and not to accept anything in faith unless it has been passed on to us by the succession of the churches.[109] He stresses particularly the importance of the tradition preserved in the Church in order to distinguish the truth from falsehood:

Seeing there are many who think they hold the opinions of Christ, and yet some of these think differently from their predecessors, yet as the teaching of the Church, transmitted in orderly succession from the apostles, and remaining in the churches to the present day, is still preserved, that alone is to be accepted as truth which differs in no respect from ecclesiastical and apostolic tradition.[110]

The great champion of orthodoxy, Athanasius, equally emphasizes the need of sound teachers and the importance of the Church's grasp of tradition in explaining Scripture.[111] Cyril of Jerusalem writes in similar vein.[112] The ideas of the Western Fathers are not dissimilar. According to Hilary, "those who are outside the Church cannot understand the Word of God."[113] Augustine is quite outspoken when the acceptance of the gospel is concerned: "For my part, I should not believe the gospel except as moved by the authority of the Church."[114] Only the authority of the Church can guarantee the right interpretation of biblical texts in the light of the rule of faith.[115]

Vincent of Lerins in a masterly way explained how and why Scripture, tradition, and Church are interrelated. On this occasion he elaborated his famous rule for discerning the Catholic truth from heretical falsehood:

I have often then inquired earnestly and attentively of very many men eminent for sanctity and learning how and by what sure and so to speak universal rule

[107] *Strom.* 1, 11, 3 (Congar, *Tradition and Traditions*, p. 28).
[108] *Strom.* 6, 15, 124–25 (Congar, p. 32).   [109] *In Matt.* serm. 46.
[110] *De princ.* 1, praef. 2 (Willis, *Teaching of the Church Fathers*, p. 121).
[111] *C. gent.* 1; *C. Ari.* 3, 58.   [112] *Cat.* 4, 33; 5, 12.
[113] *In Matt.* 13, 1.   [114] *C. Manich.* 4 (Willis, p. 102).
[115] *De doctr. chr.* 2, 12; 3, 2· *C. ep. Manich.* 6; *C. Faust. Manich.* 22, 79.

I may be able to distinguish the truth of Catholic faith from the falsehood of heretical pravity; and I have always . . . received an answer to this effect: . . . Fortify our own belief in two ways: first, by the authority of the divine law, and then, by the tradition of the Catholic Church. But here some one perhaps will ask, since the canon of Scripture is complete, and sufficient of itself for everything, and more than sufficient, what need is there to join with it the authority of the Church's interpretation? For this reason, because, owing to the depth of Holy Scripture, all do not accept it in one and the same sense, but one understands its words in one way, another in another. . . . Therefore it is very necessary, on account of so great intricacies of such various error, that the rule for right understanding of the prophets and apostles should be framed in accordance with the standard of ecclesiastical and Catholic interpretation. Moreover, in the Catholic Church itself all possible care must be taken that we hold that faith which has been believed everywhere, always, by all. . . . This rule we shall observe if we follow universality, antiquity, consent.[116]

So far we have studied Scripture and tradition, those media, identical in content and different in form, through which the original revelation or apostolic tradition has been transmitted to the Church. Besides these two modes of transmission, numerous Fathers claimed to have known purely oral traditions of equally apostolic origin. Some of them even laid claim to secret traditions of the same source. There arises the question to what extent the first kind of information has contributed to the doctrinal heritage of Christian revelation, and how reliable the second kind of claim is. This will be the subject of discussion in the next section of this essay.

EXISTENCE OF PURELY ORAL TRADITIONS IN EARLY CHURCH

In addition to the oral tradition doctrinally coinciding with Scripture, numerous Fathers were acquainted with some merely oral or extrascriptural traditions which were supposed to have supplied some information not to be found in the Bible. Tertullian was the first to mention some oral traditions of this kind: e.g., the renunciation of Satan at baptism, threefold immersion, tasting of the mixture of milk and honey after the rite, abstention from the daily bath for the whole week after the baptismal ceremony, the reception of the Eucharist only at the assemblies before the dawn and only from the hands of the presiding celebrant, the anniversary offerings for the dead and in honor of the martyrs, the prohibition of fasting and praying on one's

[116] *Common.* 2 (Willis, pp. 119 f.)

knees on Sunday and during Eastertide, the custom of signing one's forehead with the sign of the cross on various occasions during the day.[117] Origen specified such customs as infant baptism, praying on one's knees while facing the east, the baptismal and Eucharistic rites.[118] Cyprian saw in the offering of the chalice of wine mixed with water a custom instituted by Christ.[119] He also viewed the rule of electing the bishop in the presence of the people and in the assembly of the bishops of the province as of "divine tradition and apostolic practice."[120] Epiphanius speaks of an ancient immemorial usage prohibiting marriage after the vow of virginity.[121] Jerome invokes an apostolic origin for the imposition of hands and invocation of the Holy Spirit after baptism, the threefold baptismal immersion, giving milk and honey to the newly baptized, the practice of praying in an upright position and of not fasting during Paschaltide.[122] Augustine quotes infant baptism as an apostolic tradition,[123] then such baptismal rites as aspersion, exorcisms, and insufflation,[124] the celebration of the Passion, Resurrection, Ascension, and Pentecost as liturgical feasts.[125] Leo puts forward as apostolic traditions the Ember day fasts,[126] the custom permitting a priest to have only one wife,[127] the celebration of baptism only on Easter and Pentecost,[128] the consecration of bishops on a Friday.[129] John Damascene appealed to apostolic tradition in defense of the devotion to images. Furthermore, he referred to the oral traditions of Basil. He backed up as apostolic the threefold baptismal immersion, the veneration of holy places, the adoration of the holy cross, the institution of the sacraments.[130]

A careful study of these so-called purely or extrascriptural traditions makes it clear that they concern themselves almost exclusively with customs and rites, not doctrines—at least not directly. Perhaps an exception could be made for the practice of infant baptism. Augustine concluded from this practice to the belief of the primitive Church in the presence of original sin in infants.[131] Unfortunately, no historical

[117] De cor. 3–4.   [118] In Lev. hom. 8, 3; In ep. ad Rom. 5, 8; In Num. hom. 5, 1.
[119] Ep. 63, 9–13.   [120] Ep. 67, 5.   [121] Panarion 61, 6.   [122] Dial. adv. Lucif. 8.
[123] De Gen. ad litt. 10, 23, 39; De bapt. c. Don. 4, 24, 31.
[124] De nupt. et concup. 2, 50.   [125] Ep. 54, 1 ad Januar.
[126] Sermo 8; 10, 1; 12, 4; 81, 1.   [127] Ep. 4, 2; 5, 3; 12, 3.   [128] Ep. 16, 1; 168, 1.
[129] Ep. 111, 2.   [130] De imag. or. 1, 23; 11, 16; De fide orthod. 4, 12.
[131] De nupt. et concup. 1, 22.

reason justifies his conclusion. It is also impossible to ascertain that all of the ancient customs and rites mentioned above are of apostolic origin.

In addition to the oral traditions specified so far, some later Fathers laid claim to a secret extrascriptural tradition containing esoteric teaching allegedly coming from Christ. Clement of Alexandria and Basil are the main representatives of this opinion. The *disciplina arcani*, developed probably by the middle of the third century, belongs here. It is a peculiarity of this claim that earlier Fathers like Irenaeus and Tertullian vehemently opposed the Gnostics of their time exactly on this issue. Irenaeus was the first to deny firmly that the apostles concealed some esoteric knowlege in order to impart it to a privileged group.[132] He is quite outspoken when he writes: "There is no gnosis other than the teaching of the apostles,"[133] entirely public and accessible to everyone, transmitted by them to the churches they had founded.[134]

Anyone who wishes to discern the truth may see in every church in the whole world the apostolic tradition clear and manifest. We can enumerate those who were appointed as bishops in the churches by the apostles and their successors to our own day, who never knew and never taught anything resembling their [the Gnostics'] foolish doctrine. Had the apostles known any such mysteries, which they taught privately and *sub rosa* to the perfect, they would surely have entrusted this teaching to the men in whose charge they placed the churches. For they wished them to be without blame and reproach to whom they handed over their own position of authority.[135]

Tertullian rejected no less strongly the Gnostics' claim to a secret apostolic tradition.[136]

Clement of Alexandria was the first among the Fathers to allege the possession of a secret knowledge coming from Christ,[137] which he probably confused with the rule of faith.[138]

On the basis of scattered testimonies[139] some scholars are inclined to admit that the so-called *disciplina arcani* developed in the Church after the middle of the third century. This rule of secrecy consisted

---

[132] *Adv. haer.* 3, 5. 1; 2, 40, 2.   [133] *Adv. haer.* 4, 33, 8.   [134] *Adv. haer.* 3, 2–5.
[135] *Adv. haer.* 3, 3, 1 (Quasten 1, 301).   [136] *De praescr.* 22–27.
[137] *Strom.* 1, 1, 11–12; 6, 7, 61; 6, 8, 68.   [138] *Strom.* 7, 15, 92–93; 7, 16, 105.
[139] Aristides, *Apol.* 16, 2; *Ep. ad Diogn.* 4, 6; 6, 4; 7, 1; Minucius Felix, *Octavius* 10, 1; 9, 4; 19, 15; *Epitaph of Abercius*; Hippolytus, *Apost. trad.* 23, 13–14; Cyprian, *Testim.* 3, 50; *Didasc. apost.* 15.

mainly in keeping secret the religious gatherings and rites, particularly those of baptism and Eucharist, from the eyes of outsiders. The reason for the secrecy was more often than not the fear of persecution, of arrest and trial, the desire to avoid profanation by pagans, and later, probably under the influence of mystery religions, a wish to encourage in newcomers a healthy curiosity and veneration for Christian mysteries. However, it must be emphasized that the secrecy concerned only outsiders and never Christians, as if some mysteries were accessible only to an elite.[140] The character of that secrecy is insinuated (unjustly) by a pagan as represented by Minucius Felix in his *Octavius*:

For why do they [Christians] make strenuous efforts to veil and hide away whatever it is that they worship, since things that are innocent always rejoice in publicity, but crimes are secret? Why do they have no altars, no temples, no recognized images, why do they never speak openly, never meet freely, unless what they worship and suppress deserves either punishment or shame?[141]

One of the most puzzling views on the existence of extrascriptural secret traditions is that of Basil. He compiled a dossier of customs and rites and insisted that they were transmitted by the apostles in a secret way. Further, on account of their apostolic origin they deserved, according to him, the same respect as the Scriptures themselves. The object of these secret traditions includes such customs as signing with the sign of the cross, turning to the east for prayer, the epiclesis in the Eucharistic celebration, the blessing of baptismal water and oil and the baptized person himself, the threefold baptismal immersion, etc.[142] With these customs and rites we are well acquainted, since they were already referred to by Tertullian, Origen, and others. What is new and puzzling is the fact that, according to Basil, they were secretly transmitted by the apostles and that they deserve the same reverence as Scripture itself. After having enumerated the religious customs and rites referred to above, he insists that they are known to us not from written documents but

from the sacred and mystical tradition . . . from this unpublicized and secret teaching which our fathers preserved in a silence proof against the meddlers and busybodies, having well learnt the lesson that the holy nature of the mysteries is preserved in silence. For how could it be likely that the teaching of what it is not

[140] R. P. C. Hanson, *Tradition in the Early Church*, pp. 27–35.
[141] *Octavius* 10, 1 (Hanson, p. 30). [142] *De Spiritu Sancto* 27, 66.

permissible for the uninitiated to gaze upon should be advertised in writings . . . ? The apostles and fathers who were ordering the institutions in connection with the churches in the beginning used to preserve that which was sacred in the mysteries by a secret and undivulged method. For that which is published for common and chance hearing is not properly a mystery. This is the reason for the tradition of unwritten things, to prevent the knowledge of secret doctrines becoming neglected and through familiarity becoming contemptible in the eyes of the majority.[143]

It is disconcerting to see the customs and rites which were known publicly two centuries earlier without the aura of mystery and secrecy become for Basil mystical and hidden and deserving the same respect as Scripture itself. Christianity seems to have become suddenly for Basil a mystery religion, and all customs, rites, and beliefs have assumed the same value. A hundred years later Vincent of Lerins was more cautious when he set up a criterion for Catholic belief: universality, antiquity, and consent.

In conclusion, one can say that so far no historian has been able to produce a doctrine which has reached us exclusively through an extra-scriptural oral tradition. This view is shared today by all those scholars who let themselves be convinced by the force of historical reasons alone. Yves Congar writes on this subject:

In all honesty it is difficult to see what *truths of faith* there could be that had been handed down secretly through the ages, whispered in the ear. Apart from the fact that the testimony of the earliest Fathers expressly contradicts the idea of an esoteric tradition, any such secret transmission would be a complete historical improbability. The discipline of the *arcanum*, which did exist, never had this sense. It merely applied, either to the maintenance of a discreet silence with regard to pagans or, after the organization of a catechumenate, to a liturgical observance within the community . . . .

Now revelation is of its nature public; it was made through the prophets, in Christ and through the apostles, once and for all, and Scripture is its sufficient and perfect record. Tradition is not a second source, alongside Scripture, from which comes a *part*, not contained in Scripture, of the truths of the faith, but another and complementary way of handing on of these truths.[144]

So far, so good. A Catholic scholar, however, is faced with a special difficulty. Within the last hundred years several dogmas have been proclaimed in the Catholic Church. Now, according to the customary

---

[143] *De Spir. S.* 27, 66 (Hanson, pp. 181 f.).
[144] Congar, *Tradition and Traditions*, pp. 63–64.

interpretation, a dogma is a doctrine solemnly proclaimed as divinely revealed by a pope or a general council. Thus the definition of the Assumption of Mary has created particular difficulties (to take only one example), since neither scientific exegesis nor a history of the first centuries of the Church has been able to discover even traces of this doctrine. To get out of the impasse, some theologians such as Benoit and R. Brown have defended the so-called fuller sense of Scripture,[145] which would explain the appearance of the new dogmas. Some theologians-historians, e.g., Congar, have tried to introduce a new concept of tradition, some kind of Christian midrash, i.e., a constantly developing understanding of Scripture in the Church and by the Church.[146] The objections leveled against these two attempts are serious, and no one seems to have proposed a sufficient solution. The fuller sense seems to reintroduce into exegesis the highly subjective and arbitrary method of the school of Alexandria, which has wrought such havoc in Christian biblical scholarship. The expansion of the concept of tradition seems to admit the emergence of a new revelation—another ominous phenomenon which may lead to the divinization of the papacy as it did towards the end of the Middle Ages.[147]

Still another attempt has been made by some theologians to solve the problem. They believe they are authorized to conclude from the unanimity of the Church's ordinary and universal teaching of a doctrine to its authenticity or apostolicity.[148] From this point of view, this theory seems related to the concept of expanded tradition. This argument is evidently based on the argument of Vincent of Lerins, with only one difference: it lacks a very important element, i.e. the element of antiquity. It can be objected to this method that as far as sound history is concerned, it is a blind leap into the darkness. No serious historian will feel authorized to conclude from the existence of a contemporary consensus concerning a doctrine to the presence of

[145] Cf. P. Synave and P. Benoit, *Prophecy and Inspiration* (New York, 1961) pp. 149–51; R. Brown, *The Sensus Plenior of Sacred Scripture* (Baltimore, 1955); "The Sensus Plenior in the Last Ten Years," *Cath. Bib. Quart.* 25 (1965) 262–85; R. North, "Scripture Trends in 1964," *Amer. Eccl. Rev.* 152 (1965) 361–97.

[146] Congar, *Tradition and Traditions*, pp. 18, 63ff., 6, 434–56.

[147] G. H. Tavard, *Holy Writ or Holy Church* (New York, 1959) chap. 10: "The Permanent Revelation."

[148] Cf. James Gaffney, "Scripture and Tradition in Catholic Thought," in *Vatican II*, pp. 147–50.

that doctrine in the preaching of the apostles. Many would also object to the assumption of the existence of a genuine consensus in the Church. The concept of consensus, according to them, implies the free expression of some kind of belief or decision. Now an unbiased historian well knows that any kind of consensus in the Church has been strictly controlled and even imposed on the faithful by highly centralized authority. Msgr. Drinkwater has ably and with great humor shown how much that consensus is worth: "There is heard only, so to speak, a single gramophone record playing on and on."[149]

Some theologians suggest a more radical solution. They assume the fact of the development of doctrines in the Church—a fact which only extremists would deny. They call it a legitimate and healthy phenomenon in the living Church. However, they would never view the results of the development as the apostolic teaching but rather as an ecclesiastical interpretation.

To recapitulate the argument of the second part of the present essay, one can say that, according to the Fathers of the third century and of the golden age, the gospel or apostolic tradition as contained in Scripture and interpreted by the Church in the light of her tradition is the criterion of teaching and the norm of faith.

CONCLUSION

The task of the present essay was to determine the criterion of teaching and the norm of faith in the patristic Church. We have arrived at the conclusion that Scripture and tradition played this role, but not in the same measure. Scripture was for the Fathers the ultimate criterion and norm, supreme wisdom, and all-sufficient for salvation—but Scripture guarded and interpreted in the Church and by the Church in the light of tradition. The concept of tradition, as contrasted with Scripture, developed gradually. At first, in the latter half of the second and the earlier part of the third century, it meant the rule of faith, i.e., the pattern or summary of the Church's teaching in whatever form of worship and life it might have been expressed. In the third and the following centuries the concept of tradition was expanded to comprise not only the preaching and catechetical instruc-

[149] F. H. Drinkwater, "Ordinary and Universal," *Clergy Review*, Jan., 1965, pp. 2–22; cf. p. 19.

tions of the Church, but also the liturgy, the Apostles' Creed, the decisions of synods and general councils, the appeal to the Fathers—all recognized as depositories of the Church's living patrimony, as either emanating from the apostles or confirming and explaining their teaching. To be sure, Scripture and tradition were always viewed as modes, identical in content and different in form, of the transmission of the original gospel or apostolic tradition. In addition to this kind of tradition, there emerged in the early third century the concept of purely oral traditions to be developed in the following centuries. However, those traditions were confined rather to ancient customs and rites. From the doctrinal point of view, they have not contributed anything new, at least not directly. As has been hinted, the Church and its ministers (magisterium) played an increasingly important role in preaching, guarding, and interpreting the norm of teaching and faith. Now it is important to keep in mind the fact that by the Church the Fathers meant the new People of God, the mystical Body of Christ inhabited by the Holy Spirit as its soul, served and guided by its ministers.

Vigiliae Christianae 21 (1967) 137–140; *North-Holland Publishing Co., Amsterdam*

PAPIAS AND ORAL TRADITION

BY

A. F. WALLS

Οὐκ ὀκνήσω δέ σοι καὶ ὅσα ποτὲ παρὰ τῶν πρεσβυτέρων καλῶς ἔμαθον καὶ καλῶς ἐμνημόνευσα, συγκατατάξαι ταῖς ἑρμηνείαις, διαβεβαιούμενος ὑπὲρ αὐτῶν ἀλήθειαν. οὐ γὰρ τοῖς τὰ πολλὰ λέγουσιν ἔχαιρον ὥσπερ οἱ πολλοί, ἀλλὰ τοῖς τἀληθῆ διδάσκουσιν, οὐδὲ τοῖς τὰς ἀλλοτρίας ἐντολὰς μνημονεύουσιν, ἀλλὰ τοῖς τὰς παρὰ τοῦ κυρίου τῇ πίστει δεδομένας καὶ ἀπ' αὐτῆς παραγινομένας τῆς ἀληθείας. ... οὐ γὰρ τὰ ἐκ τῶν βιβλίων τοσοῦτόν με ὠφελεῖν ὑπελάμβανον ὅσον τὰ παρὰ ζώσης φωνῆς καὶ μενούσης.[1]

The frequent preoccupation of the modern reader of Papias with gospel origins has perhaps favoured the assumption that in this famous passage Papias is expressing a uniform preference for oral as against written tradition and reflecting a contemporary lack of interest in the literary preservation of tradition. It has even been quoted as explaining why the canonical gospels were not written earlier than they were, and a disparaging note has been detected in the references by Papias to the gospels of Matthew and Mark.[2]

On the face of it, there are difficulties in this assumption. If ever there was an age of such intense apocalyptic fervour as to render the composition of books otiose – and this is, to say the least, questionable – it must have been long past in the time of Papias. A conservative he may have been, but he is not an erratic survival. Further, Papias is himself writing a book – and a very large one – containing a great amount of tradition about the Lord and, to judge from the allusions to it of later writers, many other people as well. Despite all that has been written about Papias, it may be worth considering yet once again the context of his words.

Papias belongs to a generation for whom the apostles, though not necessarily very distant in time, represented a distinct and now com-

---

[1] Papias in Eusebius *EH* III, 39, 3–4.
[2] Cf. B. H. Streeter, *The Four Gospels* (1924) pp. 19 ff.

107

pleted stage of God's dealings with His people; a view that pervades the letters of Ignatius to other churches of Papias' province.[3] The apostles, the accredited interpreters of Christ's words and work, are the clearly marked intermediary stage between Christ and the contemporary Church.

Accordingly, when Papias sets out to write an *Exposition of the Oracles of the Lord*, "setting down alongside" (συγκατατάξαι) his interpretations the things he has carefully learnt from the past, he will be concerned that the traditions he records are apostolic: that is the guarantee of their truth. This is the background against which he tells us of his interviewing processes; how any hearer of "the elders" was closely examined as to any apostolic utterances he might have heard. "Elders who saw John the disciple of the Lord", provided him with that agraphon of the Lord which so impressed Irenaeus about the agricultural revolution to be introduced by the millennium,[4] the daughters of Philip are the authority quoted for a happy issue out of ordeal by poison (from an exposition of *Mark* 16,18 or something like it?).[5] This is no doubt what Papias means by διαβεβαιούμενος ὑπὲρ αὐτῶν ἀλήθειαν. To guarantee the truth of traditions was to demonstrate that they derived from an apostolic or quasi-apostolic source.

Perhaps this affords some clue as to the sense in which his words about the origin of the gospels of Mark and Matthew are to be taken. While much about these enigmatic sentences remains obscure, it is clear that Papias associates each gospel with an apostle: one with Peter and the other with Matthew. That is, the gospels of Matthew and Mark meet his basic test of authenticity. They are apostolic: their truth is guaranteed.

What, then, of his apparent preference for the living and abiding voice? While we naturally tend to read this statement in conjuction with his statements about Matthew and Mark, the immediate context shows that Papias has in mind works of a different character: works that are prolix but superficial (τοῖς τὰ πολλὰ λέγουσιν) or suspicious in doctrinal tendency (τοῖς τὰς ἀλλοτρίας ἐντολὰς μνημονεύουσιν). To these Papias opposes his own standards. He delights in those who teach the truth (τοῖς τἀληθῆ διδάσκουσιν) and in those who provide com-

---

[3] *Magnesians* 6,1; 13,1–2; *Trallians* 2,2; 3,1; 12,2; *Philadelphians* 5,1; *Smyrneans* 8,1.
[4] In Irenaeus, *adv. Haer.* XXXIII, 3–4 (Harvey II, pp. 417f.).
[5] Eusebius *EH* III, 39,9; cf. Philip of Side *Christian History* (C.de Boor, TU V. 2. 1888, p. 170).

mandments given by the Lord to the faith, and deriving from the Truth itself (τοῖς τὰς παρὰ τοῦ κυρίου τῇ πίστει δεδομένας καὶ ἀπ' αὐτῆς παραγινομένας τῆς ἀληθείας). That is, in orthodoxy and authenticity as guaranteed by pedigree – in fact, apostolicity. Instead of taking all traditions at face value, he has carefully noted the accounts of reliable people with known access to apostolic teaching. Papias, then, is thinking of works of whose apostolic origin there is no proof. With Matthew, Mark, and any other demonstrably apostolic work he is not here concerned. For Papias, what matters is the quality of the source, not whether it is oral or written. A written work known to be apostolic provides "oracles of the Lord", which may be taken as authentic, ready for exposition. But Papias wants more. He knows that such works contain only a fragment of the Lord's words and deeds, and he is ready to expound any oracles that are certainly authentic. There are other teachers and other books which present oracles ostensibly from the Lord; but their manner or their matter is dubious. Papias has a test for them, and a source superior to them: the voice, still living and abiding, of the hearers of the elders, who can relate what the apostles themselves used to say.

By the time of Papias, Christianity had, to use Goodspeed's phrase, already gone to press, and there were evidently an embarrassing number of works purporting to provide authentic tradition. And they were popular (οὐ γὰρ ... ὥσπερ οἱ πολλοί). Perhaps the "many" of *Luke* 1,1, is not as rhetorical as has sometimes been thought. At any rate, Papias is as desirous as Theophilus could be to have the ἀσφάλεια.[6] Despite the celebrated estimate of his intelligence by Eusebius, he is not completely gullible. He recognizes that some of the alleged traditions keep very strange company; and we have only to think of the Gospel of Thomas to realize how readily quite authentic material could be modulated, transformed or corrupted by bad company at the hands of people with a particular *tendenz*, and to guess what Papias may have meant by "those who relate alien commandments".[7] For him, authenticity meant apostolicity; and apostolicity was patient of historical verification. Far from being uninterested in the literary preservation of the tradition, he is wrestling manfully with the problems involved in it.

How far he was right in his particular judgments is now irrelevant,

---

[6] *Luke* 1,4.
[7] Cf. R. M. Grant, *The Earliest Lives of Jesus* (1961) p. 16.

especially as his book is almost entirely lost. But it is worthwhile to notice that his generation was the last which could think of applying his methods in his way. When the last people to hear the apostles were dead, who was then to sort out the true from the false traditions about the Lord? Then it was the Gnostic teachers, the descendants of "those who relate alien commandments" who claimed apostolicity by pedigree; and their opponents increasingly located the tradition in those written collections believed to be apostolic or to derive from an unimpeachably "apostolic man".

University of Aberdeen
King's College

ORIGEN'S DOCTRINE OF TRADITION

THAT which is handed over from one generation of Christian believers to the next, the Christian teaching and gospel, the method by which it is handed over, and the sources from which it is derived, and its authoritative guardians and interpreters, in a word, Christian tradition in its widest sense, forms a subject which ought to be the concern of all scholars of theology. One would moreover expect those who had made a special study of Origen, one of the most able, influential, and voluminous of the Fathers of the Church, to pay particular attention to his doctrine of tradition. But in fact few of those who, in recent years, have written upon Origen[1] have dealt with his doctrine more than incidentally, as a subordinate part of their exposition of what they considered his more important doctrines, such as the relation of the Son to the Father, or the origin and destiny of the soul, or the allegorization of the Bible. Those who have given special attention to his doctrine of tradition (such as Prat and Migne) have sometimes not sufficiently examined their sources. One notable exception to this rule is Dr. Prestige who in his *Fathers and Heretics* has included a valuable essay on the doctrine of tradition in the Fathers generally, and later in the book has attempted very sketchily to exemplify his general conclusions from Origen's works. This article is simply an endeavour to work out in greater detail than Dr. Prestige was able to afford Origen's doctrine of tradition, taking Prestige's conclusions about the doctrine in the Fathers in general as a convenient starting-point.

The Fathers, says Dr. Prestige in the first chapter of his book (p. 6), spoke of two sorts of tradition. In one sense of the word they meant 'an accretion, enlargement, confirmation of the faith', which 'is to be expected and welcomed in the process of transmitting Christian truth', 'the accumulating wisdom of philosophically grounded Christianity'; this the Fathers called διδασκαλία. The other type of tradition they called παράδοσις. This was the faith handed down from Christ to the Apostles and from them to the Church for it to keep (p. 13), and 'for most practical purposes the tradition is enshrined in the Bible' (p. 26). But in cases of dispute or ambiguity in the Bible itself, appeal is made to tradition as enshrined in Christian institutions and witnessed

---

[1] e.g. G. W. Butterworth, Preface and Introduction to his translation of Origen's *Concerning First Principles*; G. L. Prestige, *Fathers and Heretics*; R. B. Tollinton, Essay prefixed to *Selections from the Commentaries and Homilies of Origen*; B. F. Westcott, article 'Origen' in *D.C.B.*; C. Bigg, *The Christian Platonists of Alexandria*; W. R. Inge, article 'Origen', *Encyc. Religion and Ethics*; F. Prat, *Origène, le Théologien et l'exégète*; E. de Faye, *Origène, sa vie, son œuvre, sa pensée* (3 vols.) ; P. Koetschau, Introduction to his edition of *Against Celsus*; J.-P. Migne, Editor's Preface to *Origen*, vol. ii.

to in the Christian *cultus*, and as always held in the Church. It should be interesting, and even valuable, to see how far Origen's views on tradition correspond to these.

But before we approach this task we must issue a warning. The Latin translators of Origen's works will have to be used very sparingly in evidence because it is clear that both Rufinus and Jerome, the chief ancient translators of Origen's works, altered the sense of Origen's words when they thought fit; and we have definite evidence that they both did so in cases where his words referred to tradition. In his Preface to his translation of Origen's *Concerning First Principles*, Rufinus expressly tells us that he omitted or altered to suit the orthodox rule of faith various passages in Origen's works on the grounds that they were later interpolations by heretical and malevolent persons.[1] He claims that he is in this practice only following the example of St. Jerome in his translations of Origen. That Rufinus applied this policy of alteration in order to make Origen appear to have more respect for the tradition of the Church than his original text justified is clear from a later passage in his translation of *Concerning First Principles*[2] where Origen has ὥστε κατὰ τοῦτο with no reference whatever to the Church's rule of faith; Rufinus translates this 'ex quo magis convenit regulae pietatis'. Later still in the same work a Greek fragment enables us to observe that Rufinus omits a particularly daring speculation by Origen suggesting that Christ is crucified still in the heavenly places, and begins the next paragraph: 'Verum in his omnibus sufficiat nobis sensum nostrum regulae pietatis aptare et ita sentire, &c.'[3] The Greek fragment stops before the next paragraph begins, but we may shrewdly suspect that this is another example of an insertion by Rufinus of a reference to the Church's tradition. Again, Dr. J. E. L. Oulton in an article on 'Rufinus' Translation of the Church History of Eusebius'[4] has pointed out how, in his summary of Origen's *Letter to Africanus* about the History of Susanna, Rufinus described Origen as saying 'that that alone should be deemed true in the divine Scriptures which the seventy interpreters had translated, since it had been confirmed by apostolic authority'; but in fact what Origen wrote was πρὸς ταῦτα δὲ σκόπει εἰ μὴ καλὸν μεμνῆσθαι τοῦ· οὐ μεταθήσεις ὅρια αἰώνια ἃ ἔστησαν οἱ προτεροί σου. Rufinus' claim that Jerome carried out similar alterations of Origen's text can be verified by references to Jerome's translation of Origen's *Commentary on Matthew*, for the first part of which the Greek text survives. In one passage here Origen

---

[1] *Con. First P.* (ed. P. Koetschau, Leipzig, 1913), Rufinus' Preface 2, 3; compare his equally candid admission in his Preface to his translation of Origen's *Comm. on Romans*.

[2] Op. cit. iii. 1–23 (Migne, 21).   [3] Op. cit. iv. 3–13, 14.

[4] *J.T.S.*, Vol. XXX, No. 118 (for Jan. 1929), p. 164.

belittles the 'doctrine of the resurrection of the dead as it is believed in the Church'. Jerome's translation significantly omits this passage.[1] The discovery that both Rufinus and Jerome are capable of altering Origen's references to tradition in the interests of their orthodoxy does not mean that we can entirely ignore the Latin translations of Origen as sources for our inquiry. It does mean that we must take his works extant in Greek as our primary authorities, and realize that any reference to tradition in a translation by Rufinus or Jerome may very well have been touched up or even interpolated by the translator.

With this caution in mind, let us return to Prestige's two forms of tradition, παράδοσις and διδασκαλία. In all the works and fragments of Origen that survive in Greek, the word παράδοσις occurs 44 times; 30 instances of it signify Rabbinic or Jewish tradition, and 6 mean traditions independent of the Bible connected with the Christian faith; 1 instance may refer to the Bible, and 7 occurrences have meanings quite irrelevant to our inquiry. Origen never uses the phrase 'apostolic' nor 'ecclesiastical' παράδοσις. His instances of tradition outside the Bible are small and comparatively unimportant pieces of information, such as that 'the brothers of Jesus' were sons of Joseph by another wife,[2] or details concerning the death of John bar-Zebedee and the exile of the other John in Patmos.[3] Twice, indeed, Origen quotes a saying of our Lord not found in the N.T.,[4] and once a saying which he calls apostolic but which is not in the N.T.;[5] but he does not call any of these a παράδοσις. Some of these traditions, whether called παραδόσεις or not, are probably intelligent guesses,[6] and some perhaps derived from popular legend or gossip.[7] The one occasion where παράδοσις probably means the Bible is in a comment on Ps. i, ver. 5,[8] where his phrase τὴν τῶν ἀρχαίων παράδοσιν apparently means the Scriptural doctrine of the resurrection of the body. But this instance is not, of course, sufficient to prove against the testimony of the others that Origen uses the word παράδοσις to express the sense of tradition which, in Dr. Prestige's account, attaches to it in the Fathers generally. In fact, as I have shown, Origen quite demonstrably does not so use it. If further proof is needed, it is supplied by a passage in *Against Celsus* (ii. 13), which runs: 'For [the enemies of Christianity] surely will not assert that those who knew Jesus and heard Him handed

---

[1] *Comm. on Matt.* xvii. 9; cf. pt. ii, 46, where the survival of a Greek fragment enables us to see how much Jerome has elaborated upon Origen's reference to the Church's rule of faith.

[2] *Comm. on Matt.* x. 17.   [3] Ibid. xvi. 6.

[4] *Con. Prayer*, ii. 2 (repeated in *Comm. on Ps.* iv. 4 and referred to *Against C.* vii. 44) and *Hom. on Numbers*, xxiii. 4.

[5] *Hom. on Leviticus*, x. 2.   [6] Cf. *Hom. on Genesis*, xiv. 3.

[7] Cf. *Against C.* i. 51; ii. 62, 68; *Hom. on Jeremiah*, xx. 8.

[8] Migne, *Origen*, ii. 1092 et seq.

down the teaching of the gospels without committing it to writing'
(χωρὶς γραφῆς τὴν τῶν εὐαγγελίων παραδεδωκέναι διδασκαλίαν). According to Prestige's theory this should have been δεδιδαχέναι παράδοσιν.

But this instance, with its strong suggestion that what the first
disciples (to use Dr. Prestige's term) 'traditioned' was to be found in
the Bible, serves to illustrate the fact that Origen does derive the sort
of tradition to which Dr. Prestige gives the name παράδοσις from the
Bible, though he does not call it παράδοσις.[1] That he looks for tradition in this primary sense nowhere outside the Bible is clear from
almost every passage of his works.[2] He quotes no other source of
doctrine except the Scriptures or documents which were held to be
inspired by at least parts of the Church. Here he is entirely at one
with the other Fathers quoted by Dr. Prestige.

That his sole source of primary doctrinal teaching is the Bible
applies even to Origen's conception of secret tradition. At first sight
this statement seems highly unlikely and even contradictory, because
it is clear that on the one hand Origen believed that our Lord and
His Apostles gave special secret doctrines to various people, some of
which at least were never written down; and on the other hand he
says repeatedly that there is secret teaching available in the Church of
his day for those who are spiritually and intellectually fit to receive it.
The conclusion seems ready that he believed in a continuous unwritten
tradition deriving from our Lord. But in fact a close examination of
his words compels us to discard this conclusion. Certainly his references to a tradition of secret teaching given by our Lord and His
Apostles are frequent. Writing in *Against Celsus*[3] of the disciples, he
says ὁρῶντες δὲ ταῦτα [viz. the doctrine of the Atonement] οἱ τοῦ
'Ιησοῦ μαθηταὶ καὶ ἄλλα τούτων πλείονα ἃ εἰκὸς αὐτοὺς ἐν ἀπορρήτῳ
ἀπὸ τοῦ 'Ιησοῦ μεμαθηκέναι; and later in the same work he says that
John xvi. 12, 13, 'I have yet many things to say unto you, but ye
cannot bear them now, &c.', meant that Christ after His Passion and
Resurrection taught His disciples the allegorization of the old law
(*Against Celsus*, ii. 2). Again, in his *Homilies on Joshua* (xxiii. 4), he
speaks of the unspeakable mysteries which Paul learnt when he was
caught up to Heaven, and suggests that though he could not disclose
them to ordinary men, 'perhaps he used to tell them to those who do
not walk according to man. He used to tell them to Timothy, he used
to tell them to Luke and to the other disciples whom he knew to be

---

[1] He does, however, frequently use the verb παραδιδόναι in connexion with
it, as in the instance quoted above; cf. *Against C.* iii. 17; *Comm. on Matt.* xiii.
1, &c.

[2] Cf. especially *Con. First P.* i, Origen's Preface 3 and 10; *Comm. on Matt.*,
pt. ii, 47; *Hom. on Numbers*, ix. 1.   [3] i. 31.

fit to receive unspeakable mysteries.'¹ Two examples of what Origen imagined to be the content of this secret teaching we have already seen, the doctrine of the Atonement and the allegorization of the law. Other examples are the doctrine of the pre-existence of souls,² some points of soteriology and some of Christology, knowledge about angels (fallen and unfallen), and about the differences of souls, the origin and nature of the world, and the origin and extent of evil.³

The word εἰκός, however, which occurs in two of the passages already referred to (*Against Celsus*, i. 3 and *Concerning Prayer*, ii. 5), suggests that in attributing a secret tradition to Christ and His Apostles Origen was not relying on any continuous delivery of that tradition in the Church, but on his own speculation. In fact, this conclusion is inescapable, because on several occasions Origen makes it clear that the secret doctrines of his own day and his own school are to be found in the Bible, and never at any point does he even surmise that they are to be found in any other source. In *Against Celsus* (iv. 8, 9) he says that 'there are certain secret and inexplicable systems and logical trains of argument about the dispensation of different destinies to different souls', to be derived only by the really intellectual Christian from such passages as Deut. xxii. 8, 9; and for these and similar doctrines, 'the educated man will need to calculate the principles of the doctrine by various sorts of explanations, both from the inspired writings and from the logical developement of the principles themselves' (τὰς ἐν τοῖς λόγοις ἀκολουθίας). In his *Commentary on Romans* (v. 2) he suggests that 'though the Apostle Paul as a wise steward of the word of God wished these doctrines to be secret and hidden in his letters, still he did put them in', and 'he who is instructed in the law of the Lord knows how to understand a dark saying and the words of the wise and riddles'; and he is here almost certainly referring to his own special doctrines of the salvation of all men and of the pre-existence of souls.⁴ The only conclusion which will fit all these facts is that Origen believed that the intellectual Christians of his day were intended to derive from their study of the Bible a number of secret doctrines beyond the understanding of the average believer (and in fact identical

---

¹ For similar statements see *Against C.* iii. 37, 58; vi. 6; *Comm. on Matt.* xii. 17; xiv. 12; *Con. Prayer*, ii. 5.

² *Against C.* v. 29; *Comm. on John*, vi. 12, 13; *Comm. on Matt.* xv. 34.

³ *Con. First P.* iv. 2, 7; this Origen calls διδασκαλία, and Prestige (*Fathers and Heretics*, p. 120) apparently wants to identify it with his secondary form of tradition, and make it equivalent to the creed of Origen's day. But a close examination of the passage (which Dr. Prestige can hardly have made) makes this view impossible. These are the articles of Origen's esoteric teaching, not of the Church's διδασκαλία. He calls them in the same passage τῶν ἀπορρήτων μυστηρίων.

⁴ For similar passages see his *Comm. on Romans*, vi. 8 and x. 43.

with the speculations of Origen himself and his school of thought), and that he assumed that Christ and His Apostles had taught such doctrines privately to their more intelligent disciples as Origen was teaching them to his; but that there is no evidence that any continuity of delivery in the Church existed between such alleged secret teaching by Christ and His Apostles on the one hand and Origen's secret teaching on the other, nor even that Origen believed such continuity to exist.

An investigation of the occurrences of the word διδασκαλία in Origen is not much more rewarding than that of the word παράδοσις, and serves to bring us to much the same conclusion, namely, that in the narrowly philological field Origen does not very obviously bear out Dr. Prestige's conclusions about the meaning which the Fathers attached to the word. Διδασκαλία occurs 210 times in Origen; 46 instances are quite irrelevant to our study; 102 instances refer to the teaching of our Lord, and 12 to that of evangelists, Apostles, or disciples; in 2 cases it means the teaching of the Bible generally, in 6 that of the law or the O.T., and in 31 that of Christianity or of God, so generally as to be of no use in our inquiry. In 4 instances it signifies the teaching of Christianity in particular relation to those outside the Church, and in 7 explicitly the teaching of the Church. But once more, where Origen does not clearly support the Fathers generally in the word which he uses for tradition, he does so in his conception of that tradition. For he leaves us in no doubt that the primary doctrinal tradition (which is to be found only in the Bible) is the tradition *of the Church*, and that the Church alone has the right to interpret that tradition through its instruction. As has been said, he does refer [1] to this function of the Church as ἐκκλησιαστικὴ διδασκαλία or as ὑγίης διδασκαλία,[2] or as κατήχησις ἐκκλησιαστικὴ καὶ διδασκαλία,[3] or as ἐκκλησιαστικὴ γνώμη καὶ διδασκαλία.[4] He also refers to the Church's βούλημα,[5] to the Church's κήρυγμα,[6] and to the ἐκκλησιαστικὸς λόγος.[7] On one occasion, however, he explicitly belittles the Church's teaching; in his *Commentary on Matthew* (xi. 15) he says: 'And even that which is thought to be ecclesiastical teaching [ἐκκλησιαστικὴ διδασκαλία], if it becomes servile on the score of flattery, or as an excuse for greed, or when someone is seeking glory from men on account of his teaching, does not carry any weight with those who are placed by God in the Church as first apostles, then prophets, and thirdly teachers.' [8] This tendency to suggest that

[1] *Comm. on Matt.* x. 12.   [2] *Hom. on Jeremiah*, v. 4.
[3] *Comm. on Matt.* xv. 7.
[4] *Comm. on Ps.* v. 7; cf. *Comm. on Ps.* xlviii. 12.   [5] *Against C.* v. 22.
[6] *Con. First P.*, Origen's Preface, 10; iii. 1, 1.
[7] *Comm. on Matt.* xii. 23; xiii. 2.
[8] Cf. *Comm. on Matt.* xvii. 29, a passage already referred to.

the real judgement of the Church should be left to its intellectual *élite* appears also in his references to ὁ ἐκκλησιαστικός, who is sometimes the average churchman truly representing the mind of the Church,[1] but sometimes the average churchman who had better leave the interpretation of Scripture to the professors.[2] Similarly, though he does clearly claim that the Church alone has the right to interpret Scripture,[3] he tends to identify this interpretation with the allegorization of Scripture, and to claim that this allegorization was handed down as the true method of interpretation by the Apostles.[4] It is clear, of course, that his only source for this belief (or rather, speculation) is the Bible itself.

One more word used by Origen in this connexion must be noted, and that is κανών. In Origen this always means 'rule of faith' and never 'canon of Scripture'. Indeed, according to H. Oppel, who has written a monograph upon the word,[5] κανών does not occur meaning 'the list of the writings acknowledged by the Church as documents of the divine revelation' until we reach Athanasius.[6] In one passage Origen, characteristically, uses κανών as 'the rule of faith prevalent among the majority of the Church' which the man who is perfect and holy can transcend.[7] Elsewhere he links this κανών with the Apostles, claiming that he himself in using allegory holds fast to τοῦ κανόνος τῆς Ἰησοῦ Χριστοῦ κατὰ διαδοχὴν τῶν ἀποστόλων οὐρανίου ἐκκλησίας.[8] A Greek fragment of the *Commentary on Matthew* (pt. ii, 46) speaks of ὁ μὲν ἔξω τῆς πίστεως καὶ τοῦ τῆς ἐκκλησίας κανόνος καὶ τῆς γραφῆς, where of course no reference to the canon of Scripture can be intended. And in a long passage in the *Homilies on Jeremiah* (v. 14) he equates τὸν λόγον τὸν τῆς ἐκκλησίας, τὸν ἐκκλησιαστικὸν κανόνα, and τὴν πρόθεσιν τῆς ὑγιοῦς διδασκαλίας. It is remarkable that in the whole of his *Letter to Africanus*, which is entirely devoted to discussing the canonicity of the History of Susanna, he does not use the word κανών once.

Indeed Origen's attitude to what was later known as the 'canon' of the N.T. is significant of his whole view of the tradition of the Church. For him there is no official imposition of canonicity. The

---

[1] e.g. *Hom. on Luke*, xvi (on Luke ii. 34).
[2] e.g. *Fragment on Exodus*, xx. 5, 6.
[3] *Comm. on Matt.* xvii. 35; *Hom. IV on Ps.* xxxvii, 1.
[4] Cf. *Hom. on Exodus*, v. 1; *Hom. on Leviticus*, v. 5; *Hom. on Numbers*, xxvii. 2; *Hom. on Genesis*, vi. 3; *Hom. on Joshua*, xv. 1.
[5] '*KANΩN*, Zur Bedeutungsgeschichte des Wortes und seiner lateinischen Entsprechungen (Regula–Norma)', published in *Philologus*, Supplement-band xxx, Heft 4, Leipzig, 1937.
[6] Op. cit., pp. 70 and 71, where he derives his information from Zahn's *Grundriss der Geschichte des Neutestamentlichen Kanons*.
[7] *Comm. on John*, xiii. 16.   [8] *Con. First P.* iv. 2, 2.

only point where he approaches this conception is in his conviction that there can be only four gospels (though he is not nearly as emphatic upon the subject as the earlier Irenaeus). Πολλοὶ ἐθέλησαν γράψαι, he says,[1] ἀλλ' οἱ δόκιμοι τραπεζῖται οὐ πάντα ἀνέκριναν, ἀλλὰ τὰ τέσσαρα μόνον ἐξελέξαντο. Then after mentioning five rejected gospels he adds τὰ δὲ τέσσαρα μόνα προκρίνει ἡ θεοῦ ἐκκλησία.[2] One would very much like to know whom exactly Origen imagined ' the experienced money-changers ' to be; one suspects (as one always suspects with Origen) that they would turn out to be the intellectual *élite.* In all other references in Greek (for in this point the Latin translators come within the circle of suspicion) Origen preserves a very open mind, and makes the general judgement of the whole Church his only criterion for deciding the genuineness of writings, fully admitting its inconclusiveness.[3] In his *Commentary on John* (xiii. 17), he divides the books claiming to be inspired into γνήσιον, νόθον, and μικτόν, and puts the ' Gospel of Peter ' into the last class, without decisively rejecting it as spurious; and in his *Commentary on Matthew* (x. 17) he seems inclined to believe a tradition which he finds in the same gospel (and also in the 'Book of James'). In a fragment of the *Commentary on John* (No. 107, ed. Brooke) he discusses the authenticity of several books, and his verdict on 2 Peter, 2 John, and 3 John is ἀμφιβάλλεται. His most characteristic phrase for describing books as what we would now call 'canonical' is αἱ φερόμεναι ἐν ταῖς ἐκκλησίαις τοῦ θεοῦ γραφαί,[4] or κατὰ τὰ ἀναντίρρητα τῶν ἀναφερομένων βιβλίων θεοπνεύστων[5] (though this is in the context applied to the O.T. canon). His attitude to the 'Shepherd' of Hermas makes an interesting study. Five times he refers to it without commenting on its inspiration (and therefore presumably supposing it to be inspired).[6] In his *Concerning First Principles*, however, he does in one place admit (iv. 2, 4) that it is τῷ ὑπό τινων καταφρονουμένῳ βιβλίῳ, but he is himself obviously not among these despisers. In his *Homilies on Luke,* xxv (on Luke xii. 59) he is still very sure of its inspiration, for, having quoted an apocryphal work which he knows may be

[1] *Hom. on Luke,* i (on Luke i. 1–4).
[2] Cf. the words μαθὼν περὶ τῶν τεσσάρων εὐαγγελίων ἃ καὶ μόνα ἀναντίρρητά ἐστιν ἐν τῇ ὑπὸ τὸν οὐρανὸν ἐκκλησίᾳ τοῦ θεοῦ, *Comm. on Matt.* i, quoted by Eus. *H.E.* vi. 25.
[3] This is not intended as an exhaustive account of the apocryphal books which Origen quotes (such as can be found in M. R. James's *The Apocryphal Gospels*), but as an estimate of Origen's attitude towards what was later known as the N.T. canon.
[4] *Against C.* vi. 20; cf. *Comm. on John,* xix. 23, ὡς ἐν τῇ φερομένῃ 'Ιακωβοῦ ἐπιστόλῃ.
[5] *Comm. on Ps.* iv. 2.
[6] *Con. First P.* i. 3, 3; iii. 3, 4; *Hom. on Joshua,* x. 1; *Comm. on Ezekiel,* xiii. 3; *Fragment of Hosea* (*Philocalia* viii. 3).

disputed, he adds that if this work offends anybody he can find the same doctrine in Hermas' 'Shepherd', as if it were a much more widely acknowledged source. In his *Commentary on Romans* he calls it (x. 31) 'a work which seems to me very useful, and, as I believe, divinely inspired'. But in his *Commentary on Matthew* he describes it as 'a document in circulation among the churches, but not allowed by all to be inspired' (xiv. 23), and says of it later in the same work 'si cui placeat etiam illum legere librum'.[1] It is not perhaps fanciful to trace in Origen a growing caution in his references to the 'Shepherd'. *Concerning First Principles* is an early work and betrays perhaps something of the dogmatic quality of a young mind. The *Commentary on Matthew* was certainly written much later, though it is difficult to date the order of composition of the other works in which he refers to the book. A similar cooling of his approval can perhaps be traced in his references to the 'Acts of Paul'. In *Concerning First Principles* (i. 1, 3) he quotes this book with evident belief in its genuineness; but in his *Commentary on John*, xx. 12 (written when he had left Alexandria for Caesarea, several years later) his verdict on the book becomes, 'if anybody likes to admit them'. He uses an almost identical phrase with this last one twice of the 'Gospel according to the Hebrews'.[2] On the other hand, he apparently accepted the 'Epistle of Barnabas' as genuine without question, for he quotes from it twice without comment on its inspiration, once in one of his earliest works (*Concerning First Principles*, iii. 4, 7) and once in one of his latest (*Against Celsus*, i. 63).[3]

His attitude to the Epistle to the Hebrews is the most revealing of all for a study of his views on canonicity. In the vast majority of his references to the book he assumes without question that it was written by St. Paul. Once he admits the possibility of its not being written by Paul (though he tells us that he himself believes in the Pauline authorship),[4] and once, in a well-known fragment of his *Homilies on Hebrews* preserved by Eusebius, he discusses the whole question fully.[5] After discussing the book's style and contents and concluding that the style is un-Pauline but the ideas in the book are quite as magnificent as Paul's, he goes on:

> 'If I were to give my opinion I would say that the ideas are those of the Apostle, but the style and composition are due to someone who is recalling the words of the Apostle and writing, so to speak, a commentary upon what was said by his teacher. If

[1] Pt. ii, 69; there is no particular reason to suspect the translator here. Cf. *Hom. on Numbers*, viii. 1, where a very similar phrase is applied to the book.

[2] *Comm. on John*, ii. 2; *Hom. on Jeremiah*, xv. 4.

[3] In this passage he certainly would have disowned it had he thought its genuineness suspect, for Celsus had apparently referred to it.

[4] *Comm. on Matt.*, pt. ii. 28.   [5] Eusebius, *H.E.* vi. 25.

therefore any church possesses the letter on the grounds that it is by Paul, let it give its approval to the letter even on the grounds that it is Paul's, for the men of old did not hand it down to us as Paul's for nothing. As for who wrote the Letter, God knows the truth. The story which has reached us says, following some authorities, that Clement who was bishop of Rome wrote the Letter ; but, following others, Luke who wrote the gospel and Acts.'

This frank statement makes perfectly clear what we might infer from Origen's references to other works whose genuineness was disputed, that the question of authorship was not the only test, in his eyes, of a book's genuineness. In this case the Epistle's νοήματα θαυμάσια commend it to him, and it is likely that this too was true of Hermas' 'Shepherd'. Secondly, the tradition current in the Church concerning a book was something which, in Origen's view, should be given its true weight, but was not by any means decisive. Thirdly, the final standard of judgement in this matter was the fluctuating and indefinite one of the use of any book in question in the Church of Origen's day, and Origen was content to leave it so without betraying any signs of wanting an official list of books of the N.T. canon.

One more possible source of tradition in Origen must be noted, and that is tradition as enshrined in Christian institutions and as witnessed to in the Christian *cultus* (see *Fathers and Heretics*, pp. 31 and 32). Does Origen recognize this type of tradition ? His references to Christian institutions in his works are not very frequent, and to the Christian *cultus* surprisingly rare. In many cases where he does mention them it is obvious that he presumes them to derive from rules to be found in the Bible. For instance, in his little work *Concerning Prayer*, he takes all his examples of prayer from the Bible and bases his rules for private prayer and his suggestions for its order entirely on the Bible.[1] Again, in his *Commentary on Romans* he calls the necessity of Baptism *ecclesiastica regula* and speaks of the holy kiss being 'handed down as the Church's custom ',[2] but it is clear that to him the Church's authority was in the first case John iii. 5 and in the second Rom. xvi. 16. In spite of this, however, we do find in a few passages an undoubted recognition of Christian institutions and the Christian *cultus* as a source of authoritative tradition. For instance, in his *Commentary on Romans* (v. 8, 9) he clearly recognizes infant baptism as a tradition given to the Church by the Apostles, and he does not try to find Scriptural authority for it; similarly in his *Homilies on Isaiah* (vi. 3) he argues that our Lord's command to the disciples to wash one another's feet could not have been intended literally because nobody in the Church obeys it literally, which constitutes something of an appeal to ecclesiastical tradition.

---

[1] See *Con. Prayer*, xv. 1 ; xxxiii. 1.   [2] *Comm. on Romans*, ii. 7 ; x. 37.

The clearest reference is in his *Homilies on Numbers* (v. 1), where he says that 'most of those who observe many customs of the Church, such as turning to the East for prayer, kneeling to pray, the manner of celebrating the Eucharist, or the words, actions, questions, and replies in baptism, do not know the reason for them. But the people do them all the same, ' according to the way in which they have been handed down and entrusted by the Great High Priest and his Sons' (which probably means Christ and His bishops). He goes on to say that there are of course some people who know the reason for these things, and he is here almost certainly referring to the intellectual *élite* who would be capable of giving the true allegorical meaning of such customs. It seems reasonable to conclude, therefore, that while Origen recognized an authoritative tradition derived from Christian institutions and the Christian *cultus*, his knowledge of the origins of both was so uncertain that we cannot put much confidence in such a tradition; and the examples given here can readily be seen to confirm this suspicion.

We may then sum up Origen's doctrine of tradition by saying that to Origen the Bible *is* the tradition of the Church. In practice he makes no distinction between the two; but he is quite clear that it is the tradition *of the Church*, and the Church alone has the right to determine what is its tradition and to interpret that tradition. There are, as we have seen, exceptions to this rule, but they are not very significant. Perhaps the most important modification of it is that Origen is always inclined to identify the Church's interpretation of its tradition with the speculations of his own particular highly intellectual and rationalizing school of thought. The question of what precisely are the organs whereby the Church determines and interprets tradition he is content to leave almost unanswered, and the limits of that tradition were in his conception only loosely defined. His essentially speculative mind was always ready to leap over the boundaries set by the list of inspired books and the articles of a creed which the Church of his day was in process of forming.

R. P. C. HANSON

BASIL'S DOCTRINE OF TRADITION IN RELATION TO THE HOLY SPIRIT

BY

R. P. C. HANSON

The following texts have been used in this essay:

ATHANASIUS *De Synodis* and *Historia Arianorum*, herausg. H.G.Opitz *Apologia contra Arianos*, ed. W.Bright, *Athanasius' Historical Writings* (Oxford 1881) *Orations against the Arians*, ed. W.Bright (Oxford 1884) *Epistles to Serapion*, Migne, *P.G.* 26 (col. nos. in text), and C.R.B.Shapland, *The Letters of Athanasius concerning the Holy Spirit* (London 1951) *Festal Epistles*, tr. from Syriac by H.G.Williams (Oxford 1854) (page nos. in text)

BASIL *De Spiritu Sancto*, ed. B.Pruche (Paris 1946), and Migne, *P.G.* 32 (col. nos. in text) *Adversus Eunomium*, Migne, *P.G.* 29 (col. nos. in text) *Letters*, ed. Y.Courtonne (Paris 1957) and R.J.Deferrari, for later letters (with col. nos. of text of Migne, *P.G.* 32) *De Fide*, Migne, *P.G.* 31 (col. nos in text)

EUNOMIUS *Liber Apologeticus*, Migne, *P.G.* 30 [col. ref. in text]

GREGORY OF NAZIANZUS *Five Theological Orations*, ed. A.J.Mason (Cambridge 1899)

The Christian writers of the fourth century all shared the tendency, which had originated long before their day, of ascribing an apostolic foundation to all contemporary doctrine and practice whose origins went back beyond living memory. The Arians were no exceptions in this particular. The Creed of the Dedication (341) begins with the words, "We believe, following the evangelic and apostolic tradition..."[1] Eunomius, who would have regarded the Dedication Creed as dangerously modernist, described the colourless creed upon which, according to his

---

[1] Athanasius, *De Synodis* 23.2 πιστεύομεν ἀκολούθως τῇ εὐαγγελικῇ καὶ ἀποστο-λικῇ παραδόσει.

123

own account, he had been brought up, as "the orthodox tradition which has prevailed from the beginning from the Fathers"[2] and he characterised it as a κανών and a γνώμων and appealed to the "Fathers' " teaching as authority for his doctrine of God.[3] When he places the Holy Spirit third in rank and nature he claims to be following in all things "the teaching of the saints",[4] a phrase which Basil, no doubt correctly, takes to refer to the doctrine of the Fathers. And Arius and his supporters claimed that the statement of faith which they voluntarily submitted to Alexander of Alexandria was "our creed which we have learnt from our ancestors and from you, blessed Pope".[5]

Athanasius himself is a good example of the extent and the limits of appeals to tradition made by writers before Basil. Athanasius appeals to tradition in a number of forms at various points in his works. He can appeal to the κανών or the κανόνες, meaning the traditional rules and customs of the Church.[6] He regards these rules as apostolic.[7] He has the greatest respect for the doctrinal tradition which had formed in the history of the Church before his day. Unless we are to prove bastards, he says, we must approve of what the Fathers say: "we have the traditions from them, and from them the teaching of orthodoxy."[8]

In this traditional teaching he emphatically includes the decisions of the Council of Nicaea of 325. When the Arians attack this council, he says, they are attacking their own fathers in the faith and disregarding tradition.[9] He cites Christian baptism several times as authoritative traditional practice from which doctrinal consequences can be drawn, though practice based on the commandment of the Lord given in Scripture.[10]

---

[2] Eunomius, *Apologeticus* 4 (480); Basil, *Adversus Eunomium* 1.4 (509) τὴν κρατοῦσαν ἄνωθεν παρὰ τῶν πατέρων παράδοσιν.

[3] Eunomius, *Apol.* 7(841); Basil, *Adv. Eunom.* 1.5(513).

[4] Eunomius, *Apol.* 25(861); Basil, *Adv. Eunom.* 3.5(653).

[5] *De Synodis* 16.2 ἡ πίστις ἡ ἐκ προγόνων ἦν καὶ ἀπὸ σοῦ μεμαθήκαμεν, μακάριε πάπα. But we must remind ourselves that the Arians were ready on occasion to reverse this tendency. The "Dated Creed" of 359 described the action of the Fathers at Nicaea as "rather stupid" (ἁπλούστερον, *De Synod.* 8.6).

[6] E.g. *Apologia contra Arianos* 11,21, 25, 29 (the last three quoting Julius of Rome), 69 (quoting Arsenius); in 29 the Eusebians are quoted as making the same appeal.

[7] *Ibid.* 30 (κανὼν ἀποστολικός and παράδοσις ἀποστολική) 34, 35 (these first three quoting Julius); *Hist. Arian.* 14.1, 36.1, 74.5; *Festal Epistles* II (19–21).

[8] *De Syn.* 47.4 ἐξ αὐτῶν ἔχομεν τὰς παραδόσεις καὶ παρ' αὐτῶν τὴν τῆς εὐσεβείας διδασκαλίαν; cf. 7.1, 43.2–3, 54.3; *Epistle to Serapion* 1.33 (605).

[9] *De Syn.* 13.1–5, 14.1–3.

[10] E.g. *Orations against Arians* II.41; *Ep. to Serap.* 1.28(593, 596), 3.6(633). Cf. Eusebius Caesariensis, *Adv. Marcellum* I.1 (*PG* 24, 728); he appears to have been the first to use this argument.

He insists that an understanding of the *skopos*, the general burden or drift, of Scripture, as the Church understands it, is necessary for sound belief.[11] Orthodoxy is for him the message of the Bible interpreted in the way in which the Church has always interpreted it. He says, for instance, of the Melitians: "Their conduct is not orthodox, and they do not know sound faith in Christ, nor generally what Christianity is, nor what sort of Scriptures we Christians possess."[12]

But we must modify this account of Athanasius' respect for tradition by two considerations. In the first place, in those uncritical times tradition formed very quickly. The Council of Nicaea had taken place when Athanasius was a young man, but not too young to be an archdeacon, and he had attended it himself. But in a comparatively short time he was referring to its decisions as part of the tradition of the Fathers. In one instance, we can precisely calculate the length of time it had taken for contemporary decision to become immemorial tradition – thirteen years! In his Festal Letter for the year 338 Athanasius refers to "the custom which obtains among you, which has been delivered to us by the Fathers".[13] There can be no doubt that Athanasius is here alluding to the observance instituted by the Council of Nicaea whereby each year the bishop of Alexandria should announce in advance the date of Easter to all parts of the Church.

In the second place, Athanasius unmistakably believed in the sufficiency and primacy of Scripture for doctrinal purposes. Having spoken of "the burden of Scripture and the characteristic idea of Christianity",[14] he continues, showing that he desires to prove tradition from Scripture: "This characteristic idea came from the apostles through the Fathers; it is our task now to search the Bible and to examine and judge when it is speaking about the divinity of the Word, and when about his humanity."[15] Elsewhere[16] he makes a strong plea that the traditional faith (τὰ τῇ πίστει παραδιδόμενα) associated with baptism must content itself with the words

---

[11] E.g. *Orat. against Arians* III.28,29,58; *Ep. to Serap.* 2.7(620).

[12] *Hist. Arian.* 78.1 οὐκ ἀπὸ θεοσεβοῦς ἀγωγῆς εἰσιν, οὐδὲ γινώσκουσιν τὴν εἰς Χριστὸν ὑγιαίνουσαν πίστιν, οὐδ᾿ ὅλως τί ἐστιν Χριστιανισμὸς ἢ ποίας ἔχομεν ἡμεῖς οἱ Χριστιανοὶ γραφάς.

[13] *Festal Epistles* X (66–67).

[14] *Ep. to Serap.* 2.7(620) σκοπὸς τῆς θείας γραφῆς and χαρακτὴρ τοῦ Χριστιανισμοῦ.

[15] *Ibid.* 2.8(620) ὁ μὲν οὖν χαρακτὴρ οὗτος ἐκ τῶν ἀποστόλων διὰ τῶν πατέρων· δεῖ δὲ λοιπόν, ἐντυγχάνοντα τῇ γραφῇ, δοκιμάζειν καὶ διακρίνειν πότε μὲν περὶ τῆς θεότητος τοῦ Λόγου λέγει, πότε δὲ περὶ τῶν ἀνθρωπίνων αὐτοῦ.

[16] *Ibid.* 4.5(644).

of Scripture and not curiously enquire why they are as they are. When he recommends silence and belief rather than disbelief and enquiry in the face of profound and difficult doctrines about God, he makes it clear that the object of belief is the Scriptures.[17] The material which provides the doctrine expressed as the *skopos* is the Scriptures.[18] Let the Arians, he says, invent another Word or another Christ rather than their own, "for theirs is not in the Bible".[19] To believe that the Word was made by himself "is in enmity to God and in opposition to the Scriptures which came from him".[20] Athanasius, then, has a profound, indeed an uncritical respect for tradition. But he never regards it as a substitute for Scripture in doctrinal matters. He certainly believes that Scripture must be interpreted by tradition, but he never imagines that in doctrinal matters it must be *supplemented* by tradition.

In order to illustrate Basil's thought on the subject of tradition, we shall consider the *Adversus Eunomium*, a work written about 364, and then some passages in his letters which may be said roughly to span the period of time between the *Adversus Eunomium* and the *De Spiritu Sancto*, and then the *De Spiritu Sancto* itself. In his *Adversus Eunomium*, Basil's attitude to tradition is very much like that of Athanasius. He begins by saying that if everybody who was called Christian made no attempt to deviate from the truth but was ready "to be content with the tradition of the apostles and the simplicity of faith",[21] then the treatise need not have been written. He describes the course of Christian doctrine up to his day as "the tradition which has been held fast during all the past time by so many saints".[22] He combines Scripture and tradition when he asks rhetorically in what account was it ever known for anyone to claim that we can know the *ousia* of the earth (far less of God): "What sort of an account is this? Where can it be found in the Bible? By which of the saints was it handed down?"[23] And, like Athanasius, he betrays clearly that he thinks that Scripture is doctrinally sufficient. He does not, for instance, refuse the title *agennetos* to God, but describes it as "found

---

[17] τὰ γεγραμμένα *Orat. against Arians* II.36.
[18] *Orat. against Arians* III.28,29.
[19] οὐ γὰρ γέγραπται *ibid.* III.64.
[20] τῷ Θεῷ μάχεται καὶ ταῖς παρ' αὐτοῦ γραφαῖς ἐναντιοῦται *ibid.* III.65.
[21] τῇ παραδόσει τῶν ἀποστόλων καὶ τῇ ἁπλότητι τῆς πίστεως *Adv. Eunom.* 1.1(500).
[22] τὴν ἐν παντὶ τῷ παρελθόντι χρόνῳ ὑπὸ τοσούτων ἁγίων κεκρατυῖαν παράδοσιν *ibid.* 1.3(508).
[23] ποίῳ τούτῳ; ποῦ τῆς γραφῆς κειμένῳ; ὑπὸ τίνος τῶν ἁγίων παραδοθέντι;

nowhere in Scripture" (quoting Matt. 28:19).[24] Later he declares that there is no necessity to call the Son a *gennema*, as Scripture does not do so. We should not give the Son names which may easily occur to us simply because they are a literal development (ἐκ τῆς τῶν ῥημάτων ἀκολουθίας); we should confine ourselves to the names given in Scriptures.[25] Why do you not, he says to his opponent, "knowing how great is the danger in subtracting anything from or adding anything to the things handed down by the Spirit, abandon your ambition to produce new doctrines of your own, and rest content with the things which have already been declared by the saints?".[26] It is interesting to note that in the Homily *De Fide*, which is usually dated 374/5, Basil repeats these sentiments. He insists that it is clearly a sin of pride and arrogance ἢ ἀθετεῖν τι τῶν γεγραμμένων, ἢ ἐπεισάγειν τῶν μὴ γεγραμμένων, and declares that at Gal. 3:15 the apostle has forbidden us τὸ προσθεῖναι ἢ ὑφελεῖν τι ἐν ταῖς θεοπνεύσταις γραφαῖς.[27] This doctrine of the sufficiency of Scripture is not easy to reconcile with the words of the *De Spiritu Sancto* which we shall be examining presently. Perhaps this is an argument for placing the Homily *De Fide* at a rather earlier period than the *De Spiritu Sancto*.[28]

Eunomius, in his rationalist Unitarian way, had been quite confident about what the Spirit is. He described the Spirit as τρίτον... ἀξιώματι καὶ τάξει... τρίτον... καὶ τῇ φύσει. His nature is accordingly different from that of the Father and from that of the Son. He distinguishes between τὸ προσκυνούμενον and ἐν ᾧ προσκυνεῖται (quoting John 4:24). He thinks that John 14:16, 26 sufficiently assures us that the Spirit has his own ὑπόστασις (which he does not seem to distinguish from οὐσία). He describes the Spirit as "third in nature and order, coming into existence

---

[24]   *Ibid*. 1.5(517).

[25]   *Ibid*. 2.7(584–585).

[26]   εἰδότα ὅσος ὁ κίνδυνος ἀφελεῖν τι, ἢ προσθεῖναι τοῖς παραδεδομένοις ὑπὸ τοῦ πνεύματος, μὴ παρ' ἑαυτοῦ φιλοτιμεῖσθαι καινοτομεῖν, ἀλλὰ τοῖς προκατηγ-γελμένοις παρὰ τῶν ἁγίων ἐφησυχάζειν *ibid*. 2.8(585).

[27]   *De Fide* 1(680).

[28]   But in one respect at least Basil has changed his mind since writing the *Adversus Eunomium*, because in the *De Fide*, in a passage to which Dr. E. A. de Mendieta has recently drawn attention, he distinguishes between non-Scriptural language which he thinks it right to use in controversies and simpler language drawn from Scripture itself (1(677)). See de Mendieta, *The Unwritten and Secret Apostolic Traditions in the Theological Thought of St Basil of Caesarea* (Scottish Journal of Theology Occasional Papers, No. 13, Edinburgh 1965), pp. 19–20. This work will henceforward be referred to as *UAT*.

by the command of the Father and the operation of the Son, honoured in the third place as first and greater than all and sole creation (ποίημα) of this only-begotten Son described above (τοιούτου), inferior indeed (ἀπολειπόμενον) in godhead and creative power but complete in sanctifying and instructing power". It is absurd to regard the Spirit as an ἐνέργεια of the Father and at the same time to put him in the category of οὐσίαι.[29] Basil has little difficulty in exposing the weakness of Eunomius' account of the Holy Spirit, but he does not find it easy to match Eunomius' confidence in stating the nature of the Spirit. He frankly declares that we do not know what exactly the Spirit is and we must admit our ignorance. He is not *agenneton* (for Basil agrees with Eunomius that there can be only one such). He is not a Son. But we can be sure that he is beyond creatureliness, as the source, and not the receiver, of holiness and instruction and revelation. Then he goes on to describe, without defining, the Spirit.[30] He ends his treatise a little later by saying that it is the mark of an orthodox mind "to be careful to interpret the silence of Scripture as acclaiming the Holy Spirit".[31] These passages leave the impression that Basil is troubled about the deficiency of evidence in Scripture on the subject of the Spirit, even though Eunomius had laid no great stress upon the necessity of confining the argument to Scriptural evidence. Basil never uses the argument from extra-Scriptural tradition in this work, and though he has two references to baptism[32] he does not develop them.

Basil's Letters enable us to obtain an ampler view of his attitude to tradition. He shows, as we should expect, considerable respect for established custom; he calls, for instance, the traditional rules about the examination of candidates for holy orders "the canons of the Fathers".[33] His three Canonical Letters[34] provide many instances of his support for already established custom. He has a firm respect for the tradition of doctrine already established in the Church. The man who exalts the Holy Spirit above the Father and the Son, he says, is "alien from sound faith and does not preserve the manner of cult which he has received".[35]

---

[29] Eunomius, *Apol.* 25(861).
[30] *Ibid.* 3.6(668).
[31] τὰ ἀποσιωπηθέντα ἐν ταῖς ἁγίαις γραφαῖς εὐλαβεῖσθαι ἐπιφημίζειν τῷ ἁγίῳ πνεύματι *ibid.* 3.7(669).
[32] 3.2(657) and 3.5(665).
[33] οἱ τῶν πατέρων κανόνες *Letters* LIV.
[34] *Letters* CLXXXVIII, CXCIX, and CCXVII.
[35] *Ibid.* LII.4.

Enumerating the woes of the Eastern church of his day, he writes, "the decisions of the Fathers have been despised, the apostolic tradition has been set at naught, the inventions of the modernists are controlling the churches, they teach, in short, the devices of men and not the doctrine of God".[36] Though he regarded dogma as only a necessity to be invoked in order to settle disputes[37] (just as Athanasius did), he unhesitatingly included the doctrinal decisions of the Council of Nicaea among "the traditions of the Fathers",[38] the Nicene Creed is "what we have been taught from the holy Fathers".[39]

In fact Basil has a remarkably strong consciousness, evidenced in several places in his letters, of the traditional nature of the Christian faith, that he has been, as a Christian, entrusted with a divine deposit preserved intact by those who went before him. "We have been taught in the tradition of the faith", he says, "that there is only one Only-begotten"[40] and he uses the phrase "the traditional rule of orthodoxy".[41] On two occasions he recounts with pride the care shown by his mother and his grandmother (and he seems particularly to emphasize the part played by his grandmother) to bring him up in the orthodox faith.[42] Consistent with this is the argument which occurs again and again in his letters drawn from Christian baptism. "May the good teaching of our Fathers who assembled at Nicaea shine out again", he says, "so that the ascription of glory (δοξολογία) to the blessed Trinity may be completed in a manner harmonious with the saving baptism."[43] When he is giving a kind of rule of faith to a group of deaconesses to whom he is writing, he ends it with the clause "as also the tradition of saving baptism witnesses".[44] His argument, of course, is that we cannot be baptised into any name that is less than the name of God, and that it is absurd to imagine that we are

---

[36] καταπεφρόνηται τὰ τῶν πατέρων δόγματα, ἀποστολικαὶ παραδόσεις ἐξουθένηνται, νεωτέρων ἀνθρώπων ἐφευρήματα ταῖς ἐκκλησίαις ἐμπολιτεύεται, τεχνολογοῦσι λοιπόν, οὐ θεολογοῦσι ibid. XC.2.

[37] See ibid. CXXV.3, CXL.2.

[38] Ibid. LII.1.

[39] ἅπερ παρὰ τῶναγίων πατέρων δεδιδάγμεθα ibid. CXL.2 (cf. XC.2, CXXV.1).

[40] ἕνα γὰρ μονογενῆ ἐν τῇ παραδόσει τῆς πίστεως δεδιδάγμεθα ibid. CXXV. 3.

[41] τῇ παραδοθέντι κανόνι τῆς εὐσεβείας ibid. CCIV. 6.

[42] Ibid. CCIV.6 and CCXXIII (825). Dehnhard (Das Problem der Abhängigkeit des Basilius von Plotin (Berlin 1964), pp. 20–21, 32–38) has shown that this doctrinal tradition which was so strongly entrenched in Basil's family went back to the Symbolum of Gregory Theodorus (later called Thaumaturgus).

[43] Ibid. XCI.

[44] Ibid. CV ὡς καὶ ἡ τοῦ σωτηρίου βαπτίσματος παράδοσις μαρτυρεῖ.

baptised into the name of two divine beings and one creature, and that therefore the Holy Spirit must enjoy divinity equally with the Father and the Son. Many more examples of this argument might be given.[45]

We find Basil in his letters, therefore, displaying a readiness to appreciate the value of Christian tradition and to understand its possibilities for arguing even theological points which we could hardly have expected had we confined ourselves to the *Adversus Eumonium*. This observation is significant when we turn to the *De Spiritu Sancto*.

The quite new step which Basil was to take in his greatest work, the *De Spiritu Sancto*, is not evident at the beginning of the treatise. He is anxious, in the course of his argument about the divinity of the Holy Spirit, to establish as authoritative the doxological expression current in his church, "Glory be to the Father along with the Son with the Holy Spirit" (δόξα τῷ πατρὶ μετὰ τοῦ υἱοῦ σὺν τῷ πνεύματι τῷ ἁγίῳ) as opposed to the expression "through" the Son (διὰ). His opponents quote church custom in support of their formula, but Basil is convinced that his form is the more ancient and ranks as "the tradition of the Fathers".[46] But he hastily adds, "but this is not sufficient for us, that it is the tradition of the Fathers; they too followed the intention of Scripture," and proceeds to quote appropriate texts.[47] Later, however, he reveals that the sources of his doctrine about the Spirit are general ideas (κοιναὶ ἔννοιαι) derived both from the Scriptures and from the "extra-Scriptural tradition of the Fathers".[48]

The "general ideas" he expounds in a noble passage which Dehnhard has shown to owe much to the earlier document which also came from his pen, the *De Spiritu*. This document was greatly influenced by Gregory Theodorus' *Symbolum*, by Origen, and by Eusebius of Caesarea, and only to a relatively small extent by the work of Plotinus.[49] It is impossible to exclude from these "general ideas" a contribution from Greek philosophy.[50] That by the phrase ἀγράφου παραδόσεως Basil meant in this work

---

[45] E.g. *ibid*. CXXV.3; CLIX.2; CLXXXVIII.1; CCXXVI(849). The fact that *Letters* CLXXXIX.3 contains a passage decrying custom in contrast to Scripture adds to the suspicion that this letter is from the hand of Gregory of Nyssa and not of Basil.

[46] *De Spiritu Sancto* VII.16(93–96).

[47] *Ibid*. VII.16(96).

[48] (ἔννοιαι) τάς τε ἐκ τῶν γραφῶν περὶ αὐτοῦ συναχθείσας ἡμῖν, καὶ ἃς ἐκ τῆς ἀγράφου παραδόσεως τῶν πατέρων διεδεξάμεθα *ibid*. IX.22(108).

[49] *De Spiritu Sancto* IX.22(108–109). Dehnhard, *op. cit.*, passim. See also de Mendieta, *UAT*, pp. 25–26. For an interesting and typical use of κοιναὶ ἔννοιαι see *Letters* CCXXXVI.1(877).

[50] See Dehnhard, *op. cit.*, pp. 85–86.

"extra-Scriptural" and not "unwritten" tradition has been amply demonstrated by de Mendieta.[51] It is, of course, perfectly possible for Basil elsewhere to use the word ἄγραφος and its cognates in a different sense, meaning "oral" as opposed to "written". He can, for instance, contrast his writings with what he has spoken ἀγράφως in church.[52] Shortly after expounding these "general ideas" Basil emphasises strongly the necessity of preserving the baptismal formula intact during the whole of the Christian's life and even says that the loss entailed in receiving something from tradition in a deficient state is as great as that entailed in dying without baptism.[53] He deals with the Scriptural evidence briefly, without much success or conviction, and then comes to the subject of extra-Scriptural tradition.

In the twenty-seventh chapter therefore he boldly defends his own formula of doxology by claiming that tradition independent of the Bible is important, indeed essential, in doctrinal matters as well as merely practical. "Secret doctrines (δογμάτων) and public teachings (κηρυγμάτων) have been preserved in the Church, and some of them we have from Scriptural teaching (ἐγγράφου διδασκαλίας), and others we have handed down in a mystery from the tradition of the apostles (ἐκ τῆς τῶν ἀποστόλων παραδόσεως). Both sets have the same value for piety ... if we were to try to disregard the extra-Scriptural ordinances of custom (τὰ ἄγραφα τῶν ἐθῶν) on the ground that they had no great force, we would be unawares damaging the Gospel in the most important points themselves (εἰς αὐτὰ τὰ καίρια), or rather, reducing the public teaching to a mere name."[54] Instances of this extra-Scriptural tradition are the custom of Christians crossing themselves, turning to the east for prayer, the words of the consecration-prayer (ἐπίκλησις) at the eucharist, the formula for blessing the water for baptism and the oil of anointing, and indeed the anointing with oil itself and the triple immersion in baptism.[55] Later he adds to this list the custom of praying in a standing posture on Sundays, the observance of Pentecost, the confession of faith (ὁμολογίαι τῆς πίστεως) at baptism and (as climax) the doxology.[56] He insists that this extra-Scriptural tradition is secret, using such phrases as "the esoteric

---

[51] UAT, pp. 23–29.
[52] Letters CCXXIII.4(828).
[53] De Spiritu Sancto X.26(113).
[54] Ibid. XXVII.66(188).
[55] Ibid. 66(188–189).
[56] Ibid. 66(192); 67(193).

and mystical tradition" (ἀπὸ τῆς σιωπωμένης καὶ μυστικῆς παραδόσεως) "unpublicised (ἀδημοσίευτον) and secret teaching", and "the teaching of that which it is not permitted to the uninitiated to gaze upon" (ἐποπτεύειν τοῖς ἀμυήτοις) – all phrases reminiscent of the mystery-religions.[57] A little later he makes it quite clear that he regards these traditions as deriving independently of the Bible from the apostles.[58]

In two recent works de Mendieta has thrown much light on what Basil means by this extra-Scriptural apostolic tradition.[59] The contents of this secret tradition can be divided into three categories:

I Extra-Scriptural traditions in
   (i) sacramental rites and prayers, and
   (ii) ecclesiastical customs and practices.
II Extra-Scriptural traditions of doctrines implied in these rites and prayers.
III Extra-Scriptural traditions of the Fathers about some theological *dogmata* of an advanced sort, and especially about the Holy Spirit.

Under I, (ii) come Trinitarian doxologies, of which Basil, though greatly attached to his favourite formula σὺν τῷ πνεύματι, is ready to accept all current ones. Under II Basil includes the equality of the Father, the Son and the Holy Spirit in honour and dignity and godhead, a doctrine derived from the use of the Trinitarian doxology. Under III Basil includes extra-Scriptural doctrine about the dignity and operations of the Holy Spirit derived largely from κοιναὶ ἔννοιαι.[60] Basil probably meant the more advanced of the secret doctrines to be reserved for specially pious and meditative souls, for the most part monks. The other doctrines were confined to "the initiated", i.e. all baptised and communicating Christians.[61] What in fact Basil was describing in these terms was a union (but not necessarily a confusion) of two things:

(i) The *disciplina arcani*, which had been imposed by the Church of the fourth century as a necessity forced upon it by the increased interest taken by pagans in the doctrines and rites of the Church.

(ii) The practice of reserve in communicating advanced or difficult

---

[57] *Ibid.* 66(189).
[58] *Ibid.*, XXIX.71(200).
[59] *UAT* (referred to already) and "The Pair κήρυγμα and δόγμα in the Theological Thought of St. Basil of Caesarea", *Journal of Theological Studies*, Vol. xvi(NS)I(1965), pp. 129–145), henceforward referred to as *PKD*.
[60] *UAT*, pp. 60–70; *PKD*, pp. 135–138.
[61] *UAT*, pp. 41–42; *PKD*, p. 136.

doctrine, so that weak or badly educated Christians should not be shocked or upset by what was only fit for mature and educated and intellectual people. This reserve had been taught and practised by Clement of Alexandria and Origen, and was associated with the *disciplina arcani* by Basil in his day. Basil applied this reserve more specifically than had Origen to the interpretation of rites and customs.[62] De Mendieta admits that Basil did think that these traditions had been transmitted *secretly* (and that this is the meaning of μυστήρια in *De Spiritu Sancto* XXVII.67 (193)),[63] and that Basil did use concerning them the language of the mystery-religions.[64] He allows that Basil did think that the secret tradition of which he spoke had come down originally from the apostles and that the situation was in his day much as it had been in theirs, that he did not clearly distinguish between what the apostles established and what the Fathers established, and in particular that he nourished the illusion that his own cherished Trinitarian formula (δόξα τῷ πατρὶ μετὰ τοῦ υἱοῦ σὺν τῷ πνεύματι τῷ ἁγίῳ) had been instituted by the apostles and that by this institution they had intended to transmit the doctrine of the perfect equality of the Father, Son and Holy Spirit. And de Mendieta concedes that these convictions on Basil's part cannot bear historical investigation.[65]

Even reduced to the moderate and precisely-defined terms in which the careful scholarship of de Mendieta has presented it, Basil's doctrine of secret tradition is a startling innovation. He is not content to say that the Scriptures must be interpreted by the mind of the Church and in accordance with the Church's traditional way of interpreting them, as all Christian writers had claimed since Irenaeus. He is not content to say that customs and rites which had been established beyond living memory must be regarded as deriving from the apostles, as had been unreflectingly but harmlessly assumed everywhere long before his day. He claims that the extra-Scriptural traditions which he is concerned to defend not only had been handed down by the apostles and preserved intact from their time, but that this had been done secretly and that to reject them would be to damage the gospel in the most important points and to reduce the public teaching to a mere name. Had Irenaeus or Tertullian encountered

---

[62] *UAT*, pp. 39–50.
[63] *UAT*, pp. 30–31.
[64] *UAT*, p. 43, especially n. 3. Cf. *De Spiritu Sancto* XXVII.66(189) ἃ γὰρ οὐδὲ ἐποπτεύειν ἔξεστιν τοῖς ἀμυήτοις.
[65] *UAT*, pp. 43, 52, 55, 57, 58.

this doctrine, they would have branded it as typical of the Gnostics. Whether he is aware of the fact or not, Basil is introducing a new doctrine. In spite of de Mendieta's deprecatory words,[66] it is idle to deny this fact. Why did Basil produce this new doctrine, so little consistent with the words of his Homily *De Fide* which he had apparently written not long before? The answer to this lies in the subject of the work in which he had propounded this new doctrine, his greatest, the *De Spiritu Sancto*. It is significant that it was not in connection with a defence of the position of the Son in the Trinity, but of the Spirit, that Basil felt the need of having recourse to a theory of secret tradition. We have seen that Basil, in writing against Eunomius, gave signs of uneasiness at the scarcity of Scriptural evidence to support a doctrine of the Spirit as a fully divine independent hypostasis within the Trinity. But Eunomius, at least in his *Apologeticus*, had not laid much emphasis upon the necessity of producing Scriptural evidence for doctrine about the Spirit. His main arguments were in fact philosophical, and he could well have described them as κοιναὶ ἔννοιαι. The case was different with the opponents against whom Basil was defending his doctrine of the Spirit in the *De Spiritu Sancto*. These were Eustathius, bishop of Sebaste, and his followers. Indeed, if we accept the thesis of H. Dörries in his book on the *De Spiritu Sancto*, we may conclude that behind chapter X–XV, XX–XXI, XXIV–XXV, and the beginning of chapter XXVII of this work lies the "protocol", the proceedings of the conference held between Basil and Eustathius in Sebaste in Armenia Prima in June 372. We must not unreflectingly identify Eustathius' position with that of Eunomius. According to Basil, Eustathius had taken a variety of viewpoints towards the great subject of controversy during his career, among them one very like that of Nicene orthodoxy and, at another time, a semi-Arian position. But it is clear that Eustathius and his followers distinguished themselves by insisting upon proofs from Scripture for Basil's (or anybody else's) doctrine of the Spirit. Eustathius would not go further than the letter of the New Testament, and the appeal to τὴν ἄγραφον πατέρων μαρτυρίαν made no impression on him.[67]

Basil could not meet Eustathius' demand for a full documentation from Scripture of his doctrine of the Holy Spirit. The methods of interpreting the Bible which were accepted and conventional in the fourth-

---

[66] *UAT*, pp. 58–59.
[67] *De Spiritu Sancto* X.25(112). De Mendieta, *UAT*, pp. 23–24.

century Church simply did not admit of such a possibility. Basil was quite perspicacious enough to realize this. So he took the alternative course of developing to an extent not previously achieved the support which extra-Scriptural tradition could give to the Church's doctrine. The Church's practice and the Church's experience could combine with the ideas of Scripture to produce κοιναὶ ἔννοιαι, general ideas about the Holy Spirit clothed in philosophical language and articulated by the aid of recent philosophy. Stated like this, Basil's strategy devised to circumvent the Eustathians sounds innocent and justifiable. But in the form in which Basil presented it, that of secret extra-Scriptural tradition deriving from the apostles, it was a doctrine which was destined to cause a great deal of confusion and mischief in later ages.

It is instructive to compare the manner in which Basil's great friend and fellow defender of Nicene orthodoxy, Gregory of Nazianzus, deals in one of his works with exactly the same problem. Towards the end of the fifth of his *Theological Orations*, delivered in Constantinople not long after Basil's death and within perhaps five years of the writing of Basil's *De Spiritu Sancto*, Gregory comes to deal with the Holy Spirit. He is just as aware of the difficulty of the problem of finding Scriptural evidence to support the doctrine of the *homoousia* of the Spirit as an hypostasis within the Trinity as was Basil, but he solves it in quite a different way. He argues first that we are bound by the logical consequences of Scripture, even though they are not stated in Scripture. If his opponents said "twice five" or "twice seven", he would be justified in concluding that they meant "ten" or "fourteen", and these would be virtually his opponents' words even though they had not stated them: ὥσπερ οὖν ἐνταῦθα οὐκ ἂν τὰ λεγόμενα ἐσκοποῦν ἢ τὰ νοούμενα.[68] Then he launches into a fine exposition of the gradualness of God's revelation, very largely borrowed from Origen, but put to good use here in explaining our gradual understanding of the significance of the Holy Spirit. He insists that the reason for this gradualness was that God would coerce nobody. Gregory divides history into two great epochs, each introduced by a σεισμὸς γῆς, but so gradual an earthquake that it was not immediately noticed – the giving of the Law and the coming of the gospel. There is to be a third earthquake – τὴν ἐντεῦθεν ἐπὶ τὰ ἐκεῖσε μετάστασιν, τὰ μηκέτι κινούμενα μηδὲ σαλευόμενα (Heb. 12: 28). What is voluntarily accepted lasts, that which is imposed by coercion does not do so. First,

---

[68] Gregory of Nazianzus, *Five Theological Orations*, V.24.

in order to abolish idolatry, God instituted sacrifices but allowed circumcision to be retained voluntarily until it was gradually abolished.[69] Similarly, Gregory continues, in teaching doctrine God acted gradually, but in an opposite direction, by adding new revelations of himself, not by subtracting (as in the case of sacrifices and circumcision). The Old Testament could suffice to reveal fully only the Father, the New to reveal fully the Son, but even the New could only suffice to give a faint impression of the Spirit: ἐκήρυσσε φανερῶς ἡ παλαιὰ τὸν πατέρα, τὸν υἱὸν ἀμυδρότερον, ἐφανέρωσεν ἡ καινὴ τὸν υἱόν, ὑπέδειξε τοῦ πνεύματος τὴν θεότητα. ἐμπολιτεύεται νῦν τὸ πνεῦμα σαφεστέραν ἡμῖν παρέχον τὴν ἑαυτοῦ δήλωσιν. οὐ γὰρ ἦν ἀσφαλές, μήπω τῆς τοῦ πατρὸς θεότητος ὁμολογηθείσης, τὸν υἱὸν ἐκδήλως κηρύττεσθαι· μηδὲ τῆς τοῦ υἱοῦ παραδεχθείσης τὸ πνεῦμα τὸ ἅγιον, ἵν' εἴπω τι καὶ τολμηρότερον, ἐπιφορτίζεσθαι.[70] "You perceive", he goes on, "stages of illumination gradually shining on us and neither indiscriminately revealing nor entirely obscuring the order of the knowledge of God which it is better for us to preserve." Perhaps the divinity of the Spirit was one of those things which the disciples could not bear "now" (John 16: 12), but which were to be disclosed later.[71]

Gregory does later very briefly mention the argument from baptism; his words do not go beyond what Athanasius had suggested and betray no influence from Basil.[72] All these arguments drawn from the gradualness of revelation and from baptism he describes as τὸ ἄγραφον, in other words, arguments not directly drawn from Scripture. He then expounds the testimonies from Scripture in a densely packed and beautifully expressed cento of biblical allusions, none of which, of course, directly involves the divinity of the Holy Spirit as a separate hypostasis, a doctrine for which in fact Gregory does not attempt to produce Scriptural evidence.[73] It is difficult to imagine that Gregory had not read Basil's work De Spiritu Sancto when he composed this Oration. But he deliber-

---

[69] Op. cit., V.25.
[70] Op. cit., V.26.
[71] Op. cit. V.27. The words which have been here translated from the Greek are ὁρᾷς φωτισμοὺς κατὰ μέρος ἡμῖν ἐλλάμποντας καὶ τάξιν θεολογίας ἣν καὶ ἡμᾶς τηρεῖν ἄμεινον, μήτε ἀθρόως ἐκφαίνοντας μήτε εἰς τέλος κρύπτοντας.
[72] Op. cit., V.28 εἰ μὲν γὰρ οὐδὲ προσκυνητόν, πῶς ἐμὲ θεοῖ διὰ τοῦ βαπτίσματος; εἰ δὲ προσκυνητόν, πῶς οὐ σεπτόν; εἰ δὲ σεπτόν, πῶς οὐ θεος;
[73] The nearest he comes to dealing with this point is to say, elliptically (op. cit., V. 30) ἴσον γὰρ εἰς ἀσέβειαν, καὶ Σαβελλίως συνάψαι καὶ Ἀρειανῶς διαστῆσαι, τὸ μὲν τῷ προσώπῳ, τὸ δὲ ταῖς φύσεσιν. The allusion to τὸ ἄγραφον occurs at V.29.

ately chose quite a different way of defending the same doctrine which Basil had formulated. The twentieth-century reader is likely to conclude that Gregory's method was a much preferable one to Basil's.

Basil and Gregory were facing a problem which faces us today. It is not simply the distinction between "what is the nucleus or core of Christian knowledge and truth, the accepted faith, and what is its full theological development".[74] It involves the delicate and complex task of articulating a doctrine of the place of the Holy Spirit within the Trinity. This subject is rendered all the more difficult because it involves the intimate and subjective field of the individual's and the Church's experience, and it is one for which the Bible supplies the essential materials for the doctrine but gives very little help towards formulating it. We may well sympathize with the demand of the Eustathians for a doctrine which should be Scriptural, as we sympathize with Basil's predicament in face of this demand. We can understand his good intentions in meeting the predicament by the argument for secret, extra-Scriptural apostolic tradition, set forth in the De Spiritu Sancto, and we may think that what he was trying to express corresponds in some sense to something which we can recognize as true and necessary. But that the expression of this necessary truth should have taken the form of a claim for secret, extra-Scriptural, apostolic tradition we must regard as unfortunate and unnecessary.

Nottingham University

---

[74] De Mendieta, *PKD*, p. 140.

THE RULE OF TRUTH IN IRENAEUS.

A DANISH author, Mr S. A. Becker, has dedicated a very elaborated study to the problem, what *The Rule of Truth* is to Irenaeus. Through his thorough exegesis I think he has contributed a good deal to bringing to an end the dissension amongst scholars on that point, and readers of the JOURNAL may be glad to have his work brought to their notice. ('Ο κανὼν τῆς 'Αληθείας. *Regula veritatis* eller Sandhedens Regel. Et Bidrag til Belysning af dette Udtryks Forekomst og Betydning hos Irenaeos. Copenhagen, G. E. C. Gad, 1910, 280 pages.)

I do not agree with Becker in all details. Although generally very careful, he has, I think, not been careful enough in interpreting a few passages, which affect the result itself. But instead of giving here

---

[1] *Histoire ecclésiastique* liv. LXXIV ch. 34 ; nouv. éd., x (1777) 622.

a review of the book, I prefer to point to the problem itself and how it is to be solved according to my opinion. We begin with an analysis of the passages in which the expression *Rule of Truth* is to be found, and a few others of importance for the question. I quote in *Adv. haer.* the chapters according to Massuet, the pages according to Harvey; for the *Epideixis* the edition of Harnack.

I ix 4; Harvey I p. 87 f. The argument of Irenaeus is as follows. Suppose a man to destroy a mosaic image of a king and arrange the stones so as to form the picture of a fox, declaring it to be the same picture (I viii 1; Harvey I p. 67), or to take some verses by Homer and out of them make a new poem (a so-called *Cento*). This is just what the Gnostics do: they take expressions from the Scriptures, especially from the Prologue to the Gospel of St John, and use them in quite another connexion and meaning. But he who knows the true picture of the king will not accept that of the fox; he who knows his Homer will detect the *Cento* to be false. Οὕτω δὲ καὶ ὁ τὸν κανόνα τῆς ἀληθείας ἀκλινῆ ἐν ἑαυτῷ κατέχων, ὃν διὰ τοῦ βαπτίσματος εἴληφε, τὰ μὲν ἐκ τῶν γραφῶν ὀνόματα, καὶ τὰς λέξεις, καὶ τὰς παραβολὰς ἐπιγνώσεται, τὴν δὲ βλάσφημον ὑπόθεσιν ταύτην [αὐτῶν] οὐκ ἐπιγνώσεται ... ἐν ἕκαστον δὲ τῶν εἰρημένων ἀποδοὺς τῇ ἰδίᾳ τάξει, καὶ προσαρμόσας τῷ τῆς ἀληθείας σωματίῳ, γυμνώσει καὶ ἀνυπόστατον ἐπιδείξει τὸ πλάσμα αὐτῶν.

Ὁ κανὼν τῆς ἀληθείας must be something which includes the terms abused by the Gnostics (such as Pater, Charis, Monogenes, Aletheia, Logos, Zoë, Anthropos, Ecclesia). Then it must be either *the Scriptures* or *the main content of the Scriptures*. That it is said to have been received at Baptism cannot overthrow this explanation and lead us to think of a short formulated Creed. But in some way or other there must have been given at the Baptism or at the baptismal instruction some knowledge of the principal content and expressions of Scripture. And then the Christian, who knows these expressions, will again make them harmonize with the *The Body of Truth*, i.e. the principal Christian doctrine, especially contained in Scripture. For shewing that the diminutive form σωμάτιον is not to be urged I must refer to Becker, p. 19 ff.

I xxii; Harvey I p. 188 f 'Cum teneamus autem nos regulam veritatis, id est quia sit unus Deus omnipotens, qui omnia condidit per Verbum suum . . . quemadmodum Scriptura dicit . . . Hanc ergo tenentes regulam . . . facile eos deviasse a veritate arguimus'.

The content of *The Rule of Truth* is here: the belief in one God the Creator proclaimed in Scripture.

II xxv 1; Harvey I p. 343. We ought to interpret details in Scripture from its main content. 'Non enim regula ex numeris, sed numeri ex regula.' In a musical composition we ought to catch the principal theme. So in Scripture we must glorify its compositor (i.e. God) 'nusquam transferentes regulam, neque errantes ab artifice, neque abiicientes fidem quae est in unum Deum qui fecit omnia'.

II xxvii 1 ; Harvey I p. 347 f. In interpretation of the Scriptures we ought to begin with the clear passages, then we shall be safe, 'et veritatis corpus (the correction of Kunze and Becker instead of the meaningless *a veritate corpus*) integrum . . . perseverat'. If on the other hand we combine uncertain passages with others just as uncertain, 'sic enim apud nullum erit regula veritatis'.

II xxviii 1 ; Harvey I p. 349 'Habentes itaque regulam ipsam veritatem'.

In these last three passages there can be no doubt of the explanation : *The Rule of Truth* is the main, unambiguous content of the Scriptures. And the last quoted passage shews that at least here the κανών *is* the ἀλήθεια, so that the genitive may be explained as gen. appos.

The first chapters of lib. III are generally taken as a proof that Irenaeus fights against the Gnostics, taking his stand rather on tradition or on the Baptismal Creed than on Scripture. But rightly understood they say just the opposite.

III i 1 ; Harvey II p. 2 'Non enim per alios dispositionem salutis nostrae cognovimus, quam per eos per quos Evangelium pervenit ad nos : quod quidem tunc praeconaverunt, postea vero per Dei voluntatem in Scripturis nobis tradiderunt, fundamentum et columnam fidei nostrae futurum'.

The proclamation of the first witnesses of Christ is according to the will of God continued and perpetuated in Scripture ; *fundamentum . . . futurum* relates not simply to *Evangelium*, but to *Evangelium in Scripturis*.

III ii 1 ; Harvey II p. 7. The assertion here, that the true tradition is not to be found in the Scriptures themselves, but transmitted *per vivam vocem*—this assertion is not that of Irenaeus himself, but of the Gnostics. And they by means of their secret traditions spoil *The Rule of Truth* (*regulam veritatis depravans*), which also here seems to indicate the true, genuine Christianity.

But then Irenaeus follows the Gnostics on the battle-ground they prefer : tradition outside Scripture. He is sure he shall be able to refute them on that ground. For there is a true Catholic tradition handed down through the Bishops ; as examples he quotes Rome and Asia Minor. This tradition, he says III iv 1 ; Harvey II p. 15 f, is so full and valid that it would be sufficient even if we had no apostolic writings. But this is only an imaginary situation. Very few really depend upon tradition alone, only (*a*) The Churches outside the Greek-Latin world, who have no translations of the Bible in their tongue :

(*b*) all Christians in smaller questions (*de aliqua modica quaestione*), probably such as to which Scripture gives no certain evidence. Now let us see the surroundings of the chapters in question.

II xxxv 3 ; Harvey I p. 387 'Sed ne putemur fugere illam quae ex Scripturis Dominicis est probationem, ipsis Scripturis multo manifestius et clarius hoc ipsam praedicantibus . . . ex Scripturis divinis probationes apponemus in medio omnibus amantibus veritatem'.

So ends lib. II, i. e. in lib. III Irenaeus will give the evidence from the Scriptures.

III v 1 ; Harvey II p. 18 'Traditione igitur quae est ab Apostolis sic se habente in Ecclesia et permanente apud nos, revertamur ad eam quae est ex Scripturis ostensionem . . .'

So Irenaeus says having finished the evidence from tradition. *Ergo*, this passage about tradition is a parenthesis. Before going on to develope his proper subject in lib. III, the evidence from Scriptures, Irenaeus will strengthen his position against an eventual appeal from Scripture to tradition. This parenthesis is surely interesting, but it can by no means be allowed to dominate the understanding of Irenaeus's principal views and methods.

III xi 1 ; Harvey II p. 40 f 'Omnia igitur talia (i. e. the statements of the Gnostics) circumscribere (exclude) volens discipulus Domini et regulam veritatis constituere in Ecclesia, quia est unus Deus omnipotens, qui per Verbum suum omnia fecit . . . sic inchoavit in ea quae est secundum Evangelium doctrina : In principio erat Verbum ', &c.

The Rule of Truth here is the belief in God's creation and salvation, and this is proclaimed in the Gospel of St John.

A little later (III xi 7 ; Harvey II p. 46 f ; the Greek text is here to be corrected by the Latin) Irenaeus gives his proof, that there can only be four Gospels as there are four corners of the earth. The pillar of the Church, he says, is (1) the Gospel (i. e. the four Gospels), (2) the Spirit of Life, always breathing eternal life out from the four Gospels. This is a very strong instance that to Irenaeus Scripture is the principal objective basis of the Church.

III xii 6 ; Harvey II p. 59. The Gnostics try to evade the demonstration from the Acts of the Apostles by assuming an accommodation by the Apostles. 'Secundum hunc igitur sermonem apud neminem erit regula veritatis, sed omnes discipuli omnibus imputabunt . . . Superfluus autem et inutilis adventus Domini parebit . . .'

The Rule of Truth is also here the genuine Christianity. A more special meaning (the content of the Acts or of the writings of St Luke) is to be found in III xv 6 ; Harvey II p. 79. The Gnostics reject the statement of the Acts about St Paul ; but God has just arranged it so that in the Gospel written by the same author there are to be found many necessary details 'ut sequenti testificationi eius, quam habet de actibus et doctrina Apostolorum, omnes sequentes, et regulam veritatis inadulteratam habentes salvari possint'.

IV xxxv 5; Harvey II p. 276 'Nos autem unum et solum verum Deum doctorem sequentes et regulam veritatis habentes eius sermones ...'

In this clearest of all passages *The Rule of Truth* is the Words of God contained in Scripture (A.T. and N.T.).

In the *Epideixis* we find in c. 1 the expression *Body of Truth*, as in the above-mentioned *Adv. haer.* I ix 4. Twice (c. 3 and 6) we find *The Rule of Faith*. If we may trust the Armenian translator it is not correct then to assume that Irenaeus always uses the expression *Rule of Truth*. *The Rule of Faith* in both places is the main content of Christianity (as an exposition of the belief in Father, Son, and Holy Ghost).

Our result is :—

I. *The Rule of Truth primarily* is not an institution, a formula, or a book ; it is Christianity itself, the genuine, apostolic Christianity.

II. That κανών or *regula* may be used for not a formal rule, but a body of doctrine, we may prove from the Latin translation. For there very often (compare Dr Kunze: *Glaubensregel, Heilige Schrift und Taufbekenntniss*, 1899, p. 322, and Becker, p. 212 f) *regula* (or *regulae*) is used of the doctrine or the main principles of the Gnostics. Only in one passage (I xx 3 ; Harvey I p. 180) the Greek text is preserved ; there *regula* stands for ὑπόθεσις.

III. *The Rule* is *the Truth* itself. The genitive is generally to be taken as gen. appos. as indicated in the above-quoted passage, II xxviii 1 'Habentes itaque regulam ipsam veritatem'. Still we shall perhaps not press such a dilemma too strongly. *Rule of Truth* may *perhaps also* mean the Rule, which decides what is to be regarded as Truth. In the connexion *Rule of Faith* the gen. may also be taken as gen. appos. (Faith = *fides quae creditur*), but here more probable as gen. obj. = *regula credendi* (this expression is used by Novatian *De trin.* c. xvi).

IV. *The Truth*—which is the Rule—has a central place in the theology of Irenaeus. It comprehends the whole revelation, nay even nature, which also gives testimony to the Creator. Its main points are : the creation—the dispensation and prophecies in the Old Testament—Christ as the second Adam, His supernatural birth, His words, His death, His resurrection and ascension—the Holy Ghost—the Church—the Christian Ethics—the Eschatology. *The Rule of Truth* is something positive, leading to salvation. It is not—as generally assumed—formed as against the heretics ; but of course it excludes heresy just as truth excludes error.

V. This *Truth* is first to be found in Scripture, so that Scripture or some part of it occasionally may be called *The Rule of Truth.* The idea of separating Scripture from the Church never occurs to Irenaeus. But how strongly he insists on Scripture as the basis may be proved from nearly every page he wrote. Characteristic is the passage :—

V xx 1 ; Harvey II p. 379 ' Fugere igitur oportet sententias ipsorum (the heretics) . . . confugere autem ad Ecclesiam, et in eius sinu educari, et dominicis Scripturis enutriri. Plantata est enim Ecclesia Paradisus in hoc mundo. Ab omni ergo ligno Paradisi escas manducabitis, ait Spiritus Dei, id est, ab omni Scriptura dominico manducate . . .'

VI. The same *Truth* can be found outside the Scriptures in the tradition of the Church, for materially tradition coincides with the Scripture. But never does Irenaeus call the tradition *Rule of Truth,* although we should not have been astonished if he had done so.

VII. The question of a formulated Creed by Irenaeus seems to be quite doubtful. In several passages scholars generally have found a creed. Those from *Adv. haer.* have often been collected (comp. Harnack in *Patrum apostolicorum opera,* ed. major. I p. 122 f ; Hahn *Bibliothek der Symbole* 3 Aufl. p. 6 f ; C. A. Swainson *The Nicene and Apostles' Creeds,* 1875, p. 28 ff ; A. C. McGiffert *The Apostles' Creed,* 1902, p. 48 ff) ; to be added are Epid. c. 3, 6, 7, 97, 100. It may be that sometimes Irenaeus hints at a Creed, but I do not see that it has been proved, and still less do I see how a reconstruction is possible.

On the question of *The Rule of Faith (Truth)* Caspari called Irenaeus the classical author. It would be interesting to see if the explanation we have found in his case could be justified also in the case of other authors.

I think it is the case with Polykrates of Ephesus. He says (Euseb. *hist. eccl.* V xxiv 6) that the great Christian leaders of Asia Minor kept Easter *according to the Gospel,* and the following *according to the Rule of Faith* probably means the same. I also think it is the case with Novatian (*De cib. jud.* c. VII ; *De trinitate,* c. I, IX, XVI, XVII (Moses has put the *regula veritatis* in Gen. I), XXI, XXVI, XXIX). Only it is here more evident that Novatian uses a formulated Creed — not as identical with, but as a means of arranging the description of, *The Rule of Truth.* Cyprian also (Ep. LXVIIII 7 ; Hartel II p. 756) supposes him to use a formulated Creed ; and he certainly is right in that, although he may be mistaken in assuming Novatian to use just the African formula (*per sanctam ecclesiam*).

In regard to Hippolytus and Tertullian I have at present formed no judgement. But if originally *The Rule of Truth* is a thing so elastic as we have found, it would be no wonder if later its meaning may have been modified.

In the Danish *Theologisk Tidskrift* I have tried to prove more in detail the opinion stated shortly here, and I have examined some points of the history of the interpretation of Irenaeus from Erasmus to the present time. As this Danish periodical will be found in few public libraries, I shall be glad to send this article to scholars on application.

VALDEMAR AMMUNDSEN.

SOME RIDDLES IN THE APOSTLES' CREED

Hardly any document of the Christian tradition outside the New Testament has been the subject of a more painstaking research than the Apostles' Creed (AC) [1]). Even if one omits the studies devoted to single authors and to the single articles of the Creed and limits oneself to general studies, the bibliography is impressive [2]). The reasons for this exceptionnal interest

---

[1]) Te following abbreviations are used :
AC: the Apostles' Creed
H: the Creed of Hippolytus
R: the Roman Creed as attested by Marcellus of Ancyra and Rufinus
T: the textus receptus of AC as in use from the 8th century on
O: the hypothetic basic form of an Oriental Creed.

[2]) Select bibliography

I. — Collections of texts
A. HAHN, Bibliothek der Symbole und Glaubensregeln der alten Kirche, Breslau [3]1897.
H. LIETZMANN, Symbole der alten Kirche (KlT 17/18), Berlin [6]1968.
H. DENZINGER-A. SCHÖNMETZER, Enchiridion Symbolorum, Freiburg [32]1963.
II. — New Testament
O. CULLMANN, Le premières confessions chrétiennes (Cah. Rev. Hist Phil Rel. 30), Paris [2]1948.
V. H. NEUFELD, The earliest Christian Confessions, Leiden, 1963.
III. — The old Church
A full discussion of the previous studies with an exhaustive bibliography is given by: J. DE GHELLINCK, Les recherches sur les origines du Symbole des Apôtres (Patristique et Moyen-Age I), Gembloux [2]1949. Therefore, of the older studies, I mention only:
F. KATTENBUSCH, Das Apostolische Symbol, 2 Bde, Leipzig, 1894-1900, a goldmine of information and reflection.
H. LIETZMANN, Kleine Schriften (TU 74), Berlin 1962, a postumous reprint of his epoch-making articles:
— Die Anfänge des Glaubensbekenntnisses, 1919
— Die Urform des Glaubensbekenntnisses, 1919
— Symbolstudien I-XIV, 1922-1927.
B. CAPELLE, Les origines du Symbole romain, in: RechThAM 2 (1930) 5-20.
J. LEBRETON, Les origines du Symbole baptismal, in: RechScRel 20 (1930) 97-124.
Recent studies:
J. N. D. KELLY, Early Christian Creeds, London 1950; [2]1960, the most authoritative and synthetic study.
C. EICHENSEER, Das Symbolum Apostolicum beim hl. Augustinus (Kirchengeschichtliche Quellen und Studien 4), St. Ottilien 1960, covers a wider field than Augustine.
D. L. HOLLAND, The earliest Text of the old Roman Symbol; a debate with H. Lietzmann and J. N. D. Kelly, in: Church History 34 (1965) 262-281.
P. Th. CAMELOT, art. Symbola, in: Sacramentum Mundi, IV, Freiburg 1969, col. 789-795.
A. BREKELMANS, Geloofsbelijdenissen in de oude kerk, in: Concilium 6 (1970) n. 1, 30-39.
IV. — Some recent theological commentaries:
P. BRUNNER a.o., Veraltetes Glaubensbekenntnis, Regenburg 1968.

146

are many. The history of the AC offers an intrigueing and challenging field to historians of Christian texts and institutions: fascinating because of the rich diversity of its sources, challenging because of the many gaps in our documentation. This profession of faith which has been in common use in the Roman Catholic Church of the Latin rite for more than a thousand years was also upheld by the Reformation, thus providing one of the basic pronouncements of faith which they have in common. Last but not least, in the present crisis of the teaching authority and of the docility of the faithful, one's interest turns almost automatically to one of the oldest and most venerable documents of Christian teaching. This old Creed, in a certain measure, provided the pattern for the later counciliar definitions, and even in recent times, the teaching authority of the Church has promulgated professions of faith which in some way look back towards this ancient model. Evidently, the Profession of Faith promulgated by Pope Pius IV as a result of the Council of Trent or the Oath against Modernism of Pius X [3]) are poles apart from the AC. And yet, the road which lead to such documents began with a profession of faith of that primitive type [4]). Might perhaps one of the sources of the present uneasiness be sought in the twists of history, which made this long road deviate too far from its original direction?

The present study will focus on discovering the direction of the AC in its original setting by reflecting on and, it is hoped, solving some of the riddles which the previous studies have not satisfactorily answered. Two obvious riddles are: why does the AC not profess explicitly the faith in ONE God and why could it, in its original form, lack the qualification OUR LORD ? In connection with this last point, one may ask what motive could have dictated the choice of articles in the christological part: birth, crucifixion, burial, resurrection, ascension, enthronement, future judgment? In order not only to answer those questions but also to show their urgency,

---

J. RATZINGER, Einführung in das Christentum, München, 1968.

W. VON LOEWENICH a.o:, De Geloofsbelijdenis; poging tot een nieuw verstaan, Baarn 1969.

G. RUHBACH a.o., Bekenntnis in Bewegung, Göttingen 1969.

H. DE LUBAC, La foi chrétienne; essai sur la structure du Symbole des Apôtres, Paris 1969.

V. — On Baptism and its rites:

W. F. FLEMINGTON, The New Testament doctrine of Baptism, London 1948.

A. BENOIT, Le baptême chrétien au second siècle, Paris 1953.

A. STENZEL, Die Taufe; eine genetische Erklärung der Taufliturgie, Innsbruck 1958.

Th. MAERTENS, Histoire et pastorale du rituel du catéchuménat et du baptême (Coll. Past. lit. 56), Bruges 1962.

G. KRETSCHMAR, Die Geschichte des Taufgottesdienstes in der alten Kirche, in: Leiturgia, Handbuch des Evangelischen Gottesdienstes, fasc. 31-35, Kassel 1964-1966, the most adequate history of the baptismal rite in the ancient Church.

[3]) DENZINGER-SCHÖNMETZER, n. 1862ff; 3537ff.

[4]) An indication is the positive form of those documents, by which they differ from canons and other documents condemning errors and heretics. But in their case, this positive form veils a deeply negative attitude, for the focus of interest lies in the errors to be excluded.

a sketch of the history of the Creed is indispensable. After this search for the origins, a second part will pass in review the elements of its prehistory and then focus on its main articles. The conclusion will attempt to bring out the fundamental intention of the AC and let it point out its own original orientation.

I. IN SEARCH OF THE ORIGINS

In sketching this history, one has to steer a middle road. Such details as the use of the accusative or the ablative after „I believe in", the different wording of the article on Jesus' conception and birth, and so on, may be revealing to establish minor families of Creeds, but they may also obscure more important facts. In credal research the danger of overlooking the forest because of the trees is not illusory. On the other hand one may read, even under the pen of serious students, the statement that the AC, although not composed by the Apostles themselves, faithfully reflects the thought and even the wordings of New Testament times. This is to clothe the AC with an unwarranted authority, and moreover to neglect the light history may shed on its setting and meaning.

That the Apostles themselves, before going out over the earth, composed the AC, is a legend first found in Ambrose († 397) and rendered popular by Rufinus († 410) [5]. That every Apostle contributed his own article is an even later embroidery [6]. As a matter of fact, the definitive and universally accepted text of the AC, the *textus receptus* (T) was only imposed on the Latin church by the strong hand of Charlemagne [7]. He prescribed to the whole of his vast empire a Creed which had been introduced in the Frankish and Alemanian churches in the beginning of the 8th century, especially by the activity of Priminius († 753), the apostle of the Alemans, who brought it from his native country in the south-west of Gaul or northern Spain [8]. There T originated sometime in the sixth century [9].

During the fifth to the eighth centuries, local and regional churches of the Latin speaking world used Creeds which, although very similar, even in many details, still show definite characteristics of their own. Before Carolingian times there did not exist any rigid uniformity in the Creed. All Western Creeds, as will appear in the tables on p. 242-243, followed a common pattern and no doubt derived from a common source, but still they had a fairly large margin of variations.

This is to say that the Catholic Church lets the *status quaestionis*, in a large measure, be dictated to her by non-catholic thought.

[5]) AMBROSIUS, *Explan. Symb.*, 3. ed. CONNOLLY, p. 6; *Ep.* 42, 5, PL 16, 1125; Rufinus, *Expos. Symb.*, 2, CChr 20, 134.

[6]) C. BÜHLER, *The Apostles and the Creed*, in: Speculum 28 (1953) 335-339.

[7]) B. CAPELLE, 20; KELLY, 420-426.

[8]) PIRMINIUS, *Scarapsus*, PL 89, 1034-1036; HAHN § 92.

[9]) On the origin of T in Gaul/Spain: KELLY, 398-420.

1. Latin Creeds between 400 and 700

The main source for our knowledge of the Latin credal customs and texts in the period between about 400 to 700 are, besides of a few liturgical books from the last part of this period, sermons at the occasion of the „tradition" and „rendering" of the Creed [10]). A few weeks before the baptism service

---

[10]) In geographical/chronological order, such sermons have been conserved:
Northern Italy
AMBROSE, *Explan. Symb.*, ed. CONNOLLY, 1952; CSEL, 73, 3-12.
MAXIMUS OF TURIN († ca 415), *Hom.* 83, PL 57, 433-440. This homily is not considered as authentic by A. MUTZENBECHER, *Bestimmung der echten Sermones des M.*, in: Sacr. Er. 12 (1961) 197-293.
PETRUS CHRYSOLOGUS OF RAVENNA († 450), *Sermones* 56-62, PL 52, 354-375. This is the only Western sequence of sermons on the Creed, but its character does by no means contradict the observation made in the text.
RUFINUS, *Expositio Symboli*, CChr 20, 133-175, written about 404, is an important witness to the Creeds of Aquileia and Rome. Is does not contain sermons, but is a literary composition.
Illyricum
NICETAS OF REMESIANA, *De Symbolo*, ed. BURN, 1905, 38-52.
Africa
AUGUSTINE OF HIPPO († 430), *Sermo* 214, PL 38, 1065-1072, which he delivered as a priest.
Sermo 213, PL 38, 1060-1065; and in a more complete text: *Sermo Guelferb.* 1, Misc. Ag. I, 441-450. Held before 410.
Sermo 212, PL 38, 1058-1060. Held 411/412.
Sermo 215, PL 38, 1072-1076, and in a better edition: P. VERBRAKEN, in: RevBén. 68 (1958) 18-25. Date uncertain.
School of Augustine, *Sermo de symbolo ad catechumenos*, CChr 46, 185-199. Although considered as authentic by most authors, I feel fully convinced that this sermon, as Kattenbusch said, cannot belong to the master himself, but must come from his „school" (KATTENBUSCH, II, 447, Anm. 26). It exaggerates the augustinian mannerisms, and labours under a general flatness which in Augustine is extremely rare.
De fide et symbolo, CSEL 41, 3-32, is a commentary on the Creed, held not before baptismal candidates, but before a Synod of bishops, october 8, 393.
It is to be observed that Augustine commented on the Creed of Hippo only in *Sermon* 215. Elsewhere, he takes his own baptismal Creed of Milan (EICHENSEER, 473-475).
QUODVULTDEUS OF CARTHAGE († 453), to whom four pseudo-Augustinian sermons must be ascribed: *Sermones de Symbolo*, PL 40, 637-668; *Sermo contra Iudaeos* etc. de *Symbolo*, PL 42, 1117-1130.
FULGENTIUS OF RUSPE († 533), Fragm. 36 from *Contra Fabianum Arianum* X, CChr 91A, 854-860. Kelly, 176, quotes his Creed as reconstructed by C. CASPARI, *Ungedruckte...*
Quellen, II, 247-257; but it should be noted that some of his wordings repose on mere conjectures, e.g. PER ecclesiam.
Gaul
PS.-EUSEBIUS, *Sermo* 9-10, ed. CASPARI, *Ungedruckte... Quellen*, II, 185-199. Those sermons might belong to Faustus of Riez († ca 490): L. A. VAN BUCHEM, *L'Homélie pseudo-eusébienne de Pentecôte*, Nijmegen 1967.
CAESARIUS OF ARLES († 542), *Sermo* 9, CChr 103, 47.
The *Confessio*, 4, 4, of Saint Patrick ((† 461), ed. BIELER, *Liber Epist.*, I, 58-59, in a certain sense belongs to Gaul, where he was baptized; but his paraphrase, although highly revealing, is so free as to allow hardly any reconstruction of the credal wording.

during the Easter Vigil the bishop solemnly communicated the Creed to the candidates, who were admonished not to write it down but to learn it by heart. On the following Sunday(s) they then had publicly to recite, to „render" it [11]). A sermon given on those occasions would of course embrace the whole Creed. This fact is noteworthy. In several churches of the East, the Creed provided, although in a fairly artificial way, the pattern of the whole series of instructions given to the candidates [12]). It does not seem that the Creed in the West fulfilled a similar role. One might try to explain the absence of whole series of instructions on the Creed in the Western documents by the fact that such series were not conserved as the solemn sermons of the bishop at the tradition or rendering were; but this

---

Spain
The documents from Spain are of a different nature. They are not sermons, but quotations of the Creed in books. Yet all of them explicitly refer to the fact that this was the faith received and professed at the occasion of Baptism:
PRISCILLIAN OF AVILA († 385) or a disciple, *Liber ad Damasum*, CSEL 18, 34-37.
MARTINUS OF BRAGA († 579), *De correctione rusticorum*, 15-16, ed. BARLOW, 196-197. M gives an interrogatory form of the Creed.
ISIDORUS OF SEVILLA († 636), *De cognitione baptismi*, 36-83, PL 96, 127-142.
The baptismal Creed is extensively quoted in the Mozarabic *Liber Ordinum*, composed before the Arab conquest in 712, ed. FÉROTIN, MonEcclLit, V, 184-185.
Rome
The Roman Creed of the fourth century is attested to by documents of different order, the convergence of which establishes the text and its Roman use beyond any doubt (DS 11-12):
— Several English manuscripts of the VII/IX century;
— Rufinus' (see above) remarks on the divergencies between his Aquileian and the Roman Creed;
— a profession of faith in Greek, inerted in a leter of Marcellus of Ancyra to Julius of Rome, written in 337 or 341: EPIPHANIUS, *Haer*. 72, 3, 1, GCS 37, 258.
Two Roman rituals of the seventh century have conserved the baptismal rite, the *Gelasian* in the redaction of the manuscript Vat. Reg. 316 (ca 650), ed. WILSON, and the *Ordo* XI, ed. ANDRIEU, II, 417-447, which seems to be slightly younger (C. Vogel, *Introduction aux sources du culte chrétien au M. A.*, no date, 138-141). But they do not have the AC, but the Niceno-Constantinopolitan Creed, which in Rome, as in most Eastern churches, had supplanted the simpler baptismal Creed (KELLY, 344-348, 426-434).

[11]) The first explicit mention of a public „rendering" of the Creed before the whole congregation seems to be the eyewitness narrative of the conversion at Rome of Marius Victorinus (ca 355), related by AUGUSTINE (*Conf.*, VIII, 2, 5). Both Augustine and RUFINUS, *Expos. Symb.*, 3, 135, show that this custom was not then universal in the Latin churches. Cf. STENZEL, 176; MAERTENS, 135. For the East, Council of Laodicea (between 341 and 381), can. 46, JONKERS, 94.

[12]) CYRILL OF JERUSALEM († 386) or his successor, *Catecheses*, PG 33; I will quote the edition of REISCHL-RUPP, 1848-1860.
THEODORE OF MOPSUESTIA († 428), *Catechetical Homilies*, ed. TONNEAU-DEVREESSE, Rome 1967.
PROCLUS OF CONSTANTINOPLE († 446), *Baptismal Mystagogy*, ed. F. LEROY, *L'homilétique de Proclus* (SteT 247), Rome 1967, 188-194. This is a one-sermon commentary on the Creed; from our point of view it is unfortunate that the commentary is so free, that only the wording of a few articles can be established.
JOHN CHRYSOSTOM OF ANTIOCH AND CONSTANTINOPLE († 407), *Huit catéchèses baptismales*, SChr 50, on the contrary hardly alludes to the Creed.

would not account for the fact that nowhere in those episcopal sermons any allusion is made to the previous familiarity of the candidates with the wording of the Creed. Systematic instructions preparatory to Baptism must certainly have been in common use during the fifth century; but they probably followed a pattern such as recommended in Augustine's *De catechizandis rudibus* or as reflected in Irenaeus' *Demonstration*: a survey of the history of salvation interspersed with instructions on the Christian „way" of life. A fair amount of knowledge of the Old Testament and Gospel narratives and of the Lord's commandments was no doubt demanded of the baptismal candidates. And those topics must have been — at least where and when a good number of catechumens came from paganism, and had not for a longer time belonged to the „hearers" — an important stock subject-matter of the baptismal instructions. This supposition is confirmed by the room such topics often took in the solemn comments on the Creed themselves. Yet not a single Creed contains allusions to those topics.

This observation leads to a weighty conclusion. The function of the Creed was not to provide the instructor with a certain pattern, nor to give the catechumens a summary of what they had learned and should know about Christianity. The statement of Kelly that „declaratory creeds . . . were compendious summaries of Christian doctrine compiled for the benefit of converts undergoing instruction," [13]) seems to be unwarranted and misleading. *The Creed was less a teaching than a liturgical text.* Maertens is much nearer to the mark in noting that the instruction of the catechumens, insofar as it centred on the Creed, was not „une instruction scolaire" [14]). The handing over and giving back of the Creed was much more than a question of knowledge, unless one takes the word in its full biblical sense. It was one of the high points of a prolonged baptismal celebration, culminating in baptism proper, to which exorcisms, prayers, the laying on of hands and other rites gave a highly dramatic note. In the period under review, as during the foregoing centuries, the pronounciation of the Creed was considered the counterpart of the threefold renunciation of the devil, his pomps and works, that is to say of the pagan ways of life and thought [15]). This parallelism of abrenuntation and Creed, and the related qualification of the Creed as the document of our „contract" or „alliance" with God, which belong to the stock phrases of all comments on the Creed [16]), point to a deep-rooted identification of the profession of the

---

[13]) KELLY, 50, quoting A. SEEBERG and C. H. TURNER. In the same sense STENZEL, 160.
[14]) MAERTENS, 104f.
[15]) STENZEL, 98-104.
[16]) Almost all commentaries listed in note 10, speak of the „pactum". The idea of baptism as an initation into the new alliance with God belongs of course to the oldest baptismal concepts. But even the more juridical turn given to this idea by the conception of a „contract", goes far back. It is present in Tertullian in explicit connection with the interrogations and answers at Baptism (TERTULLIAN, *De pudicitia*, 9, 15, CChr 2, 1298; 12, 9, 1303), and in CLEMENT OF ALEXANDRIA, *Stromata*, VII, 15, 90, GCS 17, 64; compare QUASTEN, *Patrology*, II, 25; ORIGEN, *Exhort Mart.*, 17, GCS 2, 16.

Creed with baptism itself. As a matter of fact, as we will see, in Hippolytus the speaking of the Creed by the bishop and its acceptance by the baptizand make the baptismal ,,formula" itself.

Another consideration may confirm our conclusion that the Creed was not a summary of teaching. In the period under review, the struggle with the Arians in Northern Italy, Africa, Spain and Gaul stood far more on the foreground than that against a dying paganism. An elaborate doctrine of the Trinity therefore occupies a major part in almost all the episcopal comments on the Creed [17]). Frequently, they stress the neat Trinitarian doctrine of the Creed, which is a solid bulwark against the Arian and other errors. But in fact, those comments appear to be very much artificial. The traditional Creed did not of itself exclude Arianism, as Ambrose and Augustine remarked [18]). But, although the anti-Arian bias was so much in the foreground of catechetical instruction, none of the Western churches modified the AC in that sense. Even the churches of Spain, who produced a wealth of anti-Arian and elaborately Trinitarian counciliar creeds, maintained the old baptismal Creed. One might submit that the Creed, by that time, was so much a sacrosanct formula, that it did not admit of any modification inspired by the actual controversies. But the comparison of the Creeds of the fifth century shows that their local forms possessed as yet a fairly large margin of elasticity, which allowed them to borrow felicitous wordings from other churches. The local Creeds were not yet rigidly fixed. The reason of the refusal of anti-heretical additions or elaborations must lay elsewhere. *The baptismal Creed, to the western churches, was not the right place for polemics, however vital.*

2. The Prehistory of R and Hippolytus

We may for the moment assume that during the fourth century the church of Rome made use of a baptismal Creed (R) of the tenor witnessed to by Rufinus and Marcellus of Ancyra. The essential arguments for this assumption will soon appear. It would, of course, be an anachronism to conceive such a Creed as rigidly fixed up to the last detail in the way Charlemagne's authority established one authentic text of T. The Creed was not a shiboleth, as Rufinus seems to have imagined it, of which the exact wording and even pronunciation might be distinctive. It admitted of a certain plasticity, as shown by the detached manner in which Augustine could take either the Milan or the Hippo Creed as the starting point of his comments. But even

---

[17]) One of the few exceptions is AUGUSTINE, *Sermo Guelf.* 1. The spontaneous flow of this beautiful sermon with its very slight allusions to heretical doctrines brings out clearly, by contrast, what is said in the text on the forced character of the anti-heretical elaborations in most comments on the Creed. Here, the Creed finds its true setting.

[18]) AMBROSE, *Explan. Symb.*, 5-7, p. 7-8, comments on the refusal of the Roman (and the Milanese) church to change the AC in view of errors. On the other hand, AUGUSTINE, *De fide et symbolo*, 1, 1, p. 4, is fully aware that the heretics use the same Creed.

so, it must have acquired by that time a remarkable stability, not only with regard to the general pattern, but also to the single articles and many details of their wording.

This is an essential element in the study of R's pre-history. As a matter of fact, the historian does not have at his disposal any direct document on the history of the Creed at Rome between the end of the fourth century (with the one exception of Marcellus' letter of about 340, which does not give any information on the function of the Creed) and Hippolytus at the beginning of the third. Yet, scholars have succeeded in lifting much of the cloud which covers those extremely important hundred and fifty years. This was done by combining the Roman data of Hippolytus, Marcellus and Rufinus, respectively from the years about 210, 340 and 400, with those from the other provinces *after* 400. And it can be established, with a reasonable degree of certainty, that the other Latin churches borrowed their Creeds — with a certain liberty — from Rome. This will clearly come out in a table (p. 242-243) comparing the different local Creeds witnessed to by the documents indicated in note 10, with R as found in Marcellus and Rufinus, and with the baptismal interrogations of Hippolytus.

But first a word about Hippolytus (ca 210). In his booklet on church order, which bore the characteristic name of *Apostolic Tradition*, this schismatic bishop of Rome inserted a baptismal order. The original Greek text has been lost, but the passage of interest here can be reconstructed with sufficient certainty from an old Latin version and several Oriental adaptations [19]. Hippolytus lets the baptizand get down into the font. Then the bishop lays his hand on him and asks: „Do you believe in God Father Almighty"; the baptizand answers: „I believe", and is then baptized. The same rite is repeated with the interrogations about Jesus Christ and about the Holy Spirit. The bishop does not speak other words. The three interrogations and answers constitute the very „form" of the sacrament [20]. The meaning of such a rite we will return to later. First let us turn to the text of the baptismal interrogations (H), which is printed below (p. 242) in the first column. The second column gives R, the Roman Creed as witnessed to by Marcellus and Rufinus, the third one the noteworthy particularities of the younger Latin Creeds as contained in the documents of note 10.

---

[19] I cannot enter into the questions of the Roman origin and Hippolytan authenticity of the *Traditio Apostolica*. I quote Hippolytus according to B. BOTTE, *La Tradition Apostolique de saint Hippolyte* (*Liturgiewiss. Quellen u. Forsch.* 39), Münster 1963. See also: Gregory DIX, *The Treatise on the Apostolic Tradition of St. Hippolytus of Rome*, reissued . . . by H. CHADWICK, London 1968; E. TIDENER, *Didascaliae Apostolorum, Canonum Ecclesiasticorum, Traditionis Apostolicae versiones latinae* (*TuU 75*), Berlin 1963.

[20] The opinion of J. CREHAN, *Early Christian Baptism and the Creed*, London 1950, 170, who supposes that Hippolytus wrote down the part of an assistant minister, whereas the bishop's words, „including the pronunciation of the formula of baptism" were not put into writing, is desperate.

Baptismal Interrogations of Hippolytus (H)	Roman Creed according to Marcellus of Ancyra and Rufinus (R)
1. Do you believe in God the Father Almightly? — I believe	I believe in God Father Almighty [1])
2. Do you believe in Christ Jesus, the Son of God,	and in Christ Jesus, [2]) his only Son, our Lord,
3. who was born of Holy Spirit and the Virgin Mary	who was born of Holy Spirit and the Virgin Mary
4. who was crucified under Pontius Pilate, and died [and was buried] [3])	who was crucified under Pontius Pilate and buried
5. and rose the third day living from the dead,	and rose the third day from the dead,
6. and ascended into the heavens,	and ascended into the heavens
7. and sat down at the right hand of the Father	and sat down at the right hand of the Father,
8. and will come to judge the living and the dead? — I believe.	whence he comes to judge the living and the dead.
9. Do you believe in Holy Spirit,	And in Holy Spirit,
10. and (or: in) the Holy Church, [4])	Holy Church,
11. [6])	remission of sins,
12. and the resurrection of the flesh? — I believe.	resurrection of the flesh, [5])

---

* This table neglects minor, even if significant details.

[1]) Marcellus omits FATHER; to all probability this is a copyist's distraction: KATTEN-BUSCH, I, 72.

[2]) Marcellus has: μονογενής, ONLY-BEGOTTEN; Rufinus: UNICUM, ONLY.

[3]) AND WAS BURIED in Hippolytus is uncertain.

[4]) On the uncertain construction of this article, see below.

[5]) Marcellus adds: ETERNAL LIFE. But this article probably did not belong to any Western Creed of the early fourth century: Kattenbusch, I, 72. It may be a distraction, either of the copyist or of Marcellus himself. who added it from his Oriental Creed.

[6]) The presence of this article in H is not absolutely certain.

Divergencies from R in other Western Creeds and in T

1. WE BELIEVE: Hippo? [1])
   in ONE God etc.: Priscillian.
   add: INVISIBLE AND IMPASSIBLE: Aquileia.
   CREATOR OF HEAVEN AND EARTH: Remesiana?, Arles, T.
   INVISIBLE IMMORTAL, KING OF THE CENTURIES, CREATOR
   OF VISIBLE AND INVISIBLE THINGS, or similar words: Hippo?,
   Carthage?, Ruspe. [2])

2. a. JESUS CHRIST: all, except Ravenna.
   b. ONLY-BEGOTTEN: Arles.
      omit ONLY: Remesiana, Hippo, Carthage, Riez, Patrick.
   c. *omit* OUR LORD: Remesiana, Arles, Patrick.

3. Born FROM the H. G. OUT OF V. M.: Turin, Ravenna, Carthage, Ruspe, Braga
   CONCEIVED FROM the H. G. born OUT OF V. M.: Milan?, Arles, Riez, T.

4. a. *omit* CRUCIFIED: Milan, Remesiana?
      add: SUFFERED: Milan, Remesiana, Arles, Priscillian, Braga, Lib. Ord., T.
      DIED: Remesiana?, Arles, T.
   b. *add:* DESCENDED TO HELL: Aquileia, Arles, Braga, Sevilla, Lib. Ord., T.

5. *add:* rose LIVING: Hippol., Remesiana, Braga, Sevilla, Lib. Ord.
   omit: FROM THE DEAD: Ruspe?, Riez.

7. *add:* of the ALMIGHTY Father: Arles, Priscillian, Sevilla, Lib. Ord., T.

10. a. *omit it here* (*see 12b*): Hippo, Carthage, Ruspe.
    holy CATHOLIC Church: Remesiana, Riez, Arles, Braga, Sevilla, Lib. Ord., T.
    b. *add:* COMMUNION OF SAINTS: Remesiana, Arles, Riez, T.

11. *add:* SAVING BAPTISM: Priscillian.

12. a. *add:* ETERNAL LIFE: Marc. of Anc., Ravenna, Remesiana, Hippo, Carthage,
       Braga, Sevilla, Lib. Ord., T.
    b. *add:* THROUGH HOLY CHURCH: Hippo, Carthage, Ruspe.

---

[1]) After CASPARI, *Ungedruckte ... Quellen*, II, 253 Anm. 8, it is commonly assumed that Hippo used the plural, which was the common use of the greek churches. The fact is then quoted as proof of Greek influence. But the fact is not so certain: 1° Augustine, *Sermo* 215, 1, p. 18, tells us that he exposed the Creed to the gathered catechumens, but that every single one of them had to hand it back; in this last case the singular would be indicated. Augustine may have adopted the plural when speaking to a group. 2° This supposition is confirmed by the fact that Augustine uses the plural even in commenting on the Milan Creed, which certainly read the singular.

[2]) In Augustine, *Sermo* 212, 1, col. 1058, and Quodvultdeus, *Sermo* II, 3, 3, col. 654, words of this tenor occur, but it is not sure that they belong to the text of the Creed and not to the commentary. But linked with Fulgenius' testimony, the occurrence of a sentence of this kind points to a place in the Creed itself. Probably we witness here the progressive entering of a certain wording in the text of the Creed.

This table brings out several interesting facts: (1) that there exists an extremely complicated pattern of mutual borrowings; (2) that there existed a neat tendency toward regional forms, which in several cases had, in an early phase already, acquired a certain measure of stability (this would appear even more clearly if the translation had been able to conserve minor details of wording and word-order); and most importantly (3) that all those local and regional Creeds descended from a common stock. A comparison with the Eastern Creeds of our period would bring out even more emphatically the thoroughgoing consent of the Western ones (see below p. 253). The Creeds of all Latin churches known to us are cousins.

This sheds a definite light on the pre-history of R, since the common ancestor must have been a Creed which was exceedingly similar to R, although not quite identical with it. The similarity can be seen from the fact that almost every divergence from R appears to be an ulterior development of a passage which in R could seem to be excessively jejune; a dogmatic precision such as the formula: CONCEIVED FROM THE HOLY SPIRIT BORN OUT OF THE VIRGIN MARY, or the adding of CATHOLIC; an addition, such as DESCENDED TO HELL [21]), COMMUNION OF SAINTS and ETERNAL LIFE. By subtracting the passages on which the various local Creeds vary, one arrives almost exactly at the wording of R [22]).

Yet R in its precise form is not itself the common ancestor. This may be established by the uncertainty connected with the word ONLY in 2b, by the omission of OUR LORD in some Creeds in 2c, and by the insertion of LIVING in 5. Once such words had firmly established themselves in the mother Creed, they could not be changed in the borrowing. The last item was too innocuous for that, and especially the omission of ONLY and OUR LORD would have provoked a violent outcry. Those points have one thing in common, namely they are points at which H differs from R. This fact, which to my knowledge has not yet been commented upon, establishes a solid conclusion: the borrowing from Rome, at least by the churches of Illyricum, Africa and Gaul occurred somewhere between Hippolytus and Marcellus of Ancyra, when the Creed of Rome was at least as yet hesitant about the wording of those passages.

It is difficult to narrow down this space of time. Still some indications are to be found which might help. The article REMISSION OF SINS is unknown to H, but present in R and is found in all Western Creeds. By the time of the borrowing, therefore, it must have been firmly established

---

[21]) On this article, RUFINUS, *Expos. Symb.*, 26, 161, remarks: „The meaning of those words seem to be identical with the mention of his burying." But then he continues to comment on it with the help of 1 Peter. 3, 18ff.

[22]) That the Creed of Rome was the common ancestor of all Western baptismal Creeds, was clearly brought out by KATTENBUSCH, I, 79-84. But then he supposes this mother Creed to haven been R in its definite form.

at Rome. And here one might think of the violent disputes at Rome on the remission of postbaptismal sins provoked by Novatian in 251 [23]). That almost all later commentators explain this article of baptism is no decisive argument against such an interpretation. It is well known that the bishops, speaking for baptismal candidates, had heavy scruples about mentioning the „laborious Baptism" of Penance. A second consideration flows from the language of the Creed. The church of Rome became widely Latin speaking about the middle of the third century [24]). The original redaction of the Creed was in Greek: even as late as 340 Marcellus does not translate from Latin, but quotes a current Greek Creed of Rome. But all Western Creeds stem evidently from the same Latin translation [25]). The borrowings therefore could not take place before a Latin version of the Creed had, in Rome, established itself firmly enough to become the common model to all its daughters. This points to a date in the second half of the third century. A third consideration may be added here. The characteristic place given to HOLY CHURCH in the Creeds of Africa may well reflect Cyprian's effort to elaborate ecclesiology. It is therefore probable that this african way of inserting the mention of the church in a more organic way is due to him [26]). On the other hand, this redactional refinement would be less probable after the simple juxtaposition of articles 9-12 in R had established itself. This borrowing also points to a period, somewhere between H and R, when the redaction of this article was yet in some confusion. I think that the convergence of those considerations point to an origin of the Western Creeds out of a pre-R Roman form somewhere in the last half of the third century. This does not, however, say that those churches did not have texts which were similar to R (a following chapter will study this point). But, for some undefinable reason, during the last half of the third century an exceptional activity took place in the field of Latin Creeds. The various churches adopted Creeds modeled on the Roman one, which they adapted to their local traditions or even personal tastes.

Studying the table printed on p. 242, one is forced to ask whether Hippolytus' baptismal interrogations were the direct ancestor of R, and at the same time of the other Western texts? In the first enthusiasm over H's discovery, most scholars answered in the affirmative, but soon a reaction

---

[23]) A similar dispute had shaken the Roman church as early as the first decades of the century; this was one of the factors of Hippolytus' schism. The article in question therefore might have been added at that time, perhaps at the occasion of the reconciliation of Hippolytus' followers in the thirties. But the following argument militates against a borrowing by the other churches at such an early date.

[24]) G. BARDY, La question des langues . . ., Paris 1948.

[25]) This has been established by Kattenbusch, I, 80f, and especially by LIETZMANN, Symbolstudien II, 192-194; Kelly, 111-113. The Latin text, it is to be noted, is not a servile translation, but a rendering such as to be expected in the live liturgical use of a church which, at the moment, was bilingual.

[26]) CYPRIAN, Ep. 69, 7, ed. BAYARD, II, 244, gives „Do you believe in the remission of sins and eternal life through the holy church" as one of the baptismal interrogations.

set in. Lebreton and Capelle pointed to the anachronism which might be underlying the question: one should not, at the time of Hippolytus, imagine a rigid fixity in any liturgical text, not even the baptismal Creed. Liturgical codification of a sort only began with Hippolytus, and he himself allowed for a certain margin of creative improvisation by the bishop. This is certainly true. But granted this, one must ask if a Creed which, with small fluctuations, sounded very much like H, has been the direct ancestor of R. If the answer is in the affirmative, the further problem arises as to whether the interrogatory form of H represents the original.

Kelly definitely opted for the negative. According to him, H cannot be considered the ancestor of R, but represents a sideline [27]). Holland tried to refute him, but did not succeed in fully demolishing Kelly's arguments. Nonetheless, only some of Kelly's arguments are convincing. He is right in stating that, if H was the direct ancestor, the word DIED in H could not have been replaced by BURIED in R, nor could the meaningful IN THE HOLY CHURCH, which Kelly rightly assumes to be H's real reading, yield to the colourless article of R. His main argument, though, seems to lie in the second article. He supposes that ONLY in 2b and OUR LORD in 2c must have belonged, at Hippolytus' time, to pre-R. The last one, because this was nothing less than the most primitive and original Christian confession, which just could never be absent; the first one, because, in Kelly's theory, the title Monogenes was introduced about 170, in order to counteract the Valentinians' distinction between the divine Monogenes and Jesus Christ [28]). This main argument seems to me to have been devoided of its foundation by the foregoing. Half a century after Hippolytus, when the great borrowing process took place, there circulated in Rome a Creed with sufficient authority to be taken as a model, in which on the other hand neither the word ONLY, nor the title OUR LORD had firmly established themselves [29]). The only points therefore, where H could not be the direct ancestor of R are the words DIED (4), LIVING (5) and IN *the holy Church*. Now this last point has been, with a good deal of plausibility, brought home to Hippolytus' personal theological and liturgical idiosyncrasies: he likes to end his doxologies by ,,in the church", and he sees an intimate connection between the Spirit and the Church [30]). This, therefore, could well be his personal modification of an existing Roman Creed. The two other divergencies between H and R are hardly of any importance: that he replaced BURIED, which already must have been solidly established (see below, on the christological elaboration), by DIED may just reflect a desire for greater explicitness. The addition of LIVING in the article on the resurrection is one of those redactional fineries which, under

---

[27]) KELLY, 113-119. HOLLAND, a.c.
[28]) KELLY, 142.
[29]) We will, of course, have to offer a plausible explanation for the late insertion in R of that most venerable confession OUR LORD.
[30]) P. NAUTIN, *Je crois à l'Esprit Saint* (*Unam Sanctam* 17), Paris 1947, especially p. 17f.

scriptural influence (for instance Rom. 6:13) may turn up now and again. We may therefore conclude that Hippolytus took over an existing Roman Creed of good standing, in which he made a few smallish modifications, the only important one of which tended to build in the mention of the church (attested to already by older authors) in a more organic way, according to his personal theology. But — and this is the essential thing — *this Roman Creed of good standing did lack the words ONLY and OUR LORD in the second article* [31]).

Hippolytus' fundamental fidelity to a pre-R thus established, the question arises if the interrogatory form of H is the original one. In other words, did the AC, a pre-R form of which we postulated for Hippolytus' times, originate as an interrogatory Creed, which had as with him its place at the very heart of Baptism, or must it be conceived at its origin as a declaratory Creed, such as the later Creeds, which by Hippolytus himself or perhaps even at an earlier date was adapted for use in the baptismal act itself? In order to answer this question, one has to consider what is known about baptismal rites in the second century, and even so we may hardly hope for certainty. Let us try to marshall the facts.

But first it must be noted that the pre-R Creed of good standing which underlies H could not, at Hippolytus' time, be very old. Most scholars would now agree that a Creed which fuses into one a Trinitarian and a Christological profession of faith, such as is characteristic for the Creeds we studied and for their Eastern parallels, could not be situated before the second half of the second century, somewhere in between Justin Martyr († 165) and Irenaeus, who wrote about 180/200. But this consideration works two ways. On the one hand, one cannot suppose a very complicated history of such a Creed before Hippolytus: developing from the Trinitarian baptismal invocation to a declaratory Creed, and then reshaped into the interrogatory form and function it has in Hippolytus. On the other hand, if this declaratory Creed was fairly young and its use in the baptismal rites not yet well established, Hippolytus, although a traditionalist, may have allowed himself a certain liberty in assigning to it an organic function.

One consideration may tell in favour of the priority of H's interrogatory form. In Hippolytus, as we already saw, the three main articles of the AC had their place at the very heart of Baptism. At the end of the Vigil the baptizand descends naked into the water, and with him a deacon. Then the bishop imposes his hand on him and asks: „Do you believe in God Father Almighty?" The baptizand answers: „I believe", and is then baptized. This is repeated three times, with the threefold interrogation of the Creed. This elaborate rite has a striking resemblance with that of proselyte Baptism. The kinship between the Jewish and the Christian rite has frequently been

---

[31]) The late insertion of ONLY is confirmed by the hesitations of the daughters: ONLY or ONLY-BEGOTTEN, before or after the word SON. At the time of the great borrowing, it was not yet firmly established.

recognized, but the importance this resemblance has for the setting of the rite of Hippolytus has to my knowledge never been commented upon [32]). Strack-Billerbeck describes the admission of the proselyte in the following way: If somebody presents oneself, the seriousness of his step is pointed out to him. If he persists, he is circumcised. After the wound of circumcision is healed, he is, at daytime, not at night, conducted to the bath, which must preferably consist of „living" water. Two or three rabbi's disciples assist him, and after he is already half covered by the water which covers him up to the loins, they explain to him some heavy and light commandments. If he persists in his proposal, he is made to submerge himself, so that the water covers his whole body [33]). There can be little doubt that the rite as described by Hippolytus, is modeled on this Jewish rite. The introduction of this type of baptismal liturgy may have happened around the middle of the second century, when at Rome the relations of Christians to their Jewish brethren seem to have been quite friendly and a renewal of Jewish influence can be observed. The baptismal interrogations and answers of Hippolytus' rite would be the exact counterpart of the commandments, which the rabbi's disciples exposed to the proselyte standing in the water, and of his acceptance of them [34]). By the way, this sheds an interesting light on the function of interrogations and answers. By the middle of the second century, proselyte baptism had, in Jewish circles, widely superseded circumcision as the act of entrance into the Elect People and its Alliance. The interrogations and answers of Hippolytus are the conclusion of the „contract" with God, the participation in the New Alliance and the new People of God, the baptizand's „pact". Such a conception of baptism would provide a perfectly natural setting for the molding of the credal profession in interrogatory form. And from this point of view this form might very well have been the original one.

But, on the other hand, the character of the baptismal interrogations in H opposes itself to that conclusion. The second main article, especially, seems just too long to have originated as a question. One does not see how a

---

[32]) BENOIT, 12-27, comes near to it, but his comparison being made with the Didache, does not make the point.

[33]) STRACK-BILLERBECK, I, 109-110. A reminiscence of the proselyte rite and its borrowing by the Christians may be seen in the traditional representations of Christ's Baptism by John in old christian art: Christ stands in the water up to his loins.

[34]) Some affinity with those rabbinic prescriptions may already be distinguished in the Didache's preference for cold and „living" water i.e. as in a stream or at a source (Didache, 7, 1). The same affinity is also found in Justin. In his description of Baptism he alludes to an acceptance of the christian teachings and commandments: „As many as are persuaded and believe that those things which we teach and describe are true, and undertake to live accordingly, are taught to pray ... Then they are led by us to a place where there is water ..." (Apol., I, 61, translation WHITAKER, 2). But here this adherence does not take place in the water as in the proselyte and the Hippolytan rite, but before. And as the liturgy avoids doubles, it is not to be assumed that after this preparatory profession of faith a second one took place. Since Justin wrote in Rome, we are justified in concluding that around 160 that church did not yet have the interrogatory rite of Hippolytus.

single interrogation, consisting of seven parts some of which touch on more than one topic, could arise within the live liturgical situation. The bishop's breath would have given out. From this point of view it is more plausible that the pre-R Creed — at least in its elaborate christological section — originated in its declaratory form and was only afterwards transposed into an interrogatory one.

These two considerations balance one another. The solution may lay in the theory, the conjectural character of which should not however be forgotten, that two formulas were fused together. As we will see, there existed on the one hand, from the first half of the second century on, short Trinitarian Creeds, which in a few words commented on the Father, the Son and the Holy Ghost, much in the same way as R and H do in the first article. As to the other hand there circulated, from the very beginning of the second century on, short summary statements of the Gospel message about Christ. A fusion of both would result in the unnatural interrogation of the second main article. That such a fusion took place during the second half of that century, can be established, as we will see. But our argument here supposes that already before this fusion the Trinitarian Creed with its short elaborations existed in interrogatory form. This is the hypothetical element in our solution.

The only passage, as a matter of fact, one could quote, is found in Tertullian's *De corona*, written about 210. After mentioning the abrenuntiation, Tertullian continues: „We are then immerged three times, answering something more than the Lord prescribed in the Gospel" [35]). It is clear that questions and answers about Father, Son and Holy Ghost are, as in Hippolytus, situated after the baptizand has entered the water. But what is the „something more"? Elsewhere, Tertullian gives to understand· that the Church is mentioned [36]). Earlier students assumed that, since Tertullian certainly knows creed-like summaries of the faith, by „something more" he meant a full Creed in interrogatory form. But Restrepo-Jaramillo has shown that one is not justified in assuming the identity of Tertullian's Creeds with the baptismal interrogations [37]). We do not know therefore whether, in the rite described by Tertullian, the interrogations on Trinity and Church already comprised any elaboration on the three names. Tertullian's testimony does not, therefore, solve the question about the priority of either the declaratory or the interrogatory form of the Creed in Rome. But at least it shows that Baptism by interrogation was not just an invention of Hippolytus: a few years earlier it was in use at Carthage.

Perhaps the balance may be weighted in favour of the declaratory Creed's priority by the witness of the East. The next paragraph will establish a

---

[35]) TERTULLIAN, *De corona*, 3, 2-3, CChr 2, 1042f; cf. *De spectac.*, 4, 1-3, CChr, 1, 231. E. DEKKERS, *Tertullianus en de geschiedenis der liturgie*, Brussels 1947, 191.

[36]) TERTULLIAN, *De baptismo*, 6, 1-2, CChr 1, 282.

[37]) J. RESTREPO-JARAMILLO, *Tertuliano y la doble fórmula en el símbolo apostólico*, in: Gregor. 15 (1934) 3-58.

connection, at an early stage of the birth history of the Creeds, between
Rome and the East. One might feel confident that, if Rome at the time used
the interrogatory form, some traces of this would appear in the East. But
neither do such traces appear in R's western daughters!

Before turning to the problem of second century Creeds, we have to study
those of the East. Not only do they help us, by contrast, to focus more
sharply on the characteristics of the Latin AC, but they also provide important material for its pre-history.

3. Eastern fourth century Creeds

The principal churches of the East during the fourth century had baptismal Creeds which show an over-all resemblance to the Latin ones. They
are built on the same Trinitarian scheme, and several articles correspond
to their Latin counterparts, if not in the exact wording, at least in subject-
matter. But the Greeks never dreamt of a direct Apostolic origin. That may
be one reason why they were more willing to transform their Creeds according to the last dogmatic developments, and why they allowed their local
Creeds to be replaced by one of the many formulas which arose in the wake
of the Council of Nicea and finally by the Niceno-Constantinopolitan Creed.

The historian therefore has at his disposal a poorer material in the East
than in the West. In the Eastern material it is often difficult to distinguish
between what stems from the traditional local Creed and what is borrowed
from a more learned conciliar one. Some Greek authors of this period
proclaimed individual Creeds, which were heavily remodelled forms of their
baptismal Creed. Most of the Creeds conserved come from the region of
Antioch and its sphere of influence. But we never have, as in the West,
successive Creeds of one single church or region. Yet a comparison of those
Eastern Creeds with one another and with R brings out significant facts,
but only on the condition that one prescinds from details and centers one's
attention on the main points. With regard to the Eastern Creeds some
scholars have, with a global approach, reached wholly unfounded conclusions; others have been completely lost in the forest of details.

The following table tries to steer a middle course. It neglects variations,
such as the alternance of MAKER OF HEAVEN AND EARTH with
CREATOR OF ALL VISIBLE AND INVISIBLE THINGS, the multi-
plication of concepts around the Lord's eternal birth, GOD OF GOD,
LIGHT OF LIGHT ecc.; the different order of the last articles. Such details
may be important for the mutual relationship of local Creeds, but our main
object here is to give an insight into the topics mentioned. By leaving out
more dogmatic developments, especially on the burning topic of the Son's
eternal generation, the main lines of the Creeds appear more clearly.

In the following table (p. 253) the left column gives the text of R (above
p. 242) for easier comparison. The following columns represent:

1. — The Creed of Eusebius of Cesarea († 339), inserted in a letter
on the Council of Nicea. Since Eusebius declares this to be the Creed with

which he was baptized, one may assume that it represents the baptismal Creed of Cesarea around 270. But, in view of the cavalier way the bishops of the period treated their Creed, this should not be urged. The article on the Holy Ghost lacks all further elaborations; they may have been absent, but Eusebius may have cut short, those articles not being in question. — Text: OPITZ, *Athanasius Werke*, III, *Urkunde* 22, 4-6, p. 43; HAHN § 123; DS 40.

2. — The Creed of Jerusalem which with some margin of uncertainty may be culled from the *Catechetical Homilies* of Cyril of Jerusalem († 386) or his successor John. — Text: REISCHL-RUPP, 1848-1860; HAHN § 124; DS 41.

3. — The Creed of Mopsuestia, commented upon by Theodorus of Mopsuestia († 428). As the work is known only in a Syriac version, the exact wording is not always certain. — Text: TONNEAU-DEVREESSE, *Les homélies catéchétiques de Th. M.*, 1949; DS 51.

4. — The Latin version of the Creed of Antioch, quoted by Cassian († ca 430). One may suspect some reminiscences of Cassian's own Latin Creed, especially in the passages which were not under debate. — Text: Cassiani *Opera*, ed. PETSCHENIG, CSEL 13, 327; HAHN § 130.

5. — The Creed contained in the baptismal rite of the *Apostolic Constitutions*, VII, 41. This compilation was composed around 380, probably in Syria. — Text: FUNK, *Didascalia et Constitutiones Apostolorum*, 1905, I, 444-446; HAHN § 129; DS 60.

6. — The second Creed of the Council of the Church Dedication, held at Antioch (341). This Creed is ascribed by ancient authors to the martyr Lucian of Antioch († 312). It may, indeed, be a worked-over redaction of his Creed; but this cannot be established. — Text: G. BARDY, *Recherches sur saint Lucien d'Antioche et son école*, 1936, 92-94; HAHN § 154.

7. — A few credal quotations found in the sermons of two bishops of Constantinople, John Chrysostom († 407) and Proclus († 446). — Texts: Joh. Chrysostomus, *Hom. 40 in 1 Cor.*, PG 61, 347-349; *Hom. 4 in Col.*, PG 62, 342; see A. WENGER, SChr 50, 94 f. — F. J. LEROY, *L'homilétique de Proclus*, 1967, 188-194.

8. — The shorter Creed, found in the *Ancoratus*, written in 374, of Epiphanius of Salamis († 403). This Creed is to all intents identical with the so-called Niceno-Constantinopolitan Creed, which is supposed to have been promulgated by the Council of Constantinople in 381. The latest study of the question, A. M. RITTER, *Das Konzil von Konstantinopel und sein Symbol*, Göttingen 1965, 159-169, is of the opinion that it is the work of the Council, working over an older baptismal Creed, and that its presence in the *Ancoratus* is due to a later copyist. Whatever its origin, this is a good example of a moderately „learned" Creed of the late fourth century. Moreover, its insertion in our table reveals an interesting point on its character. — Text: GCS 25, 146 f.; HAHN § 125; DS 42.

R	Catchwords	1. Euseb.	2. Cyr.	3. Theod.	4. Ant.	5. Ap. Const.	6. Dedic.	7. Procl. Chrys	8. Epiph.	9. Greg.	10. Alex.	11. Arius	12. Mac.
1. I believe in God Father Almighty	I believe	X	X	X	X	X	X	X	X	X?	O	X	X
	We believe	X	X	X	X	X	X	one true God	X	O	O one unbegotten Father	X	X
	in one God Father					one true God Alm. the Father of Christ							
	Almighty												
1b.	maker of ...	X	X	X	X	X	X	O	X	O	—	—	—
2. And in Christ Jesus his only Son our Lord	in one Lord J.C.	X	X	X	X	X	X	X the Son of God	X	O the Son of God	X	X	X
	in the Lord J.C.	X	X	X	X	X	X	O	X	O	X	X	X
	his only (begotten) Son							O		O			
	Word	X		X				O	X	¿		X	X
	God of God ecc.	X		X	X	X	X	O	X	O			X
	Firstborn of Creation	X		X				O	X	¿			
	Through whom all ...	X	X	X	X	X	X	O		O		X	X
3. Who was born of Holy Spirit and V.M.	for our salvation	X		X				O	X	¿		X	X
	came down		X		X	X	X	O	X	O		X	X
	became man	X	X?	X	X	X	X	O	X	O			X
	became flesh		X?	X	X	X	X	O	X	¿	X	X	
	born from V.(M.)	X	X?					O	X	O	X		X
	and H. Spirit				X	X		O	X	O	X		
	dwelt among men	X				X		O			X		X
4. Who was crucified under P.P. and buried	suffered	X		X	X		X	O	X			X	
	crucified		X		X	X	X	O	X	X			X
	died	X		X	X	X		O		X	X	X	X
	under P.P.					X		O	X	X	X		
	buried	X	X?	X	X		X	O	X		X		X
5. And rose the third day from the dead	rose	X	X	X	X	X	X	O	X	X	X	X	X
	the third day	X	X	X	X	X	X	O	X	X			X
6. And ascended into heavens	ascended into heavens	ascended to	X	X	X	X	X	O	X	X	X	—	— ?
7. And sat down at the right hand of the Father	sat down at the right hand of the Father	the Father	X	X	X	X	X	O	X	O	X	—	X

164

		C1	C2	C3	C4	C5	C6	C7	C8	C9	C10	C11
8. Whence he comes to judge living and dead	Comes to judge living and dead	X	X	X	X	X	O	X	X	X	X	X
8b.	whose reign has no end	—	X	—	—	—	O	X	X	—	—	—
9. And in Holy Spirit	in one H. Spirit (1)	X	X	X	O	O	X	O	X	X	X	X
	in Holy Spirit	O	X	X	O	O	O	O	X	—	X	—
	paraclete/sanctifier ecc.	O	X	—	O	O	O	O	X	X	—	—
	spoke through prophets								X			
10. Holy Church	holy church (1)	O	O	O	O	O	O	O	one holy cath. and apost. ch.	one cath. apost. ch.	one cath. church of God	—
	one cath. church	O	O	X	O	O	X	O				—
	holy cath. and apost. ch.	O	O	—	O	O	O	O				—
10b.	baptism	O	X	—	O	O	—	O	X	—	—	—
11. remission of sins	remission of sins	O	X	X	O	X	X	X	X	—	—	—
12. resurrection of the flesh	resurrection of flesh/body	O	X fl.	X b.	O	X fl.	O	X		X	X	X
	resurr. of the dead											
12b.	eternal life	O	X	X	O	X	X	X	X	—	X	—
12c.	Kingdom of heavens	O	—	—	O	X	X	X	—	—	X	—

Signs: X : the catchword is present; in alternative readings the one present.
— : the catchword is absent.
c. : the catchword is absent in the credal quotation, but is commented upon.
o : the document skips this part of the Creed.
(1) The variation of order of articles 10-12 is not noted in this table.

165

9. — A few quotations from the Creed, found in Gregory Nazianzus *Hom. 40 in S. Bapt.*, 44-45, PG 36, 421-425; HAHN § 135.

10. — Fragments of a Creed, inserted in letters of Alexander of Alexandria († 324). — Text: OPITZ, *Athanasius Werke*, III, *Urkunde* 14, 46 and 53, p. 27 f.; 15, p. 30.

11. — A Creed of Arius († 336), which he offered to Constantine as a proof of his orthodoxy. — Text: OPITZ, o.c., *Urkunde* 30, p. 64.

12. — A Creed contained in some manuscripts of the *Apophtegmata* of Macarius of Egypt († 390). — Text: LIETZMANN, 25 f.; DS 55.

In order to bring out the contribution of this table to the history of the AC, we will have to go through the single articles. But a few comments can be made beforehand. A first glance reveals several important features common to East and West, but others that mark a neat distinction between the two groups. These distinctive features are definitely less pronounced in Egypt. It is therefore commonly assumed that the Creed of Egypt stood somewhere midway between the Western and the Oriental world. This is quite plausible. Yet one should not forget that the evidence we have on Egyptian Creeds is extremely weak. „Macarius"'s background is utterly unknown, and toward the end he certainly skipps phrases. There is no way of knowing whether Alexander quotes the first articles in full, and both he and Arius may have remodeled the text in view of the present controversy. On the absence of articles 10-12 in Eusebius, and in the Creed of Nicea for that matter, I will argue below that Eusebius is omitting them. The table brings out a curious feature of the Creed of Epiphanius: it is complete. Almost nothing found anywhere is lacking; in fact it gathers together just about everything which could possibly be gleaned from the different Creeds of the East. Might it perhaps be an artificial composition, skilfully compiled to make everybody happy? The result is an unmistakeable redundance in articles 3, 4 and 10, but in the long run a splendid success.

Now for the single articles.

1. — In contrast to the West, the first article always runs: in ONE God, and out of Egypt adds: MAKER OF HEAVEN AND EARTH or something to that effect. This points to a stronger influence of a passage like 1 Cor: 8. 6: „one God the Father, from whom are all things . . ., and one Lord Jesus Christ, through whom are all things." Yet, the influence of this Pauline passage should not be exaggerated: Paul writes THE Father, but in all Creeds the article is absent; ALMIGHTY, never found in Paul outside one Old Testament quotation, is standard in all Creeds; God's creative activity is not expressed in the words of Paul, but by MAKER or CREATOR. The words GOD FATHER ALMIGHTY, without articles, will call for further comment when we turn to the original setting of the Creed.

2. — In the second article, several points must be noted. — As in the West, the profession is directed toward JESUS CHRIST, the words ONLY-BEGOTTEN SON being an apposition or a predicate.

This is, as we will see later, significant for the over-all orientation of the Creed. And it speaks against a direct derivation from the Matthean baptismal formula.

— At the same time, a neat line of distinction between East and West appears. Whereas the Latin Creeds run: JESUS CHRIST, HIS ONLY SON, OUR LORD, thus considering SON and LORD as appositions of the proper name JESUS, the Greek Creeds have: ONE (or THE) LORD JESUS CHRIST, HIS ONLY-BEGOTTEN SON. To the Greeks LORD JESUS CHRIST make up almost one name. As in the first article, the influence of 1 Cor: 8. 6 is unmistakable in the wording ONE LORD JESUS CHRIST, but appears to be secondary. If, as a matter of fact, Paul's profession was at the source of the credal wording, the qualification ONE could never be absent. For once this qualification had entered into the standard credal material, it could not drop out.

— As against the Latin Creeds, the pre-existence of the Lord is brought out emphatically. Not only is ONLY-BEGOTTEN the rule with the Greeks, whereas in the West ONLY is the more common reading; but moreover FIRSTBORN OF CREATION (cf Col: 1. 15) and THROUGH WHOM ALL THINGS WERE MADE (cf 1 Cor: 8. 6), which were unfrequent in the Latin Creeds, are the rule here (the absence of FIRST-BORN in Alexander, Arius and Epiphanius may well be an intentional omission).

3. — The third article represents perhaps the most striking difference with the West. The Latins were content with the simple formula BORN OF HOLY SPIRIT AND THE VIRGIN MARY or the somewhat more refined CONCEIVED OF HOLY SPIRIT, BORN FROM THE VIRGIN MARY; but the Greeks have a rich variety of expressions. Several of those seem directly connected with the explicit preexistence-doctrine of the foregoing article: CAME DOWN, and BECAME FLESH or MAN are the deeds of a heavenly being. The absence of any mention of the HOLY SPIRIT in this article is strikingly in contrast with the Latin Creeds, where it was the absolute standard.

4-8. — Those articles need little comment. The most striking feature is the very low rate of variation in articles 5-8, in which East and West go together. This summary of the Gospel message about Jesus Christ gives evidence of a far greater degree of stereotyping than the rest of the Creed. This confirms, what will be proven afterwards, that this summary circulated widely before it was inserted into the three-member Creed.

9. — The qualification ONE with the HOLY SPIRIT is fairly frequent, whereas the West ignores it. According to Theodore, it was not traditional in the church of Mopsuestia, but was introduced by the Council of Constantinople of 381 [38]). Was it a Pauline reminiscence? (cf 1 Cor: 12. 11-13; Gal: 3. 2-5, 26-29; Eph: 4. 2-4). The *Apostolic Constitutions* refer it to the unity between the Old and the New Testament, a theme which is under-

---

[38]) THEODORE OF MOPSUESTIA, *Hom. cat.*, 9, 16, p. 239.

lying Cyrill's and Epiphanius' WHO SPOKE IN THE PROPHETS.
This was a main issue in second century church life and teaching, and since
it turns up quite frequently in the old „Rules of Faith", this may very well
have been its original point.

10-12. — With the exception of Eusebius (and the Council of Nicea),
all witnesses mention CHURCH and RESURRECTION, most REMIS-
SION OF SINS and ETERNAL LIFE, very much the same situation we
found in the West.

The absence of those articles in Eusebius and in the Council of Nicea
has been frequently commented upon. Most scholars assume that they were
not present in the Creed of Cesarea, and then quote this as an example
of a Creed ending on the words HOLY SPIRIT, without further additions.
A glance at our two tables shows that this is highly improbable. I am convinced for the following reasons that at Nicea and in Eusebius' letter, this
part of the Creed was omitted for brevity's sake and because, in the Arian
dispute, those articles were not a stake:

— Eusebius had already abrigded by fusing articles 6 and 7 into the compound ASCEND TO THE FATHER. In view of the high rate of stability
of those articles in all Creeds, this compound cannot possibly have been
the real reading of the Creed of Cesarea.

— If, as late as 325, the article CHURCH had been lacking in the Creed
of an important metropolis like Cesarea, its presence in all other Creeds
at exactly the same place (the exception of Africa has been explained; Arius
may very well have borrowed it from there) is hard to explain. A late addition would have left some traces.

— Our two tables establish that the Fathers of Nicea never intended to
write down a full Creed, but limited themselves to the articles on Father
and Son, which were at stake, adding for good measure the profession of the
Holy Spirit. Much the same was done by theologians of the mid fourth
century, such as Hilary of Poitiers, who certainly knew the closing articles [39]. If, as a matter of fact, the Nicene Fathers had intended a full
Creed, the vast majority would have vigorously protested against the absence of subjects like CHURCH, REMISSION OF SINS, RESURREC-
TION, which they professed in their local Creeds. Especially to the Latins
present, among whom the influential Ossius of Cordova, Caecilian of Carthage, the Roman priests, and to Constantine himself, who had been recently
engaged in the Donatist controversies, the profession of CHURCH and
REMISSION OF SINS was of a glowing concern. A full Creed in which
those subjects were lacking would have been unacceptable to them.

It must therefore be assumed that neither the Council of Nicea, nor Eusebius
comparing his local Creed with that of the Council, intended to lay down
a full Creed. This witness cannot, therefore, be considered as an example
of a Creed ending on the words HOLY SPIRIT, without further additions.

---

[39] P. SMULDERS, La doctrine trinitaire de saint Hilaire de Poitiers (Anal. Greg. 32),
Rome 1944, 109-111, 262f.

The table of Eastern Creeds suggests a complicated pattern of mutual influences which is impossible to unravel. Yet, a general conclusion imposes itself which we can best discuss by briefly reviewing and discussing the opinions of other scholars.

1° *Eastern Creeds stem from a common root.* Kelly is of a different opinion. Commenting on the basic resemblances between our Creeds, he suggests that the various Eastern Creeds developed on parallel lines and had no ancestor in common: „Creeds grew up in the baptismal rite, their ground-plan being prescribed by the threefold questionnaire and triple immersions. Their content was supplied from the Trinitarian and Christological outlines of basic Christian truths imparted in catechetical instruction" 40). This is assuming quite a lot. No doubt, the trinitarian form of baptism had come in universal use at least during the second century 41), but a threefold questionnaire is hardly attested outside a fairly narrow circle of western witnesses 42). We do not know much about catechetical instruction in the

---

40) KELLY, 200.

41) Baptism in the name(s) of Father, Son and Holy Spirit, is attested to by *Didache*, 7, 3; *Kerygmata Petrou* in Ps.-CLEM., *Hom.* IX, 19, 4; XI, 26, 6, GCS 42, 141 and 167; JUSTINUS, *Apol.* I, 61, ed. GOODSPEED, 70f.; it is confirmed by evidence from Gnostic sects, such as the Valentinian wordings quoted by IRENAEUS, *Adv. Haer.*, I, 21, 3, ed. HARVEY, I, 183; cf. F. SAGNARD, *La Gnose valentinienne et le témoignage de saint Irénée*, Paris 1947, 423; CLEMENT OF ALEXANDRIA, *Excerpta ex Theodoto*, 76, 3, SChr 23, 200; 80, 3, p. 205. The evidence of Kretschmar, 35, for the persistance of one- or two-member forms in the second century, is extremely weak.

42) That some interrogation on the faith preceded baptism, seems self-evident from the time of the development of a catechumenate on (i.e. from around 150). But the content of such interrogations in early times cannot be established: the western interpolation in Acts 8, 37, suggests: JESUS THE SON OF GOD; JUSTIN, *Apol.*, I, 61, ed. GOODSPEED, 70, gives to understand that the catechumen's willingness to accept the commandments is one of the main subjects of the examination.
The first „Trinitarian questionnaire" is that found in Hippolytus. It should be noted, that Baptism by Trinitarian interrogation, as in Hippolytus, is attested to in fairly narrow circle: TERTULLIAN, quoted in note 35; CYPRIAN, *Ep.* 69, 7, ed. BAYARD, II, 244; *Council of Carthage*, 348, can. 1, ed. JONKERS, 74f. The witness of FIRMILIAN OF CESAREA, among the letters of CYPRIAN, *Ep.* 75, 10, 5, BAYARD, II, 298, is liable to suspicion, because Cyprian, in translating it, allows himself a large margin of liberty. The words of Dionysius of Alexandria, quoted by EUSEBIUS, *HE*, VII, 8, are ambiguous or suppose an interrogation preceding Baptism. Did Rome for centuries maintain this rite described by Hippolytus? The *Gelasian Sacramentary*, ed. WILSON, 86, which was compiled about 650, knows such a rite. One may suspect an archeologist's revival of an ancient rite. If Rome had, until the middle of the seventh century, continued to baptise according to the rite of Hippolytus with the interrogations at the immersion itself, it is hard to believe that no author would have commented upon it and that such a custom would not have left more traces in the liturgies and creeds of the West. Against this, the witness of MARTINUS OF BRAGA (above, note 10) should not be called on. In a small treatise of his on *The Threefold Immersion*, 2-3, ed. BARLOW, 256, he appears himself as an archeologist who called on Roman and Constantinopolitan customs and letters in order to justify his baptismal rite.
The first witnesses to a formal and public „rendering" of the Creed and to a „Trinitarian questionaire" are the instance of the baptism of Marius Victorinus and the Council of Laodicea (see note 11).

second and third century, but the one thing which is explicitly witnessed to is that the commandments were taught and the relationship between the Old and the New Testament exposed, two topics which do not enter into the Creeds. Kelly is right in stating with all modern scholars, that a Christological scheme embracing Birth - Passion - Resurrection - Ascension - Enthronement - Final Judgment, was in use; but the absence, in this summary of any allusions to the prophecies about Jesus, to his baptism, his teaching and his commandments hardly allows us to consider this scheme as an outline for catechetical instruction. Finally, even granted Kelly's assumptions, one does not see how a mere parallel development could result in such a wide consent in many articles and in the over-all construction of our Creeds: ONE GOD FATHER ALMIGHTY, MAKER OF . . ., ONE (or THE) LORD JESUS CHRIST, his dignity as FIRSTBORN and his role in creation, the constant mention of CHURCH and RESURRECTION, and the way articles 4-8 are grafted on to the threefold pattern. It was established that passages like 1 Cor 8, 6 and Mt 28, 19 were not at the root of those schemes (above p. 255).

The lastnamed point needs comment. By the familiarity with later Creeds we are so much accustomed to the grafting on of the Christological articles after the profession of Jesus Christ and before that of the Holy Spirit, that this seems quite natural. But the next section of our study will establish that, toward the end of the second century, this was by no means obvious. If, from that time on, all Creeds agree in the position of those articles [43]), a common root is indicated.

2° *This common root cannot be identified with any known or reconstructed Creed.* Three identifications of this common ancestor have been proposed.

Kattenbusch and Harnack thought to find it *in R itself.* After the deposition in 268 of the bishop of Antioch, Paul of Samosata, the church of Antioch would have adopted the Creed of Rome, adapting it to the local needs. From Antioch, it would have spread over the other churches of the East. But this supposes, as Kelly pointed out, that the antiochene adapters hacked about R in a way which defies any rational explication [44]). Moreover, as the next section will establish, creed-like summaries circulated in the East before the middle of the third century.

Lietzmann, by subtracting those points on which the Eastern Creeds vary, reconstructed a basic Eastern formula, inspired by 1 Cor: 8. 6; then, in the course of his studies, he gradually elevated this construction to the

---

[43]) The only apparent exception is the credal quotation of ALEXANDER OF ALEXANDRIA. But there can be no doubt that Alexander is juggling with the sequence of the articles. He writes: Along with Father and Son „we profess one Holy Spirit and one catholic Church and the resurrection of the dead, of which our Lord and Saviour became the hansel who vested himself with a body from Mary the Mother of God etc." (OPITZ, *Urk.* 15, p. 30). This is just too artificial ever to have been the construction of a Creed.

[44]) KELLY, 201f.; not all his arguments are equally well founded, but his reasoning is correct.

dignity of common ancestor to all Creeds of East and West [45]). But we already saw that the wording of the first article speaks against a direct inspiration by the pauline passage (above, p. 252). Moreover, in Lietzmann's theory, the roman bishop adapting this basic Creed would have excised the qualification ONE in the first and second article, the title LORD (but Lietzmann did not recognize that this title had ever been absent from the Roman Creed), the Son's role in creation [46]). Even if toward the end of the second century Creeds were not yet canonized and could be treated in a fairly cavalier way, even if the menace of Monarchianists and the confusion between DESPOTES as title of the Father and KYRIOS as that of Jesus Christ might render such surgical operations desirable, Lietzmann's theory demands too much, even of the most willful bishop.

Capelle, in his last article, agreed with Lietzmann that our longer Creeds were preceded by a shorter one of Trinitarian pattern. It would have run somewhat like this:

I believe in God the Father Almighty,
and in Jesus Christ, his Son,
and in the Holy Spirit, holy church, the resurrection of the flesh [47]).

In the course of the second century, a Christological summary which already was widely accepted (possibly, according to a suggestion of Kattenbusch and Lietzmann, in the setting of the anaphora and its prayer of thanksgiving), was gradually grafted on the second article of this basic Creed. Two strong points in favour of Capelle are that Creeds of more or less the type he postulates are in fact known, and that he takes seriously the absence of OUR LORD in the early Roman Creed, a fact which earlier scholars had bagatellized. Something like the process Capelle analyzes must have taken place. But he failed to explain two striking features of his reconstructed basic Creed: the absence of the qualification ONE with the name of God, and that of the title OUR LORD. Moreover, because of the scope of his article, he did not touch on the proper characteristics of the Eastern Creeds; and yet their agreements and divergencies as compared with the roman Creed are factors in the history of the latter.

Must we, in the end, despair of retracing the AC back to its original wording and setting? Perhaps an effort to analyze in more detail the text of R, H, and their Eastern counterparts, together with the study of precredal formulas will allow us to penetrate somewhat further into the mysterious birth history of the AC. This will be the subject matter of a further article, which for redactional reasons will appear not in the next, but in the following issue of this review.

---

[45]) LIETZMANN's successive studies, *Die Urform*, 184; *Symbolstudien III*, 194-212; *Symbolstudien XII*, 244, 281, show many fluctuations on this point. But in *Geschichte der alten Kirche*, ³II, 100-110, he seems to be quite sure of himself.

[46]) KELLY, 203f.

[47]) CAPELLE, 19; on the absence of OUR LORD and ONLY-BEGOTTEN in a Roman Creed of good standing about 200: CAPELLE, 13-14.

PROVISIONAL CONCLUSIONS

The results of this first part of our inquiry may be summed up as follows:
1. — The AC is less a doctrinal than a liturgical text. This is not weakened, but on the contrary confirmed by the way, the Latin Fathers made use of it in their doctrinal stand against Arianism.
2. — All Latin Creeds from the third century on stem from a common ancestor, which was nothing else than an pre-R Creed. Several indications may point to the last half of the third century as the period in which this borrowing from Rome took place.
3. — H does not exactly represent this pre-R. Hippolytus made some alterations in its wording. But since several of those alterations can, with a fair amount of probability, be identified, H may be used as a document in the history of R. Although the interrogatory form of H finds a perfect setting in the jewish antecedents of Christian baptism, weighty arguments speak for its derivation from a declaratory form.
4. — Pre-R lacked the qualification ONE with God and with SON, and also the profession OUR LORD.
5. — The Creeds of the East have some basic features in common with those of the West. These agreements cover all parts of the Creed. A common root must therefore be admitted, but it has as yet not been possible to identify it.
6. — On the other hand the Greek group distinguishes itself from the Latin one by a neat diversity in some fundamental features. Most of these characteristic Greek features appear in articles 1-3, and refer to Father and Son in their relationship to creation and to the pre-existence of Christ. This agreement of the Greeks among themselves is not adequately explained by the influence of 1 Cor: 8, 6.

Amsterdam, June 1970   P. SMULDERS

SOME RIDDLES IN THE APOSTLES' CREED

II. CREEDS AND RULES OF FAITH

An earlier article [1]) established that the Roman Church toward the middle of the third century possessed a Latin version of an originally Greek Creed, which enjoyed enough authority to serve as the model for the creation or reshaping of the other Creeds of the West. Its text can with sufficient certainty be reconstructed from three sources: the baptismal interrogations of Hippolytus (H), which however do not, as older studies often supposed, represent the main stem of Roman credal development, but a side branch; the Roman Creed of the fourth century (R), as found in Marcellus of Ancyra and Rufinus, which offers a later development; and the comparison with the other Latin Creeds, in use in the late 4th and 5th centuries in the various Churches of the West. The interpretation of those different sources is delicate. We applied by analogy one of the surest principles of textual criticism. There, whenever not the main stem, but only side branches are conserved, the *lectio difficilior*, if represented at least by one side branch and one later manuscript of independent tradition, is certain to be the original reading. If, in our subject for *lectio difficilior* one reads: the dogmatically less satisfying text, a safe rule is obtained: whenever a choice must be made between H and R, the less satisfying reading is certain to be the original reading of the pre-R Creed, if it turns up in one of the later Creeds.

Thus we were able to establish that around the middle of the 3d century the Roman Creed did for instance lack the adjective ONE with GOD, that the beginning of the second article simply ran: CHRIST JESUS THE SON OF GOD, without adding ONLY or ONLY-BEGOTTEN and without the title OUR LORD, and that the article REMISSION OF SINS had already established itself in the Creed of Rome [2]).

A first comparison of this pre-R Creed with the various 4th century Creeds of the Eastern Churches brought to light some conclusions which ran counter to the modern current of credal studies. Although there exists a clear dividing line between the Western and the Eastern groups, they have features in common which point to a common, although as yet unidentifiable root. A spontaneous parallel development as championed for instance by Kelly, does not fit the facts. Among the most characteristic features pointing to a common source are, besides the overall pattern of the Creeds, the basic

---

[1]) See: *Some Riddles in the Apostles' Creed*, in: Bijdragen 31 (1970) 234-260, quoted below as *Some Riddles* I. There the abbreviations used, the essential bibliography and documentation are listed: p. 234 f., 237 f., 250-254. I will frequently refer to the synoptic tables of the Latin and the Greek Creeds, printed p. 242 f., 252 f.

[2]) *Some Riddles* I, p. 244-247; p. 254.

threefold title given to the Father: GOD FATHER ALLSOVEREIGN, the way the Creeds address JESUS CHRIST, and profess his sonship by way of an apposition, and the highly standardized sequence of what may be called the Gospel Summary, from birth to second coming [3]). Those features, it was claimed, cannot be explained by the influence of Scripture passages such as the baptismal command in *Matthew* 28, 19 or the pauline confession of 1 *Cor* 8, 6 [4]). Those and similar facts point to a proper credal tradition. The identification of this credal tradition may shed definitive light on the original setting and meaning of the Creed. But, in order to bring out with greater clarity and certainty the existence and the nature of such a credal tradition, another line of argument imposes itself: a comparison between the Creeds on the one hand and on the other what by contemporary authors was called the „Rule of Faith" and similar documents. It is to this matter that the present article devotes itself. But by way of an introduction, another question must be considered.

1. The Origin of the AC, a false problem?

Hans Freiherr von Campenhausen, in a suggestive and stimulating paper read on April 27th 1971 before the Theology Department of the Vrije Universiteit of Amsterdam, concluded that the quest into the origins of the AC was on the wrong track [5]). The work of Von Harnack, Seeberg, Lietzmann and the other historians of the Creed started from false suppositions, in that they tried to discover the common ante-nicene sources of the different Creeds. According to this outstanding historian, before the Council of Nicea no authoritative and commonly accepted Creeds were in existence. Only the authority of Constantine imposed such a Creed on the Churches of the Empire. Of course, the Creed of Nicea did not simply drop from the skies. Two categories of factors had prepared it in the course of the foregoing centuries. On the one hand, the Churches knew what was called the *Kanon* or *Regula* of Faith. This was not any written text, but a commonly accepted summary of the main truths of Christianity. This Rule of Faith generally followed a triadic pattern inspired by the baptismal formula, and gave some elaboration on the christological theme along the familiar lines of birth, death and resurrection, enthronement and future coming. The paper established this theory by the example of Tertullian and other contemporary authors who, when referring to the Rule of Faith, follow a certain pattern, but allow themselves a fair margin of liberty with regard to the topics mentioned and the wordings used, according to the actual needs of their writings. On the other hand, there were in existence several Professions of Faith which, however, — and this is the

---

[3]) *Some Riddles* I, p. 254-259.
[4]) *Some Riddles* I, p. 254 f.
[5]) As the hoped for publication of this paper has not yet come to pass, I refer to my personal notes.

important novelty in Von Campenhausen's paper, — lacked any public authority, but were of a private character. Only insofar as their authors were widely known, such Professions of Faith could gain a wider circulation and a certain weight. As examples of such private Professions of Faith Von Campenhausen quoted the Creeds of Gregory Thaumaturgus or Lucian of Antioch. He explained the origin of such private Professions of Faith by means of what Origenes' *Discussion with Heraclides* [6]) reveals about the customs of his times. Frequently, Origen relates, when a difference of opinion about the faith arose, the accused were invited to put into writing a Profession of their faith, which was then subscribed by the accused and the bishop in the presence of the faithful [7]). The Professions of Faith prior to the Nicene Council were, according to Von Campenhausen, occasioned by this custom. They did not, therefore, enjoy more than an extremely limited validity, although, when composed by a famous and respected teacher, they might be widely circulated. Such would also have been the nature of the Creed written down by Eusebius of Cesarea. In order to placate the suspicions of Constantine and of his fellow bishops, the metropolite of Cesarea would have composed his personal Profession of Faith. When the Council of Nicea, on Constantine's initiative, the paper concluded, created its Creed by fusing into one several such private Professions of Faith, it introduced a fundamentally new kind of Creed: an authorized, public document which could serve as a touchstone of orthodoxy for the entire Church.

One may object Eusebius' own witness, who declares this Profession of Faith to have been the one on which he had been baptized and which as a bishop he had always taught [8]). But Von Campenhausen replied that this cannot be the meaning of Eusebius' words. If, he argued, Eusebius were speaking of the public Creed of his Church, he would not have felt the need to write it out in a letter to his faithful, who would have been perfectly familiar with it.

It is no small merit of the paper under discussion to have discerned the importance of Origenes' *Dialektos* for a proper understanding of credal history. Some of the more personal Professions of Faith ascribed to the ancient Fathers may well have originated in occasions such as described by Origen. Moreover the paper seems right in seeing the Creed of Nicea as a funda-

---

[6]) First published by J. Scherer, *Entretien d'Origène avec Héraclide et les évêques ses collègues sur le Père, le Fils et l'âme* (*Publications de la Société Fouad Ier de Papyrologie, Textes et Documents, 9*), Le Caire, 1949. We make use of the edition with translation edited by the same J. Scherer, in: SChr 67, Paris, 1960. The english translation by H. Chadwick, printed in: J. E. L. Oulton and H. Chadwick, *Alexandrian Christianity* (*The Library of Christian Classics, 2*), London, 1954, I did not have at my disposal.

[7]) Origen, *Entretien avec Héraclide*, 4, SChr 67, p. 62. Scherer, in his introduction, p. 16 ff., gives some more information on this custom, attested to mainly for the Churches of Arabia.

[8]) Eusebius of Cesarea, *Letter to his Church*, 3, ed. Opitz, *Athanasius' Werke*, III/1-2, Urk. 22, p. 43. On this Creed, see: *Some Riddles* I, p. 250 f.

mental innovation, not only in that it was destined for the entire Church and acquired, by the authority of the Emperor, a juridical validity, but above all in that it adopted some highly technical anti-arian pronouncements which made it into a touchstone of orthodoxy. Von Campenhausen's observations on the Rules of Faith need not retain us, because they run parallel to the commonly accepted conclusions of recent credal studies.

His main thesis, however, which denies the existence, before the Council of Nicea, of any authoritative public Creeds, even on diocesan or regional level, oversteps the mark and fails to explain a number of well established facts. To our intent it is of minor importance that his last argument is unconvincing. Eusebius, it should be noted, does not just quote his Creed for the information of his faithful, but he transcribes for their benefit the document he had submitted to the Emperor, and in this document the Creed in question, with a short dogmatic argumentation, was contained. Here, his quoting of their familiar Creed made excellent sense. In face of the rumors about his behavior spread in his Church, he justifies himself by showing that he had by no means compromised its traditional faith. Yet, it must be granted that Eusebius' words admit of the novel reading championed by Von Campenhausen, *if* one supposes that the Churches did not, before the Council of Nicea, know any publicly recognized and authoritative Creeds.

But this supposition is in contradiction with a number of well established facts, which, in part were exposed in the earlier article and, in part, will be discussed in the following paragraphs. Von Campenhausen, as a matter of fact must suppose that the remarkable affinity between the Creeds either must have come about only after the Council of Nicea, or is to be explained by the common Rule of Faith, or by that spontaneous parallel growth we found unacceptable in Kelly [9]). In comparing the various Rules of Faith with the Creeds, the following paragraphs will establish that there must have existed a credal tradition, proper to the Creeds, and not primarily related to the Rules of Faith. Here is. the place to discuss once more the chronology of the Creeds. We will first discuss the latin ones, than those of the East.

Although all our evidence on the Creeds of the West, with the one exception of Hippolytus, dates from the period after the Council of Nicea [10]), the earlier article suggested that the time in which the various Churches of the West adopted, with a certain liberty, the Roman model was to be sought somewhere in the second half of the 3d century [11]). Now Von Campenhausen forces us to take a better look at this timing.

The *terminus a quo* can be established by the means of two data. First, it must be after Hippolytus writing around 220. For, where in Hippolytus the article REMISSION OF SINS is lacking, it is found in all later Latin Creeds without any exception or hesitation. Second, it must be after the latinization

---

[9]) *Some Riddles* I, p. 257 f.
[10]) See the sources listed in: *Some Riddles* I, p. 237 f., note 10.
[11]) *Some Riddles* I, p. 244 f.

of the Roman Church. For, as the wording of the younger Latin Creeds shows, all of them stem from one identical rendering of the originally Greek text of the Creed of Rome [12]). This supposes that a standard rendering of it had already so solidly established itself in Rome, that it could be taken as an unquestioned model for the other Churches of the West. Now, such a degree of latinization of the Roman Church can hardly have been reached before the middle of the 3d century.

In face of Von Campenhausen's thesis, the *terminus ante quem* is of greater importance. He must suppose, as a matter of fact, that the borrowing from the Roman Creed took place only after the Council of Nicea, nobody conceiving of an authorized and public Creed before Constantine's innovation. One might generally point out the inner contradiction of his standpoint. No Creed existed before the Council of Nicea, yet after that Council and impelled by its example, no Church of the West adopted its Creed. But is it possible to determine the *terminus ante quem* with any precision?

Since all traces of the influence of Pre-R date from a later period, external evidence for the refutation of Von Campenhausen's theory is lacking. But the internal evidence is strong enough.

First, the Western Churches, especially those of Africa and Spain, could not have reshaped their local Creeds on the Roman model after the Council of Nicea. Moreover, by the time the Council's doctrine penetrated the West, those remodeled Creeds must have been deeply rooted in the local tradition of the various Churches.

The first argument is based on the fact that on the two central points of the Arian controversy the Pre-R Creed which served as the model for the different Latin Creeds was jejune to the extreme. Its profession of God kept its old simplicity and just said: GOD FATHER ALLSOVEREIGN. This can be established with complete certainty from the fact that most of its younger daughters retained just this wording. The adjective ONE is found only in Priscillian's Profession of Faith. Several Creeds, those of Africa and Arles and perhaps of Remesiana elaborate somewhat on the theme of creation, but then they use different formulas [13]). This is a conclusive argument for the absence of any such elaboration in the common ancestor. Is it by any means probable that after the Council of Nicea such an elementary Creed would have been considered a model to be imitated?

With regard to Christ's sonship the same reasoning is even more convincing. By any standard of Nicene orthodoxy, the pre-R Creed was highly deficient. It was absolutely reticent on the transcendent and eternal character of that sonship, but with Hippolytus just professed: CHRIST JESUS THE SON OF GOD. This appears once more from the comparison between the later Creeds [14]). Quite a few of them have only those words without any

---

[12]) *Some Riddles* I, p. 245, n. 25.
[13]) See the tables: *Some Riddles* I, p. 243.
[14]) See the tables: *Some Riddles* I, p. 243.

addition (Remesiana, Hippo, Carthage, Riez, Patrick). The other Creeds add ONLY-BEGOTTEN (Arles) or more commonly ONLY; but even here they vary in that the adjective either precedes or follows the word SON. This proves beyond doubt that their common ancestor lacked any such determination. And the conclusion imposes itself: after the Council of Nicea a Creed which was so very reticent on the great question of the day could not stand model.

One may object that it took some twenty or more years before the Churches of the West became aware of the Arian controversy and the Council of Nicea. Hilary of Poitiers confesses having learnt about it only in the fifties [15]), and Poitiers was no obscure outpost of the Church. This would leave several decades after 325 in which the Latin Churches, unaware of the storm raging in the Greek half of the Empire, could have shaped their Creeds on a definitely pre-nicene model. Once more, the contradiction is blatant. Under the influence of Constantine's novel conception of the Nicene Creed, the Churches would have adopted Creeds which completely ignored the Nicene issue! Moreover, it should be noted that, in whatever way the remodeling on the Roman example happened, it could hardly come about without the bishops of Rome on the one hand, and of Carthage or Cordoba on the other, being involved. And those bishops had, personally or by representatives, taken part in the Council. The remodeling, of course, should not be imagined as imposed by a decree of the Roman bishop. Such an image would be anachronistic, and it would have resulted in a far more thoroughgoing uniformity of the daughter-Creeds. But even if the remodeling was a more spontaneous move, it could hardly be achieved without the active collaboration of the bishops of Rome and the major sees in the provinces. And how could the Roman bishop, after the Council of Nicea, favour the diffusion of a Creed which was so very defective compared with the modern standard of orthodoxy? We may, therefore, conclude that the remodeling of the Creeds on the Roman example came about before the Council. This is the ultimate *terminus ante quem*.

I think, however, that the historian must go further back. Although the Churches of the West, at least from the forties on, — the Council of Serdica (343) and the accession to the monarchy of Constantius (350) are the turning points [16]), — were profoundly disturbed by the Arian controversy, their Creeds proved impermeable to the influence of that of Nicea. Only at a much later date, under the Byzantine domination, did Rome for a time abandon its traditional Creed in favour of the so-called Niceno-Constantinopolitanum [17]). This solid resistance against a penetration of the Nicene Creed seems to suppose that before the fourties the local Creeds remodeled on the Roman pattern were deeply rooted and solidly established in the local

---

[15]) HILARY of POITIERS, *De Synodis*, 91, PL 10, 545.
[16]) See: M. MESLIN, *Les Ariens d'Occident (Patristica Sorbonensia,* 8), Paris, 1967.
[17]) KELLY, p. 346-348.

traditions. To all probability, such a process would take at least two or three generations. This brings us back to the last half of the third century, which other arguments already suggested to us [18]. For the Churches of the West, therefore, an authoritative and public Creed was not an innovation of Constantine's: such Creeds were in existence several decades earlier.

As for the Churches of the East, this fact is more difficult to establish beyond any doubt. The 3d century Creed of Gregory Thaumaturgus may very well be a private document as postulated by Von Campenhausen; that of Lucian of Antioch [19] is subject to so many incertainties as not to provide any solid foundation; that of Eusebius is precisely under discussion. There is no direct evidence for the existence of authoritative Creeds in the East before the middle of the 4th century, and by that time it is not always easy to decide how much they are influenced by the Nicene Creed. Even so, a good case for the existence of official Creeds, long before the Council of Nicea, can be made. The main argument would run somewhat like this. The Creeds of the East, as known in the second half of the 4th century, present several layers of different antiquity: that of the pre-existence doctrine which might reflect the triumph of origenist orthodoxy on the point of Christ's sonship around the middle of the 3d century, and the older one of credal material they share with the West, such as the triple title GOD FATHER ALLSOVEREIGN, the way JESUS CHRIST is addressed and his sonship expressed by way of apposition, the Gospel summary, the mention of the CHURCH in the third main article. This then points to a long development. This argument can be confirmed by the existence, as early as the 2d century, of primitive Creedlike elements in different regions of the Eastern Church. But in order to be conclusive the argument supposes that such credal material was not, at a late date, borrowed from the Roman Church, as Kattenbusch and Von Harnack thought [20]), and above all that it was not derived from the Rule of Faith. Therefore a comparison between those Rules and the Creeds now imposes itself. From this comparison it will appear that the existence of a proper credal tradition must be admitted. Moreover this comparison will suggest that this credal tradition is older than the heyday of the Rules of Faith. If this can be established, not only the untenability of Von Campenhausen's thesis will be proven, but much more important: the contrast with the Rules of Faith will bring to light the characteristic nature of the Creeds.

Our comparison will proceed by two steps. In a first paragraph we will try to bring out what those Rules, when written down looked like; in the second the comparison between the Creeds and the Rules of Faith as to their subject matter will be made.

---

[18]) *Some Riddles* I, p. 245.
[19]) On this Creed, see *Some Riddles* I, p. 251, n. 6.
[20]) See: KELLY, p. 201 f.; *Some Riddles* I, p. 258.

2. The Rule of Faith

References to what they call the *Rule* (kanon, regula) of *Faith* [21]) or *Truth*, the *Ecclesiastical Rule*, sometimes the *Ecclesiastical Logos* or simply the *Kerygma* or the *Faith*, occur regularly in all major ecclesiastical authors from around the end of the 2d to the middle of the 3d century. Sometimes, this Rule of Faith covers what one would now call disciplinary matters, such as the apostolic tradition about the Easter date or the casuistic rules (largely derived from the Christian reading of the Bible) on forbidden foods [22]). But more often the Rule is quoted in a doctrinal context; it then refers to the orthodox faith and teaching, and is considered a guideline saveguarding against heretical aberrations. Of the last passages a few, under the heading *Ecclesiastical Rule* mention only one single, but fundamental and all-embracing hermeneutics principle, which separates Christian orthodoxy from all kinds of Gnostic schools, Marcionites and Jews, to wit the consent of the Old Testament with the New. It then refers both to the Christian's keeping in honour the Old Book, as against Gnostics and Marcionites, and to his reading it as a prophecy, typology or allegory of the new Christian reality. In this sense Clement of Alexandria wrote: ,,The ecclesiastical rule is the harmony and symphony of Law and Prophets with the Testament given us at the time of the Lord's presence [23])''. More often however the ancient writers, when

---

[21]) The fundamental study on the Rules of Faith remains: D. VAN DEN EYNDE, *Les normes de l'enseignement chrétien dans la littérature patristique des trois premiers siècles* (*Univ. Cath. Lov. Diss. Mag. Th.* Ser. II tom. 25), Gembloux, 1933, p. 282-313. See moreover: V. AMMUNDSEN, *The Rule of Truth in Irenaeus*, in: JThSt 13 (1912) 39-49; G. BARDY, *La Règle de Foi d'Origène*, in: RechScRel 9 (1919) 162-196; J. M. RESTREPO-JABAMILLO, *Tertuliano y la doble fórmula en el simbolo apostolico*, in: Gregor 15 (1934) 3-58; H. HOLSTEIN, *Les formules du Symbole du l'oeuvre de saint Irénée*, in: RechScRel 34 (1947) 454-461; A. BENOIT, *Saint Irénée, introduction à sa théologie* (*Et. d'Hist. et Phil. Rel.*, 52), Paris, 1960, p. 207-215; J. MOINGT, *Théologie trinitaire de Tertullien* (*Théologie*, 68), vol. I, Paris, 1966, p. 66-86; R. CH. BAUD, *Les <règles> de la théologie d'Origène*, in: RechScRel, 55 (1967) 161-209.

The question of the role of the Rules is discussed in most modern studies on Tradition, such as: E. FLESSEMAN-VAN LEER, *Tradition and Scripture in the Early Church*, Assen, 1954, p. 125 ff., 161 ff; H. E. W. TURNER, *The Pattern of Christian Truth*, London, 1954, p. 348-378; H. HOLSTEIN, *La tradition dans l'Eglise*, Paris, 1960, p. 70-76; J. BEUMER, *Die mündliche Überlieferung als Glaubensquelle* (*Hdb. d. DG*, I/4), Freiburg, 1962, p. 32; R. P. C. HANSON, *Tradition in the Early Church*, London, 1962, p. 75-129; Y. CONGAR, *La tradition et les traditions*, 2 vol., Paris, 1960-1963, I, p. 44 ff., with the references, p. 95 ff.

[22]) Polycrates of Ephesus (ca. 190), *Letter to Victor of Rome*, quoted by Eusebius, HE, V, 24, 6: Easter date.

NOVATIAN, *De cibis iudaicis*, 7, PL 3, 964: ,,Quorum ciborum rations perspecta (. ,. by weighing the meaning of the Old Covenant and the Gospel, the demands of temperance and the defilement of sacrificial foods) regulam veritatis per omnia custodientes...''

[23]) CLEMENT OF ALEXANDRIA, *Strom.*, VI, 15, 126/3, GCS 52, p. 495. The same meaning underlies the title of a lost work of Clement's: ,,The ecclesiastical rule or against the Judaizants''. (Eusebius, HE VI, 13, 3).

The harmony of both Testaments as Rule of Faith already in Irenaeus, *Adv. Haer,*, II, 25, 2 Harvey I, p. 343; cfr. 27, 1, p. 348; 28, 3, p. 352; and later in Origen, *Comm. Joh.*, V, fragm. from Philokalia, PG 14, 196.

referring to the Rule, present some kind of summary of the basic Christian doctrine. Such summaries, especially in Irenaeus and Tertullian, resemble so much to what soon would be called a *Symbolum* or Creed, that older students did hardly distinguish between both kinds of documents, and freely made use of the various Rules in reconstructing the Creeds. The resulting confusion has not yet been completely cleared, and persists especially in German studies [24]). To my knowledge, the first to draw a line of demarcation was Damiaan van den Eynde, in his classical work on the norms of Christian teaching in the early Fathers. Later studies have confirmed and more solidly established the distinction, but the precise nature of the Rule of Faith has not yet been defined without ambiguity. For our present purpose it is superfluous to enter into the much debated questions on the nature and authority of the Rule of Faith. Did the 2d and 3d century authors, when speaking about the Rule of Faith, primarily think of a fundamental hermeneutical principle, a basic insight and general viewpoint, or on the other hand of a ,,series of ideas" [25]) and some more or less vaguely defined and solidly established ,,body of doctrine" [26])? How about its authority and its relation to Scripture, Tradition or the teaching ministry?

A consideration of the contents of the written Rules will be sufficient, and, it is hoped, enlightening for a comparison with the Creeds. By its very nature, a Rule of Faith was not, by itself, an established text. Even in one and the same author it could take widely different forms, according to the preoccupations or necessities of the moment. Yet, whenever the writers of the time felt the need to put it down in writing, they were inclined to follow certain patterns, which enabled them to organize somewhat the fundamental articles of Christian teaching. It is, therefore, possible to get a general view of the contents of those written down Rules. This study of the contents has been

---

[24]) See for instance the contributions of both O. Cullmann and K. Aland, in: *Das Neue Testament als Kanon*, hrsg. E. Käsemann, Göttingen, 1970, p. 105 f. and 146 respectively. Also N. Brox, *Altkirchliche Formen des Anspruchs auf apostolische Kirchenverfassung*, in: Kairos 12 (1970) 113-140, especially p. 138 n. 93. In this context of German thought, Von Campenhausen's paper (above p. 351) was a discovery indeed!

[25]) The words are of E. Evans, whose characterization of Creeds and Rules of Faith, even if heavily exaggerated, illustrates the general trend: ,,The Rule of Faith ... is not the same thing as the Creed. The Creed is a liturgical document ... It was a jealously guarded form of words: in different Churches ... verbal details might differ; but in the same Church verbal accuracy was insisted on. It was a very brief document ... The Rule of Faith is not a form of words but a series of ideas, a guide for teachers rather than a test of the neophyte's faith" (Tertullian, *Treatise against Praxeas*, London, 1948, p. 189). By now, the reader knows what to think about the ,,verbal accuracy" in the Creeds and their role as ,,tests of the neophyte's faith". As for the Rules, they were not so much longer, and that they were meant as a guide for teachers is in direct contradiction with the most outspoken declarations about their function: the faithful received it through baptism (Irenaeus, *Adv. Haer.*, I, 9, 4, Harvey I, p. 88) and even the Barbarians kept it (ibid. III, 4, 2, vol. II, p. 16).

[26]) Irenaeus, *Adv. Haer.*, I, 9, 4, Harvey I, p. 89; II, 27, 1, p. 347; Origenes, *De Princ.*, I, praef., 10, GCS 22, p. 16. See, on Irenaeus' use of the expression ,,body of truth": E. Scharl, *Recapitulatio Mundi; der Rekapitulationsbegriff des hl. Irenäus (Freib. Th. Stud., 60)*, Freiburg, 1941, p. 2 Anm. 3.

sadly neglected, probably because scholars were more interested in the formal aspects of those Rules, such as their nature and authority. For our purpose, however, a provisional study of their contents is indispensable for several reasons. First, their contents provide some background to the Creeds by establishing what, in the eyes of the contemporaries, were the „major doctrines" as Origen calls them [27]), the fundamental teachings on which the orthodox Christian's life, faith and hope were built. Second, the study of the contents of the Rules may help to distinguish what may be considered as strictly credal material and tradition, proper to the Creeds. Finally, by comparison, and sometimes by contrast, this study may shed some light on the intentions, the setting and the meaning of the Creeds.

The following table therefore, endeavours to give an overall view of the pattern and the contents of all summaries which by their authors are called or by their setting appear to be a „Rule of Faith". For reasons, which will be obvious to a reader of those tables, some documents of a different kind have been added, such as Justin Martyr's paraphrase of the baptismal rite, the fragment from the closing chapter of Melito's *Homily* and the final doxology of the *Didascalia*. The first texts are added, because they resemble the well known First Mandate of Hermas: „First of all, believe that God is one" [28]), and so illustrate the transition from Jewish to Christian professions of faith. One may hesitate about the passage from 1 *Clem.* This may be only an adaptation of the pauline *Eph* 4, 3-6, but, even so by the way it continues the One God profession by pointing to the Christian way of life, it closely resembles the texts of Polycarp and Hermas, and the Jewish professions of faith. On the other hand, the several christological professions of Ignatius of Antioch, studied by Crehan [29]), are left out; although highly important for the development of christological summaries, their very character would demand a fuller and complicated study, out of proportion with the results they promise for the study of the Creeds and Rules as such.

The table brings out, first to what category the text belongs: is it a commandment, in the manner of Hermas' first Mandate, a Rule of Faith, a paraphrase of Baptism, or a doxology or other prayer-like text? Second, its general pattern. Here two questions may be distinguished: first, is the text what one may call „monarchical", in that the whole is directly a profession of God, or „dyadic", *viz* built on the scheme God — Christ, which does not always exclude an explicit mention of the Holy Spirit, or trinitarian? Second, how is the Gospel summary inserted: either in the familiar way (not noted in the tabels), or as the deeds of God, or as foretold by the Holy Spirit inspiring the prophets? For a few of our texts, especially for that of Justin Martyr, seemingly credal topics and expressions found elsewhere in his works are noted, mainly for later reference, but also because they manifest a surprising degree of standardization.

---

[27]) Origen, *Matt. Comm. Ser.*, 33, GCS 38, p. 61.
[28]) Hermas, *Mandata* I, 1, n. 26, Apost. Fathers, vol. VI, p. 63.
[29]) J. CREHAN, *Early Christian Baptism and the Creed*, London, 1950, p. 49.

Sources used in the table

1. — 1 *Clem.*, 46, 6, SChr 167, p. 176. Clement, taking up ideas of the pauline corpus, opposes the divisions at Corinth with the unity of God's grace.

2. — Polycarp, *Ad Philipp.*, 2, 1, SChr 10 bis, p. 204. Polycarp develops the first commandment of God's service by recalling the Christian's moral duties, much as Hermas does. But, in contrast with Hermas, he adroitly inserts a Christological confession in the following way: „Serve God who has raised up our Lord etc." and by continuing, after the mention of the final judgment, with the words: „Who will also raise us if we do his will . . ."

3. — *Kerygmata Petrou*, as contained in Ps-Clem., *Hom.*, II, 45-46, GCS 42, p. 53 f, and quoted by Clement of Alexandria, *Strom.*, VI, 5, 39, 2, GCS 52, p. 451. Another development of the first commandment of the Law, the setting of which cannot be determined.

4. — Justin Martyr, *Apology* I, 61, 1-13, Goodspeed, p. 70 f. His famous description of baptism and paraphrase of the baptismal formula. We add references to other passages of the *Apology* and the *Dialogue with Trypho* (D), which attest Justin's familiarity with expressions which later will turn up in Rules and Creeds.

5. — Justin Martyr, *Acts of Martyrdom*, 2, 5, Knopf-Krüger, *Ausgewählte Märtyrerakten*, ³1929, p. 15 f. Justin's answer to the judge's interrogation: What kind of opinion is this?

6. — Melito of Sardes, *Paschal Homily*, 104, SChr 123, p. 124; part of the same sequence in n. 70, p. 98. Towards the close of his homily, Melito sums up the mystery of Christ in a sequence of short sentences, which is of the highest importance in credal history, but hitherto neglected.

7-12. — The various summaries, found in Irenaeus, most of them qualified by him as „Rules of Truth": *Adv. Haer.*, I, 10, 1, Harvey, I, p. 90; 22, 1, p. 188 f; III, 4, 2, vol. II, p. 16; III, 16, 5-6, p. 87; IV, 33, 7, p. 261 f; V, 20, 1, p. 378. This is the „Faith", which the Church received from the apostles, which she confesses „as with one mouth" over the whole earth (I, 10, 1-2, p. 90 ff), which through baptism she imparts to her children (I, 9, 4, p. 88), who conserve it written on their hearts' tables (III, 4, 2, vol. II, p. 16).

13. — Irenaeus, *Demonstratio Apostolicae Praedicationis*, 6, SChr 62, p. 39 f; cfr. n. 3, p. 32. What he calls a „systematic instruction of our faith", subdivided in three „articles".

14. — Clement of Alexandria, *Strom.*, VI, 15, 127, 1, GCS 52, p. 496. A short christological summary, contained in an exposition on the hidden prophecy in Scripture. This explains the strange pattern, and may make one suspect a fragmentary character.

15. — Origen, *De Princ.*, I, praef., 4-5, GCS 22, p. 9-11. His summary of the basic truths which are without ambiguity taught by the apostolic preaching.

16-19. — Several summaries found in Origin's exegetical works: *Comm. Joh.,* XXXII, 16, 187-193, GCS 10, p. 451 f; *Hom. Jer.,* 5, 13, GCS 6, p. 42; *Fragm. in 1 Cor.,* 4, ed. Jenkins, in: JThSt 9 (1908) 234; *Matt. Comm. Ser.,* 33, GCS 38, p. 60 f. The *Comm. Joh.,* which begins by quoting Hermas' first Mandate, and the *Matt. Comm. Ser.,* in their setting resemble the preface to *De Princ.*

20. — Origen, *Contra Cels.,* I, 7, GCS 2, p. 60 f. A few standard credal expressions found in Origen's defence against the accusation of being esoteric.

21. — Origen, *Dialektos with Heraclides,* 1, SChr 67, p. 53 f. The accused, on the demand of the bishops present, professes his faith in Christ. The titles given to God, are found in Origen's interrogation of Heraclides.

22-24. — Hippolytus, *Fragment against Noetus,* 1; 4; 8; ed. Nautin, *Hippolyte, Contre les Hérésies,* p. 235 f, 241 f, 249. The first text is the profession the presbyters of Smyrna opposed against Noetus; the last is Hippolytus' own summary.

25-28. — Tertullian, *De Praescr.,* 13, 1-6, CCL 1, p. 197 f; 36, 5, p. 217; *De Virg. Vel.,* 1, 3, CCL 2, p. 1209; *Adv. Praxeam,* 2, 1, p. 1160. The several „Rules" which Tertullian considers as originating from the Apostles' preaching and from Christ himself.

29. — Novatian, *De Trinitate,* I, 1; IX, 46; XXIX, 163 ed. Weyer, p. 34, 74, 182. Broaching the subject of the Father and the Son respectively, Novatian begins: „The Rule of Truth demands . . ." As to the Holy Spirit, „the order of reason and the authority of faith" demand that we believe in him also.

30. — *Didascalia,* VI, 12, 1, Funk, p. 326; c. XXIV, Achelis-Flemming, p. 122. This Church Order, compiled around the middle of the 3d century, probably in Syria, here pretends to give the catholic doctrine as laid down by the Apostles when last gathered in Jerusalem. The passage is lost in the Latin translation; its authenticity is guaranteed by its exploitation by *Const. Apost.,* VI, 14, 1-5, Funk, p. 336 f(!).

31. — *Didascalia,* VI, 23, 8, Funk, p. 382; c. XXVI, Achelis-Flemming, p. 145; § 64, Tidener, p. 103. In the final doxology of the book a christological confession is interwoven. The text is conserved in the latin version only, and one might suspect the influence of the translator's latin Creed, if the *Apost. Const.* (Funk ibid.) did not guarantee it.

See annex, p. 361a-361d.

Leaving the various titles given to God and Christ for the comparison, in the next paragraph, between Rules and Creeds, we here limit ourselves to a short comment on the main patterns of the Rules summarized in those tables. Three questions may be considered.

1. — *Monarchical, two member and trinitarian Rules.* The tables show a marked predilection for a trinitarian pattern. Yet, after Clement's elaboration on the first commandment (n. 1), which may be directly inspired by such pauline formulas as *Eph* 4, 3-6, and Justin Martyr's paraphrase of the baptismal rite (n. 4), it is only with Origen and Novatian that this pattern comes to dominate to the exclusion of other patterns.

The *Kerygmata Petrou* present a monarchical Rule (n. 3), which differs from traditional Jewish confessions only in the explicit profession of God's eschatological, achieving act. Polycarp's exhortation to keep to the faith in God who raised up and glorified Our Lord (n. 2) is also basically monarchical. While the glorification sequence, which will retain us in the comparison with the Creeds, is fully developed, the steps of Christ's glorification, with the exception of the last member, are professed as God's mighty deeds. Traces of this archaic approach may be found in the passive tense in which Christ's resurrection and ascension are expressed in later Rules, especially in Tertullian (n. 27, 28). An exceptional type of monarchical Rule is found in one of Irenaeus' passages (n. 8), which mentions the Word and Spirit as the instruments of God's activity in creation and salvation.

A two member formula is more common: One God and Jesus Christ with the incarnation sequence. So Justin Martyr before his judge (n. 5), Irenaeus in two of his Rules (n. 9, 10), the professions of faith of both Heraclides (n. 21) and the Smyrnean presbyters (n. 22) and two Rules of Tertullian's (n. 26, 27).

A trinitarian pattern is found as early as Clement of Rome (n. 1), and gradually becomes the rule. The development in both Irenaeus and Tertullian would merit a detailed study, because one can discover there a series of attempts to combine organically a trinitarian with a two member formula. Irenaeus' first Rule (n. 7) is basically trinitarian, and introduces the christological sequence under the heading: the Holy Spirit prophecied the birth etc. of Christ. From a literary point of view this is quite satisfactory. But theologically it has two major setbacks: the economy of salvation, the kernel of the Chistian message, is mentioned in an indirect way only, and the Holy Spirit is professed only in his prophecying, pre-christian activity. In the two following Rules, therefore, Irenaeus inserts the christological sequence in its traditional and natural place, even if this results in silence about the Holy Spirit. Thereafter, he takes up once more the trinitarian pattern. But he must have felt the need to bring out better the Spirit's role. First (n. 11), he turns to a rare word (σκηνοβατέω = bring on the stage, exhibit publicly), which was able to embrace the entire gamut of the Spirit's work: revealing the future to the prophets, realizing the incarnation, illuminating the believers. Later (n. 12), he professes the gift of the Spirit only. Finally, the *Epideixis* (n. 13)

	1 1 Clem. 46, 6	2 Polyc. 2, 1 cfr. 7, 1; 9, 2	3 Ker. Petrou	4 Justin M., Ap. I 61 cfr. 13; 21; 67; Dial. 30; 63; 132	5 Just. Acta Mart. 2, 5
C(ommand), R(ule), B(aptismal), P(rayer)	C	C	C	B	R
Pattern	trinit.	monarch. Christology dependent from God	monarch.	trinit.	
	One God	God	One God	God	One
				Father	
				of all	
			Creator and Judge	(Creator: Ap. 13; 67)	Creator
	One Christ	Our Lord Jes. Chr.		(his Son: Ap. 67) D. 132 Jesus Christ our Saviour (teacher: Ap. 13; 21)	Lord Jesus Christ Gods παῖς teacher
					foretold
		(come in flesh: 7, 1)		(born from the Virgin: Ap. 46; D. 63)	
		(died for us: 7, 1)		crucified Ap. 13; 21; 46; 61 D. 30; 63; 132 under Pontius Pilate Ap. 13; 61; D. 30	
		God raised him		(rose: Ap. 21; 46; D. 63; 132)	
		gave him glory		(ascended into heavens: Ap. 21; 46; D. 63; 132)	
		gave him throne			
		He will come to judge living and dead		(future coming to judge: D. 132)	
	One Holy Sp.			H. Spirit who foresaid the events of Jesus	
	given us				
	one vocation				
		future judg- ment and resurr. (cfr. 9, 2)	God achiever		

187

6	7	8	9	10 Irenaeus	11	12	13
Melito Hom. Pasch 104 cfr. 69-70	A.H. I 10	A.H. I 22, 1	A.H. III. 4,2	A.H. III 16, 6	A.H. IV, 33. 7	A.H. V, 20. 1	Epid. 3: cfr. 6
P	R (cfr. 9. 4)	R	R		R		R
christolog.	trinitar. Christology dependent from H. Spir.	monarch. Christol. and Pneumatol. dependent from God	dyadic	dyadic	trinitar.	trinitar.	trinitar.
							Unique
	One God	One God	One God	Truely God	One God	One God	God
							Father
	Father	[Father of O Lord J. Chr.]		[Father]		Father	
	Allsovereign	Allsovereign			Allsovereign		Creator
	Creator	Creator through God of Abraham ecc.	Creator		from whom all things		
				only begotten Word Jes. Christ	the Son of God Jes. Christ	the Son of God	the Word, the Son of God Jes. Christ our Lord
	One Christ Jesus Son of God [our Lord]	his Word and	Christ Jesus Son of God	[Son of God] our Lord	our Lord		
who made all things					through whom all things		through whom all things
foretold	[foretold]			always present			who appeared to the prophets
incarnated in Virgin	become man		born from the Virgin	from Mary	his economy incarnation	economy of incarn.	become man born from men
crucified	[his passion]		suffered under P.P.	suffered for us			death
buried							
rose	[resurrection]		rose	rose for us			life
taken up into heavens	[taking up]		taken up in glory				
sits on right hand of F							
judge and saviour	[future coming to judge]		future coming as saviour and judge	future coming as saviour and judge		future coming	
						one gift of	
	H. Spirit who foresaid the economy	his Spirit			H. Spirit who manifests the economy	H. Spirit	H. Spirit who prophecied and
							is given
	resurrection			judgment	salvation of body and soul		

188

14 Clem., Str. VI.15	15 Orig.. Pr. I R	16 Comm. Jo XXXII R	17 Origenes H. Jer. 5,13	18 Fr. 1 Cor. R	19 Mt. Com. S. 33 R	20 C. Cels., I, 7
God Father mentioned in dependence of Christol.	trinitar.	trinitar.	trinitar.	trinitar. Economy after H. Spirit	trinitar.	
[God]	One God	One God			One God	
			Father	Father		
[Creator]	Created from nothing					
	God of the justs	[of law and Gospel]			who gave Law and Gospel	
the Lord the Son of God			the Son	the Son		
	Christ Jesus born from Father served the Father God	Jes. Christ Lord			Christ Jesus first born of creation	
		Godhead and manhood				
fore told					foretold	
incarnated in Virgin	become man from Virgin and Holy Spirit	born from Virgin and Holy Spirit		his economy	true man born from Virgin	birth from Virgin
suffered	truely suffered and died	crucified under P. P.			death on the cross	crucified
rose	rose				rose	resurrection
					deified	
	taken up					
	[judgment] (cfr. III, 1, 1	[judgment]	[judgment]	[judgment]		
	the same Spirit in prophets and apostles	H. Spirit	H. Spirit	H. Spirit	the same H. Spirit in patriarchs, prophets and apostles	
	(Old and New Testament) man's responsibility ... judgment and resurrection ...		Old and New Testament resurrection judgment	resurrection judgment	resurrection	judgment

189

21 Heraclides Dial. 1	22 1	23 Hippolyt., C. Noetum 4	24 8	25 Praescr. 13	26 Tertullian Praescr. 36	27 Virg. Vel. 1
R	R		R	R	R	R
christological	dyadic		trinitar.	dyadic H. Spirit in Christology	dyadic	dyadic
[God]	One God		Father God	One God	One God Lord	One God
[Allsovereign]			Allsovereign			Almighty
[Creator]				Created through	Creator of all	Creator of the world
the Word		Word	Christ Jesus			
	Christ Son of God	Son of God	Son of God God	Word Son [become Jesus Chr.]	Christ Jesus [Son of God]	his Son Jesus Chr.
through whom all things						
				who appeared to the patriarchs		
took flesh born		from H. Spirit and Virgin	become man	who by the Spirit of God descended in Virgin born preaching	from Virgin Son of God	born from Virgin
	suffered died			miracles		
				crucified		crucified under P. P.
	rose on third day			rose on third day		raised
ascended into heavens	ascended into heavens			taken up into heavens		taken up
sits on right hand of Father	sits on right hand of F.			sits on right hand of Father sent H. Spirit		sits on right hand of Father
future coming as judge of living and dead	future coming as judge of living and dead			future coming as saviour and judge		future coming to judge living and dead
			H. Spirit (who mani- fested: 14)	[H. Spirit]		
				who moves the faithful		
				resurrection of body and soul	Old and New Testament	resurrection of the flesh

28 Adv. Prax. 2	29 Novat., Trin. c. 1, 9, 29	30 Didasc., VI. 12, 1	31 Didasc., VI 23
R	R	R	P
trinitar. (monarch.- dyadic)	trinitar.	trinitar.	Christological dyadic
Only God	God	God	
	Father and Lord Almighty	Allsovereign	
Son Word	Son of God Christ Jesus Our Lord God	Jesus his Son Christ	Jesus Christ the Nazorean
through whom all things God and man			
sent into Virgin born			
suffered died buried			crucified under P. P. „dormivit"
raised			rose
taken up			taken up by God's power and Spirit
sits on right hand of Father			sits on right hand of Father
future coming to judge			coming to judge living a. dead
who sent the			
H. Spirit Paraclete Sanctifier	H. Spirit promised	H. Spirit	
	given		
		Old and New Testament resurrection use of creatures and marriage	

[...] The words are read in this passage, but not at the point where indicated

(...) The words are not in the passage quoted, but elsewhere

191

settles for two attributes: inspiration of the prophets and gift to the faithful. A similar effort seems to underlie Tertullian's Rules. That of *De Praescr.* (n. 25) is basically a two member Rule, and professes the Holy Spirit only within the christological sequence, and then in its chronological order: between his enthronement and second coming, Christ sent the Holy Spirit as his caretaker. But this inclusion of the Holy Spirit in the framework of the christological sequence is unsatisfying, because it gives little relief to his role and name. So, after two Rules in which, as Irenaeus, Tertullian falls back on the two member pattern (n. 26, 27), he returns to his earlier profession: Christ sent the Spirit (n. 28). But now he abandons the chronological order in such a way that this sending of the Holy Spirit is the last member of the christological sequence. This enables him to close on a final chord which accentuates the role of the Holy Spirit, paraclete and sanctifier. Whatever part must here be ascribed to Tertullian's Montanism, there can be no doubt but that, as Irenaeus, he is groping for a way to put a trinitarian in line with a two member profession of faith.

2. — *The Christological Sequence.* This sequence can sometimes be reduced to a single word: his dispensation (n. 11, 12, 18), sometimes it mentions only Christ's birth, death and resurrection (n. 13; Clement and Origen, n. 14-20), but even such short sequences most of the time profess his future coming. But most Rules have a fully developed six or seven member Christological profession, running from the Virgin birth to the second coming. As in the Creeds (*Some Riddles* I, p. 255), this sequence shows a remarkable stability. No alien matters are taken up: Tertullian's attempt (n. 25) to insert a profession of Christ's teachings, miracles and sending of the Spirit was abortive. This sequence may be abridged, but not added to. This pleads for the highly traditional character of this Gospel summary, and especially of the glorification sequence. The matter will be further discussed in the comparison between Creeds and Rules.

In contrast with its contents, the place of the Gospel summary in a trinitarian confession was not, as yet, completely settled. This is manifest from Irenaeus' attempt to make it dependent on the profession of the Holy Spirit, and seems to be confirmed by Justin Martyr's testimony. In his paraphrase on baptism, only the crucifixion under Pontius Pilate is mentioned; but the way he quotes on various occasions different combinations of several members of the Gospel summary is sufficient proof that he knew this summary as a whole.

3. — As compared with the Creeds, the absence of any mention of the Church is striking. Even more remarkable is the importance, in the Rules, of the *harmony of the Old with the New Testament.* This doctrine was very much in the limelight in 2d century apologetics and controversies. In the dialogue with the Jews it established that Christ was the one prophecied, in that with the Pagans, the venerable age of the Christian message. And the controversy with all kinds of Gnostics and the Marcionites demanded a de-

monstration of the identity of the God Creator of this world and Lawgiver of the Jews with the Father of Jesus Christ. Above all, this doctrine was essential for the Church's internal life, because it commanded the Christian reading of the Bible.

But the expression of this doctrine could take widely different forms. It could turn up under the chapter on the Father, who created and will achieve the world (*Kerygmata Petrou*, n. 3), who already was the God of the saints of old (Irenaeus, n. 8; Origen, n. 15), and who is the God of both the Law and the Gospel (Origen, n. 16, 19). Although it is impossible to decide, what the „One God" profession meant precisely in the Rules, — an abjuration of polytheism, or as in hellenistic acclamations, the profession of the God who is unique, or the identity between Jahweh of old and the Father of Christ, — this last meaning is probably frequently understood. Another form of the same doctrine is the teaching that Christ has been foretold (Justin Martyr, n. 5; Melito, n. 6; Irenaeus, n. 7; Clement of Alex., n. 14; Origen, n. 19), that he was the servant of God in the whole course of history (Origen, n. 15), or that he was present and appeared to patriarchs and prophets (Irenaeus, n. 10, 12; Tertullian, n. 25). The doctrine of the harmony of both Testaments may also be connected with the Holy Spirit, who prophecied the incarnation (Justin Martyr, n. 4; Irenaeus, n. 7; 11; 13), inspired both the prophets and the apostles (Origen, n. 15; 19), is the same gift (Irenaeus, n. 12), once promised, now given to the Church (Novation, n. 29). Finally, several of our authors make an independent article of the harmony between the Old and New Testaments and of the Christian's duty to keep the old Book (Origen, n. 15; 17; Tertullian, n. 26; *Didascalia*, n. 30).

Quite a few of the Rules, beginning with Polycarp (n. 2), wind up by professing the final *resurrection and judgment*, although they had already professed Christ's future coming as the judge of the living and dead. Sometimes, this profession of the final achievement is turned against the widespread Dualism of the times (Irenaeus, n. 12; Tertullian, n. 25; 27; *Didasc.*, n. 30), sometimes, as in Origen, it serves to underline man's free will and responsibility, as against fatalistic tendencies (Origen, n. 15; 16).

3. Conclusion

The century preceding the taking shape of the Roman Creed around the middle of the 3d century was a period of a surprising fertility and fermentation in the field of Rules of Faith. Most major theologians of the times found occasion to refer to the Rule and put it in writing. Those authors who, like Irenaeus, Tertullian or Origen, wrote down a Rule at different occasions offer abundant proof that the Rule, to them, was nothing like an official text or even an official summary of the fundamental orthodox teaching. One and the same author could produce either a markedly trinitarian Rule or one which did not even mention the Holy Spirit. It is only with Origen that the trinitarian pattern does not admit of any exception. The same variability is seen in the christological summaries: they could, in one and the same author embrace a long list of members, or mention only the Virgin birth, the death and resurrection, or just profess Christ's salvific work. In other words, those Rules were private compositions, composed according to the actual interests and perhaps whims of their authors.

Yet there is no doubt that those various Rules spring from a shared conviction of what Christianity was about. First, the One God profession, with a few varations such as ,,Truely God'' (Irenaeus, n. 10), always is the starting point: the only exceptions are two of Origen's Rules where he almost completely falls back on the simple baptismal formula (they are also the only ones which have the Fathername only, and not that of God) (n. 17, 18). With very few exceptions, God is explicitly confessed to have created the world, though only once in the wording ¡of 1 Cor 8, 6 (n. 11). With the one exception of the *Kerygmata Petrou* all Rules continue by professing Jesus Christ, but after Justin Martyr there is a very marked tendency to profess him as the Word and/or Son of God before his incarnate name. Here also it is noteworthy that the pauline title ,,One Lord Jesus Christ'' of 1 Cor 8, 6 is not found even once. With only one exception in Origen (n. 17) a profession of the dispensation of salvation follows. This closes regularly on Christ's future coming as the eschatological judge, and the profession of the final judgment and/or resurrection is the final chord of the Rule. Although a profession of the Holy Spirit is part of most of the Rules, it can be absent, and his attributes can vary; his prophecying the mystery of the incarnation is the most frequently mentioned. From Justin Martyr's *Acts* on, the harmony of the Old with the New Testament is, in some way or other, regularly professed.

It seems apparent that the New Testament texts, which by most scholars are considered the starting points of the credal development did not play any such role with regard to the Rules. Of 1 Cor 8, 6 only the words ,,One God'' are regularly found in the Rules, and those words could originate as well from the Jewish confessions. Nor does the baptismal command of *Matthew* 28, 19 appear as the fountain head of the Rules. The invocation of the three names at baptism strongly favoured the trinitarian pattern, as is apparent already in Justin Martyr (n. 4) and in Origen, whose Rule could at times be almost reduced to the baptismal formula. But this influence was secondary and it found a tradition already firmly established. This is manifest from the facts that the name ,,Father'', in the Rules, definitely cedes pride of place to that of ,,One God'', and that the place of the Holy Spirit is by no means secured. Most of the single articles, read in the Rules, have of course their parallels in the New Testament, and their wording is generally inspired by or even derived from Scripture.

But the Rules as a whole are a different affair. Taken generally, they present a fairly clear basic pattern, which embraces: One God — Creator — Jesus Christ and his dispensation of salvation — Final Judgment and/or Resurrection — and, interwoven in the whole, the Harmony of the Old and New Testaments. To this general pattern, it is not easy to find any clear-cut parallel in the New Testament literature. The nearest parallels might be found in such relics of archaic preaching as 1 *Thess* 1, 9 f. or *Acts* 3, 13 ff. That the origin of the Rules is to be sought in that ambiance could be confirmed by an, at first sight, surprising feature of our oldest Rule-like text, that of Polycarp (n. 2): the passion and death of Christ is not mentioned, and the christological sequence begins with God's raising him. Now, something of the kind occurs in both New Testament passages. It seems therefore that the basic pattern of the Rules points to a highly archaic scheme of kerygmatic preaching.

This primitive pattern was soon enriched by a fusion with a trinitarian sequence, which also goes back to the early Christian origins (see for instance 1 *Cor* 12, 4 ff.), and especially by the taking up of a developed Gospel summary. This summary, as Irenaeus shows, had by his times not yet secured a fixed place in the pattern of the Rule, and Justin Martyr seems not to have known its fusion with what soon would be called the Rule. But this summary existed, at least in the Asian churches, before its insertion in the Rules and had already acquired, especially in the four or five member glorification sequence, a certain stability. Its original setting is by modern scholars generally supposed to have been the prayer of thanksgiving. The whole question of the Gospel summary must be taken up in the comparison between Creeds and Rules. It may, however, already be noted that the material at our disposal does not favour this theory of an originally anaphoric setting. Its origin might very well be an homology of the lordship of Jesus Christ, not so much as a title, but as an event and function.

P. SMULDERS S.J.

Amsterdam, August 11th 1971

ΓΝΩΜΑΙ ΔΙΑΦΟΡΟΙ.*

THE ORIGIN AND NATURE OF DIVERSIFICATION
IN THE HISTORY OF EARLY CHRISTIANITY.

HELMUT KOESTER

HARVARD DIVINITY SCHOOL

I. THE CRISIS OF THE HISTORICAL AND THEOLOGICAL CRITERIA.

ALREADY Walter Bauer, well known as a lexicographer, but unfortunately little known as a historian of the Ancient Church, in his ingenious monograph Rechtgläubigkeit und Ketzerei im ältesten Christentum (1934),[1] had demonstrated convincingly that such Christian groups which were later labelled "heretical," actually dominated in the first two or three centuries, both geographically and theologically. Recent discoveries, especially those of Nag Hammadi in Upper Egypt, have made it definitely clear that Walter Bauer was essentially right and that a thorough and extensive re-evaluation of early Christian history is called for.

The task is by no means just a fresh reading of the known sources and a close reading of the new texts in order to redefine their appropriate place within the existing schemes of the conventional picture of early Christian history. It is this conventional picture itself that is called into question. At the same time, the convenient and time-honored labels for the distinction of heretical and orthodox prove to be very dangerous tools since they threaten to distort the historian's vision and the theologian's judgment. The term "canonical" becomes useless when the New Testament books themselves emerge as a deliberate collection of

* This term is used by Hegesippus with reference to the seven doctrinal divisions among the Jews: Essenes, Galilaeans, Hemerobaptists, Masbothei, Samaritans, Sadducees, and Pharisees (apud Euseb. hist. eccl. iv.22,7). From these sects, Hegesippus apparently derives the seven Christian heresies (op. cit. iv 22,5). The word γνώμη, though not used as a technical term, elsewhere designates doctrines of Christian heretics; cf. Ign. Phld. 3:3; Justin Dial. 35:4,6.

[1] A second edition with appendices was published in 1964 by Georg Strecker; cf. also G. Strecker, "A Report on the New Edition of Walter Bauer's Rechtgläubigkeit und Ketzerei im ältesten Christentum," Journ. of Bible and Rel. 31 (1965), 53-56. For a positive evaluation of W. Bauer's book in this journal, see Arnold Ehrhardt, "Christianity before the Apostles' Creed," HTR 55(1962), 73-119 [now in idem, The Framework of the New Testament Stories (1964), 151-99].

writings representing various divergent convictions which are not easily reconciled with each other. The criterion "Apostolic" is useless when Christian movements that were later condemned as heretical can claim genuine Apostolic origin. It is certainly untenable that the orthodox Church and only this orthodox Church was the direct offspring of the teachings, doctrines, and institutions of the Apostles' times and that only this Church was able to preserve the Apostolic heritage uncontaminated by foreign influences.

On the other hand, the criteria designating heresies, such as "Jewish-Christian" and "Gnostic" are questionable. The assumption implied in such criteria that heresies always derive from undue foreign influences is absurd and misleading, since Christianity as a whole, whether labelled "heretical" or "orthodox," has assimilated and absorbed a staggering quantity of outside influences. Christianity in all its diversified appearances is a thoroughly syncretistic religion including its so-called orthodox developments. Furthermore, a label such as, for example, "Jewish-Christian" [2] is misleading insofar as everyone in the first generation of Christianity was a Jewish-Christian anyway, and as Jewish traditions and Jewish thought (not to speak of the Old Testament) continued to exert considerable influence upon almost all developments of early Christian theology for a long time.

No less ambiguous and vague is the use of the term "Gnostic" as a convenient tag for early Christian heresies. There may be different opinions about the origins of Gnosticism, whether it antedates Christianity and arose out of Judaism, oriental syncretism, or Hellenistic philosophy, or whether it is an inner-Christian development in the second century A.D. Such questions are secondary. More important is the recognition of the indebtedness of Christianity as a whole to a theological development that bears many marks of what is customarily designated as "Gnostic." Where to draw the line between heretical and

---

[2] This term is again freely employed in the recent History of the Ancient Church by J. Daniélou and H. I. Marrou "The First Six Hundred Years" (1964). Early heretical movements are understood as remnants of, or tendencies towards Jewish sectarianism; heresies of the second century A.D. are seen as developments on the edges of Christianity. See also J. Daniélou, Théologie du Judéo-Christianisme. Histoire des doctrines chrétiennes avant Nicée, Vol. I (Paris, 1958).

orthodox is not a matter of external appearance but of theological evaluation.

This leads into the question of prolific theological criteria. Unless this question is taken seriously, the new texts will only serve further to encourage the production of ingenious hypotheses [3] whose pretentious claims to objectivity are usually matched only by their historical uselessness and theological aloofness. On the other hand, the search for theological criteria cannot be avoided by means of a retreat into dogmatic or religious propositions. Such propositions often attempt to fill the gaps and try to bridge the inconsistencies in the history of orthodoxy by postulating a primitive orthodox church which, apparently, was concealing the true beliefs in certain practices and institutions, and in the — theologically mute — "lex orandi." [4] Any such construction bars further questioning, since it takes for granted that which is actually the challenging task of the theological quest.

In the quest for criteria, the task of the historian and of the theologian are identical and cannot be divided into the free inquiry of the one and the dogmatic security of the other. The search for the decisive criterion for the distinction between true and false belief coincides with the historical quest for the essential characteristics of Early Christianity as such. We have to do here with a religious movement which is syncretistic in appearance and conspicuously marked by diversification from the very beginning. What its individuality is cannot be taken as a matter of course.

The quest for criteria which could serve to recognize the essen-

---

[3] See the complaint of Ernst Käsemann, "Neutestamentliche Fragen von heute," in Exegetische Versuche und Besinnungen II (1964), 11.

[4] This is the position of H. E. W. Turner, The Pattern of Christian Truth. A Study in the Relations between Orthodoxy and Heresy in the Early Church (Bampton Lectures, 1954), x; cf. 474f. Thus, in this only systematic treatment of the question of heresy in the Early Church since W. Bauer, Turner maintains that heresies always are specific types of deviation from a still undeveloped core of more original true beliefs, e.g. Gnosticism is their "dilution," Marcion's doctrines a "truncation," Montanism a "distortion," and Arianism an "evacuation"; see 97–148. For further criticism of Turner's very learned and instructive study, see G. Strecker in the appendix to W. Bauer, Rechtgläubigkeit und Ketzerei, 2nd ed. (1964), 293–300; W. Schneemelcher, "Walter Bauer als Kirchenhistoriker," NTStud. 9(1962/63), 21; A. Ehrhardt, op. cit., 93.

tial characteristics of that which is distinctively Christian, inevitably leads to a resumption of the discussion of the problem of the historical Jesus. It is beyond dispute that the historical origin of Christianity lies in Jesus of Nazareth, his life, preaching and fate. Consequently, the quest for the individuality and singularity of Christianity is inevitably bound up with the problem of the historical Jesus. The so-called "old" quest of the historical Jesus, however, has failed in this respect. The "new" quest,[5] on the other hand, implies exactly the question we are concerned with. Ernst Käsemann, in a paper published only recently, has stated the question thus (discussing the problem of the criteria for the legitimacy of the Christian proclamation = kerygma): "The center of the problem as it is put before us can be summarized plainly in this way: Does the kerygma of the New Testament count the earthly Jesus among the criteria of its own legitimacy?"[6] Accordingly, we are not confronted with the quest for a new image of Jesus to be used as the yardstick for true belief, but with the question, whether and in which way that which has happened historically, i.e. in the earthly Jesus of Nazareth, is present in each given case as the criterion — not necessarily as the content — of Christian proclamation and theology. Only in this way can our inquiry arrive at an evaluation of the orthodox and heretical tendencies of each new historical situation[7] — certainly not in order to open a new heresy trial of the early Christian literature, but in order to recognize in which way the criterion for true Christian faith, consciously or unconsciously, structured the re-interpretation of the religious traditions and presuppositions upon which Christianity was dependent, whether such religious inheritance was of Jewish, pagan, or — which becomes more and more important in the course of history — of Christian origin.

The complexity of this task cannot be overestimated, although

[5] For this see J. M. Robinson, A New Quest of the Historical Jesus (Studies in Bibl. Theol. 25; 1959).

[6] Ernst Käsemann, "Sackgassen im Streit um den historischen Jesus," in Exegetische Versuche und Besinnungen II (1964), 53.

[7] For the question of the interrelation of the problem of the historical Jesus and the question of heresy, see also pp. 70–73 of my article "Häretiker im Urchristentum als theologisches Problem," in Zeit und Geschichte (Dankesgabe an R. Bultmann zum 80. Geburtstag; 1964), 61–76.

the structure of our question is identical with the problem of systematic theology today. Inasmuch as no generation of Christian theologians has direct access to the criterion of its own legitimacy, the result of the historical work should never try to assume the attitude of such questionable achievements. The historical criterion Jesus of Nazareth remains embedded in the historical witness that surrounds him, and cannot be separated from it. For the historical inquiry, the New Testament itself has no prerogative with respect to the correct and orthodox use of the criterion of true faith. The canonical writings of the New Testament must be part and parcel of the historical questioning. Fortunately, we can rely here on a number of detailed studies, to a large extent influenced by Walter Bauer's book, which are concerned with the question of the heretical front in various writings of the New Testament.[8] At the same time, it is by no means necessary that these canonical writings will emerge as the direct predecessors of later orthodoxy, and their opponents always as the fathers of the late heretics. But, certainly, the early controversies reflected in the New Testament may not be without relation to the great battle against heresy in the subsequent centuries. New sources from recent discoveries, first of all the (coptic) Gospel of Thomas, must be considered on a par with the canonical writings, and they cannot be depreciated by reason of their non-canonical nature.

The following sketch has to remain both hypothetical and frag-

[8] For bibliographical references see my article "Häretiker im Urchristentum," in Die Religion in Geschichte und Gegenwart III (3rd ed., 1959), 17–21. Publications since 1958 include: on the Corinthian correspondence: G. Bornkamm, "Herrenmahl und Kirche bei Paulus," in Studien zu Antike und Urchristentum (1963²), 138–76; U. Wilckens, Weisheit und Torheit (1959); D. Georgi, Die Gegner des Paulus im 2. Korintherbrief (1964); on other Epistles from the Pauline corpus: H. Koester, "The Purpose of the Polemic of a Pauline Fragment" (Phil. III), NTStud. 8(1961/62), 317–32; W. Schmithals, "Die Irrlehrer von Rm. 16, 17–20," Studia Theologica 13(1959), 51–69; on Polycarp of Smyrna and the Pastoral Epistles: H. von Campenhausen, "Polycarp von Smyrna und die Pastoralbriefe," in Aus der Frühzeit des Christentums (1963), 197–252 [first published in Sitzungsberichte der Heidelberger Akademie der Wissenschaften, phil.-hist.Klasse 1951, 5–51]; on the whole question see: G. Strecker, Appendix to W. Bauer, Rechtgläubigkeit und Ketzerei im ältesten Christentum, 2nd ed. (1964), 243–306; W. Schmithals, "Zur Abfassung und ältesten Sammlung der paulinischen Hauptbriefe," ZNW 51(1960), 225–45; see also my article above, note 7. — Complete collections of all older materials and sources about heretics in Early Christianity will be found in A. Hilgenfeld, Die Ketzergeschichte des Urchristentums (1884 [reprint 1963]).

mentary. It is limited to the areas of Syria (both West and East, i.e. Antioch and Edessa) and Asia Minor, including the area of the Pauline mission in Greece across the Aegean Sea. One of its primary aims is to draw the lines from the developments of the "Apostolic age" and the first century A.D. — seldom considered in Walter Bauer's study [9] — into the subsequent history of the Ancient Church.[9a]

II. PALESTINE AND WESTERN SYRIA.

Our evidence for the Christian beginnings in Palestine and Syria is very fragmentary. There are, however, sufficient indications for a rather rapid dissemination of the Christian proclamation in this area. Moreover, there was, from the beginning, no uniformity in beliefs and institutions, and disagreements must have led to debates and controversies very early. Since, on the whole, these early Christian congregations understood themselves as part of the religious community of Judaism, such controversies were not exclusively internal Christian affairs, but rather discussions in which non-Christian Judaism participated as a silent or even rather loquacious partner. This aspect is a conspicuous element throughout the early controversies, especially in the Syro-Palestinian realm.[10]

In the first two decades there are three events which reveal the existence of such conflicts: 1. the circumstances of Stephen's martyrdom; 2. the Apostle's council in Jerusalem; and 3. the incident in Antioch. As to Stephen's martyrdom, the original account of the source used by Luke in Acts 6:1–8:5 is still clear enough to disclose that only the group of the "Hellenists" (Greek speaking Jews from the Diaspora) was persecuted and forced to

[9] I am, of course, heavily indebted to W. Bauer's work throughout, and the reader will have no difficulty in finding the respective sections in his book.

[9a] The structure of the theological question will be explicated only at certain points of the following historical outlines. This article does not claim to present final solutions with complete documentation. It is, as my friend and colleague Krister Stendahl aptly remarked, a blueprint for further work in the history of early Christian theology. The Gospel of Thomas will receive more detailed attention, since solving some of the problems of this newly discovered text will doubtlessly have far-reaching consequences for the study of Early Christianity as a whole.

[10] See also below on the Gospel of Matthew, p. 287f.

leave Jerusalem, whereas the circle around Peter and James remained there unmolested. The reason for this difference in the Jewish attitude overagainst the two Christian groups seems to have been that the circle around Peter and James remained within the realm of Law observance and Temple cult, whereas the Hellenists did not. Stephen was not martyred because he was a Christian, but because as a Christian he rejected the Law and ritual of his Jewish past.[11]

The Apostles' council presupposes that the mission of the Christian Hellenists had not only grown in number, but had created Christian churches that included in their membership numbers of uncircumcised Gentiles. This constituted a threat to the continuation of the Law which was considered essential by the Christians in Jerusalem. The problem was not solved, but only settled by a compromise in praxis, namely the distribution of the areas of missionary activity and the obligation for Paul's churches to make a collection of money for the church in Jerusalem (Gal. 2:7–10).

It is apparent from our sources that this compromise between the two leading exponents of the Christian missionary enterprise could not eliminate all conflicts, either in praxis or in theory. A third group in Jerusalem (Gal. 2:4) had not signed the agreement anyway, apparently because they were convinced that especially the ritual Law of the Old Testament had a remaining and essential significance for the Gentile Christians also. Paul, very shortly thereafter, was to be troubled seriously by such theological insistence upon the continuation of the ritual Law.

But also in praxis problems arose, precisely among those who had participated in the Jerusalem agreement and who were genuinely sympathetic to the cause of the Gentile mission. This was certainly the case with respect to Peter. While visiting at Antioch, in a display of true liberal attitude, he ate with the Gentiles (Gal. 2:12).[12] After the arrival from Jerusalem to Antioch of some "people from James," who were not willing to forego the demands of the dietary laws, Peter, and with him Barnabas and

[11] For further discussion of the Stephen problem, see the two most recent commentaries on Acts by Ernst Haenchen and Hans Conzelmann.
[12] For the understanding of Gal. 2:11ff., I am greatly indebted to my friend, Dr. Dieter Georgi of Heidelberg, Germany (presently at Harvard).

all other Jews, withdrew. For Peter and his friends this must have been a quite consistent display of open-minded concern, in this case directed towards the Jewish guests from Jerusalem. Quite different for Paul. To him, this is hypocrisy, motivated by fear (Gal. 2:12f.).

On the surface, this is a conflict over praxis. Paul's argument in Gal. 2:15ff., however, illuminates the underlying theological problem which is based upon his concept of the Law: The road from law-observance to the existence "in Christ" only allows a one-way traffic. His concern is not that a withdrawal such as Peter's disrupts the documentation of the unity of the one church of Jews and Gentiles. In this case he should have urged also "the people from James" to join the common (sacramental?) meals. This he did not do. On the contrary, it was Peter and his friends who were interested in such a show of unity in which also the Gentiles in a truly liberal gesture accepted Jewish dietary laws as long as James' people were present.[13] Paul grants that Jews who become Christians continue faithfully in their Law observance, but he protests against Peter's understanding of Christian existence and Law, since in the case of Peter the demands of the Law are made irrelevant through an enlightened (Jewish-Hellenistic) attitude that gives sufficient liberality to return into Law observance if this is opportune in order to serve higher aims.

The basis of Paul's argument is his interpretation of the death of Jesus and the Christian's participation in it (Gal. 2:18ff.). The precise structure of this argument will be discussed below (see p. 308f). It will do for our purposes here to state that Paul, by the criterion of the crucifixion of Jesus, which is seen in the context of the traditional Jewish concept of Law (and Covenant, Gal. 3), establishes the rule that return into Law observance reverses the direction of the act of salvation and justification. He who does so stands condemned (Gal. 2:11). This remarkable theological rigidity, bare of all liberality, forced Paul to depart from Antioch, since he obviously lost in the showdown with Peter and Barnabas. For the time being, this solved the controversy without involving a radical break. But his independ-

[13] This is the only possible interpretation of Gal. 2:14; cf. also H. Schlier, Der Brief an die Galater, ad. loc.

ent missionary work in Asia Minor and Greece did not protect
Paul from further confrontations with a hostile Christian propaganda even in the churches he had founded. For this, we have
ample evidence in Paul's letters to which we will have to return.
But even in Antioch and Syria (i.e. Coelesyria) the controversial issue was by no means eliminated through Paul's departure in A.D. 49. We know that Paul himself returned for a brief
visit (Acts 18:22f.), and there is enough evidence that "Pauline"
Christianity continued to play a significant role in Antioch:
Ignatius, bishóp of Antioch A.D. ca. 100, represents an Antiochian Gentile Christianity that is emphatically Pauline.[14] Striking
is Ignatius' complete indifference to the values of Old Testament
interpretation, and his suspicion of judaizing heretics, whose
Christology is at the same time the first gnostic docetism that
we know. The center of Ignatius' theology is apparent at this
point, and it cannot be evaluated by the yardstick of true continuation of Pauline (and thus Apostolic and Canonical) doctrine alone. The creedal formulae (Ign. Sm. 1:1f.; Trall. 9:1f.;
etc.), especially in their particular Ignatian interpretation, reveal
a new emphasis upon the reality of the earthly Jesus. In a context of increasing metaphysical systematization of the Christology, Ignatius tries to recapture not only the human reality of
Jesus' crucifixion, but also the truly human essence of Jesus'
appearance. Whether he succeeded must remain an open question here. Inasmuch as his understanding of martyrdom seems
to crown the fruitfulness of this return to the earthly dimension
of the revelation in Jesus, his reliance upon essentially un-histor-
ical language, his sacramentalism, and his lack of interest in the
Old Testament pose puzzling problems.

Ignatius' continuation of Paulinism in Antioch has to be seen
overagainst the background of an equally strong development of
traditions under the authority of Peter in the same area. Its
earliest witness, roughly contemporary with Ignatius, is the "Jewish-Christian" Gospel of Matthew.[15] Here Peter is the primary

[14] R. Bultmann, "Ignatius and Paul," in Existence and Faith (1960), 267–77
[first in Studia Paulina (Festschrift de Zwaan, 1953), 37–51].
[15] G. Bornkamm, "Der Auferstandene und der Irdische," in Zeit und Geschichte
(Dankesgabe an R. Bultmann, 1964), pp. 171–91, gives a thoughtful evaluation of
the differences of Matthew's and Paul's theology.

authority of the church (Mt. 16:13ff.). His "power of keys"
documents a tightly organized church of non-episcopal character
— in striking contrast to Ignatius. The positive role of the results of Old Testament interpretation for the understanding of
the Gospel and the emphasis upon the renewed Law of the Old
Testament as the rule of life for the church leave no doubt that
the Gospel of Matthew has no intention whatsoever of agreeing
with the dangerous development of Paul's (and Ignatius') radicalism. The conflict in matters of church offices which arises
here is not only an external one. The most powerful institutional
weapon against the heresies was very soon to be the monarchical episcopate. Matthew, however, understands the Apostolic
authority of Peter as the power of keys analogous to the Rabbinic authority of teaching and church discipline, represented in
the offices of Prophets and Teachers (= Scribes; also Wise Men,
as a third category of offices?).[16] The Didache, also from Syria,
gives evidence to the predominance of the same offices (Did.
11:1-2,7-12; 12;13; but also Apostles, 11:3-6). At the same
time, their authority is only accepted with certain reservations,
and the churches are advised to elect bishops and deacons who
are — as local officers — expected to replace prophets and teachers (Did. 15:1-2).

It is hard to assess the different theological approaches and
traditions which underlie the conflict between what the Didache
considers the older offices of prophet and teacher — so also Matthew — and the newer offices as represented by Ignatius. The
wandering of these prophets certainly was connected with a theology of the sojourner whose prototype was Jesus in his earthly
life. This concept was very widespread in Syria through many
centuries (cf. The Gospel and the Acts of Thomas, and the
pseudo-Clementine letters *De virginitate*). Even if this theology is
labelled "heretical," its worthy predecessors like Abraham in
Philo's interpretation and in the Epistle to the Hebrews as well
as its powerful heirs, the later Monastic movements, should not
be forgotten.[17] It is characteristic for the development of anti-

[16] See R. Hummel, Die Auseinandersetzung zwischen Kirche und Judentum im
Matthäusevangelium (1963), 27f., and, for the question of Peter's rule, especially
59-64.
[17] For a discussion of the Gospel of Thomas, see below, p. 299ff.

heretical weapons that the Roman church, which at the time of
the Gospel of Matthew did not even dream of the monarchic
episcopate (see 1 Clem.), should later borrow the concept of
Peter's power of keys in order to strengthen the theory of the
episcopate, while the power of keys originally was designed to
bolster those offices which became typical of the major heresies:
The Prophet in Montanism, and the Teacher in Gnosticism.[18]

Although it may be possible to reconcile the basic intentions of
Matthew's and-Paul's theology, further developments of "Jewish-
Christian" Petrine tradition in Syria excluded such peaceful co-
existence. In the Kerygmata of Peter (source of the pseudo-
Clementines),[19] in which rigorous insistence upon the continuation of the Old Testament Law and gnosticising tendencies (both
typical for Ignatius' opponents) are combined, Paul (Simon
Magus) has become the prime scapegoat for all satanic falsifica-
tions and aberrations. Related Jewish-Christian traditions in
Syria under the authority of Peter have produced the Gospel of
Peter and the Apocalypse of Peter.[20] These writings, however,
do not express the same theological concerns as the Kerygmata
of Peter.

Only the oldest document of these Syrian Peter traditions, the
Gospel of Matthew, has been accepted by the orthodox church,
whereas all others finally were rejected. But the high esteem in
which these "heretical" traditions were held for a long time is
expressed for example in bishop Serapion's (of Antioch, ca. 200)
reluctant rejection of the Gospel of Peter (Eusebius, hist. eccl.
VI.12). On the other hand, it should be remembered that the
Gospel of Matthew is not rooted in the same soil as the orthodox
concept of Church and episcopate, represented by Ignatius, even
if later orthodox circles found it convenient to use Matthew for

[18] For further detail on the development of these offices, see Hans v. Campenhausen, Kirchliches Amt und geistliche Vollmacht (1953), passim.
[19] For the discussion of this debated subject matter, see G. Strecker in E.
Hennecke, Neutestamentliche Apokryphen II (1964³), 63–69. The origin of the Kerygmata in Coelesyria is widely accepted.
[20] G. Quispel and R. M. Grant, "Note on the Petrine Apocrypha," Vigiliae
Christianae 6(1952), 31–32, give convincing evidence for the use of the Apocalypse
of Peter in Theophilus of Antioch ad Autolyc. I. 14; in my own judgment, however, the evidence for Theophilus' use of the Kerygma of Peter (quoted first by
Clement of Alexandria) is much less striking, although this does not exclude the
possibility of the Syrian origin of the Kerygma of Peter.

their own benefit. A fresh evaluation of the place of these West Syrian writings in the history of early Christian theology is still a crying need.[21] The books are not yet closed, neither concerning the survival of traditions which are independent of our canon-ical Gospels (e.g. the Gospel of Peter, and the Gospel traditions of the pseudo-Clementines), nor concerning the integrity of the-ological effort which has gone into the continuation and reinter-pretation of such traditions in an environment that remained an enigma to the Western world. That the question of the Law plays a significant role, especially in the pseudo-Clementines, does not, in itself, call for the label "Jewish-Christian." It is difficult to see why the partly allegorical, partly ascetic under-standing of the Law in the pseudo-Clementines is so much more "Jewish" than the Western messianic and moralistic interpreta-tion of the Old Testament.[22]

III. EDESSA AND THE OSRHOËNE.

What can be said about the Christian beginnings in the Os-rhoëne, especially in its capital Edessa? When W. Bauer de-stroyed the wholly legendary edifice of orthodox wishful think-ing,[23] there could be no doubt that for several centuries Christian-ity in Edessa was dominated by the controversies between several major heresies, as W. Bauer believed, the Marcionites, the Bar-

[21] G. Strecker, Das Judenchristentum in den Pseudo-Clementinen (1958) is only a beginning. The presentation of H. J. Schoeps, Theologie und Geschichte des Judenchristentums (1949) is, in all its erudition, too programmatic to be of much help.

[22] We know very little about the rest of Palestine and Western Syria. The existence of Christian churches in Galilee is probably presupposed in Mk 16:7 (cf. Jn 21). Acts 8:5ff. uses a tradition about the beginnings of a church in Samaria that was independent of the Twelve (see also Jn 4 in comparison with the op-posite view in Lk. 9:51-56). Perhaps Lk. 6:17 gives evidence of Christian com-munities in the region of Tyre and Sidon. Acts 10:1ff. presupposes that the church in Caesarea was from the beginning Gentile Christian. There is not much material which permits us to guess the character of the Christian communities in the Jordan valley (baptismal sects? predecessors of the Mandaeans?) and in Damas-cus (pre-Pauline). Certainly, Paul had once been active as a missionary in "Arabia" (Gal 1:17; i.e. Nabataea, South of Damascus), but no traces of this work of Paul are left.

[23] See W. Bauer, op. cit., 6-48; see also most recently A. F. J. Klijn, The Acts of Thomas (1962), 30-33. Turner's critique (op. cit., 40-46) of W. Bauer's argu-ments is not convincing, as A. Ehrhardt has shown (op. cit., 94-95). That, in the light of new findings, W. Bauer's reconstruction has to be revised, is another question; see below.

desanites, and, last but not least, the Manichaeans. Compared
with these, Orthodoxy, a late-comer anyway (probably not much
before the year A.D. 200), appeared as only a small and insignifi-
cant group still in the third and fourth centuries.

Bauer was, however, probably mistaken in his assumption that
the Marcionites were the first Christians to come to Edessa, presumably soon after the middle of the second century A.D.[24] The
only substantial piece of Thomas-tradition known to Bauer in
1934 was the 3rd century Acts of Thomas. Since the discovery
of the gnostic library at Nag Hammadi, more important Thomas-
material has come to light, a Gospel of Thomas and a book of
Thomas the Athlete. It seems that also this coptic Thomas material originates from Edessa or its surroundings.[25] The reasons
for this thesis are:

a) The author of the (coptic) Gospel of Thomas [26] is named
"The Twin (Didymos) Judas Thomas," and in the book of
Thomas the Athlete [27] Jesus' words (written down by Matthew)
are being spoken to "Judas Thomas." This unique appellation of
the Apostle Thomas has parallels only in the tradition of the
Osrhoëne.[28] In the Acts of Thomas he is introduced as 'Ιούδας
Θωμᾶς ὁ καὶ Δίδυμος.[29] Also in the catholic Abgar legend from

[24] W. Bauer, op. cit., 27-29; his primary evidence, the mention of Marcion in
the Edessene Chronicle and the stereotyped attacks against Marcion (and Mani
and Bar Daisan) by Aphraates and Ephrem — whereas other heretics are seldom
mentioned — only proves that the Marcionites played a role in Edessa at least
in the late third and in the fourth centuries.

[25] Arguments for Edessene origin of the Gospel of Thomas were first set forth
by H.-Ch. Puech in his studies of this document, see the articles quoted in H.-Ch.
Puech, "Gnostic Gospels and Related Documents" in E. Hennecke, N. T. Apocrypha I (Engl. transl. 1963), 282; also W. C. van Unnik, Newly Discovered Gnostic Writings (1960), 49f.

[26] Coptic text with English Translation by A. Guillaumont, H.-Ch. Puech, G.
Quispel, W. Till and Yassah 'Abd Al Masih (1959). A good translation into Latin,
German and English is easily accessible in K. Aland, Synopsis Quattuor Evangel-
iorum (1964), 517-30.

[27] Still unpublished; see the note of H.-Ch. Puech in E. Hennecke, N. T. Apocrypha I, 307.

[28] It would be misleading to speak of "Syria" in general, since Matthew, from
Western Syria, knows only the simple name Thomas for this Apostle (Mt. 10:3;
following Mk). — Some of these and the following observations regarding the
significance of this particular form of the name of the Apostle Thomas were first
made by H.-Ch. Puech; see in E. Hennecke, N. T. Apocrypha I, 286f., and the
literature quoted p. 282.

[29] According to the Greek text. The Syriac reads "Judas Thomas the Apostle,"
see also below.

Edessa Thomas is called Ἰούδας ὁ καὶ Θωμᾶς.[30] While nowhere in
the New Testament is there any connection of the names Judas
and Thomas, in Jn 14:22 instead of "Judas, not Iscariot" sy[c]
reads "Judas Thomas" (sy[s] reads Thomas). For control we can
refer to the non-Edessene Infancy Gospel of Thomas in which
the writer is called "Thomas, the Israelite (Philosopher)."[31]
Thus it is obvious that this tradition of "Judas Thomas (the
Twin)"[32] is a peculiar part of Early Christianity in the Osrhoëne.[33]

b) It is known that the Acts of Thomas, which itself shows
several Manichaean elements, i.e. it stands half way between
Christian and Manichaean Gnosis, was — together with other
Acts of Apostles — used by the Manichaeans. Now, however,
it can be affirmed with respect to the (coptic) Gospel of Thomas,
as H.-Ch. Puech says, "that it is identical with the document of the same title which our ancient authorities number
among the Manichean Scriptures."[34] There can be little doubt
that the Gospel of Thomas came to the Manichaeans from Edessa
rather than from Egypt.

c) As has been pointed out several times, the Gospel of Thomas
is used by the author of the Acts of Thomas,[35] which certainly
was written in the Osrhoëne in the early third century A.D.,
and which is the direct continuation of the East-Syrian Thomas
tradition as it is represented in the second century by the Gospel
of Thomas.

[30] It is interesting to note that "Judas Thomas" only appears when Eusebius
quotes the text of the Abgar legend verbatim (hist. eccl. I.13.11), whereas in his
own summaries he uses the simple "Thomas" (hist. eccl. I.13.4; II.1.6). According to A. F. J. Klijn, op. cit., 158, the Syriac translation of Eusebius has "Judas
Thomas" in all instances referred to above.

[31] The Syriac translation of this Infancy Gospel has only the title "Infancy
of the Lord Jesus," see O. Cullmann, in E. Hennecke, op. cit. I (1963), 390.

[32] The Acts of Thomas understands the designation "the Twin" as referring to
Thomas as the twin brother of Jesus. This is usually considered as an interpreta-
tion of the word "Twin" which arose from the peculiar interests of the Acts of
Thomas. But also this tradition is older, since according to H.-Ch. Puech (in
Hennecke, op. cit. I, 308) also in the book of Thomas the Athlete, Jesus addresses
Thomas as "his twin brother."

[33] For further reference to traditions about the Apostle Thomas, see W. Bauer,
Das Leben Jesu im Zeitalter der neutestamentlichen Apokryphen (1909), 444f.;
G. Bornkamm, in E. Hennecke, op. cit. II (1964³), 298f.

[34] In Hennecke, op. cit. I (1963), 283, see also 299f.

[35] A good survey of the passages in question is found in H.-Ch. Puech, op. cit.,
285–87.

If this Gospel had its origin in the Osrhoëne, but was already known in Egypt in the second half of the second century, as the Oxyrhynchus Papyri 1, 654 and 655 testify, the time of its writing must have been A.D. ca. 150 or earlier.[36] This proves that the Thomas tradition was the oldest form of Christianity in Edessa, antedating the beginning of both Marcionite and orthodox Christianity in that area. The greatest obstacle, however, to an evaluation of the history and theology of Christianity in Edessa still is the uncertainty about the character of the Gospel of Thomas and the nature and origin of the tradition incorporated in it. In order to attempt a brief description of Edessene Christian history in the first centuries, it is unavoidable to discuss critically some of the primary controversial issues connected with the Gospel of Thomas.

1. *The origin of Thomas' Gospel tradition.* Already in 1908 E. Wendling had proved beyond doubt that the Saying in Pap. Oxyrh. 1:6 ("No prophet is acceptable in his fatherland, and no physician performs healings among those who know him") is more primitive than the present narrative in Mk 6:1–6.[37] This result was confirmed through form critical analysis by R. Bultmann long before the discovery of the Gospel of Thomas.[38] Since the complete text of this Gospel, to which Pap. Oxyrh. 1 belongs, has come to light, an unusual lineup in scholarship has occurred.[39] G. Quispel, from the beginning, had the right intuition, when he argued that the sayings of the Gospel of Thomas must have "come from a different and independent Aramaic tradition."[40] His arguments receive convincing support from his acute awareness of the problems of non-canonical tradition in other early

[36] W. C. van Unnik (op. cit., 49f. and 53f.) dates the Gospel of Thomas not earlier than A.D. 170, since he follows Quispel's improbable suggestion that it made use of the Gospel according to the Hebrews; on this question, see below.

[37] Emil Wendling, Die Entstehung des Marcus-Evangeliums (Tübingen, 1908), 53–56.

[38] Rudolf Bultmann, Die Geschichte der synoptischen Tradition, 1st ed. 1921; for the discussion of Mk 6:1–6, see pp. 31f. of the English translation (1963).

[39] For the discussion of this question up to 1960, see E. Haenchen, "Literatur zum Thomasevangelium," Theol. Rundschau, N.F. 27(1961), 147–78, 306–38, especially 162–78. It is not my intention here to bring Haenchen's bibliography up to date, nor to present a complete survey of my own. I merely want to indicate some trends and preoccupations in the treatment of the problem.

[40] G. Quispel, "The Gospel of Thomas and the New Testament," Vig. Christ. 11(1957), 189–207; cf. also his article "Some Remarks on the Gospel of Thomas," NTStud. 5(1958/59), 276–90.

Christian literature (pseudo-Clementines, Makarios, Diatessaron),[41] but, unfortunately, Quispel's assumption that the source for these primitive and independent Sayings of the Gospel of Thomas was the so-called Gospel according to the Hebrews,[42] as well as his resplendent disdain for form critical methodology,[43] and his contention that the Gospel of Thomas is not gnostic in character [44] have failed to enhance the persuasive power of his hypothesis.

On the other hand, scholars who wanted to prove the Gnostic character of the Gospel of Thomas have usually tried to intensify their arguments for the secondary and heretical character of this Gospel by the hypothesis of its dependence upon the canonical Gospels. The list of authors who have thrown their weight on this side of the controversy is very impressive.[45] However, Wendling's and Bultmann's proof for the primitive character of the saying Pap. Oxyrh. 1:6 = Gospel of Thomas 31 has never been refuted, nor even been given serious consideration.[46]

[41] Cf. also his articles in Vig. Christ. 12(1958), 181–96; 13(1959), 87–117; 14(1960), 204–15; 18(1964), 226–35.

[42] Vig. Christ. 11(1957), 189ff.; cf. Haenchen's critique, op. cit., 162ff. To conceive of this Gospel as a very primitive synoptic-type writing is impossible, as Philipp Vielhauer has shown recently in his treatment of the "Jewish-Christian Gospels" in Edgar Hennecke, New Testament Apocrypha I (1963), 117–65. Relations, of course, cannot be denied; but since the Gospel of Thomas migrated from Syria to Egypt, the Egyptian Gospel according to the Hebrews is more likely to depend upon the former, if not free tradition explains the similarities.

[43] See, e.g., Quispel's glowing remarks, Vig. Christ. 11(1957), 206f.

[44] Most strongly this view was propounded in a paper given at the 100th Meeting of the Society of Biblical Literature in New York, December 29, 1964 (to be published by the Society in the near future).

[45] E.g. R. M. Grant and D. N. Freedman, The Secret Sayings of Jesus (1960); E. Haenchen, op. cit., and Die Botschaft des Thomas-Evangeliums (1961); B. Gärtner, The Theology of the Gospel according to Thomas (1961). H. E. W. Turner, "The Theology of the Gospel of Thomas," in H. Montefiore and H. E. W. Turner, Thomas and the Evangelist (Studies in Bibl. Theology 35; 1962). See also H. K. McArthur, "The Gospel according to Thomas," New Testament Sidelights (1960), 43–77. The wisdom of the methodological procedure of the latest publication on this question is beyond my comprehension: W. Schrage, Das Verhältnis des Thomas-Evangeliums zur synoptischen Tradition und zu den koptischen Evangelienübersetzungen (Beihefte zur ZNW 29, 1964). Schrage tries to prove the secondary character of the tradition contained in the Gospel of Thomas by a comparison with the Sahidic translation of the Synoptic Gospels (and John). His understanding of form critical method is glaringly evidenced in his comments on Saying 31 (= Pap. Oxyrh. 1:6, quoted above): "Thomas has detached the saying from the historical situation to which it was assigned by the Synoptic Gospels, and has again made it a 'free Logion'" (p. 76).

[46] G. Quispel did not exactly dream of the possibility of weighty support from these quarters.

Furthermore, the employment of rigorous form critical analysis is strikingly nonexistent in a great number of the studies referred to above,[47] except for one area: the evaluation of the parables of the Gospel of Thomas.[48] It is evident that the form critical work of J. Jeremias on the parables has had a much greater impact, especially on the English speaking world, than R. Bultmann's form criticism. Especially H. Montefiore's detailed and careful study proves clearly "that Thomas's divergences from synoptic parallels can be most satisfactorily explained on the assumption that he was using a source distinct from the Synoptic Gospels. Occasionally this source seems to be superior . . ." [49] Meanwhile, some scholars have assigned a higher possibility to the derivation of the entire (or almost entire) tradition contained in the Gospel of Thomas from an independent early stage of the Sayings tradition [50] and so they have returned to a confirmation of the original suggestion of G. Quispel. It is my opinion that this view is correct.[51] The methodology called for in further studies also requires a fresh analysis of the parallel sections in the Synoptic Gospels, mainly the collection of parables and Sayings underlying Mk 4 and Mt. 13; the basis for the Markan Sayings used in Mk 2 and 3; Q sections underlying Mt. 5–7 and Lk. 6 as well as other Q material now occurring in Mt. 11:7ff. // Lk. 7:24ff.;

[47] A rare exception is the article of H.-W. Bartsch, "Das Thomas-Evangelium und die synoptischen Evangelien," NTStud. 6(1959/60), 249–61; also O. Cullmann, "Das Thomasevangelium und die Frage nach dem Alter der in ihm enthaltenen Tradition," Theol.Lit.Ztg. 85(1960), 321–34 [Engl. Trans. in Interpretation 16(1962), 418–38]. Both these authors, consequently, ascribe a much higher probability to the existence of independent tradition.

[48] In addition to authors quoted above who base their judgment largely upon the parables (like Quispel and Cullmann), see C.-H. Hunzinger, "Aussersynoptisches Traditionsgut im Thomas-Evangelium," ·Theol.Lit.Ztg. 85(1960), 843–46; idem, "Unbekannte Gleichnisse Jesu aus dem Thomas-Evangelium," Judentum, Urchristentum, Kirche (Festschr. f. J. Jeremias), = ZNW, Beih. 26(1960), 209–20. H. Montefiore, "A Comparison of the Parables of the Gospel According to Thomas and of the Synoptic Gospels," in H. Montefiore and H. E. W. Turner, op. cit., 40–78; first published in NTStud. 7(1960/61), 220–48.

[49] H. Montefiore, op. cit., 78.

[50] Cf. R. McL. Wilson, "Thomas and the Growth of the Gospels," HTR 53(1960), 231–50; idem "Thomas and the Synoptic Gospels," Exp. Times 72(1960/61), 36–39; idem, Studies in the Gospel of Thomas (1960); R. A. Spivey, The Origin and Milieu of the Gospel According to Thomas [Dissertation Yale University, New Haven (1962), unpublished]; see also E. W. Saunders, "A Trio of Thomas Logia," Biblical Research 8(1963), 43–59; R. North, "Chenoboskion and Q," Cath.Bibl.Quart. 24(1962), 154–70.

[51] I hope to be able to publish the results of my own studies in a not too distant future in a different context.

Mt. 21, 22 and par. etc.; finally the sources for the special Lukan material in Lk. 12 (Lk. 11:27–12:56 is paralleled by no less than thirteen sayings in the Gospel of Thomas, seven of these have parallels only in Lk.). In such a comparison of our sources the present Synoptic Gospels are not only to be used as reference material, convenient to state agreements and deviations and to discuss priorities, but as a parallel development of the same tradition of Sayings, containing probably just as much primary and just as much secondary material as the Gospel of Thomas. "Gemeindetheologie," not necessarily hellenistic mythology,[52] was indeed the power of the formation of the tradition of Sayings in both cases.[53]

2. *The nature of the tradition under the authority of Thomas.* The pattern of "Apostolic" tradition which appears under the name of the Apostle Judas Thomas in Eastern Syria may be compared to the Peter tradition in Coelesyria which we discussed above, and the Paul tradition in Asia Minor which will be discussed later. There is no doubt that those traditions had their ultimate origin in the actual historical missionary activity of these Apostles in such areas in which their names survived. This pattern of tradition under the name of a specific Apostle must be distinguished from later catholic-orthodox claims on the names of the Apostles in order to establish the legitimate Apostolic doctrine and succession in the antiheretic controversy, as was the case with the Roman claim on Peter (distinct from the survival of the West-Syrian Peter tradition), or the later orthodox attempt to establish the authority of Thaddaeus as the authority of true Christianity in Edessa. Thomas, however, seems to have been the authority for an indigenous Syrian Christianity already before the formation of stronger orthodox influence in that area. Unfortunately, we have not, as in the case of Peter for Antioch and of Paul for Asia Minor, any further historical evidence to confirm the assumption that Judas, the (twin) brother of Jesus,

---

[52] Cf. G. Quispel's remarks in Vig. Christ. 11(1957), 206.

[53] I can only add briefly that also the Gospel of John is not very likely to have served as a source for the Gospel of Thomas. However, parallels are remarkable, as Raymond E. Brown has shown ["The Gospel of Thomas and St. John's Gospel," NTStud. 9(1962/63), 155–77] which, in my opinion, points to some connections in the tradition and environment of both writings.

actually was the Apostle of Edessa. This must remain a mere conjecture. It is, however, a legitimate historical question to ask for the reason of the early existence of Thomas' authority in that area. For this question it is necessary to consider once more the name Judas͜Thomas. The simple "Thomas," the only form that occurs in the canonical tradition, is the transliteration of the Semitic surname תאמא, meaning "the twin," into a widely used Greek name. That "twin" was the original meaning of the underlying Aramaic tradition is still evident in the Greek ὁ λεγόμενος Δίδυμος (Jn 11:16, etc.). What is lost in the canonical tradition, however, is the actual, original name of this Apostle: Judas.[54] That this was his true name is as probable as is the fact that Peter's given name was Simeon. Yet, this Judas is also called the (twin) brother of the Lord, which raises the question whether the canonical tradition did not after all preserve the original name of this Apostle elsewhere: in the name of the author of the Epistle of "Judas [Jude], the brother of James," since this James is certainly the brother of the Lord. Though not desiring to indulge any further in the complex problem of the *desposynoi*, I would like to affirm that the identity of Judas, the brother of the Lord, and the Apostle Thomas is more likely a primitive tradition than a later confusion — a primitive tradition which was, to be sure, suppressed by later orthodox developments; already 2 Peter, by incorporating the Epistle of Jude, takes a second step in this development; the initial step is reflected in the *incipit* of Jude itself, where "brother of the Lord" is avoided in favor of "brother of James." In any case, it is not impossible that the origin of the primitive designation "Judas Thomas, the brother of the Lord," in the Gospel of Thomas is the actual historical activity of this Apostle in Edessa or in another area of Palestine-Syria from which Edessene Christianity derives its beginnings. The alternative would be that an early Christian group adopted the name of one of the *desposynoi* at a later date. This is quite possible in view of the role of Jesus' family in the early decades of Christianity. But since this group thus would have preserved

---

[54] תאמא is not recorded as a Jewish name anywhere in the Mishna and Tosephta, nor in the Jewish papyri, and there is only very slight evidence that it might have been in use as a Phoenician name, as my colleague, Dr. Frank M. Cross, Jr., confirms.

an original form of his name that has been lost in the canonical tradition, such adoption must have taken place before the composition of the canonical Gospels.

It is also necessary to consider the "Gattung" of this Thomas tradition, in order to determine its nature. We are here not concerned with the specific Synoptic source Q as the literary source for the Gospel of Thomas,[55] since its basis is certainly not identical with any possible form of Mt.'s and Lk.'s common second source. It rather reflects smaller collections [56] which were partly incorporated in Q, but were otherwise directly available to Lk. and Mk. Further light can be expected from more detailed studies of the Sitz im Leben and theological function of the Sayings, or better: of the Logoi, in the early Church. An important step in this direction was taken recently by James M. Robinson.[57] A direct consequence of his study for our question can be formulated in this way: The Gospel of Thomas directly continues, even if in a modified way, the most original "Gattung" of the Jesus tradition — the *Logoi Sophōn* — which, in the canonical Gospels, became acceptable to the orthodox Church only by radical and at the same time critical alteration, not only of the form, but also of the theological intention of this primitive "Gattung"; such critical evaluation of the Logoi-Gattung was achieved by Mt. and Luke through imposing the Markan (narrative — kerygma) frame upon the Sayings tradition represented by Q.[58]

Thus, Thomas does not continue "Q," but he indeed represents the Eastern branch of the Gattung "Logoi," the Western branch being represented by the synoptic Logoi of Q, which was used in Western Syria by Matthew and later by Luke. If this paral-

---

[55] Cf. the warning of H.-W. Bartsch, op. cit., 258, although his extreme scepticism regarding Q is certainly unfounded.

[56] Possibly more like the collections of Sayings used in Clem. 13 and Did. 1. These two examples, of course, emphasize the difficulty of the problem, since the sayings in 1 Clem. 13:2 are more primitive than Mt. and Lk., whereas the collection inserted into Didache 1:3–5 may have been composed on the basis of Mt. and Lk.; see my study, Synoptische Überlieferung bei den Apostolischen Vätern [TU 65(1957)], 12–16; 220–37.

[57] James M. Robinson, "ΛΟΓΟΙ ΣΟΦΩΝ. Zur Gattung der Spruchquelle Q," in Zeit und Geschichte (Dankesgabe an R. Bultmann, 1964), 77–96.

[58] Cf. J. M. Robinson, op. cit., especially 96; cf. idem, "The Problem of History in Mark, Reconsidered," Union Sem. Quart. Rev. 20 (1965), 135, where he says about his study of Logoi and Q: "I have tried to trace this Gattung, whose gnosticizing proclivity is blocked by Matthew and Luke by embedding Q in the Markan gospel form."

kelism of Thomas' tradition of the Logoi and Q is seen correctly,
Papias' reference to the Logia which Matthew composed in "He-
brew" should not be overlooked in this context.[59] It may not be
a coincidence that Thomas and Matthew appear as a pair in the
lists of Apostles (Mt. 10:3; cf. Mk 3:18, Lk. 6:15), and the
book of Thomas the Athlete has an explicit "The book of
Thomas . . . which he wrote" which conflicts with the *incipit*
"The secret words spoken . . . to Judas Thomas, and which I
have written down, I, Matthew . . ."[60]

3. *The theological character of the Thomas tradition.* The
present battle over the question whether the Gospel of Thomas
is Gnostic or Jewish Christian is of little avail. If there is any
chance that this Gospel has preserved traditions from the first
and second Christian generations, it is very likely that such traditions were as Jewish Christian as the synoptic sayings source Q,
or Paul, or the Gospel of Matthew. The reference to James the
Righteous (Logion 12) is certainly interesting, but his commanding position is also recognized by Paul (Gal. 2; 1 Cor. 15:7),
Acts 15, or the Epistle of James 1:1–2, i.e. it is historical, and in
the Gospel of Thomas the weight and authority of James is surpassed by Thomas (Logion 13), as in the later orthodox church
(beginning with Luke-Acts) James' authority is surpassed by
Peter. Furthermore, to link the Gospel of Thomas with the
"Jewish Christian" circles of Western Syria out of which emerged
the Ebionites, who used a modified Gospel of Matthew, assigned
a high value to the Old Testament Law, and rejected the authority of Paul, would be a mistake, since neither was typical for
Edessa.[61] The designation "Jewish Christian," thus, is probably
not wrong, but it is indeterminate.

The same, however, seems to refer to the use of the term
"Gnostic," even if to a lesser degree, since E. Haenchen[62] prob-

---

[*] J. M. Robinson, art. cit., note 57, emphasizes this connection rather strongly.
[*] H.-Ch. Puech, op. cit., 307; cf. J. M. Robinson, art. cit., 82f.
[*] A collection of Pauline epistles was in use in Edessa before the arrival of
representatives of the orthodox church. This is shown indirectly through the
special introduction of the antignostic third epistle to the Corinthians into Edessa,
probably in order to fight against the existing concept of Paul; cf. W. Bauer, op.
cit., 45ff. It also is interesting to note that the sectarian heirs of the Thomas
tradition in Syria, the Manichaeans, reflect a positive evaluation of Paul; see
Kephalaia (ed. Schmidt, Ibscher, Polotsky, Böhlig [1940]), 13, lines 19–26.
[*] Die Botschaft des Thomas-Evangeliums (1961). Note that R. M. Grant, The

ably has been able to present a reading of the Gospel of Thomas as it was current, say, in Egypt in A.D. ca. 175, or even somewhat earlier in Syria.

The crucial problem of Gnosticism, however, is not how to relate second century Gnostic writings to subsequent developments — as important as this task may be — but to interpret early forms of Gnosticism with respect to their roots in early Christian and Jewish theology. Here, it seems, the Gospel of Thomas occupies a uniquely critical position, since in its tradition we can observe a re-interpretation of originally eschatological sayings and of their terminology in a very peculiar way. The question is not only that of various stages in the growth of the tradition, so as to distinguish between an older "synoptic Palestinian" core and later gnosticizing accretion. We are rather confronted also with the "gnosticizing proclivity" [63] of the Gattung Logoi itself, i.e. in its oldest and most primitive stages. It is to be remembered that "Gattung" is not just a deliberate choice of an external form, but the manifestation of a distinct subject matter.

The predecessor of the Christian collection and transmission of Jesus' sayings was the Gattung *"Logoi Sophōn,"* primarily developed in the Jewish Wisdom movement.[64] This existing form served as the focus of crystallization for the preservation of one particular aspect of Jesus' historical appearance and work: his teachings.[65] It is not practicable to discuss here the complex questions of historical and most primitive sayings or groups of sayings in these early pre-Q and pre-Gospel collections. It is highly probable, however, that Wisdom sayings, legal statements (critique of the old conduct and pronouncements regarding the

---

Secret Sayings of Jesus (1960), presents an interpretation of this Gospel based on the employment of later Gnostic writings, — a method which he has criticized vociferously whenever it was employed by students with respect to New Testament writings.

[63] J. M. Robinson, see note 58 above.

[64] Cf. the excellent analysis of J. M. Robinson, art. cit., 91–95. It is known that already Rudolf Bultmann (in The History of the Synoptic Tradition) drew his categories for the analysis of the Logia of Jesus from the Jewish Wisdom Literature, see Robinson, art. cit., 77–79.

[65] It is not possible here to enter into the controversy with B. Gerhardsson, Memory and Manuscript (1964²). As I am only too aware of the fact that my disagreements with this book can hardly be exaggerated, a few critical remarks would not do justice to Gerhardsson's work nor to the importance of this controversy.

new conduct), prophetic words (including some I-words, beatitudes, and woes), and parables dominated such collections — according to Jesus' own teaching. As is partly evident from Q, sayings predicting Jesus' suffering, death and resurrection, and the material reflecting the development of a Christological evaluation of the person of Jesus were still absent; detailed apocalyptic predictions as contained in Mk 13 are not part of such primitive collections,[66] and equally absent were specific regulations for the life of the church ("Gemeinderegeln").

What will be the theological tendency of such collections of Logoi? This entirely depends upon the Christological post-Easter frame to which they are subjected. Q domesticated the Logoi through a particular apocalypticism according to which Jesus was identified with the future Son of Man. Mark (and subsequently Mt. and Lk.) were able to accommodate the Logoi in the "Gospel" developed on the basis of the early hellenistic (Pauline) Kerygma. Neither of these developments seem to have touched the Logoi tradition that has found its way into the Gospel of Thomas. The criterion controlling its Logoi seems to be more closely connected with the internal principle of this Gattung as it served as the focus for the transmission of Jesus' sayings: the authority of the word of wisdom as such. If there is any "Easter experience" to provide a congenial Christology to this concept of the Logoi, it is here the belief in "Jesus, the Living One" (G. Thom. 1). That Jesus who spoke these words was and is the living one and thus gives life through his words permeates the entirety of the Thomas sayings.[67] On this basis, a direct and almost unbroken continuation of Jesus' own teaching takes place — unparalleled anywhere in the canonical tradition — and, at the same time, a further development ensues which emphasizes even further the presence of the revelation in the word of Jesus and its consequences for the believer.

Accordingly, the most conspicuous form of sayings [68] in the

---

[66] Whether any apocalyptic Son of Man sayings were existent at this stage, is very doubtful; cf. P. Vielhauer, "Gottesreich und Menschensohn in der Verkündigung Jesu," Festschrift für Günther Dehn (1957), 51–79; idem, "Jesus und der Menschensohn," Zeitschr.f.Theol. u. Kirche 60(1963), 133–77.

[67] This has parallels in the Gospel of John (cf. Jn 6:63 and passim), but certainly does not imply literary dependence.

[68] In the classification I follow Bultmann, op. cit., passim.

Gospel of Thomas is the Wisdom saying (Proverb), often in metaphorical forms (Bildworte etc.), and almost completely paralelled in the Synoptic Gospels.[69] All these sayings do not necessarily have allegorical functions, but certainly already in the most primitive stage of the tradition they serve to emphasize various aspects of the revelation as it is present in Jesus' words. The second conspicuous element is the use of parables,[70] the most genuine vessels of Jesus' own proclamation of the Kingdom. It is obvious, however, that the eschatological element, only present in a very qualified interpretation in Jesus' original proclamation, has not been elaborated further in the Gospel of Thomas; it is rather, almost unnoticeably, altered in such a way that the emphasis upon the secret presence now expresses a gnostic tension (the mysterious presence of the divine soul in the body) instead of an eschatological one (the secret presence of the Kingdom in the world).[71] Similarly close to the most primitive form of Logoi are a number of Law sayings which express clearly the contrast of the traditional and the new morality.[72] Finally, some prophetic sayings and I-sayings seem to preserve the original impact of an early proclamation in which the pronouncement of Jesus' word announces the presence of salvation.[73]

All these sayings, of course, are not Gnostic by any definition. Nevertheless, it seems that the unbroken continuation of such a Logoi tradition by nature is endowed with the seed of Gnosticism as soon as it falls under the spell of a dualistic anthropology; the more so, since it presupposes the secret presence of the Living Jesus in his words. The subsequent growth of the tradition, which has probably started very early and without direct influence from other Christological formations of the Gospel tradition, is only a consistent spelling out of the consequences. It is particularly conspicuous in those sayings in which eschatological

[69] G. Thom. 26, 31–35, 39b, 45, 47, 66, 67, 73, 78, 86, 93, 94. Without parallels, but probably primitive traditions are 21 (last part), 24, 33a, 40?, 74, cf. 80 and 111b.

[70] G. Thom. 8, 9, 20, 57, 63–65, 76, 107; without synoptic parallels 97, 98.

[71] E.g. in the parable of the wise fisherman (8) and of the pearl (76), as has been pointed out frequently.

[72] Especially 6, 14 in part, 25, 99, 101a, cf. 39, 102, 95.

[73] Cf. 54 ("blessed are the poor," in the "Matthean" form, but without the addition "in spirit"), 58?, 68 (but see 69!); further 16a, 17, 55, 82, the latter without synoptic parallel.

terminology receives a clearly Gnostic meaning; e.g. G. Thom. 3 (The Kingdom in heaven — the Kingdom is within you and without you), 16b (Fire in a house — they will stand as solitary ones).[74] Most clearly, this Gnostic re-interpretation of the concept of the Kingdom is present in Saying 49: "you shall find the kingdom; because you come from it and you shall go there again," parallel to 50: "We have come from the Light . . ." This is as clearly as possible a primitive equivalent to the classical definition of Gnosis in the *Excerpta ex Theodoto* 78: "The knowledge of who we have been and what we have become, where we have been, etc." The rich evidence of more detailed unfolding of gnostic language of revelation — though not a reflection of any particular system or doctrine — cannot be discussed further.[75]

A judgment about Thomas' gnostic understanding of the Christian existence should not be passed too quickly. There is one important element, derived from the life of the earthly Jesus, which controls Thomas' understanding of Christian life to a certain extent: the motif of the wandering. It is most poignantly formulated in Saying 42: "Become passers-by," and it is certainly related to the Christological implications of Saying 86: "The foxes have their holes . . . but the Son of Man has no place to lay his head and to rest." Here, a Christology related to the earthly Jesus and the Gnostic understanding of man coincide, — in order to create a most powerful image of the true Christian which has deeply influenced the further development of Syrian Christianity and has become its most important contribution to orthodox Christianity.[76]

The indigenous Thomas Christianity of Eastern Syria, growing out of such beginnings during the second and third centuries A.D., was not closely defined by any specific doctrinal and institutional limits. Considering its further development we cannot

[74] See further: 5, 6b, 11, 18a, 22, 75, 88, 91, 111, 112.
[75] See for this especially Haenchen, Die Botschaft des Thomas-Evangeliums (1961), 39–74.
[76] The resulting type of Christian morality and behavior may be labelled "encratite," but it should not be confused with such encratite developments elsewhere, which often have completely different theological roots (e.g. the Marcionites, or Jewish Christian encratites in Asia Minor); see also A. Ehrhardt, op. cit., 95, n. 9, who points out that this term in its early usage can refer to a variety of heresies, and that its later technical use "arose from experiences of the post-Constantinian period."

even call it typically gnostic, but should rather describe it as a typical example of hellenistic syncretism — wide open to further influences and developments. Characteristic of such syncretistic unfolding are the following phenomena.

The philosopher Bardesanes, after whom these Edessene Christians later were called Bardesanites, was the great theological figure-head of this type of Christian faith, sometimes rightly called the "Clement (i.e. of Alexandria) of the East." He was open to astrological and cosmological speculative mysticism, a true Hellenist, and at the same time well versed in Semitic poetry.[77] At about the same time Tatian launched his innovation, the Diatessaron, as the new form of the written Gospel. The four-fold Gospel canon had not arrived at Edessa at that time, nor had any of the canonical Gospels. But against the traditional Gospel of Thomas, the Diatessaron must have been a tremendous success. Tatian had learned about the composition of Gospel harmonies at Rome in the school of Justin Martyr. He added the Gospel of John (which was rejected by Justin because the Valentinians loved it) and probably also used the Gospel of Thomas[78] and thus created the richest "Gospel" for his time, unparalleled anywhere.[79] It took the catholic church centuries to eradicate this heretical document in the East, and the orthodox Syrian Father Ephrem still used it in the fourth century. That Tatian, certainly not a "Gnostic," was later labelled an encratite, is understandable for a member of the pre-orthodox church in Eastern Syria. Also obvious are such encratitic tendencies in the document from a third century development of Edessene Thomas Christianity: The Acts of Thomas. Its appreciation for Gnostic lore and legend,[80] however, and its distinctly pre-Mani-

[77] It is certainly wrong to see Bardesanes as a founder of a sectarian type religiosity, or to label him as a representative of Eastern Valentinianism. Both these views stem from the armory of the antignostic Fathers.

[78] This is the best explanation for the appearance of Gospel of Thomas readings in the Diatessaron which G. Quispel has pointed out in several articles, Vig.Christ. 13(1959), 87–117; NTStud. 5(1958/59), 276–90.

[79] Whether the original composition was in Syriac or in Greek, is of minor concern for our question. I would tend to believe in a Greek original because of the Roman influences which are present (here Justin is Tatian's predecessor) and because of the Western evidence for it (cf. the Dutch version).

[80] Cf. G. Bornkamm, Mythos und Legende in den apokryphen Thomasakten (1933).

chaean theology already reflect a rapid development towards the establishment of a Gnostic church,[81] as it was accomplished through Mani.

Compared with this rather colorful and supple picture of Thomas Christianity as the indigenous Christian group in Edessa, the more rigorously structured churches did not gain wide acceptance in the beginning. The Marcionites seem to have been more successful for a while. Orthodoxy, however, did not get to Edessa until about A.D. 200. Their first perceptible figure is Palut, after whom the orthodox Christians, to their great distress, were called the Palutians. Whether Palut was consecrated as "bishop" of Edessa by Serapion of Antioch, remains doubtful.[82] One can picture a situation in which the orthodox group was just starting to gain strength at a time when most of the local Christians were drawn towards Mani rather than to Palut's brand of Western orthodoxy. Thus, it is only in the fourth century that the orthodox church amounted to anything. Here we find the first bishop (Kune) and the first theologian (Ephrem) of more profile. Only now this group manages to have its own story of Apostolic succession propagated: Not Thomas, but Thaddaeus is said to have been the real apostle of Edessa, while Thomas (who cannot be suppressed completely) is said to have stayed in Jerusalem (Eusebius, h.e.I.13).[83] The completely unhistorical Abgar legend which tries to connect Thaddaeus' mission to Edessa with the time and person of the toparch Abgar V (A.D. 13–50) has effectively underscored the claims of orthodoxy upon Edessa, even for many modern scholars.[84] One century

[81] On the developed Gnosticism of the Acts of Thomas, in which the earthly Jesus has been completely replaced by the figure of the Gnostic redeemer, see G. Bornkamm in E. Hennecke, Neutestamentliche Apokryphen II (1964), 300–08.

[82] This tradition only serves the purpose of connecting Palut's succession to Peter in Rome — historically improbable for many reasons; cf. W. Bauer, Rechtgläubigkeit und Ketzerei, 22 (see also 25ff.).

[83] The conflict between Thomas and Thaddaeus is usually overlooked, but is clearly present in our sources. The claim of orthodoxy to derive from Thaddaeus as the original Edessene Apostle is perhaps already reflected in the fact that the list of Apostles in the heretical Acts of Thomas reflects Mt.'s list (Mt. 10), but drops Thaddaeus. In any case, it is in this area that we have to look for reasons and motives behind the changes in such lists, rather than looking for possible desires to "harmonize" various traditions (against A. F. J. Klijn, op. cit., 158f.; W. Bauer, Das Leben Jesu, 444f., is certainly right).

[84] To assume that the Abgar legend actually speaks of Abgar IX (A.D. 179–

later, when the brutal methods of bishop Rabbala succeeded in "converting" legions of heretics, orthodoxy is so well established that later versions of the Abgar legend can drop Edessa's original Apostle, Thomas, completely (cf. the Acts of Thaddaeus).

IV. THE COUNTRIES AROUND THE AEGEAN SEA.

For the earliest history of theological controversy in parts of Asia Minor, Macedonia, and Achaia, our sources are more plentiful. A considerable part of the writings which were later incorporated into the New Testament canon was written in this region, particularly on the west coast of Asia Minor. Most of this literature is the more or less direct result of the battles waged between the various groups of Christian missionaries throughout the second half of the first century. It goes without saying that any attempt at describing briefly the history of controversies in this area is to put one's hand into the hornet's nest of many hotly debated issues of New Testament studies today.

No doubt, the Apostle Paul was the one who started Christian missionary work in the regions around the Aegean Sea. In conformity with the kerygma of the Hellenist church [85] as it was developed in Antioch, Paul's kerygma was the message of Christ's death and resurrection. It implied a strictly eschatological orientation for the understanding of Christian life in this world, together with the insistence that the Law had come to an end and had no continuing theological significance for the Christian churches. The success of Paul's missionary labors was soon to be put to a severe test. Apparently, he had only opened the door to a new missionary field. Various competing groups of Christian missionaries, Jewish Christians as Paul himself, started their propaganda in this area only a few years later while Paul was staying (perhaps for some time imprisoned) at Ephesus. The repeated theme of Paul's controversies with these competi-

---

216) is a typical example of saving a "historical" kernel and sacrificing the real intention of a legend, since the orthodox Christians invented the legend for no other purpose than to justify their claim that they had come to Edessa in Apostolic times rather than around 200.

[85] On "The Kerygma of the Hellenistic Church Aside from Paul," see R. Bultmann, Theology of the New Testament I (1951), 63ff.

tors in the missionary enterprise is the question of the continuing validity of several aspects of the religious inheritance of Judaism: the Old Testament, the Law, the Covenant, and Jewish tradition in general.

The first threat to the success of the missionary work of Paul arose from the propaganda of a group of missionaries who most legitimately have been called Judaizers. They first appear as the opponents of Paul in Galatia, and soon after Paul's death (or departure from this area) a student of Paul tries to refute the same Judaizing antagonists in the epistle to the Colossians.[86] Paul's violent reaction in his epistle to the Galatians shows clearly that something more is at stake than only the question of imposing an unnecessary burden like the circumcision upon the newly converted Gentiles in Galatia. Nor does Paul consider freedom from the Law to be just a welcome source of greater convenience for Gentile Christians. The opponents should not be mistaken for people teaching an orthodox Jewish observance of the Law, and their message is probably understood in a wrong context if it is explained with reference to Rabbinic sources. As various references in Paul's letter (e.g. Gal. 4:9–10) reveal, these Judaizers must have emphasized the spiritual implications and the cosmic dimensions of the observance of the ritual Law of the Old Testament in particular.[87] It is equally obvious that such spiritual renewal of the Law was understood as a Gospel which must have assigned a particular role to Jesus in the context of this theological endeavor. Such a Gospel must have been a call for obedience to the law as the cosmic rule of God (perhaps: revealed through Christ). This obedience, which is a participation in this cosmic order, is primarily accomplished through the observance of certain rituals of which circumcision is the most conspicuous one, whereas aspects of morality apparently receive only secondary emphasis.

The attempt to reconstruct the opponents' concept of Law

---

[86] On the Galatian controversy, see W. Schmithals, "Die Häretiker in Galatien," ZNW 47(1956), 25–67; on Colossians, see the excellent study of G. Bornkamm, "Die Häresie des Kolosserbriefes," in Das Ende des Gesetzes (1958²), 139–56.

[87] W. Schmithals, op. cit., has described this theological dimension of the opponents' teaching in Galatia very persuasively. But he confuses the problems when he denies the central role of the Law in the thought of the Galatian opponents.

from Paul's arguments in Gal. 3 shows a mythologizing of Old Testament covenant [88] theology which has Jewish antecedents. Refuting this view, Paul argues for a historical understanding of the Old Testament covenant and of the Law as part of that covenant. The covenant for him has a beginning (the promise to Abraham); and the Law, coming only after Abraham and limited in its duration (Gal. 3:17ff.) as the slavemaster until the coming of the Messiah (Gal. 3:24), is not valid beyond the time of its historical termination: the execution of the curse in Christ (Gal. 3:13), and thereby the final opening for the blessings now realized in the church (Gal. 3:14). Thus, the present time is not understood as the renewal of the covenant (now in its cosmic dimensions), but as the final fulfilment of its original purpose. It is noteworthy that Paul's reference to the "origin" is not to the creation, but to Abraham; it is an appeal to the covenant constituting act of God at a specific time in the history of his people, rather than to a primordial act of God in the beginning of the world. It seems that Paul consciously avoids any appeal to the first chapters of Genesis which played such a vital role in the mythological re-interpretations of the Old Testament tradition in Apocalypticism and in Wisdom speculations.

The key to Paul's critical refutation of his opponents' Law mythology is his understanding of the coming of the Christ as a human being at a specific moment of history (Gal. 4:4). Certainly Paul does not try to evaluate the person of Jesus with the categories of a modern historian. Jesus is seen, no doubt, as a figure fulfilling a purpose within a divine plan which is understood in theological categories. However, the reason why Jesus fulfills this function is precisely in that he was born, lived (Gal. 4:4) and died (Gal. 3:13) as a human being. For Paul, this is epitomized in the crucifixion. Both Paul and his Galatian opponents are concerned with the question of a new understanding of the Old Testament and Jewish concept of Law and Covenant. In no way are the alternatives the word and teaching of Jesus

---

[88] I can only note in passing that for my understanding of the problem of covenant in early Christianity, I am indebted to the book of Klaus Baltzer, Das Bundesformular (1960; 2nd ed. 1964), which — after the preliminary studies of George Mendenhall — for the first time opened up an entirely new perspective also for New Testament studies.

versus the Jewish doctrine of the Law; rather: Paul sets a specific concept of Law and Covenant overagainst the Covenant theology represented by his opponents. Both speak the traditional language of Judaism; both (though for the opponents this is not clear on the surface) have very specific ideas about the place of the coming of Jesus in this traditional schema. What is the decisive difference? For Paul, what has happened historically with the crucifixion of the man Jesus is not a convenient point of departure for a renewal of Covenant theology, but it is the criterion for a critical re-interpretation. Paul's insistence upon the most striking *human* aspect of this event, the birth by a woman and the crucifixion, is at the same time the means of evaluating critically the mythical elements of the opponents' Covenant theology (as they were inherited from postexilic covenant concepts). For Paul, Jesus did not enhance the religious greatness of the old covenant into new cosmic dimensions, but he brought it to an end by suffering its consequences, the curse.

Thus, the Christian's task is not the reverence of powers beyond and above time and history through the observance of their rules (Gal. 4:10),[89] but the human responsibility to an existing, visible community: *agape* (Gal. 5:6,22; cf. 6:2ff.). In this way, the historicity of the event of the revelation becomes the decisive criterion for the understanding of traditional theologies and mythologies. The failure to apply this criterion, i.e. the failure to demythologize, is identical with the "heresy" of the opponents.

In Philippi, a few years later, we find a controversy of a related, even if somewhat different, kind.[90] As in Galatia, there is a group of foreign missionaries, Christians to be sure, who proclaim a renewal of the religious tradition of Israel through Jesus Christ. According to Phil. 3, Law obedience is their way to otherworldliness and spiritual perfection. Circumcision is part of the requirements (Phil. 3:2). The possession of the traditional qualities which distinguish Israel is an undisputed value (Phil. 3:4ff.). Paul's argument is by no means that such propaganda places obstacles in the Gentile's path into the church (this probably was not the case anyway), but that his opponents have not

[89] Cf. also Col. 2:8, 16ff.
[90] See my article "The Purpose . . .," above, note 8.

understood that the coming of the redeemer as a man who died implies a transformation of values for the believer (Phil. 3:7f.), i.e. a giving-up of religious possessions and a call for the identification with the suffering and crucifixion of Christ (Phil. 3:10–11), which renders impossible the attainment of trans-historical, supranatural and otherworldly qualities as a part of man's existence.

The further development of a Law propaganda with gnosticizing tendencies continues after Paul's death, particularly in Asia Minor.[91] In the letters to the seven churches in the Apocalypse of John, the adversaries who are labelled "Nicolaitans" (Rev. 2:6,15) claim to be true Jews (Rev. 2:9; 3:9), engage in daring interpretations of Scripture (cf. Rev. 2:14; also 2:20) and possess the mystical insight into the Divine (Rev. 2:24). Ignatius of Antioch writing to several churches in the province Asia again gives evidence of perhaps the same Christian group. As with the opponents in the epistle to the Colossians, observance of the ritual Law of the Old Testament is found among Ignatius' adversaries (Ign.Mg. 8–11; Phld. 6ff.). They stress the interpretation of Scripture (Ign.Phld. 8), but at the same time have developed a clearly docetic Christology (Ign.Trall. 10; Smyrn. 2ff.). Walter Bauer has set forth an interesting hypothesis observing that Ignatius did not write to Pergamon, Thyatira, Sardes, and Laodicea, i.e. to those of the seven churches of the Apocalypse which seemed to be hardest hit by a hostile Judaizing group. Is it possible, W. Bauer asks, that at the time of Ignatius these four churches were completely controlled by the opposition?[92] It also must be mentioned that at the same time the (Jewish?) Gnostic Cerinthus was teaching at Ephesus.[93]

Quite different from the battles with these Judaizers, who were soon to develop a docetic Christology, was the controversy in which Paul found himself with his church in Corinth.[94] The first

[91] Their "Judaizing Gnosticism" must be distinguished from later groups of encratite Ebionites.

[92] W. Bauer, op. cit., 82f.

[93] The various and often contradictory reports about Cerinthus are collected in A. Hilgenfeld, op. cit., 411–18.

[94] For the following description I am indebted to D. Georgi and to his excellent study Die Gegner des Paulus im 2. Korintherbrief. He shows convincingly that it is necessary to distinguish between the controversies in 1 and 2 Cor. With respect

disturbance among the Corinthians arose from a Jewish Hellenist Wisdom teaching which might have had affinity to their own syncretistic religious background. It led the community to ambitious boasting in the name of specific religious figures and to demonstrations of individualistic spiritual achievements. There are no theological parties in Corinth.[95] Apollos, according to Acts 18:24 a Jew from Alexandria, may have contributed to the rise of such boasting in wisdom when he instructed the church at Corinth after Paul's departure. Paul, however, has no theological or personal quarrel with Apollos, and he is confident that his letter will be successful in settling these rather internal problems in his church. We can assume that actually such was the result — in spite of fundamental theological implications of the dispute. The controversy of 1 Cor. is most illuminating, insofar as it is partly Paul's own eschatological message which must have given rise to the dispute, even though the teaching of the Alexandrian Apollos after Paul's departure may have added to the development of the theology and praxis of the "strong ones" in Corinth. The crucial problem is the question of the degree to which the future events of the eschatological timetable of Apocalypticism have become present reality through the coming of Jesus. Some people in Corinth would claim that everything had come about already, or even that, in the face of the accomplished presence of σοφία and γνῶσις through the teaching of Jesus and in the possession of the Spirit and the Sacraments, their ultimate perfection had taken place. Their practices indicate that such radicalization of the fulfilment of mythical expectations made responsibility for the οἰκοδομή of an existing Christian community as unnecessary as the expectation of future "acts of God in history" was superfluous (cf. "there is no resurrection of the dead," 1 Cor. 15:12).

to 1 Cor. W. Schmithals, Die Gnosis in Korinth (1956) offers many good observations; see, however, D. Georgi's review in Verkündigung und Forschung (1960), 90–96; further U. Wilckens, Weisheit und Torheit (1959), and my review of Wilckens in Gnomon 33(1961), 590–95. On 1 Cor. cf. also G. Bornkamm, "Herrenmahl und Kirche bei Paulus," above, note 8.

[95] Insofar J. Munck is quite right; see his chapter "The Church without Factions" in Paul and the Salvation of Mankind (1959), 135–67. I disagree with Munck, however, since I am persuaded that influence from Jewish Wisdom theology is actually evident, although it seems that such wisdom theology is closely related to Paul's own teaching and/or to Apollos' activity which in essence is not criticized by Paul.

In 1 Cor. in particular, it is evident that Paul's central argument against these developments recalls the cross of Jesus Christ (1 Cor. 1:18ff.; 2:2). It is seen as an event in a past history which corresponds to the future of the final apocalyptic acts of God (1 Cor. 11:26). Thus the present time is still "historical" time and its Christological dimension is that of the crucified Jesus. The Spirit as the eschatological gift derives from there (cf. 1 Cor. 2:16; 12:1–3), not from the anticipation of the future. The church as the body of this Jesus is an earthly community in which love rules for its "edification" (1 Cor. 12:4ff.). *Agape* is the only phenomenon in which the eschatological future is directly present in the church (1 Cor. 13:8–13). *Agape* controls the exercise of any other religious qualities and leaves no room for the demonstration of eschatological fulfilment. Thereby a dimension of responsibility to a period of this-worldly reality is opened up with which the Christian has to identify himself as Christ has done it in his coming. Contrary to traditional apocalyptic expectation, the future events do not inform the understanding of the present in a direct way, but they are part of a Christian modification of that world view, which now functions to keep the present open as historical time for human existence (1 Cor. 15 must be understood in this context).

The real threat to the Pauline mission at Corinth arose from quite different grounds. It results from a powerful Jewish Christian movement which extended decisive impulses to the further development of the Christian church. This disturbance with which Paul had to deal in various letters, a personal emergency visit to Corinth, and the sending of Titus — all of this now preserved and witnessed to in the so-called second epistle to the Corinthians [96] — was caused by the successful activity of foreign missionaries at Corinth. They represent a Jewish Christian propaganda (2 Cor. 11:22) which understands the Christian message as the renewal of the Covenant (2 Cor. 3), i.e. Christianity is the true Jewish religion. Methods and means of these

[96] Cf. G. Bornkamm, "Die Vorgeschichte des sogenannten Zweiten Korintherbriefes," Sitzungsberichte d. Heidelberger Akademie der Wissenschaften, Phil.-hist. Kl. 1961,2. A short English abstract of this study was published by G. Bornkamm under the title "The History of the Origin of the so-called Second Letter to the Corinthians," NTStud. 8 (1961/62), 258–64.

missionaries, quite different from those in Galatia, were modelled after and inherited from Hellenized Jewish propaganda and Apologetics.[97] Pneumatic demonstration of the presence of the powerful revival of the true religion of Israel was the essence of such missionary activity. In the case of 2 Cor. it is evident in the performance of miracles, the boasting of mystical experiences, artistic spiritual interpretation of Scripture. To this corresponds a Christology that sees Jesus as the primary example of such spiritual revival of true Jewish religion, i.e. as the model of the "Divine Man" who is not only imitated but at the same time essentially represented in the performance of his Apostle or "Servant" ($\delta\iota\acute{a}\kappa o\nu o\varsigma$).[98] The "Gospel" which corresponds to such a Christology must have been very similar to the narrative sources and traditions which have been used by our oldest written Gospels: the Gospel of Mark and the Gospel of John.

In 2 Cor. we can see more clearly in which way the New Covenant theology of Paul's opponents was positively informed by their understanding of the mission of Jesus. For them, Jesus was the basic example of the spiritual and religious transcending of the limitations of human existence, the $\theta\epsilon\hat{\iota}o\varsigma$ $\dot{a}\nu\acute{\eta}\rho$. Spiritual exegesis of the Old Testament opened up the road for a repetition of the religious experiences of figures like Moses. Paul, who did not even try to demonstrate his apostolic authority through pneumatic performances, had, in their view, no religious qualities. But Paul rejects their "religious" understanding of the Christian values, which implies their image of Christ, calling it a Christ according to the flesh (2 Cor. 5:16). He insists that God's real power is only present in human qualities of historical existence, the divine life hidden in the death of Jesus, and that it is revealed only in the word and the work of the Apostle for his church (see especially 2 Cor. 4:7–18). Again the criterion is the humanness and radicalized historicity of the revelation in Jesus.

The Gospel of Mark can be seen as a witness to a remarkable development in the further history of this Corinthian controversy. Mark's basic concept of the "Gospel" is Pauline,[99] and it is prob-

---

[97] D. Georgi, op. cit., 83–187.

[98] See D. Georgi, op. cit., 282–300, on the Christology of Paul's opponents.

[99] This W. Marxsen has shown convincingly; Der Evangelist Markus (1956), 83–92.

ably not only a coincidence that we find a "Mark" among Paul's company.[100] The material used by Mark is very much like the Jesus image of Paul's opponents in 2 Cor., even if Mark interprets critically the "Divine Man" Christology of his material. This is not necessarily to be taken as a statement about the place of origin for Mark's Gospel, although it seems to me advisable to connect Mark more closely with the area of Pauline mission.[101]

Considering the further development, the Gospel of Mark, which became the basis of the Gospels of Matthew and of Luke as well, is only an episode — even if its (Pauline) eschatological orientation [102] was understood and transformed into an eschatological theology of the church by Matthew in Antioch. In the area of Paul's missionary work in Asia Minor and Greece, Mark's Gospel was corrected in quite a different way by Luke.[103] Both Luke's Gospel and his Acts of the Apostles manifest the victory of Paul's Corinthian (2 Cor.) opponents in no uncertain terms.

According to Luke, Jesus in his earthly life "performs" — driven by the Spirit — the fulfillment of the true essence of the religion of the Old Testament. This fulfillment is accomplished in Jesus' ministry of powerful teaching and healing, not, however, through his passion and death (in Luke the passion narrative has become an appendix to the Gospel).[104] The powerful and successful activity of the Apostles and missionaries carries this new and true religion from Jerusalem to Rome. Nowhere else is the "Divine Man" motif so effectively used as in Luke, and that both in his Christology and in his description of the

---

[100] Phlm. 24; cf. Col. 4:10; 2 Tim. 4:11; the John Mark of Acts 12:25; 13:5ff. is probably a later Lukan construction. In any case, the tradition which connects Mark with Paul is much older than that which finds Mark in Peter's company (1 Peter 5:13; Papias apud Eusebius, hist. eccl. III.39.15).

[101] This means that Asia Minor and Achaia, perhaps Antioch, would be more likely than Rome; Galilee is, of course, not more than an imaginative error.

[102] As James M. Robinson, The Problem of History in Mark (1957), has shown. A re-statement of this interpretation and further literature to this question can be found in J. M. Robinson, "The Problem of History in Mark, Reconsidered," above, note 58.

[103] The most satisfactory explanation for the location of the writing of Luke-Acts, I believe, is Asia Minor. This, of course, does not exclude the availability of "Antiochian" traditions.

[104] See H. Conzelmann, The Theology of St. Luke (1960); cf. 201: ". . . there is no trace of any Passion mysticism, nor is any direct soteriological significance drawn from Jesus' suffering or death."

missionary. Luke's missionaries are as proficient as Paul's opponents in 2 Cor. with respect to the performance of miracles (Acts 3 and passim), inspired interpretation of the Old Testament (viz. the speeches), and spiritual experiences — in Luke-Acts Paul himself has to report his own vision twice to an astounded public, not to speak of us who also know 2 Cor. 12:1ff. No doubt, Luke was a student of Paul's opponents rather than of Paul himself.

A really new factor was introduced into Asia Minor (and perhaps Macedonia) after A.D. 70,[105] again of Jewish, and this time of more distinctly Palestinian Jewish, origin: Apocalypticism.[106] The first witness to this new impact is the (pseudepigraphical) second epistle of Paul to the Thessalonians. The opponents of this epistle, not without some justification, since Paul was in fact a proponent of a certain apocalyptic theology, use the authority of Paul for the proclamation of an apocalyptic kerygma: "The day of the Lord is at hand" (2 Thess. 2:2). During the same years (i.e. A.D. ca. 80-90) — and this is the time of the composition of such Jewish Apocalyptic literature as IV Esra — in the neighborhood of Ephesus a prophetic conventicle was formed. Its leader, a prophet of the name of John (not the author of the Gospel [107]) produced the Book of Revelation. The writing is impregnated with apocalyptic traditions from Judaism to a degree that is unparalleled in early Christianity before A.D. 70. But simultaneous developments had lead to the present form of the so-called Synoptic Apocalypse in Mark and Matthew (cf. Did. 16), probably somewhat before the writing of the Apoc-

[105] This judgment is based upon the observation that Apocalypticism as a genuine movement is not an issue in the countries around the Aegean Sea in Paul's lifetime.

[106] E. Käsemann "Zum Thema der urchristlichen Apokalyptik," Exegetische Versuche und Besinnungen II(1964), 105-31 [first published in Zeitschr. f. Theol.u. Kirche 59(1962), 257-84], is to be given full credit for reopening again the question of early Christian apocalyptic. He is certainly right in his emphasis upon the tremendous importance of apocalyptic thought in the early years of Christianity; I would add: upon both Christian heresy and orthodoxy at the same time. I understand my own attempts in this paper as a partial contribution to the task of attending to the legacy of historical inquiry which Käsemann has emphasized with genuine passion.

[107] I assume that the existence of this historical "Johannine" circle attracted the Ephesian tradition of the "Apostle" and disciple of the Lord of this name. Of course, it is not impossible that also the Gospel of John was written in Ephesus. It is known, however, that the geographical location of the origin of the Gospel of John poses the most puzzling problems to the scholar.

alypse of John. The letter to the Ephesians which belongs to the same period shows a surprising closeness to the apocalyptic terminology of the Qumran community,[108] as does 2 Cor. 6:14–7:1, a small section that was inserted into the second letter of Paul to the Corinthians when this epistle was edited by the church in Corinth at the close of the first century A.D.[109] It is certainly not impossible that the dispersion of the Qumran community after the Jewish war has contributed to these developments, since parallels to Qumran in early Christianity seem to be much more conspicuous after A.D. 70 than in the (historical) teaching of Jesus and the genuine letters of Paul.

Thus, at the close of the first century we find at Ephesus several rivaling Christian groups (not several separate churches): the originally Pauline church, supported by the Qumran-influenced Paulinist who wrote Ephesians, but also represented by the author of Luke-Acts who in his own way accommodated the tradition of the great Apostle to the expediencies of the church; — a Jewish Christian "school" engaging in a daring interpretation of the Old Testament, represented by the Gnostic Cerinthus; — a (Jewish Christian) conventicle producing the apocalyptic Revelation of the Christian prophet John.

In the second century some of these early rivaling Christian groups grew up to the stature of churches with the claim of universal validity. There is probably a continuous line running from the apocalyptic disturbances of Paul's church in Thessalonica (2 Thess.) to the rise of Montanism. Apocalyptic traditions and chiliasm are found in Papias, bishop of Hierapolis (ca. 135 A.D.), a city in Asia Minor not far from the centers in which Montanism rose between A.D. 150 and 160. As Montanism was a revival and radicalization of a primitive apocalyptic form of Christianity, the assumed original intention of Paul's theology found a most powerful advocate in Marcion, a Christian merchant and shipowner from Pontus. It would be just to acknowledge that both Montanus and Marcion were legitimate heirs of two forms of more primitive Chrisitan beliefs which both had

---

[108] Cf. F. M. Cross, The Ancient Library of Qumran (1961²), 216f.

[109] J. A. Fitzmyer, "Qumran and the Interpolated Paragraph in 2 Cor. 6:14–7:1," Cath.Bibl.Quart. 23(1961), 271–80.

a justifiable claim to represent the early times of Christianity in Asia Minor. Marcion's suspicion that the Pauline epistles had been meddled with was just as correct (cf. the number of pseudo-Pauline writings) as Montanus' basic contention that the primitive expectation of the parousia with all its powerful moral implications had vanished. That both men were shortsighted in their one-sided and biassed judgment is certainly a sane and sapient modern suggestion which should not overshadow the historical relevance of the factual existence of such primitive traditions and their surviving power.

One also has to consider the price which a more moderate abiding with the inheritance from the first generations had to pay. The "conservative" theology of Asia Minor which emerged around the year A.D. 100 provides us with typical examples. We have already discussed Luke's sacrifice of the Pauline Gospel in order to rescue the image of Paul as the great and exemplary missionary for the church as he understood it. What happened to Paul in the Pastoral Epistles is even more telling. The validity of Paul's inheritance is the central issue. The re-interpretation of Paul's theology, even its domestication, has many fascinating aspects. The author of the Pastorals understood that the real proof of Paul's Apostolic authority is his suffering rather than any invented glory of his ministry. With Paul he also knows that the decisive battleground for the authentication of Christian existence is the church in a world of hard and fast facts of social and political necessities, rather than the field of disquisitional theological verification and speculation. But it still has the appearance of a sell-out of the Pauline theology under unfavorable conditions. The eschatological tension of Paul's thought has disappeared and, on the other hand, the author of the Pastorals is unable to re-open this dimension through the adaptation of categories of space (as e.g. in Eph. and Col.), since this was the prerogative of Paul's gnostic students. The recommendation is, thus, to read Paul for edification (individual and ecclesiastical), rather than as a stimulus to creative re-interpretation in a changed situation. Since theology here has become something that can be learned by practice and exercise in godliness, certain false theological sentences by definition characterize the heretic (if he is not simply recognized by his engagement in theological discourse). In Polycarp of Smyrna (in his second letter to the Philippians [110]) we find, for the first time, a carefully formulated summary of various "heretical" doctrines (Pol. Phil. 7:1). The formulation leaves no doubt that, for Polycarp, the true believer confesses and adheres to a modest minimum of true doctrines composed of Pauline and apocalyptic traditions. Moderation in the continuation of the inheritance from earlier generations instead of a fresh return to the roots of Christianity, the earthly Jesus, has become the leading criterion. This was to last until finally the new authority of the New Testament canon provided the basis for a new theological departure. The discussion of that development, however, would require a renewed analysis of the formation of Egyptian and Western, especially Roman, Christianity in the first two centuries.

[110] Cf. P. N. Harrison, Polycarp's Two Epistles to the Philippians (1936). If Harrison is right, we have to date this second letter (=Pol.Phil. 1–12) in the time of Marcion's beginnings.

Vigiliae Christianae 30, 23–44; © *North-Holland Publishing Company* 1976

IGNATIUS, POLYCARP, AND I CLEMENT: WALTER BAUER RECONSIDERED

BY

FREDERICK W. NORRIS

Walter Bauer's attack on the classical theory of the development of heresy remains impressive. The claim of some early Christian writers that everywhere heresy was both later in time and smaller in number than orthodoxy appears to be untenable to many scholars.[1] Even H. E. W. Turner contested the report that heresy only flourished in a few places, although he vigorously defended orthodoxy's priority.[2] The historical reconstructions which Bauer offered, however, continue to be debated. His assessment of the evidence resulted in two theses. 1) In most areas of the Mediterranean basin – particularly Edessa, Egypt, Asia Minor, Antioch, Macedonia, and Crete – heresy was either earlier than and/or stronger than orthodoxy. 2) From the beginning of the second century the Roman community was singularly the dominant influence in the formation of orthodoxy.[3] My purpose is to examine Bauer's treatment of

---

[1]   Walter Bauer, *Rechtgläubigkeit und Ketzerei im ältesten Christentum*, Beiträge zur historischen Theologie, 10, zweite, durchgesehene Auflage mit einem Nachtrag, herausgegeben von Georg Strecker (Tübingen, J. C. B. Mohr/Paul Siebeck, 1964) 3–4 mentions Origen, *Comm. II in Cantic.* (see Baehrens, GCS 33, 179) and *Sel. in Prov.* (see Lommatzsch 13, 228), Tertullian, *De praescr. haer.* 36, and Hegesippus in Eusebius, *H.E.* 4,22,2–6 as espousing the so-called classical theory of the development of heresy. Reviews of and responses to Bauer are cited in Georg Strecker, Die Aufnahme des Buches, in *Rechtgläubigkeit*, 288–306. The American translation by the Philadelphia Seminar on Christian Origins, *Orthodoxy and Heresy in Earliest Christianity*, ed. by Robert A. Kraft and Gerhard Krodel (Philadelphia, Fortress Press, 1971) – published in England by SCM in 1972 – contains a "completely revised and expanded" version of Strecker's essay by Robert Kraft, 286–316. Helmut Koester, Häretiker im Urchristentum, *RGG*³ III, 17–21 has an extensive list of works influenced by Bauer.

[2]   H. E. W. Turner, *The Pattern of Christian Truth: A Study in the Relations between Orthodoxy and Heresy in the Early Church*, Bampton Lectures 1954 (London, A. R. Mowbray & Co. Ltd., 1954) 7.

[3]   Bauer, *Rechtgläubigkeit*. These theses are most easily seen in Bauer's own precis of his book, Rechtgläubigkeit und Ketzerei im ältesten Christentum, *Aufsätze und Kleine Schriften*, herausgegeben von Georg Strecker (Tübingen, J. C. B. Mohr/Paul Siebeck,

selected sources from Antioch, Asia Minor, and Rome in order to reconsider both the method by which he arrived at these theses and the theses themselves.

I. "ORTHODOXY": A MINORITY IN ANTIOCH AND ASIA MINOR

The way in which Bauer employed the terms "orthodoxy" and "heresy" has been a point of contention even for those who accepted his insights. The legitimacy of that criticism will be discussed below. Here attention is directed to the claim which Bauer makes that the supporters of Ignatius and Polycarp were probably a minority in Antioch and Asia Minor. His claim may be summarized as follows. Ignatius' frantic concern for his allies is best explained against the background of a minority whose very existence is threatened. The argumentation which he put forward for monarchial episcopacy is typical of minority groups. Although it is possible that Ignatius' friends represented a plurality in the various cities to which and about which he wrote, his frenzied activity in behalf of his supporters and his overwrought exhortations to them, suggest that this was not the case. Antiochene "orthodoxy" must have been seriously endangered. Nothing else could have called forth Ignatius' unparalleled request from every congregation known to him for representatives or at least letters to be sent to Antioch. The peril was depicted so clearly that bishop Polycarp wanted to leave troubled Smyrna and himself travel as a delegate to Antioch. On the basis of these texts, Bauer concluded that "orthodoxy" in both Western Syria and Asia Minor was of questionable size and influence.[4]

Bauer himself changed his estimation of the number of those supporting Ignatius. First, he viewed the possibility of their being a majority as unlikely because of Ignatius' frantic arguments and efforts. Then he suggested that they probably comprised smaller or larger majorities in Ephesus, Magnesia, Tralles, and Philadelphia.[5] The unquestioned concession of probable majorities favoring Ignatius in Ephesus, Magnesia, Tralles, and Philadelphia has two results. 1) Bauer's claim that Ignatius' views developed from minorities cannot be substantiated on his own reading of the evidence, unless he can prove that these three cities had

---

1967) 229–233. Hans-Dietrich Altendorf, Zum Stichwort: Rechtgläubigkeit und Ketzerei im ältesten Christentum, *Zeitschrift für Kirchengeschichte* (1969) 62–63 gives a similar summary of Bauer.

[4]   Bauer, *Rechtgläubigkeit*, 65–78.
[5]   Pp. 67, 73, and 81.

"orthodox" minorities prior to Ignatius, or demonstrate that there were no truly monarchial bishops in those communities. Bauer made no attempt to argue that prior to the time of Ignatius, Magnesia, Tralles, and Philadelphia had "orthodox" minorities. He tried to indicate that Ephesus could have been no "center or orthodoxy" before Ignatius. If that could be established – which I doubt[6] – it would still not be definitive evidence that Ignatius' argument arises from a minority situation. Bauer had already conceded that Ephesus probably had a majority agreeing with Ignatius' views when the Syrian wrote. Bauer's assertion that there were nor real bishops in these cities will be handled below. 2) He could still claim that Ignatius' arguments for monepiscopacy come from a threatened minority, if he could establish the minority status of "orthodoxy" in Smyrna and Antioch prior to and during the time of Ignatius.

The texts relating to Smyrna do indicate a struggle. It is possible that both in *Smyrneans* 6,1 and *Polycarp* 1,2 the use of *topos* refers to a significant leader or leaders who were performing cultic acts outside Polycarp's jurisdiction. The opening of Polycarp's letter to the Philippians also may be evidence for counter-leadership.[7] Bauer posited a "gnostic anti-bishop" or someone acting in that way although he did not wish to quarrel about semantics.[8] These details, however, are not enough to warrant the conclusion that in Smyrna, Polycarp and those supporting Ignatius' supporters in Smyrna also comprised a majority. Decisively, as firmly in the way of demonstrating their minority status. *Smyrneans* 10 indicates that the Smyrneans unlike the Philadelphians had received Ignatius' representatives quite well. Both Philo and Rheus wished to express their thankfulness for the way in which they were treated by the Smyrnean congregation. If, as Bauer conceded, the supporters of Ignatius were a probable majority in Philadelphia, and yet did not treat Ignatius' representatives as well as the congregation in Smyrna, it is possible that Ignatius' supporters in Smyrna also comprised a majority. Decisively, as in Philadelphia, Ignatius was so certain of the proper faith and strength of the Smyrneans that he asked them to appoint a delegate to be sent to congratulate the congregation in Antioch. If Ignatius had felt that the

---

[6]   I argue the weakness of Bauer's case concerning Ephesus in "Asia Minor Before Ignatius: Walter Bauer Reconsidered", to be published in *Studia Evangelica*, papers from the Fifth International Congress on Biblical Studies, Oxford, 3–7 September 1973.

[7]   Bauer, *Rechtgläubigkeit*, 73–74. Turner, *The Pattern of Christian Truth*, 64 contests both points.

[8]   Bauer, *Rechtgläubigkeit*, 73.

Smyrneans would have had any difficulty in appointing a faithful delegate, he certainly would not have requested them to send one to his beloved Antiochenes.[9] Furthermore, since Bauer insisted that in Smyrna during Polycarp's lifetime there was no "separation between ecclesiastical Christianity and heresy",[10] on his reading of the evidence, there was no "heretical" group outside the community to which Ignatius wrote. Therefore, Bauer has been unable to prove that ecclesiastical Christianity was a minority among the Christians in Smyrna.

The situation in Antioch reflects the same kinds of difficulties seen in Smyrna, although we have little direct evidence about conditions there. In this instance, however, Bauer misinterpreted the information we possess. Ignatius did not seek representatives or letters to be sent to Antioch from every church open to him. In his epistle to Polycarp, he did ask Polycarp to write churches on his route to Rome since the journey from Troas to Neapolis came much sooner than he had anticipated. One purpose of these requested letters was to ask congregations to send representatives or messages to Antioch.[11] The reference to "bishops, presbyters, and deacons" in *Philadelphians* 10, however, states that "the nearest churches have sent bishops, and the others presbyters and deacons". Bauer, in his handbook treating the Ignatian epistles, understood "nearest" to refer not to Philadelphia or Troas, the city from which the letter to Philadelphia was written, but rather to Antioch.[12] If this interpretation is correct, bishops were only sent from churches near Antioch. Presbyters and deacons came from the more distant churches. This interpretation is supported by the fact that nowhere in his letters did Ignatius ask a bishop to go as a messenger. The Philadelphian letter specifically requests that a deacon be appointed.[13] Ignatius sought a delegate from Smyrna, but Tralles, Ephesus, and Rome were encouraged to pray for the church in Syria.[14] The letter to the Magnesians contains a cryptic phrase of purpose, concerning the refreshment of the Antiochene congregation with the dew of the Magnesian congregation, but that purpose is related to prayer.[15] Therefore, of the six churches to which Ignatius wrote, four were in no

---

[9]   *Smyrneans* 11. Compare *Philadelphians* 10.
[10]   Bauer, *Rechtgläubigkeit*, 75.
[11]   *Polycarp* 8,1.
[12]   Walter Bauer, *Die Briefe des Ignatius von Antiochia und der Polykarpbrief*, Handbuch zum neuen Testament (Tübingen, J. C. B. Mohr/Paul Siebeck, 1920) 262.
[13]   *Philadelphians* 10,1.
[14]   *Smyrneans* 11,2; *Trallians* 13,1; *Ephesians* 21,2; *Romans* 9,1.
[15]   *Magnesians* 14,1.

way requested to send either representatives or letters. Only two were asked to send delegates. The letters written from Troas: *Philadelphians*, *Smyrneans*, and *Polycarp*, make mention of either representatives or letters.

At this point Bauer might have claimed that something important occurred just before the final letters were written which caused Ignatius to change his strategy. In that case, the purpose of the delegates and/or letters would have had to have been investigated. This, however, Bauer ignored. In both the Smyrnean and Philadelphian epistles, the purpose was to congratulate the Antiochenes for the resolution of their problems.[16] The congratulations were "that they have gained peace, and have restored their proper greatness, and that their proper constitution has been restored".[17] Such statements suggest earlier unrest in Antioch, and perhaps reflect problems Ignatius had there as bishop. The peace may have been shaky. Ignatius was indeed concerned, but he also was satisfied that the present condition was proper. The news of peace in Antioch was what prompted sending messengers. The possibility of Ignatius' supporters being "routed from the field" or being "driven back" without him,[18] would have been more likely when the first letters were written, i.e., before the news of peace had arrived. Yet it is precisely these first letters from Ignatius which ask neither for delegates nor for letters to Antioch.

Bauer was impressed also by the fact that so many delegates were requested even to the rank of bishop from churches which were themselves in danger. The only mention of bishops is in *Philadelphians* 10 which Bauer read as a reference to churches near Antioch. He did not attempt to demonstrate that these anonymous churches near Antioch were threatened. His example of a troubled bishop was Polycarp, whom Bauer thought "would have preferred to undertake the journey to Antioch in person" because Ignatius had so strongly stressed the necessity of such delegates.[19] Ignatius did ask Polycarp to call a council and select a zealous and beloved person to act as God's courier to Antioch.[20] Ignatius, however, did not ask Polycarp to go. In *Polycarp* 8 he says: "I greet him who shall be appointed to go to Syria. Grace will be with him through all, and with Polycarp, who sends him." Furthermore, Polycarp

---

[16] *Smyrneans* 11,2; *Philadelphians* 10,1.
[17] *Smyrneans* 11,2.
[18] Bauer, *Rechtgläubigkeit*, 69.
[19] P. 68–69.
[20] *Polycarp* 8,2.

was so unimpressed with the necessity of his undertaking the task, that in his letter to the Philippians he says, "I will do this if I have a convenient opportunity, either myself or the one whom I am sending representing you and me."[21] Those are not the words of a man who saw the survival of the Antiochene church endangered or one who was so worried about the state of things in Smyrna that he could not leave that city. The "orthodox" community in Antioch had experienced serious difficulties, but Bauer did not assemble evidence which proves that the conditions there prior to Ignatius' epistles demand an "orthodox" minority.[22] At the time of the writing of Ignatius' letters, neither the tone of his arguments nor the scope of his actions establish the fact that he represented a threatened minority.

In the consideration of Bauer's description of the Christian communities in Antioch and Asia Minor, three points, then, are in order. First, in both areas he has been unable to demonstrate either the priority or the majority of "heresy". Ignatius and Polycarp indicate concern about "wrong" teaching and practice, but those supporting them in the Asia Minor and Western Syrian cities which their writings reflect, probably represented majorities. Secondly, the attempt to assess minorities and priorities among "orthodox" and "heretical" communities was and is important in order to deal with the classical theory of the development of heresy. That theory will continue to hold sway until such evidence is accumulated and assessed. This assessment, however, cannot be bound to a sociological theory which views arguments for monepiscopacy to be indicative of minorities. In this period all Christians of any description were in the minority. Small groups pressured by the larger culture, may see themselves as threatened even by the smallest amount of opposition from within. One or two influential people can change the whole direction of such a group. The situation which Bauer posited, a democratic *Sitz im Leben* in which control of the council has been lost, is not necessary to explain either the deep concern of Ignatian texts, or the concern of any other texts. Since Bauer has not established an "orthodox" minority within the communities in which bishops were present, nor in Ignatius'

---

[21] *Philippians* 13,1.
[22] Bauer, *Rechtgläubigkeit*, 67 saw the dispute between Peter and Paul (Galatians 2,11–21), the fact that Paul never again spoke of Antioch, and the cryptic reference to Antioch in Acts 18,22–23 as evidence against the possibility of Ignatius being a monarchial bishop. But he did not demonstrate that "orthodoxy" was a minority in Antioch prior to Ignatius.

home Antioch, then he has not demonstrated that Ignatius' arguments for monepiscopacy come from a threatened minority within the various sectors of Christianity. Bauer attempted to shore up that description by claiming that there were no real bishops in those communities, but failed to establish that claim, as we shall see. Thirdly, none of the evidence discussed demonstrates that "orthodoxy" was a majority throughout Asia Minor and Western Syria. The texts only indicate that "orthodoxy" was probably a majority in the specific cities mentioned. Bauer cannot claim that "orthodoxy" in these cities was threatened with extinction. On the other hand, one cannot claim that "heresy" was without power and influence in the regions, and possibly in the majority in some places. The ultimate question of plurality in these areas cannot be answered. In order to distinguish these adversaries, however, the question as to whether or not the categories of "orthodoxy" and "heresy" are even applicable to early Christianity must be examined.

II. "HERESY" AND MONEPISCOPACY

In his introduction Bauer stated that he employed the terms "orthodoxy" and "heresy" in a way which was consistent with their customary usage.[23] Using the terms in that context allowed him to emphasize the strength and priority of "heresy" in particular regions of the Mediterranean basin. Still he was careful to insist that later meanings of the terms were not applicable. He specifically denied that either Ignatius or Polycarp had a conception of "heretics" being excluded from the Church, and insisted that both made unity and reconciliation their primary goals.[24] Although the phrase "catholic church" was used for the first time in ecclesiastical history by Ignatius, it was employed in an inclusive sense rather than the exclusive sense in which it was to appear in the Muratorian Canon at the end of the second century.[25] Bauer viewed the absence of a division between "inside" and "outside" as an indication that Ignatius, the "bishop of Syria", would have had to claim all the baptized believers in Syria under his hegemony. Since there were many Gnostic teachers in Antioch, as well as other strong religious influences, it then became clear to Bauer that Ignatius could not have been a bishop worthy of the title.[26] Polycarp suffered the same fate since no separation between "heresy" and

---

[23] Bauer, *Rechtgläubigkeit*, 2–3.
[24] Pp. 67 and 75.
[25] P. 231.
[26] Pp. 67–71.

"orthodoxy" occurred within his lifetime. He also must have claimed all the "heretics" in Smyrna to be under his jurisdiction, and therefore could hardly be considered a powerful monarchial bishop in light of "heretical" strength in that city. If these two champions were not truly bishops, then it is unlikely that those Ignatius mentions as bishops in other cities could properly wear the title.[27]

Bauer is probably correct in asserting that no clear separation between "orthodoxy" and "heresy" can be constructed from the Ignatian and Polycarp letters. The observation about the different meanings of the term "catholic church" in Ignatius and the Muratorian Canon is important in tracing developments in early Christianity. There are, however, developments which Bauer overlooked, precisely because he stated the issue in terms of separation or division. He insisted that the word "heresy" when it appears in Ignatius means "Sekte" rather than "Ketzerei".[28] This is consistent with his later contention that Ignatius considered the opponents to be inside the community of faith. Both Lampe and Grant, however, point out that the term means "Ketzerei". Ehrhardt suggests that particularly in Tralles a separation between Ignatius' supporters and opponents had occurred because no word of reconciliation appears in the Trallian epistle.[29] There is no call to re-

---

[27]   Pp. 75–76 and 71–72.

[28]   Bauer, *Die Briefe*, 235 concerning *Trallians* 6,1.

[29]   G. W. H. Lampe, *A Patristic Greek Lexicon* (Oxford, Clarendon Press, 1968) 51 and Robert M. Grant, *The Apostolic Fathers: New Translation and Commentary*, Vol. 4, *Ignatius of Antioch* (London, Thomas Nelson & Sons, 1966) 76 in reference to *Trallians* 6,1. Arnold Ehrhardt, Christianity before the Apostles' Creed, *The Framework of the New Testament Stories* (Manchester, University Press, 1964) 180–181 views the word "heresy" as meaning "sect" but claims that there was a separation in Tralles in which the opponents appear to have been "irretrievably lost". The comparison in which the word occurs in *Trallians* 6,1 is strong evidence for its use in the sense of "Ketzerei". *Ephesians* 6,2 is enigmatic, as is Hermas *Sim.* 9,23,5. Neither of those references supplies a clear context in which to determine the exact meaning. I Clement 14,2 has used the term to mean "strife" or "party spirit". Ἑτεροδοξία as a noun in *Magnesians* 8,1 and in verb form in *Smyrneans* 6,2 only appears in Ignatius among the so called "Apostolic Fathers" in the sense of "another or irregular opinion". His letter to Polycarp 3,1 employs ἑτεροδιδασκαλέω. I Clement 11,2 uses ἑτερογνώμων of Lot's wife, indicating a "change of mind". Hermas, *Man.* 6,1,2 contrasts the two ways with the use of ὀρθός. J. B. Lightfoot, *The Apostolic Fathers*, Vol. II. Sect. 1 (London, Macmillan and Co., 1885) 28 on the basis of the Syriac and Armenian translations emended Ignatius' *Ephesians* 1,1 with the phrase ἐν γνώμῃ ὀρθῇ καί. If his emendation were correct, that would be the closest approximation of the term "orthodoxy" to appear in the "Apostolic Fathers". The word "orthodoxy" itself does not occur. Although word studies without strong contextual evidence are misleading, this collection suggested by the references in

pentance in that letter, and the contrast in which the word "heresy" appears is one between "Christian food" and that "strange plant, which is heresy". In the same letter, further distinction is made between those who are inside the sanctuary with the bishop, presbytery, deacons, and ordinances of the Apostles, and those who are outside the sanctuary. The latter are not of pure conscience. In addition the advice is explicitly given to beware of these people, to be deaf to what they say and to flee from their teachings.[30]

The Trallian letter, then, distinguishes between outside and inside by viewing the adversaries as outside. The names which Ignatius calls his opponents throughout his epistles tend to strengthen this image. The "atheists" are referred to four times as "unbelievers".[31] Although they bear the "name" – probably "Christian" – they carry it with "wicked guile". In reality they are "mad dogs" and "wild beasts" who are very difficult to heal.[32] While it is true that those who are not called Christian are not of God, some, however, use the name without actually being Christian.[33] The teachings of these adversaries are "evil". They are a "different doctrine or view" composed of "old fables", a "poisonous oil", "wicked arts", and "the snares of the prince of this world".[34] Their actions indicate a lack of expected compassion, of not caring either for love or the unlovely.[35] The consequences of following such teachings are the loss of the "Passion" and "Resurrection", "the Kingdom of God" and

---

Henricus Kraft, *Clavis Patrum Apostolicorum* (Darmstadt, Wissenschaftliche Buchgesellschaft, 1963) tends to indicate that at least in Ignatius the problem of "heresy" and "orthodoxy" was of concern.

[30] *Trallians* 6,1–7,2.

[31] *Trallians* 10,1. *Trallians* 3,2 may refer to those in the larger culture rather than to the specific opponents. *Magnesians* 5,2; *Trallians* 10,1; *Smyrneans* 2,1 and 5,3 all refer to the antagonists as "unbelievers". This collection of Ignatius' descriptions of his adversaries may be assembled without regard to the question of whether or not he combatted one or two groups. The issue concerns the possibility of his having distinguished "inside" and "outside". Virginia Corwin, *St. Ignatius and Christianity in Antioch*, Yale Publications in Religion, 1 (New Haven, Yale University Press, 1960) 52–87 is one of the most recent attempts to suggest at least two sets of opponents. Einar Molland, The Heretics Combated by Ignatius of Antioch, *Journal of Ecclesiastical History* 5 (1954) 1–6 and L. W. Barnard, The Background of St. Ignatius of Antioch, *Vigiliae Christianae* 17 (1963) 193–206 suggest only one group.

[32] *Ephesians* 7,1.

[33] *Magnesians* 4,1 and 10,1.

[34] *Ephesians* 9,1. 10,3. 16,1. 17,1; *Magnesians* 8,1; *Philadelphians* 3,1. 3,3. 6,2; *Smyrneans* 6,2; *Polycarp* 3,1. 5,1.

[35] *Smyrneans* 6,2.

"immortality", paralleled with the gain of "death" and "unquenchable fire".[36]

The above texts serve to strengthen the suggestion that Ignatius does make a distinction between inside and outside and relegates his adversaries to a position outside the community of the faithful. Even stronger elements of his letters support this interpretation. Ignatius is the only person in this period who argued for the theological necessity of mon-episcopacy. Not only does he give a series of metaphors in which the relationship of bishop, presbyters and deacons are compared with divinity, heavenly beings, and apostles,[37] he also considers baptism and the Eucharist to be under the jurisdiction of the bishop. The Eucharist is the bread of God, the medicine of immortality. Unless a man is within the sanctuary, he lacks the bread of God. Only the Eucharist which is celebrated by the bishop or his appointee is both "secure and valid".[38] The implication is that those who participate in an "invalid" Eucharist do not receive immortality and do not share in the benefits of the faith. This implication corresponds to the description of the opponents and the consequences of their teachings.

To this point the evidence appears to demand a clear differentiation between Ignatius' friends and his enemies, which may have reached the point of separation in Tralles. Separation, however, does not appear to have been the usual situation in the cities to which Ignatius wrote. *Smyrneans* 6–8 probably provides the strongest statements about the validity of the Eucharist only under the jurisdiction of the bishop. The faithful are urged to refrain from contact with the adversaries, even to the point of not speaking of them in public or in private. This might appear to be an example of separation, particularly since Smyrna is the place in which Bauer envisioned the existence of counter meetings under a "gnostic anti-bishop".[39] Yet one must step back from this tantalizing suggestion of division by noting two important aspects of this passage. First, the antagonists have not been forced out of the Eucharist because of their understanding of it. They have not been excluded or excommunicated. Ignatius might have pictured them as absenting themselves from the service in order to put the onus of division on them. It is exactly at

[36] *Ephesians* 16,2 and 20,2; *Philadelphians* 3,3; *Smyrneans* 5,1. 7,1.
[37] *Ephesians* 3,2–6,1; *Magnesians* 2–3,2. 6,1–7,2. 13; *Trallians* 2,1–3,2. 12,2; *Philadelphians* insc., 1. 3,2. 7–8,1; *Smyrneans* 8–9,1; *Polycarp* insc. 5,2–6,1.
[38] *Ephesians* 5,2. 20,2; *Smyrneans* 8. Compare *Trallians* 7,2; *Magnesians* 4.
[39] Bauer, *Rechtgläubigkeit*, 73.

this point that he warns his supporters to "flee from divisions as the beginning of evils". This warning, however, is better explained by a second consideration. In this context Ignatius exhorts "all of them" to follow the bishop. There is still time for the offenders to return to soberness and to repent. Here is the practical application of Ignatius' aversion to division and his love of unity which is testified to throughout his letters.[40] One can see this reflected even in the vilest names he calls his adversaries. When they are viewed as "mad dogs" and "wild beasts" almost incapable of being healed, Ignatius mentions the "one Physician". The disruptive teachers from outside Ephesus are probably included in the "other men" for whom the Ephesians were to pray and to hope for repentance, living before them in love and gentleness so that they might become disciples of the faithful and thus find God. Similar advice was given to Polycarp in dealing with his antagonists.[41]

Within the letters, the tension between exclusion and inclusion cannot be resolved, not even by observing the differences in each individual community. Ignatius has the structure necessary to distinguish "heresy" and "orthodoxy". He describes who the opponents are, what they teach and how they act, and has theologically to his satisfaction justified a system of organization in which the bishop is in charge of the valid sacraments. The Trallian letter might be given as an instance of separation primarily because Ignatius offered no words of reconciliation in that epistle. It is always difficult, however, to prove that silence on a specific point is intentional. Ignatius' overall attempt appears to be to preserve unity, rather than to exclude impurity. Exclusion is an action which Ignatius accused his adversaries of taking, an action he only once suggested with no indication that those excluded were to be called to repentance. The opponents may have seen themselves as separate, that is, as not needing what Ignatius' supporters offered. On the other hand, Ignatius usually prays for their repentance and their return to the valid Eucharist. His letters do not indicate what is to be done with such people if they refuse to repent and to return to the bishop. The Trallian situation cannot be shown to be the way in which recalcitrant adversaries are to be handled since no previous attempt at reconciliation in that community can be established. Ignatius had taken a significant step, however, in

---

[40] *Magnesians* 1,2. 13,2; *Trallians* 11,2; *Philadelphians* 2,1. 3,2. 4. 7,2. 8,1; *Smyrneans* 7,2; *Polycarp* 1. s. 5,2.
[41] *Ephesians* 7. 10; *Polycarp* 1–3.

distinguishing between "heresy" and "orthodoxy", although he offered no consistent position as to what must be done with unrepentant opposition. Polycarp gives no indication of separation, in spite of the use of strong language about his adversaries, and the possibility on Bauer's reading of his epistle, that he distinguished those presbyters who were with him from those who were not. Although his list of errors is quite scathing, he calls for moderation and repentance.[42]

Bauer emphasized the lack of separation between "heresy" and "orthodoxy" in Ignatius and Polycarp as if there was no distinction made. Precisely because of Ignatius' concern for unity and reconciliation, as well as his interest in repentance and the restoration of peace, he probably did feel some kind of claim on all the baptized of Syria. Bauer, however, stressed one part of the position and then extended it as if it were conclusive. All the force of Ignatius' derisive names, his villification of teachers and teachings, his organization of valid Eucharist under the bishop, and the lack of a word of reconciliation in the Trallian epistle indicate a distinction which could be the beginning of a justified separation, if the adversaries refused to repent and return to the bishop. Polycarp also uses strong names for his antagonists, and gives a concise list of errors to be combatted. Clear separation is to be found in neither of their writings, but they would have been leary of claiming their opponents as being anything but the most wayward of brothers.

Bauer's inability to grasp the difference between the beginning of a process and its fullest development led him to emphasize the lack of separation in Ignatius and Polycarp and to miss the attempts at distinction. His logic fell into the same trap when he insisted that the fullest development of monepiscopacy must be present in its beginning in order for it to exist at all. By positing that Ignatius would have needed to claim his opponents as "inside", Bauer intended to show that Ignatius would have had strong opposition from within. Because, in Bauer's view, a monarchial biship should have had "unlimited power", and "full recognition" as well as never having been overcome with the ineffectiveness of his efforts, Ignatius was not the bishop of Syria.[43] Bauer's mention of the Gnostic teachers in Antioch only demonstrates that Ignatius was not a bishop, if Bauer's definitions of "inside" and "monepiscopacy" are

---

[42] *Philippians* 2,1. 7. 11,4.
[43] Bauer, *Rechtgläubigkeit*, 71, 72, and 75.

accepted.[44] The major methodological error occurs in tightening the definition of "monepiscopacy" not only to demand its fullest development, but beyond this, to demand such characteristics of monepiscopacy that it would be difficult to find many bishops in any period of history. The imposition of an "ideal" definition kept Bauer from reading the evidence correctly. While in the available literature of this period, Ignatius offers the single example of theological arguments for the necessity of monepiscopacy, it is not likely that he himself originated the office in Asia Minor. His letters to the Ephesians, Magnesians, Trallians, Philadelphians, and Smyrneans argue for finer distinctions between bishop, presbyters and deacons than has previously existed. He does not need, however, to suggest or contend for a difference between the place of Onesimus, Apollonius, or Zotion. They are bishop, presbyter and deacon. Other persons are given with the respective titles. Such distinctions were recognizable to his readers. The Philadelphians are to appoint a deacon to be sent to Antioch. Neighboring churches have sent bishops, others, presbyters and deacons.[45] The strong case which Ignatius made for the theological and organizational significance of the bishop probably was new, but prior to his writing, the offices existed and were distinguished from each other in Asia Minor, and probably in Western Syria.

It has become evident, then, that Bauer has a tendency to use peculiar definitions of important terms, employing them with these meanings in

---

[44] Pp. 70–71. Bauer noticed the presence of Menander, Saturninus, Cerdo, and Basilides in Antioch around the time of Ignatius. But this information, although important, does not establish Bauer's claims about Ignatius, unless Ignatius must accept all these teachers as "Christian" and could not be a bishop with such opposition. Bauer has not demonstrated the strength of the groups following these Gnostics, nor that Ignatius would have accepted them without distinction as "Christian", nor that one can only be a bishop if one has no opponents.

Ehrhardt, Christianity before the Apostles' Creed, 180–181 criticizes Bauer's same arguments, but on other grounds. He views Ignatius as too Gnostic to represent the Antiochene community which produced the pseudo-Clementines. Heinrich Schlier, *Religionsgeschichtliche Untersuchungen zu den Ignatiusbriefen*, Beihefte zur Zeitschrift für die neutestamentliche Wissenschaft, 8 (Giessen, Töpelmann, 1929) and Hans-Werner Bartsch, *Gnostisches Gut und Gemeindetradition bei Ignatius von Antiochien*, Beitrag zur Förderung christlicher Theologie, 2. Reihe, 44. Band (Gütersloh, C. Bertelsmann, 1940) most strongly argue for Gnostic influence in Ignatius. However, Hans Lietzmann, *A History of the Early Church*, Vol. I, trans. by Bertram Les Woolf (New York, Meridian Books, 1961) 236–248, Grant, *The Apostolic Fathers, Ignatius*, and Barnard, The Background of St. Ignatius of Antioch, contest the strength of such influence.

[45] *Ephesians* 1,3–2,1. 4,1; *Magnesians* 2; *Trallians* 1; *Philadelphians* insc., 10; *Smyrneans* 12,2.

such a fashion as to apparently strengthen his argumentation. Probably because of this tendency, the possibility of using the terms "heresy" and "orthodoxy" as he did for the beginning of the second century has been questioned. Bauer did employ the terms with sweeping inclusiveness.[46] If they are meant to imply later definitions, then they do not fit. If, however, they are inserted in discussions of this period to signify the beginning of those developments which led to later definitions, they then become important tools. Ignatius used forms of the terms and did make distinctions which might have led to eventual separation. What is called for in the study of the documents from this era is a closer and more accurate reading of the texts in relation to these terms. The "cutting edges" in the conflicts need to be found.[47] Suggesting that such terminology will only serve to confuse the issue, avoids the beginning of issues which are in the texts.

III. "ORTHODOXY" AS ROMAN

Bauer has been unable to demonstrate that what he terms "heresy" was prior to and/or stronger than "orthodoxy" in Antioch and Asia Minor. At the same time he has also been unable to establish that monepiscopacy did not exist in these regions. Furthermore, he has misunderstood the important distinctions between "heresy" and "orthodoxy" which appear in the literature and form a background for their later separation. Therefore, Antioch and Asia Minor represent areas in which "orthodoxy", although challenged by strong and influential adversaries, was not in disarray at the beginning of the second century. If that is true, then it can be brought directly to bear on Bauer's second thesis, i.e., that Rome alone

---

[46] Wilhelm Schneemelcher, Walter Bauer als Kirchenhistoriker, *New Testament Studies* 9,1 (1962) 18. Robert A. Kraft, The Reception of the Book, *Orthodoxy and Heresy*, 312–314 offers a series of penetrating questions and suggests the use of the terms should be limited to those points where they appear in the texts. Hans-Dietrich Altendorf, in his review of the second edition of Bauer, *Theologische Literaturzeitung* 91,3 (1966) 194 utters a warning concerning the difficulty of treating these issues.

[47] James M. Robinson, Kerygma and History in the New Testament, in: *Trajectories through Early Christianity* (Philadelphia, Fortress Press, 1971) recognizes the problems involved, but suggests that stopping the investigations at the level of overwhelming plurality may be another error of interpretation. Henry Chadwick, *Early Christian Thought and the Classical Tradition: Studies in Justin, Clement, and Origen* (Oxford, Clarendon Press, 1966) 123 notices that "the perennial issue" concerning Origen is his "orthodoxy". Yet when one asks that question of Origen, the prior question is raised, "what is the essence of orthodoxy?" Without pressing for the answers to the "orthodoxy" and "heresy" questions which Bauer posed concerning early Christian texts, it will be difficult to define these concepts.

was the important center of "orthodoxy" in the second century. Tracing Rome's unfolding influence on the "orthodox" movement in Christianity, Bauer viewed the North African intervention in c. 250, the support of Alexandrian bishop Demetrius against Origen in c. 230, Victor's attempt to cut off the Asia Minor churches in c. 190, the letter of Dionysius of Corinth to Soter in c. 180, and the encounter between Anicetus and Polycarp in c. 154 as examples of what Rome did with its intervention in Corinth through the first epistle of Clement. On the basis of his understanding of this development, Bauer saw Rome in the second century as "from the very beginning the center and chief source of power for the 'orthodox' movement".[48]

There is certainly nothing methodologically illegitimate about tracing developments in one geographical area through a given period to see changes in opinion and action, as well as continuity of position and procedure. This must be considered one of the strongest points of Bauer's presentation. The claim, however, that "orthodoxy" stems from Rome will have to be supported both by the lack of influential bases elsewhere, and the proof that I Clement interposes its interest on Corinth in a way dissimilar to that of other literature of its period, and quite similar to later Roman interventions. The deficiency of important centers of "orthodoxy" has been contested above. It is, however, significant to notice how Bauer fails to grasp the similarities of I Clement and related literature of this period. He sets the stage for his interpretation of I Clement by indicating that its interest in another center is much like that of other writings from the period, and then claims I Clement to be the basis of the peculiar Roman position of intervention.[49] He does not discuss I Peter, which is also probably from Rome and is concerned with particular regions of Asia Minor. This would indicate not only a concern on the part of Rome for Corinth, as I Clement testifies, but also in Asia Minor. Bauer noted the apparently Roman influence on some of the Asia Minor literature, particularly in the coupling of Peter and Paul as the symbol of apostolic leadership, and the development of the later pseudo-Clementines in Antioch.[50] On the other hand, the Pastorals and the Apocalypse give

---

[48] Bauer, *Rechtgläubigkeit*, 231.
[49] Pp. 93–98.
[50] Pp. 115–133 particularly indicate Roman influence throughout the Mediterranean. Karlmann Beyschlag, *Clemens Romanus und der Frühkatholizismus*, Beiträge zur historischen Theologie, 35 (Tübingen, J.C.B. Mohr/Paul Siebeck, 1966) extensively confirms such influence.

evidence of cross influences of various centers in Asia Minor. Polycarp wrote to Philippi in Macedonia in response to a letter from that community. Ignatius shows a wide geographical range of influence and concern. He not only wrote to instruct communities in Western Asia Minor about faith and practics, but also sent an epistle to Rome with instructions not to interfere in his martyrdom. The occasion of his writings was his journey to suffer death, but he used that opportunity to influence the various communities he wrote. The tone of the Roman letter is more favorable than any of the others. Ignatius does not hesitate, however, to warn that community of the consequences if they interfere in his going to God through the martyr's act. Nor does he fail to assert his own position as bishop of Syria paralleled to Rome's position in its region.[51] The literature of this period shows a pattern of territorial intervention or interpenetration from many Christian centers.

Furthermore, there are five important contributions which Asia Minor and Antioch made to orthodoxy – contributions which would most likely appear in a detailed definition of "orthodoxy". First, monepiscopacy may have originated in Jerusalem where it developed through an hereditary succession.[52] The cities represented in Ignatius' letters indicate the presence of the office with no hereditary overtones and distinguished from presbyters and deacons, before Ignatius wrote. Monepiscopacy, however, is not in evidence in Rome at the beginning of the second century.[53] Secondly, the theological justification of the place of the bishop in the life of the church is first visible in Ignatius, rather than in a Roman author. The conception of apostolic succession is not found in Ignatius, and does appear in I Clement.[54] Yet nothing from early second century Rome can equal the claim which Ignatius makes for monarchial episcopacy. Thirdly, the distinctions between "heresy" and "orthodoxy" which Ignatius used are beginnings which could later be pressed toward separation if oppo-

---

[51]   *Romans* insc., 2. 8,3.

[52]   Hegesippus in Eusebius, *H.E.* 4,22,4 notices this familial relationship.

[53]   The burden of proof for monepiscopacy in Rome at the beginning of the second century rests on the one arguing that case, since all the evidence speaks either of a plural episcopate, or none at all. I Clement 42 mentions bishop*s* (59,3 uses the singular form of the word for God) as does Hermas *Vis.* 3,5,1 and *Sim.* 9,27,2. Ignatius' Romans neither argues for monepiscopacy nor mentions a bishop in that city. William Telfer, *The Office óf Bishop* (London, Darton, Longman & Todd, 1962) 43–88 suggests that the acceptance of monepiscopacy by Rome involved a significant theological shift from the position represented at the end of the first century.

[54]   I Clement 42.

nents remained rebellious. These early distinctions are not so clearly marked in the Roman literature of the period. Bauer himself thought an example of separation could be found in I John, a text which is usually ascribed to Asia Minor.[55] Fourthly, canonical developments can be seen in this region also. Marcion appears to have been the first to consciously create a canon. Asia Minor also may have a prior claim to the creation of four gospels.[56] Finally, the first liturgical texts appear to come from Syria, particularly in the form of manuals like the *Didache*. For some reason Bauer never discussed the *Didache*. It seems, therefore, highly unlikely that the spread of "orthodoxy", seen by Bauer as emanating from Rome with its organizational genius,[57] would have been functional at its heights in later centuries without monepiscopacy developed beyond hereditary connections, theologically argued, coupled with a separation between heresy and orthodoxy, a four gospel canon, and a regularized liturgy: all Syrian and Asia Minor contributions.

Bauer's second thesis is called into question because he did not recognize the strength of centers elsewhere in the Mediterranean and their contributions to the development of "orthodoxy". He also has a questionable tendency, however, to read lines of development backwards, seeing later events in earlier texts. He based the third century interventions of Rome in the first century epistle of I Clement. Yet the evidence from the second century does not demand that Rome imposed its will on other areas far removed from its local concerns until the dramatic action of Victor. The Paschal controversy of 154 is a case in point. The difficulty seems to have involved immigrants from Asia Minor, who, after settling in the vicinity of Rome, continued to celebrate Easter according to the date and customs of their homeland. Anicetus was trying to establish a uniform practice in his own region, not attempting to intervene in Asia Minor. The immigrants apparently appealed to their champion, Polycarp. We do not know the exact circumstances under which he came to Rome, but there is no evidence that he was summoned there by Anicetus. While

---

[55] Bauer, *Rechtgläubigkeit*, 96. Bauer argues wrongly, p. 91, that the difference between Jewish and Gentile Christians in Asia Minor becomes a difference between "orthodoxy" and "heresy" in the late first or early second centuries. If he were correct, his observation would be a further contribution of the area to a classical definition of "heresy" and "orthodoxy".

[56] Hans Freiherr von Campenhausen, *Die Entstehung der christlichen Bibel*, Beiträge zur historischen Theologie, 39 (Tübingen, J. C. B. Mohr/Paul Siebeck, 1968) 174/206, particularly 202.

[57] Bauer, *Rechtglaubigkeit*, 232–233.

there, Polycarp tried to convince Anicetus of the correctness of the Asia Minor custom just as much as Anicetus tried to convince him of the correctness of the Roman custom. Both failed, and did not agree on everything, but parted in peace. Anicetus even invited Polycarp to celebrate the Eucharist.[58] Since this was Roman territory, the stronger argument most probably came from Polycarp and the Asia Minor contingent. They were not merely left in peace to follow their own customs. They practiced them in the Roman region. Bauer is incorrect to suppose that in these events the Roman powers were strategically biding their time until Asia Minor weakened.[59]

It must not be assumed, however, that all such confrontations between Rome and other areas were to have these mixed resolutions. Rome was a very important center. The letters of Dionysius of Corinth well indicate that the economic power of Rome and the influence which came from that strength had penetrated the empire. Dionysius not only praises I Clement, but congratulates Soter on following and even advancing the Roman custom of sending supplies for the poor and those in the mines.[60] Such assistance made a profound impression on Dionysius, and doubtless carried some theological implications. We are, however, unaware of exactly what those pressures toward "orthodox" development were.[61]

Victor's actions were the strongest. The Paschal question had evidently become more acute throughout the Mediterranean basin. Eusebius suggests that there were a number of synods, and specifically mentions ones in Jerusalem, Rome, Pontus, Gaul, and Osrene. Only Victor, however, made the attempt to cut off as unorthodox those who did not agree. This may have been due to his North African heritage which looked to Rome for much of its leadership.[62] In any case, such action is a clear indication of his sense of power and authority, but it was not an action

---

[58] Eusebius, *H.E.* 5,24,16–17.
[59] Bauer, *Rechtgläubigkeit*, 131.
[60] Eusebius, *H.E.* 4,23,10.
[61] Bauer, *Rechtgläubigkeit*, 125–126 suggests on the basis of this letter that in 95 during the problems which prompted the writing of I Clement, the Romans sent money to support the former leadership in Corinth. It is an interesting conjecture, but not a demonstrable position.
[62] Bernhard Lohse, *Das Passafest der Quartadecimaner*, Beiträge zur Förderung christlicher Theologie, 2. Reihe, 54. Band (Gütersloh, C. Bertelsmann, 1953) 122–127. He follows Bauer, *Rechtgläubigkeit*, 14 in suggesting that the existence of a synod in Osrene is questionable. Cyril Richardson, A New Solution to the Quartodecimian Riddle, *Journal of Theological Studies* (1973) 74–84 proposes further distinctions among the Quartodecimian parties.

which occurred without being vigorously contested. Eusebius quotes not only the replies representing various bishops from Asia Minor, notably Polycrates of Ephesus, but also the interesting correspondence of Irenaeus.[63] There is little doubt that Rome should be seen as one of the most important centers of "orthodoxy" and one of the most vital sources of its power throughout the second century. That is particularly true in the deeds of Victor, and the tradition of almsgiving which Dionysius recognized as having a history prior to Soter. Even then, the contribution and influence of other regions in the development of orthodoxy must not be underplayed. Irenaeus, who viewed Rome as the type of all orthodox churches, was himself from Asia Minor and as a young man had listened to Polycarp. Irenaeus ministered in Gaul to an area which was strongly influenced by immigrants from Asia Minor.[64] As one of the major architects of orthodoxy and opponents of heresy, he refuted Victor's right to excommunicate the churches in Asia Minor and to make them alter their apostolic customs. The beginnings of Roman dominance in orthodoxy might be found in the lifetime of Victor, but neither the Anicetus–Polycarp meeting, nor the intervention of Rome in Corinth through the epistle of I Clement indicates such dominance. Therefore, Bauer's second thesis fails to stand up to scrutiny because he underrated the strength and influence of centers in Asia Minor and Syria, and because by imputing later developments into his interpretations of earlier ones, he pushed Roman centrality back to a point in history where it did not exist.

CONCLUSION

Walter Bauer's negative assessment of the classical theory of heresy has been accepted by many scholars. The daring quality of his position in 1934 must not be forgotten. The fallacy of both his positive theses, however, has not been properly emphasized. At the beginning of the second

---

[63] Eusebius, *H.E.* 5,23–24.

[64] The account of the Gaulican martyrs in Eusebius *H.E.* 5,1,17 mentions "Attalus, a native of Pergamum". 5,1,49 speaks of "Alexander, a Phrygian by race ... who had lived for many years among the Gauls". The fact that the letter is addressed to Asians and Phrygians is probably due to an immigration of Christians from those areas to Gaul. Irenaeus claims to have seen and listened to Polycarp in *Adv. Haer.* 3,3,4) and in his letter to Florinus in Eusebius, *H.E.* 5,20. Norbert Brox, *Offenbarung, Gnosis und gnostischer Mythos bei Irenäus von Lyon. Zur Charakteristik der Systeme*, Salzburger patristische Studien des internationalen Forschungszentrums für Grundfragen der Wissenschaft, 1 (Salzburg–München: A. Pustet, 1966) 144–150 questions the exactness of Irenaeus' memory of these details about Polycarp, but supports Polycarp's influence on Irenaeus.

century, Antioch and Asia Minor give evidence of "orthodox" communities which had opponents, but have not been proved either to be minorities or to be in danger of extermination. When the strength and contributions of these centers to the development of orthodoxy is recognized, it is impossible to see Rome as the dominant center of "orthodoxy" at the beginning of the second century. Therefore, in assessing Bauer's work, even though details are conceded as incorrect, it should not be asserted that the major premise of the book stands.[65] The negative attack on the classical theory of heresy stands, but the positive reconstructions fall.

In criticizing Bauer's work, it is important to recognize that a number of his arguments are conjecture based on silence.[66] Historians of early Christianity could well learn to distinguish between evidence and lack of evidence, and more freely admit the latter. On the other hand, to avoid working in the gaps is not possible, since we possess such a small fragment of the materials which once existed. It is entirely legitimate to search for methods through which groups now without the witnesses they once had, are allowed, in fact enabled to speak. Bauer's major methodological errors, however, are not confined merely to the treatment of silence. A large proportion occur in his treatment of the texts. He postulates a democratic council in which "orthodoxy" was a threatened minority in order to explain Ignatius' concern and argumentation for monepiscopacy, but is unable to demonstrate that Ignatius' supporters were a minority in any of the communities associated with Ignatius or that they did not have

---

[65] Kraft, The Reception of the Book, 314–316 indicates that "there is much in Bauer's treatment that invites supplementation or reassessment" but makes the comment under the heading of "Specific Details". Yet he recognizes that a "fresh approach" to "North Africa, Rome and other western regions", "Asia Minor and the Aegean area", and "the whole question of east Syrian Christianity" is in order. Helmut Koester, GNOMAI DIAPHOROI: The Origin and Nature of Diversification in the History of Early Christianity, Trajectories through Early Christianity, 114 claims that "Bauer was essentially right" particularly in light of the Nag Hammadi discoveries.

[66] Kraft, The Reception of the Book, 311 is correct to insist that "*ad hominem* blasts and apologetic counter-charges" will not advance the state of the problems. Bauer cannot be dismissed because he is "conjectural". It will prove more rewarding to study the texts and create new interpretations. Investigating the texts, however, indicates that Bauer's two major theses may be rejected precisely because of the methodological problems which Kraft mentions, i.e., "that Bauer has sometimes used language suggesting more confidence in his reconstruction than the evidence would seem to warrant, and that sometimes there is no direct evidence to support his interpretation, or he has overgeneralized on the basis of ambiguous data." More damaging is the indication that he has misread the texts.

bishops. He uses terms such as "monepiscopacy", "orthodoxy", and "heresy" and strengthens or weakens their meanings according to his theory. The basic error is in reading history backwards, either by demanding that the fullest or even "ideal" stage of a development must be present at its beginning in order for it to exist, or by imposing later events on earlier ones to support his interpretations. Frankly, he misreads the texts. One should be cautious in following his lead in places where there are few texts and much silence, when it can be demonstrated that he does not proceed on good grounds with the existent texts.

Positively, Bauer divides his study into areas, attempting to treat each individually. It is perhaps wise to concentrate our efforts even further by investigating separate cities within these areas. Bauer is also to be followed in researching the lines of development of "orthodoxy" and "heresy" in early Christianity. We may take the lead of Dobschütz not only in reading the individual hermeneutic of each document, but also in sketching the social, economic, and political environment of the communities which stand behind the documents.[67] In viewing the importance of the various regions over against each other, we would do well to continue research into the traditions behind such architects of orthodoxy as Irenaeus.[68] In

---

[67] Ernst von Dobschütz, *Vom Auslegen des Neuen Testaments* (Göttingen, Vandenhoeck & Ruprecht, 1927) 16 suggests the investigation of the New Testament literature with a view to the individual hermeneutic of each book. That could profitably be expanded to all early Christian texts. His *Christian Life in the Primitive Church*, trans. by George Bemner and ed. by W. D. Morrison (New York, G. P. Putnam's Sons, 1904) studies early Christian ethics in terms of its social setting. For a penetrating analysis of the need for this latter approach see Leander E. Keck, On the Ethos of Early Christianity, *Journal of the American Academy of Religion* 42,3 (1974) 435–452. Keck and Wayne A. Meeks chair a group of the American Academy of Religion and the Society of Biblical Literature which is studying the social world of Christianity in Antioch of Syria in the first four centuries. See Meeks, The Social World of Early Christianity, *The Council on the Study of Religion Bulletin* 6,1 (February, 1975) 1, 4–5. Edwin A. Judge, St. Paul and Classical Society, *Jahrbuch für Antike und Christentum* 15 (1972) 19–36 gives an excellent survey of the possibilities for such investigations. The Disciples Institut zur Erforschung des Urchristentums, Tübingen, Germany is investigating Christianity in its urban environments in Antioch of Syria, Corinth and Ephesus.

[68] André Benoit, *Saint Irénée: Introduction a l'Étude de sa Théologie* (Paris, Presses Universitaires de France, 1960) 9–41 reviews the problem of sources with an interest in defending a synthetic attempt to study Irenaeus' theology. Brox, *Offenbarung*, 105–167 deals with these questions with a view to explaining Irenaeus, while Martin Widmann, Irenäus und seine theologischen Väter, *Zeitschrift für Theologie und Kirche* 54,2 (1957) 156–173 attempts to find a way between portraying Irenaeus as a dull traditioner or the first systematic theologian. We should avoid a concept as broad as an "Asia Minor Theology" which Friedrich Loofs, *Theophilus von Antiochien 'Adversus Marcionem' und*

this way historians indebted to Bauer's attempts can move beyond his efforts toward better reconstructions of early Christianity.[69]

Tübingen, Wilhelmstrasse 100,
Disciples Institut zur Erforschung des Urchristentums

---

die anderen theologischen Quellen bei Irenaeus, Texte und Untersuchungen, 46,2 (Leipzig, J.C. Hinrichs'sche Buchhandlung, 1930) began to propose. But the contributions of that region to the formation of orthodoxy in one such as Irenaeus and the influence Antioch may have had on Asia Minor merit the continued study of what theological themes dominated the churches in those areas.

[69] Helmut Koester's GNOMAI DIAPHOROI, *Trajectories*, 114–157 is a stimulating piece which deserves attention. What is probably most needed is more penetrating work on specific areas, as the Research Team for the Religion and Culture of the Aegean in Early Christian Times and its newsletter, *Numina Aegaea* indicate Koester is pursuing.

Marcion in Contemporary Views: Results and Open Questions

GERHARD MAY*

I
STATUS OF RESEARCH

Every scholarly endeavor with Marcion invariably has to build on Adolf von Harnack's classic monograph.[1] From our century, there is hardly a second book on an early Christian theologian that has had such a penetrating and lasting success. Probably most researchers of the present see Marcion as Harnack presented him. One forgets all too easily what shabby, fragmentary source material this picture was based on. Harnack understood with masterful, historical power of portrayal how to conjure up from tradition the vibrant image of the Christian and theologian Marcion.

Harnack's collection of fragments and testimonies has still not been superseded. However, with the passing of more time, it has become increasingly clear to what extent his interpretation of Marcion's purposes and work bears the stamp of his own thinking. Is the biblical theologian—who rejects all philosophy and metaphysics, who restores the Gospel of the pure kindness and the love of God by using a critical-philological method that rejects all allegory, who founds his reformation of the depraved church on a "symbolic book," the *Antitheses*, whose piety can be expressed in verses by Paul Gerhardt—really the Marcion of the ancient sources, or is he not rather a modern ideal picture, a projection into history? Harnack's book is not only a historical study; it represents also a document of the theology of its author.[2] This fact, of course, does not

Prof. Dr. GERHARD MAY, Goldenluftgasse 4, D-6500, Mainz 1, W. Germany.

*The English translation is by David Dowdey, Professor of German, Pepperdine University.

[1]A. v. Harnack, *Marcion. Das Evangelium vom fremden Gott* (Leipzig: Hinrichs, 1921, 1924); reprint with *Neue Studien zu Marcion* (Leipzig: Hinrichs, 1923), 1–28 (Darmstadt: Wissenschaftliche Buchgesellschaft, 1960, 1985)

[2]Harnack's personal relationship with Marcion was often emphasized. Cf. Agnes v. Zahn-Harnack, *Adolf von Harnack* (Berlin: De Gruyter, 1951), 397–401.

suggest that Harnack's interpretation of Marcion is simply to be dismissed as unhistorical or anachronistic. One should not be so quick to criticize. Harnack is not merely portraying a great religious personality isolated from his time. His work purposely has the secondary title "A Monograph on the History of the Beginning of the Catholic Church." With a unique and matchless sense for what was possible and lasting in history, he asks consequently what are the effects and meaning of Marcion for church history. And he sees the contemporary traits in Marcion's thinking: his asceticism, his inability to derive anything positive from the creation and from history, and the severity of his philological undertakings. But there remains a non-derivative element of religious originality that transcends antiquity and, according to Harnack, is able to speak directly to modern man: Marcion's basic religious experiences can be obtained from the sources and still be appreciated today.[3] Is such a psychologizing interpretation in fact possible? Can we historically grasp anything more than a radical, one-sided novel interpretation of the Christian message, i.e., doctrine not experience? These are the questions, over and above any detailed criticism, that must be at the center of a basic confrontation with Harnack's interpretation of Marcion.

In spite of the continuing effect of Harnack's portrayal, its critical revision began long ago. It occurred and occurs not only through correcting individual theories and interpretations, through new observations about the sources and new hypotheses, but also indirectly through the advance of research into early church history as a totality. New insights in adjacent fields will also cast new light on Marcion. A comprehensive research project that would present the results of Marcion research since Harnack cannot be given in this paper; it would far exceed the space limitations. I will limit myself to pointing out several trends and hypotheses: A major role is played by attempts to shed light on Marcion's relationship to the intellectual currents of his time. Most of the time Marcion is placed closer to Gnosticism, and the philosophical influences on his thinking are emphasized more strongly than occurs in Harnack.[4] Hans von Campenhausen evaluates Marcion's meaning for the history of the canon in a new

[3]Cf. especially *Marcion*, 94–97 and the essay "Die Neuheit des Evangeliums nach Marcion" in Harnack, *Aus der Werkstatt des Vollendeten: Reden und Aufsätze* (Gießen: Töpelmann, 1930), 128–143. Critical toward Harnack but likewise attempting to reconstruct Marcion's piety: J. v. Walter, "Marcion" in Walter, *Christentum und Frömmigkeit* (Gütersloh: Bertelsmann, 1941), 41–62.

[4]The closeness to Gnosis is emphasized by U. Bianchi, "Marcion: Theologien biblique ou docteur gnostique?," *Vigiliae Christianae* 21 (1967): 141–149; B. Aland, "Marcion. Versuch erner neuen Interpretation," *Zeitschrift für Theologie und Kirche* 70 (1973): 420–447; K. Rudolph, *Die Gnosis* (Leipzig: Koehler and Amelang, 1980), 337–342; ET ed. R. McL. Wilson (San Francisco: Harper, 1983), 313–317. Cf. note 62 below regarding the question of philosophical influences.

and higher degree than Harnack: Campenhausen sees in Marcion the creator of the "idea and reality of a Christian Bible," whereas Harnack shows him finding and combating a four-Gospel canon.[5] Recently R. J. Hoffmann made a determined attempt to re-date the life and influence of Marcion and, based on the new chronology, to understand anew his role in church history: Hoffmann has him being born fifteen years earlier and has him beginning his activity two or three decades earlier than Harnack and other researchers. The earlier dating offers him the peg on which to hang his hypothesis that Marcion was a key figure in the process of canonizing the New Testament. Hoffmann sees in Marcion not only the first collector of Pauline epistles, but also the writer of the Epistle to the Laodiceans which we see in a catholic version in the canonical Epistle to the Ephesians. He regards the canonical Gospel of Luke as the product of an anti-Marcionite revision of the older anonymous gospel which Marcion had accepted in his canon, and asserts that the Acts of the Apostles as well as the Pastoral Epistles were supposedly written against Marcion. According to Hoffmann, Marcion's theology is characterized by an archaic biblicism and hardly touched by the influences of Greek training. I have reviewed the book in another place.[6] It is full of improbabilities and methodological errors; I consider it a failure.

New inquiries and examinations have still not, of course, led to a consensus nor to a new, well-rounded picture of Marcion.[7] We find ourselves in a situation similar to what we know today in so many other fields of historical research: the classical representations of a subject are critically called into question, everything seems more complicated than in the past, and the new syntheses are lacking. I want to show here in a brief manner

---

[5]H. v. Campenhausen, *Die Entstehung der christlichen Bibel* (Tübingen: Mohr, 1968), 174–193; ET J. A. Baker (Philadelphia: Fortress, 1972), 148–167.

[6]R. J. Hoffmann, Marcion: *On the Restitution of Christianity. An Essay on the Development of Radical Paulinist Theology in the Second Century* (Chico, Ca.: Scholars Press, 1984). For a critical view cf. G. May, "Ein neues Marcionbild?" *Theologische Rundschau* 51 (1986): 404–413.

[7]The following lengthier presentations can be named: R. S. Wilson, *Marcion. A Study of a Second-Century Heretic* (London: Clarke, 1933); J. Knox, *Marcion and the New Testament* (Chicago: U Chicago P, 1942); E. C. Blackman, *Marcion and His Influence* (London: SPCK, 1948); A. Hollard, *Deux hérétiques: Marcion et Montan* (Paris: Nouvelle revue critique, 1935) does not yield much scholarly information; G. Ory, *Marcion* (Paris: 1980) has not been accessible to me. It is characteristic that since Harnack's work no scholarly monograph on Marcion has appeared in the German language. Further total evaluations in briefer form are given by B. Aland (see note 4); D. L. Balás, "Marcion Revisited: A 'Post-Harnack' Perspective," in *Texts and Testaments. Critical Essays on the Bible and Early Church Fathers*, ed. W. E. March (San Antonio: Trinity UP, 1980), 95–108; K. Beyschlag, "Marcion von Sinope," in *Gestalten der Kirchengeschichte*, ed. M. Greschat 1/I (Stuttgart, 1984), 69–81.

what tasks arise and what perspectives open up when, more than sixty years after Harnack's work, one wants to understand Marcion in the context of early church history.

II
PROBLEMS OF SOURCES

Harnack collected source materials about Marcion with such thoroughness that, except for a few isolated instances, it can hardly be expanded.[8] On the contrary, various witnesses, whom Harnack and earlier researchers see as highly meaningful, are today no longer regarded as Marcionite or are doubted as valuable sources, at least when it comes to anti-Marcionite texts. I mention the most important of these questionable sources: (1) The supposedly Marcionite Pauline prologues of numerous Vulgate manuscripts in all probability do not go back to Marcion or his disciples.[9] (2) The prologues to the Gospels of Mark, Luke, and John were explained by de Bruyne as being anti-Marcionite texts of the second century (de Bruyne was also the first to assert Marcionite origin of the Pauline prologues). According to the convincing study of Regul, these texts are considerably later and not directed against Marcion.[10] Only the Johannine prologue specifically mentions Marcion by name; in fact, it asserts that Marcion was rejected in Asia Minor by Papias and John because of his heresy.[11] Regul shows that no historical kernel can be peeled out of this abundantly fantastic report, but rather it is an invention of the fourth century.[12] (3) The speech of an "elder" used by Irenaeus in *Adversus haereses* IV. 27-32 is according to Orbe not against Marcion but rather is in opposition to the Simonian or Valentinian Gnosis.[13] (4) The

---

[8]Here mention should be made of the attempt of R. Riedinger to substantiate antimarcionite statements by Clement of Alexandria in the writings of Isidore of Pelusium: "Zur antimarkionitischen Polemik des Klemens von Alexandria," *Vigiliae Christianae* 29 (1975): 15–32.

[9]N. A. Dahl, "The Origin of the Earliest Prologues to the Pauline Letters," *Semeia* 12 (1978): 233–277.

[10]J. Regul, *Die antimarcionitischen Evangelienprologe* (Freiburg: Herder, 1969).

[11]Regul (p. 34) gives the text as follows: "Evangelium Iohannis manifestatum est ecclesiis ab Iohanne adhuc in corpore constituto, sicut Papias nomine Hieropolitanus, discipulus Iohannis carus, in exotoricis, id est in extremis quinque libris retulit; descripsit vero evangelium dictante Iohanne recte. Verum Marcion hereticus, cum ab eo esset inprobatus eo quod contraria sentiebat, abiectus est ab Iohanne. Is vero scripta vel epistolas ad eum pertulerat a fratribus, qui in Ponto fuerunt."

[12]Ibid., 99 and 197.

[13]A. Orbe, "Ecclesia, sal terrae según san Ireneo," *Recherches de science religieuse* 60 (1972): 219–240; see p. 220, note 8.

concept held by Zahn[14] and Harnack[15] that the anonymous heretical treatise opposed by Augustine in *Contra adversarium legis et prophetarum* contained Marcionite teachings is doubted by Maria Pia Ciccarese; according to her the author is influenced by ideas of Gnostic origin.[16] (5) Likewise the existence of a Latin translation of Marcion's Bible as early as 200 cannot, according to the judgment of Bonifatius Fischer, be documented from Tertullian, the main western witness for Marcion's Bible text.[17] In sum, Harnack's reconstruction of Marcion's Bible text is proven after closer examination to be uncertain in numerous passages.

The assumption that the "elder" of Irenaeus is supposedly polemicizing against Marcion still appears to me to be plausible; likewise, the hypothesis that the *Adversarius legis et prophetarum* is familiar with Marcionite ideas appears to be worthy of consideration.[18] The Pauline and Gospel prologues, however, can be definitely eliminated as sources for Marcion. Other witnesses will also have to be examined more accurately with regard to their historical value.

Harnack had great *confidence* in the ancient traditions: in many passages where such is not clear at all to the critical reader he believes he is able to find quotations from the *Antitheses,* and he is confident he is able to show from the extant materials what Marcion "actually wanted."[19] He combines evidences from various sources with astonishing freedom according to his viewpoint of historical probability. More recent detailed studies prefer to limit themselves to a few old witnesses, naturally fa-

---

[14]Th. Zahn, *Geschichte des Neutestamentlichen Kanons,* vol. II/2 (Erlangen-Leipzig: Deichert, 1892), 432–436.

[15]Harnack, *Marcion,* p. 390f., note 4.

[16]M. P. Ciccarese, "Un testo gnostico confutato da Agostino," *Vetera Christianorum* 15 (1978) 23–44, esp. 29–33.

[17]B. Fischer, "Das Neue Testament in lateinischer Sprache. Der gegenwärtige Stand seiner Erforschung und seine Bedeutung für die griechische Textgeschichte," in *Die alten Übersetzungen des Neuen Testaments, der Kirchenväterzitate und der Lektionare,* ed. K. Aland (Berlin: De Gruyter, 1972), 1–92, esp. 26, 30f., 44f.V. Buchheit rejects the view that Rufinus looked up a Latin Marcionite Bible for his translation of the *Dialogue of Adamantius* (c. 400): cf. *Tyrannii Rufini Librorum Adamantii Origenis adversus haereticos interpretatio,* ed. V. Buchheit (Munich, 1966), XII-XXXV. This however was never claimed by Harnack.

[18]Th. Raveaux, in his recently published book *Augustinus, contra adversarium legis et prophetarum. Analyse des Inhalts und Untersuchung des geistesgeschichtlichen Hintergrunds* (Würzburg, 1987), records the many agreements between the *adversarius* and the Marcion tradition. As Zahn and Harnack, he connects the unknown author with the Roman sect of the Patricians (cf. Ambrosiaster, *Ad Tim.* I.4.5; Filastrius 62); see pp. 28–31; 140. Ms. Ciccarese (note 16) is skeptical toward this hypothesis (p. 31, note 30).

[19]Harnack, *Marcion,* p. 21; similarly p. 93.

voring Tertullian since he used the *Antitheses* and the Marcionite Bible. Neither the former nor the latter procedure will measure up to strict methodological demands. In a much more consistent way than is usual, on the one hand contexts of traditions must be traced, while on the other hand the principles of description in the individual sources must be observed. In the reports of the opponents of heresy there is more convention and the author's own stylizing than one initially believes. Only by proceeding in this manner is there any prospect of peeling out the trustworthy traditions and disclosing their presumed origin. Regul's analysis of the evidences for "Marcion's pre-Roman activity" is in this regard exemplary.[20] It hardly needs to be emphasized that the study of secondary reports and of the anti-heretical commonplaces is valuable and indispensable: in them is reflected the church's judgment on Marcion and his church. From such sources it can be seen how a definite profile of a heretic emerges which is then handed down.

Harnack regards Marcion's Bible texts as an important source for his theology.[21] However, caution is appropriate here: the reconstruction of the wording is neither possible with confidence, as Harnack assumes (as stated), nor are we able with certainty to give the motives why Marcion retains certain passages which apparently contradict his views. It is precisely to these texts that Harnack likes to appeal. We probably may not demand too much consistency and therefore should guard against drawing sweeping conclusions from the preservation of isolated texts. The writing of the old witnesses must in any case serve as the substantial basis for the reconstruction of Marcion's doctrine.

III
BIOGRAPHICAL INFORMATION

Regul has shown that two different traditions clearly exist with regard to Marcion's person and influence: one goes back to Tertullian, the other goes back to pseudo-Tertullian, *Adversus omnes haereses,* and the anti-heretical works of Epiphanius and Filastrius.[22] The last three works, because of their numerous parallels, are claimed by the majority of scholars since R. A. Lipsius to be sources for the reconstruction of Hippolytus' lost *Syntagma Against the Heretics.*[23] According to Tertullian, Marcion

---

[20]Regul, op. cit., pp. 177–195.

[21]Harnack, *Marcion*, p. 20f. 64–66.

[22]Regul, pp. 180–195.

[23]R. A. Lipsius, *Zur Quellenkritik des Epiphanios* (Vienna: Braumüller, 1865). Sharp criticism is lodged against the thesis of this book by E. Schwartz, *Zwei Predigten Hippolyts*, Sitzungsberichte der Bayerischen Akademie der Wissenschaften, Philos.-histor. Abteilung, 1936/3, pp. 37–45.

was a shipowner (*nauclerus*) from Pontus. He became a member of the Christian community in Rome. Tertullian knows nothing of earlier contact with Christianity.[24] After lengthy disputes, Marcion was excluded from the Rome congregation.[25] Cerdo, not mentioned in *De praescriptione haereticorum*, does not occur until in the later work *Adversus Marcionem* as Marcion's teacher.[26] The portrayal in the sources for the *Syntagma* has it differently: Marcion was the son of the bishop of Sinope. The bishop disfellowshipped his own son because of his seducing a virgin from the congregation.[27] Filastrius nonetheless does not mention the excommunication by the father; rather he tells that Marcion was "subdued" by John and the elders and "driven from" Ephesus.[28] The Roman church did not receive Marcion into communion, although he requested it; after a dramatic dispute with the "elders and teachers" about the proper interpretation of two sayings of the Lord, he separated himself from the church.[29]

An analysis of the *Syntagma* tradition discloses the viewpoint of legends about heretics: in the story of the excommunication of Marcion by his own father, it is obvious there are traits of legendary style, as well as the portrayal of the Roman dispute by Epiphanius with the paternal-superior stance of the elders and the concluding outbreak of anger by Marcion. The apparent quality of antiquity which shows Marcion dealing not with the Roman bishop but with the "presbyters and elders" does not have to be based on precise knowledge of the constitutional organization of the Roman church at the time of Marcion. A source from the end of the second century or from the third century may still have formulated it this way.[30] The information that Marcion supposedly attempted to find recognition among the leading men of the Roman congregation with his doctrine may be nothing more than a variation of the report of his futile attempts with Polycarp of Smyrna (Irenaeus, *Adv. haer.* III. 3.4), Papias (the anti-Marcionite prologue to John), and John (anti-Marcionite prologue to John; Filastrius 45). The recognizable interest of all these notices consisted of having Marcion rejected by the old witnesses of church tra-

---

[24]Tertullian, *Adv. Marc.* IV.4.3: "Pecuniam in primo calore fidei catholicae ecclesiae contulit." According to this statement, it was not until he was in Rome that Marcion became a Christian.

[25]Tertullian, *De praescr. haer.* 30. 2f.; *Adv. Marc.* IV.4.3.

[26]Tertullian, *Adv. Marc.* I.2.3; 22.10; IV.17.11.

[27]Ps. Tertullian, *Adv. omn. haer.* 6.2; Epiphanius, *Pan. haer.* 42.1.3–6.

[28]Filastrius, 45.7; cf. the Johanine Prologue, note 11 above.

[29]Epiphanius, *Pan. haer.* 42.1.7–2.8; Filastrius 45.1–3; cf. Ps. Tertullian, *Adv. omn. haer.* 6.2.

[30]Epiphanius, *Pan. haer.* 42.2.2. A similar use of language occurs in Hippolytus, *C. Noetum* 1. Cf. C. H. Turner, "The 'Blessed Presbyters' who condemned Noetus," *JThS* 23 (1922): 28–31.

dition. When one considers the concurring point, even the anecdote told
by Irenaeus of Marcion's encounter with Polycarp (although possible according to time) becomes doubtful historically.[31] Tertullian's version of
the events appears more believable, although it is by no means free of
clichés. The facts reported by Tertullian on a phase of tensions between
Marcion and the Roman congregation prior to the final separation apply
likewise for Valentinus (De praescr. 30.2). After all, the accounts of
Irenaeus on Cerdo's connections to the Roman congregation sound similar (Adv. haer. III. 4.3). We are encountering here a pattern of Roman
heresy tradition. The separation between the correctly believing congregation and the heretical teachers may have occasionally taken this form;
whether it was thus in the case of Marcion cannot be said for sure. The
report that Marcion supposedly was a disciple of the Syrian Gnostic Cerdo
goes back to Irenaeus.[32] That this disciple relationship existed, also known
in the Syntagma tradition, cannot be completely ignored. I consider it,
however, more probable that Irenaeus or an earlier anti-Marcionite writer
constructed a succession relationship between the two Roman heretics,
whose contemporaneity was known.[33] There is no way to know from the
information of the sources which doctrines Marcion could have accepted
from the Gnostic; his views, of course, were thoroughly described according to Marcion's. Obviously we know only one fact about Cerdo: he
is supposed to be the teacher of Marcion.

Marcion's occupation has been handed down with reliability: he was
a ναύκληρος.[34] The common translation as "shipowner" is capable of
rendering the broad spectrum of meaning of the ancient term only partially. A nauclerus can be an owner or joint owner of a ship, or he may
only be someone commissioned by the owner. He may be conducting
business at his own expense, or he may be transporting goods and pas-
sengers. Usually he is on board, but he leaves seaman's responsibilities
up to the κυβερνήτης, at least on larger vessels. There is also the type
of major sea merchant and shipowner who owns an entire fleet of ships

[31]I treated "Marcions Bruch mit der römischen Gemeinde" in 1983 in a paper at the
Oxford Patristics Congress. Publication is forthcoming.

[32]Irenaeus, Adv. haer. I.27.1.

[33]Cf. for a more complete treatment G. May, "Markion und der Gnostiker Kerdon," in
Evangelischer Glaube und Geschichte: Grete Mecenseffy zum 85. Geburtstag, ed. A. Rad-
datz and K. Lüthi (Vienna, 1984) 233–248. A. Le Boulluec, La notion d'hérésie dans la
littérature grecque IIᵉ–IIIᵉ siècles I (Paris, 1985) 86f. thinks that the source of Irenaeus,
Adv. Haer. I.23–27 may be Justin's lost Syntagma Against Heresies and that the idea of
a succession comes from him also; yet Irenaeus had first inserted Cerdo in the list.

[34]Nauclerus: Tertullian, De praescr. haer. 30.1; Adv. Marc. I.18.4; III.6.3; IV.9.2;
V.1.2. Ναύτης: Rhodon in Eusebius, Hist. Eccl. V.13.3. The less precise term ναύτης
could be used in a derogatory way ("sailor"), yet it does not have to mean this.

and does not personally go on journeys.[35] It is probably correct to rank Màrcion somewhere in the middle of these social classes. We may well suppose that he used his travel experiences, his business connections, and his financial resources to build up his ecclesiastical organization. A portion of the rapid spread of the Marcionite church can be explained in this way. The report sounds plausible that Marcion, upon his joining the Roman congregation, gave a sum of 200,000 sestertii.[36] The sum is high, but it is not astronomical; one should not consider it fictitious.[37] The congregation was certainly proud of the fact that it was in a position to repay the money after the breach came, and it is understandable that the memory of this episode survived until Tertullian's time. At the most, one could have suspicion in case Tertullian had consciously drawn a parallel between Marcion and the archheretic Simon Magus: J. H. Waszink pointed out the relationship between the description of Simon's damnation by Peter in *De anima* and the expelling of Marcion from the Roman congregation in *Adversus Marcionem IV*.[38] Yet the agreement is not so clear that one would have to conclude that here Marcion is supposedly sketched as a new Simon Magus without historical evidence. Also, since large gifts upon joining the church are documented elsewhere,[39] one is permitted to maintain the historicity of Marcion's donation.

IV

PORTRAITS OF MARCION FROM TRADITION

When it is a matter of depicting Marcion's doctrine, the eclectic method of combining and adding source documents is even more questionable than in the case of the reconstruction of his biography. The individual sources have definite concepts of Marcion's theology; clarity must be obtained in order to evaluate the texts properly. Even such a well-informed author as Tertullian naturally does not report objectively on Marcion, but completely in a polemical manner. Form, intent, and leading

---

[35]Cf. J. Rougé, *Recherches sur l'organisation du commerce maritime en Méditerranée sous l'Empire Romain* (Paris: S.E.V.P.E.N., 1966) 229–261; also Julie Vélissaropoulos, *Les nauclères grecs. Recherches sur les institutions maritimes en Grèce et dans l'Orient hellénisé* (Genève-Paris: Droz, 1980) 48–56, 77–81.

[36]Tertullian, *De praescr. haer.* 30.2; *Adv. Marc.* IV.9.3.

[37]An abundance of comparative numbers is offered by R. Duncan-Jones, *The Economy of the Roman Empire: Quantitative Studies* (Cambridge: Cambridge UP, 1974).

[38]*De anima* 34.2 says of Simon: "Damnatus ab ipso (sc. ab apostolo) cum pecunia sua in interitum"; *Adv. Marc.* IV.9.3 says of Marcion: "Pecuniam in primo calore fidei catholicae ecclesiae contulit, proiectam mox cum ipso." Regarding this see J. H. Waszink in his edition of *De anima* (Amsterdam: H. J. Paris, 1947), 406.

[39]See examples in H. Achelis, *Das Christentum in den ersten drei Jahrhunderten*, vol. II (Leipzig: Quelle and Meyer, 1912), 424.

concepts are to be considered in the use of his and of all other references to Marcion's doctrine to a higher extent than happens in most studies. I will attempt to sketch the Marcion portrait of several important sources:

(1) For Justin Martyr, Marcion is the demon-inspired archenemy of the church himself. He mentions twice in his *I Apology* that Marcion was a living contemporary and that he was highly successful in spreading his doctrines (26.5; 58.1). The sequence of the heretics Simon, Menander, Marcion apparently shows, from Justin's Roman perspective, the route of the heresy up to its current climax.[40] The message of the "greater" God and his Christ forms the nucleus of the Marcionite doctrine.[41] The juxtaposition of the good God and the just God, common in the later sources, does not occur yet in Justin: that is an index of how unsolidified his picture of Marcion still is. In the *Dialogue with Trypho*, Justin enumerates other heretics along with the Marcionites, of whom at least the Valentinians must have been known to him through personal contacts (*Dial.* 35.6). However, what Justin in summary says concerning characterization of the heretics applies primarily to Marcion: they blaspheme the God of the creation and of the patriarchs and his Christ, moreover they deny the resurrection (*Dial.* 35.5; 80.4). For Justin, the Marcionites appear to be absolute heretics; thus, he portrays all other false teachers according to their example.[42] If we may assume with P. Prigent that Justin, in the *Dialogue with Trypho*, uses the Old Testament material of his lost writing "Against Marcion,"[43] then we can get an idea how he defended the Old Testament as a book on Christ. Apparently it is mainly with the doctrine of two Gods and the rejection of the Old Testament that Marcion for Justin called Christian truth into question.

One point is striking: in *I Apology* Justin explains that the disciples of Marcion have no proof for what they teach (*I Apol.* 58.2). This assertion can be a polemical assumption.[44] But one can as well glean from this assertion that Justin had not yet recognized the meaning of the Marcionite Canon.[45] Even if the second interpretation is not certain, it is in any case based on a correct observation: Justin knows nothing yet about a "New

---

[40]Irenaeus' catalog of heretics (*Adv. haer.* I.23–27) begins with Simon and Menander (I.23) and ends with Marcion (I.27.2–4). Even if it is not based on Justin's lost *Syntagma*, nonetheless we are dealing with a Roman source.

[41]*I Apol.* 26.5 (μείζονα τοῦ δημιουργοῦ θεόν); 58.1.

[42]Cf. W. Bauer, *Rechtgläubigkeit und Ketzerei im ältesten Christentum*, 2nd ed. (Tübingen: Mohr, 1964), 133.

[43]P. Prigent, *Justin et l'Ancien Testament* (Paris: Gabalda, 1964).

[44]Rhodon, in his polemics against the disciples of Marcion, also reproaches them for a lack of proof of their doctrines (Eusebius, *H. E.* V.13.4, 6).

[45]See Campenhausen, *Entstehung*, p. 196, note 87; ET p. 167, note 89.

Testament." Obviously it is to be assumed that he lacked the prerequisites
to understand the role played by Marcion's collection of Christian writings for Marcion. In any event, in Justin's anti–Marcionite polemics, it
is ultimately a matter of defending the Old Testament and its Christian
use.

(2) A new level of the dispute is reached in Irenaeus. That is shown
especially well by the text *Adversus haereses* I.27: Irenaeus presents here
a compressed treatise on Marcion's doctrine according to one source, perhaps Justin's *Syntagma Against Heresies*. In the appropriated description,
Irenaeus himself obviously interjected a section on mutilating the apostolic writings and the words of the Lord: "Moreover he circumcised the
Gospel of Luke, removed everything written about the birth of the Lord,
and also removed all the many passages from the teachings of the words
of the Lord in which it is clearly written that the Lord confesses the Creator of this universe as his Father. He taught his disciples the conviction
that he himself is more credible than the apostles who passed down the
gospel, and he did not give them the gospel but only a part of the gospel.
But in a similar fashion he also circumcised the epistles of the Apostle
Paul and removed everything obviously said by the Apostle about God
who created the world, that he is the Father of our Lord Jesus Christ,
and everything the apostle taught with specific reference to the words of
the prophets that announced in advance the coming of the Lord."[46] Marcion now appears as the one who abbreviated and mutilated the "New
Testament" scriptures. Thereby the conflict was shifted. The wording and
the context of the New Testament on the one hand, and on the other hand
the agreement between it and the older scripture, became central themes
of the dispute. In the treatise in *Adversus haereses* I, Marcion is portrayed
mainly as a critic of the God of the Old Testament: God is the "author
of evil, a warmonger, unstable in his opinion, and in contradiction with
himself." Jesus dissolves the prophets, the law, and the works of the
Creator of the world. And as he descends to the underworld, the notorious
godless people of the Old Testament believe him and are saved, whereas
the pious people of the Old Testament assume now that, because they
have so often been tried by God, he is testing them and therefore they
do not hasten to Jesus and do not believe in him and remain in the underworld (*Adv. haer.* I. 27.2f.). This portrayal is characterized by a striking limitation to the behavior patterns of the demiurge and to the contrasting salvific work of Jesus Christ. Statements regarding the nature of
the true God as well as all philosophically marked concepts are lacking.
To the extent that Irenaeus reproduces the source, it sketches the picture

[46]I.27.2. The items on Marcion's biblical philology interrupt the report in indirect speech
concerning his doctrine and thus show that they were inserted.

of a noticeably non-speculative theology. On his own initiative, Irenaeus adds the information on Marcion's canon and frequently in his work takes a position on Marcionite exegesis.[47] With his doctrine of the unity of God and his activity and the doctrine of the universal agreement between the Old Testament and the apostolic tradition in its oral and written form, he is opposing Marcion's criticism and one-sided radicalism.

(3) Irenaeus announces that he will refute Marcion from his own canon (*Adv. haer.*I.27.3; III.12.12). This program was implemented by Tertullian. Besides the Bible, Tertullian has Marcion's *Antitheses* before him, and he grapples with both works. Moreover, he has a letter by Marcion and is able to use the anti-Marcionite polemical writings of several older authors.[48] The *Antitheses* are apparently his most important source. He points out that these defend the Marcionite gospel and ought to open up its proper understanding.[49] The rendering of many sentences from Marcion by Tertullian awakens the hope that we would be able to hear the voice of Marcion himself. And yet matters are not favorable after all. Tertullian does not want to present the doctrine of his opponent in a documentary fashion, but wants to refute it. What at first glance appears to be a quotation is mostly only a critical discussion, often probably also snatched up, editorially enhanced, and—not to be forgotten—in every case translated from Greek. Only by means of painstaking individual analysis of language and thoughts can the authentic Marcion material to some degree be filtered out. The topic of the *Antitheses* and, as Tertullian believes, Marcion's main concern is the "separation of law and Gospel." From the evidence that these two great entities contradict each other emerges the difference between the two Gods.[50] From all appearances, the *Antitheses* were a philological, exegetical work. It must have contained long series of juxtaposed texts from the Old Testament and the Marcionite Bible. The main point of the investigation, to show the antithesis of law and gospel, was taken from Paul. In Tertullian, the antithesis appears

---

[47]Regarding the characteristics of Irenaeus' perception of Marcion see G. May, "Markion und der Gnostiker Kerdon" (note 33), pp. 235–237. The more or less definite references by Irenaeus to Marcion beyond the report in *Adv. haer.* I.27 were compiled by Harnack (see *Marcion*, pp. 320ff., note 1).

[48]Tertullian mentions the letter by Marcion three times: *De carne Christi* 2.4; *Adv. Marc.* I.1.6; IV.4.3. In this regard see Harnack, *Marcion*, pp. 21ff. and J.-P. Mahé, "Tertullien et l'Epistula Marcionis, *Revue des sciences religieuses* 45 (1971): 358–371. Regarding the question of sources see G. Quispel, *De bronnen van Tertullianus' Adversus Marcionem* (Dissertation, Utrecht, 1943).

[49]*Adv. Marc.* IV.1.1; 4.4.

[50]*Adv. Marc.* I.19.4: "Nam hae sunt Antithesis Marcionis, id est contrariae oppositiones, quae conantur discordiam evangelii cum lege committere, ut ex diversitate sententiarum utriusque instrumenti diversitatem quoque argumententur deorum."

directly as the fundamental character of Marcion's thinking: it is a matter of contrast between law and Gospel, old and new, Demiurge and good God. This impression is certainly determined in part by the use of Marcion's book, but it is also related to Tertullian's own manner of speaking and writing. The great rhetorician has a preference for expressing himself in antithetical form. In Marcion he found an intellectually related opponent. The inner affinity is to the advantage of the niveau of the dispute. Even with all the irony and derision of his polemics, Tertullian does take Marcion's thoughts seriously. Furthermore, he finds convincing arguments for his own view that, in spite of all apparent and actual differences between Old and New Testaments, one can adhere to the unity of God and to continuity of his actions.[51] Finally, the question again is: Is Tertullian's Marcion, the Marcion of the *Antitheses*, the true and complete Marcion?

(4) One encounters quite a different Marcion in Clement of Alexandria: Marcion is portrayed as a radical Platonist.[52] The passage *Stromateis* III. 12.1-25.4 is devoted to the dispute with the Marcionite hostility toward the world and the flesh. According to Clement's thesis, the Marcionites took over from Plato and Pythagoras the doctrine that "originating" (γένεσις)[53] was bad, but they went beyond the philosophers with their assertion that being born and matter are not just relatively bad but also by their very nature are bad. Clement, with a series of texts from Plato, seeks to document "that Marcion took the stimulus for his strange doctrines from Plato in an unthankful and injudicious manner" (III.21.2; cf.22.1). The assumption that Marcion was dependent on philosophy occurs as early as Irenaeus and occupies in Tertullian an even larger space.[54] It is difficult to say whether the assumption by these authors means any-

---

[51]In E. P. Meijering, *Tertullian contra Marcion: Gotteslehre in der Polemik, Adversus Marcionem I-II* (Leiden: Brill, 1977) the theological contributions of Marcion do not, in my opinion, fare too well.

[52]For more precise information on this perception of Marcion see G. May, "Platon und die Auseinandersetzung mit den Häresien bei Klemens von Alexandrien," in *Platonismus und Christentum: Festschrift für Heinrich Dörrie*, ed. H.-D. Blume und F. Mann, *Jahrbuch für Antike und Christentum*, Supplementary vol. 10 (Münster: Aschendorff, 1983), 123–132, esp. 126–128; D. Wyrwa, *Die christliche Platonaneignung in den Stromateis des Clemens von Alexandrien* (Berlin: De Gruyter, 1983), 205–224; A. Le Boulluec, *La notion d'hérésie dans la littérature grecque IIᵉ-IIIᵉ siècles*, vol. II (Paris, 1985), 290–297.

[53]Wyrwa (p. 205, note 10) suggests that γένεσις be translated as "the world that became, the creation," but does not want to exclude the possibility that the meaning "procreation" also plays a part.

[54]Cf. Irenaeus, *Adv. Haer.* III.24.2 (Epicurus); Tertullian, *Adv. Marc.* I.25.3; II.16.2f.; IV.15.2; V.19.7 (Epicurus); *Praescr. haer.* 7.3; 30.1; *Adv. Marc.* V.19.7 (Stoa); in this connection see Meijering, pp. 75–77.

thing more than an accusation based on superficial observations. When Clement asserts that Marcion was dependent on Plato, his thesis carries a different weight. For Clement is of the opinion that Plato came closer to the truth than any other pagan philosopher and that he fulfilled for the Greeks a salvific function. The affiliation with Plato is important for him, both from the apologetic viewpoint and for the dispute with heresy and its intellectual claims. He would hardly have expressed and substantiated the opinion that Marcion was directly stimulated by Plato unless he was certain of it. As a makeshift, one can turn to the assumption that Clement supposedly knew Platonically influenced Marcionites of the second generation. This explanation is made easier by the fact that Clement speaks now about Marcion, and now about Marcionites, without making a recognizable distinction. One can also suspect that Clement, from the perspective of his own philosophical presuppositions, possessed no other category for characterizing Marcion's hostility toward matter and the world than that of Platonism. Yet, we cannot exclude the possibility that Clement is showing the historical Marcion from a new angle. It would be an error of method if we permitted ourselves to be induced by the Marcion portrait of Irenaeus and Tertullian to declare out of hand the "Platonic" Marcion of Clement as unhistorical.

(5) In later times, Ephraem the Syrian, and the Armenian theologian, Eznik of Kolb, added new features to the Marcion tradition. Ephraem's references agree for the most part with the oldest Greek and Latin witnesses. At times it appears to be possible with their help to fill in the gaps of the older tradition. Yet Ephraem also mentions mythological concepts for which we possess no or only uncertain parallels in the sources of the second and third centuries.[55] Shortly before 450, Eznik of Kolb turned against Marcion.[56] Even in his explanations, the fundamental thoughts of Marcion are clearly recognizable, but they are to an even more extensive degree than in the case of Ephraem recast into a gnosticizing myth.[57] Again it is to be asked: How is that which Ephraem and Eznik report related to the thinking of the historical Marcion? In the points where we could check them, both polemicists show that they are so well informed that one hesitates to declare the undocumented mythological elements in their descriptions as products of fantasy or to trace them back

[55]Cf. the contribution by H. J. W. Drijvers, "Marcionism in Syria: Principles, Problems, Polemics," in this issue.

[56]*Against Heresies (De Deo)* IV. The newest edition is by L. Mariès and Ch. Mercier: "Eznik de Kolb, *De Deo*," in *Patrologia Orientalis* 28/3 (Text), 4 (Translation) (Paris, 1959).

[57]First, Eznik presents a coherent outline of Marcion's doctrine: IV.1 (358); cf. C. S. C. Williams, "Eznik's Résumé of Marcionite Doctrine," *JThS* 45 (1944): 65–73.

to obscure sources. But how old could these concepts be? An example will clarify the problem: Eznik tells that, according to Marcion's view, matter is juxtaposed to the Demiurge as a feminine principle, and both worked together to create earthly nature. We can probably see it as a process of procreation and birth.[58] From all appearances, Ephraem also is acquainted with this myth.[59] An older source is missing. Can one imagine that the myth was already known to Irenaeus and Tertullian, and they possibly did not mention it? Would Tertullian, who in one of his own writings declared the mythology of the Valentinians as ridiculous, have allowed such vulnerable areas in Marcion to escape his attention? That has little probability.[60] It is fairly obvious that we can assume a mythologization of Marcion's doctrine among the Syrian Marcionites. Then the question arises of how this transformation is to be evaluated: Is it a matter of a legitimate development? Do we have to speak of theological decline? The answer is difficult; it would have to take into account the possibilities of thinking and expressing which Syrian Christianity at that time possessed, as well as the entire continued development of Marcionite theology. The relationship of many views of Marcion's personal pupil, Apelles, to Gnostic doctrines shows that the step to the Gnostic myth was easily taken.

If one considers the portraits of Marcion in the ancient sources in comparison, it is seen that in them the most important modern interpretations of Marcion are already a matter of concern: Is Marcion primarily a theologian of scripture? Is he a Gnostic? Is he a Platonist? Reference to each of these interpretations is found in ancient sources. Research must accept the methodological consequences of these facts and attempt to see the original Marcion in the reflection of tradition.

V

MARCION'S INTELLECTUAL PROFILE

What is Marcion's relationship to contemporary philosophy? Is he a Gnostic? It is understandable that these two questions are always being posed anew. For upon their meaning is dependent the direction in which

---

[58]IV.1 (358); see Mariès-Mercier, p. 662: "Et pareil est l'ordre qu'il [Marcion] suit dans son exposé, touchant le monde et les créatures, à l'ordre que suit la Loi en son récit. Mais il ajoute encore que c'est en commun avec l'Hylè qu'il [le Dieu de la Loi] a créé tout ce qu'il a créé et comme si l'Hylè était en quelque sorte de sexe féminin et femme à laquelle il fût marié."

[59]Cf. Drijvers, see below.

[60]Tertullian's polemical procedure in *Adversus Valentinianos* is explained by J.-Cl. Frédouille in his edition: Tertullien, *Contre les Valentiniens*, vol. I (Paris: Cerf, 1980), 12–23.

one interprets the testimonies to Marcion's doctrine, and also the position
which Marcion is assigned within the theological currents and disputes
of the second century. The question regarding Marcion's connection with
Gnosticism especially demands a methodological reflection: our modern
concepts of Gnosis and Gnosticism are indispensable, yet they are ab-
stractions; as such they are more clear-cut than the historical reality. As
is known, into the third century the borders were in flux between heretical
Gnosticism and the attempts of orthodox theologians to penetrate system-
atically the Christian message. Thus it does not lead anywhere, depending
on what concept of Gnosticism is used as a basis, if one designates Marcion as a Gnostic of a special kind or if one no longer wants to see him
as a Gnostic. Whether this way or that, only his special historical position
is described. Therefore our question should be framed another way: In
what manner did Marcion interpret and systematize the early Christian
tradition? What possibilities of interpretation and systematization existed
in his time? By asking in this way, one can compare Marcion's propositions and solutions with those of other theologians of the second century, thereby ascertaining where he is a pioneer and where he is in agreement with the tendencies and views of contemporaries.

To be sure, Marcion was more strongly influenced by philosophy than
Harnack wanted to admit. Harnack believed that Marcion's reading of
Colossians 2:8 was διὰ τῆς φιλοσοφίας ὡς κενῆς ἀπάτης. From this
equation of philosophy and deception, he deduced a renunciation of philosophy. Marcion's biblical, nonspeculative theology, as it appears to
Harnack in the sources, seems to correspond to this interpretation. Yet
the supposition of the textual correction is untenable, and even if it were
to be true, it would remain questionable whether the passage actually had
for Marcion a programatic meaning.[61] While on the subject, theoretical
rejection of philosophy and factual dependence on it does not need to be

---

[61]Harnack, *Marcion*, pp. 51, 93, 122f. The witness on which Harnack's reconstruction
is based is Tertullian, *Adv. Marc.* V.19.7: "At cum monet (sc. apostolus) cavendum a
subtililoquentia et philosophia, ut inani seductione, quae sit secundum elementa mundi,
non secundum caelum aut terram dicens, sed secundum litteras saeculares et secundum
traditionem, scilicet hominum subtililoquorum et philosophorum, longum est quidem et
alterius operis ostendere hac sententia omnes haereses damnari, quod omnes ex subtili-
loquentiae viribus et philosophiae regulis constent." It is a matter more of an interpretative
paraphrase than of a verbatim rendering of the Pauline verse. As the reference to the same
passage in *De anima* 3.1 shows, Tertullian understands κενῆς ἀπάτης as an explanation
of τῆς φιλοσοφίας : "Ab apostolo iam tunc philosophia concussio veritatis providebatur;
Athenis enim expertus linguatam civitatem cum omnes illic sapientiae atque facundiae
caupones degustasset, inde concepit praemonitorium illud edictum." Cf. Quispel, op. cit.
(note 48), pp. 91f.; Waszink in the commentary on *De anima*, p. 115. It is thus a matter
of the interpretation by Tertullian, so the assumption of a text alteration by Marcion becomes superfluous.

mutually exclusive. There are sufficient examples of this in early Christianity. Repeatedly in recent works, Marcion's philosophical motifs and arguments have been pointed out.[62] It appears to me that Marcion made a distinction between the two Gods because he could not reconcile the anthropomorphic traits of the Old Testament God with the philosophical concept of an essentially good God. It is conspicuous that the intellectually more ambitious Gnostic outlines of doctrine issue from a single highest principle; the Demiurge only secondarily comes into being through a fall.[63] If one, in addition, takes into consideration the tendency of contemporary philosophy toward monotheism, Marcion's dualism appears at first glance to be impeded and unphilosophical. For the idea, however, of an eternal coexistence of the two Gods (taken in the strictest sense, according to the world view of antiquity, it was a spatial stacking) philosophical motifs can also be opened up: If the Demiurge is a generate being, the responsibility for his imperfection and for the imperfection of his creation goes back to the good God. For a comparison, there is the two-God doctrine of Numenius of Apamea. Numenius distinguishes the "first God" and "father" from the "Demiurge" and "lawgiver."[64] The first God is absolute good, the Demiurge is the performing creator and the God of becoming (γένεσις). He imitates the first God and is himself good only through participation.[65] Insofar as the Demiurge has a relationship of participating in and imitating the first and good God, there is an analogy to Valentinian doctrine. Insofar as the Demiurge has always been and never came into existence, there is agreement with Marcion's view. The idea of foreignness between the good God on one hand, and the Demiurge with his creation on the other hand, appears as a peculiarly Marcionite thought. The ranking "good God, righteous Demiurge, corrupt matter" indeed sets up the assumption that Marcion knows a com-

---

[62]Cf. M. Pohlenz, *Vom Zorne Gottes* (Göttingen: Vandenhoeck and Ruprecht, 1909), 20–22; also Pohlenz, *Die Stoa*, vol. I, 4th ed. (Göttingen: Vandenhoeck and Ruprecht, 1970), 410f.; vol. II, 4th ed. (Göttingen: Vandenhoeck and Ruprecht, 1972), 198f.; J. G. Gager, "Marcion and Philosophy," *Vigiliae Christianae* 26 (1972): 53–59; J. Woltman, "Der geschichtliche Hintergrund der Lehre Markions vom 'Fremden Gott'," in *Wegzeichen: Festgabe zum 60. Geburtstag von Prof. Dr. M. H. Biedermann* (Würzburg: Augustinus, 1971), 15–42; G. May, *Schöpfung aus dem Nichts. Die Entstehung der Lehre von der creatio ex nihilo* (Berlin: De Gruyter, 1978), 57–60; E. Mühlenberg, "Marcion's Jealous God," in *Disciplina Nostra. Essays in Memory of R. F. Evans* (Cambridge, Mass.: Philadelphia Patristic Foundation, 1979), 93–113, esp. 112f.

[63]Cf. H. Jonas, *Gnosis und spätantiker Geist*, Vol. I (Göttingen: Vandenhoeck and Ruprecht, 1964), 328–375; A. Orbe, *Estudios Valentinianos I: Hacia la primera teologia de la procesion del verbo* (Rome: Gregoriana 1958), 203–285.

[64]Fragment 21. 13, des Places.

[65]Fragment 16. 18, des Places.

prehensive classification of being and that for him the good God is not
the absolutely incommensurable one, the "quite different" one. The comparison with Numenius can show that the correspondences and possible
connections between Marcion's thinking and the thinking of philosophers
as well as Gnostics are more multifarious and more complicated than one
often assumes.

The sharpest contrast between Marcion and the majority of the Gnostics
is in the stance toward the Christian tradition. Whereas the Gnostics appeal to Christian as well as extra-Christian texts and traditions, and in
particular traced their special esoteric doctrines back to secret traditions,
Marcion rejects any form of oral tradition and relies solely on writings
associated with the name of Paul. The Catholic solution to the problem
of Christian tradition—legitimization of the ecclesiastical proclamation
by means of the principle of tradition and succession, as well as creating
a broader canon of the New Testament—appears to be a middle path
between the extreme positions of the Gnostics and Marcion. Nothing typical of Gnostic mythology is discoverable in Marcion in the older sources.
However, the theology of Marcion's pupil, Apelles, shows already an
inclination to Gnostic ideas. The letter of the Valentinian Ptolemaeus to
Flora shows that the problems of the origin and validity of the Old Testament law, as well as of the compatibility of the divine attributes of
goodness and justice preoccupied Marcion and the Valentinians to the
same degree.[66] Marcion's solutions were only more radical than those of
the Valentinians.

We still need to take a look at Marcion's relationship to the biblical
texts. Is it justified to label his doctrine "biblical theology?"[67] His "bib-

---

[66]A. Dihle thinks Marcion and the Gnostics, as critically reflective theologians, with
regard to surmounting the principle of retribution in the New Testament as well as in the
Platonic tradition, devalued the concept of justice: *Die goldene Regel. Eine Einführung in
die Geschichte der antiken und frühchristlichen Vulgärethik* (Göttingen: Vandenhoeck and
Ruprecht, 1962), 61–79; see also his *Der Kanon der zwei Tugenden* (Cologne-Opladen:
Westdeutscher V., 1968), 32–37. Mühlenberg (see note 62 above) suspects on the basis
of statements by Tertullian. (*Adv. Marc.* I.25f.; II.29.3f.) Marcion supposedly condemned
the justice of the Demiurge because this justice was necessarily in connection with *aemulatio*, "self-asserting zeal" (p. 107). I consider this hypothesis to be mistaken; Mühlenberg
fails to recognize that *aemulatio* is Tertullian's concept and does not, as he suspects, refer
directly to the "zealous God" of Ex. 20:5. The latter is called *zelotes* in Tertullian, not
aemulus (cf. *Adv. Marc.* IV.27.8). *Aemulatio* means simply "enmity." Cf. Waszink in his
commentary on *De anima*, p. 110 (2.5).

[67]Thus in Harnack, *Marcion*, p. 93: "Marcion's proclamation of Christianity thus claims
to be nothing more than biblical theology." C. Andresen even speaks of the "scriptural
fundamentalism" of Marcion in C. Andresen, ed., *Handbuch der Dogmen- und Theologie-
geschichte*, I: *Die Lehrentwicklung im Rahmen der Katholizität* (Göttingen: Vandenhoeck
and Ruprecht, 1982), 64.

licism" arises neither from historical-philological considerations of methodology nor from a rejection in principle of any kind of metaphysics, but rather from dogmatic motives.[68] Since the Old Testament is not sufficient for his theological demands, he traces it back to a God of low rank. The rejection of allegorical interpretation is the consequence, not the presupposition, of criticism. According to the ancient view, allegorization is not a method to be applied to random texts, but rather is only justifiable if the revelatory character and the sanctity of a text is established.[69] On the other hand, because of his distrust of all oral tradition, Marcion is obliged to rely on written documents in which the original Christian truth is contained. His philological work, by means of which he wants to free the texts of his Bible from all supposed adulterations, is anything but unbiased. It is based on dogmatic postulates and a totally unhistorical view of early Christianity.[70] Similarly, his exegesis is dependent on massive dogmatic presuppositions. One calls him a biblical theologian only inasmuch as for him his scripture canon represents the only standard of faith. He is not one in the sense that he had brought the originality of the "Gospel" and Pauline theology to bear against speculative interpretations. His assault is directed against, as he thought, the Judaistically corrupted proclamation, not against the doctrinal framework of the Gnostics. However, the standard theology of the church was in almost every regard closer to the biblical texts than Marcion's doctrine was.

If one asks what is unmistakably unique about Marcion's theology, being recognizable in all the divergence of sources, one finds it less in definite doctrines than in the asperity of his thinking, characterized by movement in radical alternatives and contrasts. The "antithesis" is for Marcion not only a rhetorical figure, but rather a theological principle. This appears to be non-Greek. The tendency of philosophy of the imperial period, and of Christian theology under its influence, was towards unity, harmony, and proving historical continuity. Where does Marcion's style of thinking come from? It is not early Christian per se. Is it the result of an ontologizing of the Pauline juxtaposing of old and new, law and grace? Biographical and psychological explanations—perhaps the assumption of

[68] When Origen (*Comm. Mt.* 15.3) ascribes to Marcion the principle μὴ δεῖν ἀλληγορεῖν τὰς γραφάς, it is not to be concluded that he has a programmatic utterance from the *Antitheses* before him; here it is simply a matter of characterizing Marcion's exegetical procedure. The same holds true for the other witnesses listed by Harnack, *Marcion*, p. 259.

[69] Cf. H. Dörrie, "Zur Methodik antiker Exegese," *ZNW* 65 (1974): 121–138, 122ff.

[70] Cf. R. M. Grant, *The Letter and the Spirit* (London: SPCK, 1957), 115–119; see also Grant, "Marcion and the Critical Method," in *From Jesus to Paul. Studies in Honour of Francis Wright Beare*, ed. P. Richardson and J. C. Hurd (Waterloo/Ontario: Wilfrid Laurier U, 1984), 207–215.

a resentful departure from his own Jewish past—lack sufficient basis in the sources.[71] In any event, the radicalism of the theologian Marcion in the church history of the second century is singular.

VI

MARCION IN HIS TIME

In contrast to the Gnostics, who recognized a relative right for the church's faith and who understood themselves as Christians of a higher order, Marcion made an exclusive claim to truth. The success of his assault on the existing church and of his propaganda for his own faith was extraordinarily great. Within a few years, he was successful at building his own church. From where did Marcion's doctrine get its recruiting force? What appears to us as a violent interpretation of the New Testament message obviously had a quite different effect on many contemporaries. Certainly the renunciation of the world and the ascetic austerity of Marcion made an impression. One should call to mind how much favor rigorous movements still found in later centuries of church history. Yet, to the same, if not higher, degree Marcion's missionary success must have been conditioned by the fact that his doctrine appeared to remove a series of difficulties and internal contradictions one encountered when considering the Christian tradition. Anti-Marcionite polemics are informative in this regard: Marcion confronted his opponents with problems that until then had not been sufficiently solved, nor partly had hardly ever been recognized as such. Marcion was ahead of his Catholic adversaries as far as consistency, internal consequence, and—not to be forgotten— the documentary certainty of his doctrine was concerned. Of course, his superiority in these respects resulted from his high-handed abbreviation and rationalization of the Christian message.

During the time of Marcion's appearance, the church was on its way to a crisis. The customary concept of the "Gnostic crisis" is not sufficient to characterize it. It was a crisis of the foundations as well as of the content of the Christian faith, and it developed gradually. What led to it? The separation of the church from its beginnings became increasingly noticeable; differing interpretations of tradition and proclamation competed with each other; secret traditions supposedly formed the basis for doctrinal oddities. The question that became more and more urgent was: How does one verify the one original truth? There was an increasing openness toward Greek education. The syncretistic systems of the Christian Gnostics are the untamed expression of this thrust of Hellenization. Other theologians sought to implement, with greater methodological dis-

[71]Contrary to Harnack, *Neue Studien zu Marcion* (note 1 above) 15f.

cipline, the ideal of a Christian philosophy. The question arose regarding what, in this connection, is permissible and what are the yardsticks of truth. One result of the development was that the Old Testament and also the early Christian writings were read with "Greek" presuppositions. The problem of the authoritativeness of the Old Testament—in spite of Paul, never uniformly solved—was raised anew and pointedly: It was no longer just a question of the validity of the law. Could the Bible of the Jews, as a matter of fact, be the revelatory book of the true God?

Marcion took up the questions that were raised and answered them in his radical way. He solved the problem of tradition through a philological, i.e. Hellenistic-scholarly, reconstruction of the "Gospel" and the texts of the Pauline epistles. He surmounted the offensiveness of the Old Testament by utilizing the doctrine of two Gods. And with his doctrine of the passionless good God, he sought to come to terms with Gnostic and philosophical demands placed on the concept of God. Marcion's theology distinguishes itself by the radicalism of its solutions to problems and the clarity of its statements. It was therefore so successful.[72] At the same time, Marcion's forced solutions tore away the veil surrounding the Gnostic speculations. With inexorable clarity they made apparent what consequences resulted from the numerous new interpretations of the old tradition. It was through Marcion that the latent crisis of Christian foundations and norms became manifest. His straightforward assault, however, also aroused the forces of defense. In the discussion with Marcion, the process of theological clarification began almost convulsively, the results of which were the Catholic canon, the Rule of Faith, and the exhaustive presentations of ecclesiastical doctrines.

Unfortunately, we know little about how Marcion's doctrine survived in his church and what transformations it went through. We are able to say almost nothing about the spiritual substance of Marcionite Christianity. Towards the end of the second century, the Catholic Rhodon specifically names a series of Marcionites who were active as teachers in Rome. Their views on the principles of being are divergent; only a single school remained true to Marcion's original thoughts.[73] For Rhodon the

---

[72]Somewhat different is Harnack, *Marcion*, p. 155, note 2: "The sources give no answer to the question of what the drawing power of Marcionism mainly rested on; thus we are dependent on suppositions: probably it was the paradox of the combination of the proclamation of the exclusively good God, Christ, along with the rejection of the Old Testament; with asceticism, which promised to lead to supermanhood; and with a furious abhorrence of the 'world,' over which one felt himself to be highly exalted." Balás (note 7 above) also suspects a reason for Marcion's success resides in the simplistic solutions to complicated problems.

[73]Rhodon in Eusebius, *Hist. Eccl.* V. 13.

splits and differences of opinion among the Marcionite theologians are a sign of the untenability of their doctrines. The modern reader gets a more positive impression from the report: Rome's Marcionite church must have been uncommonly productive and without doubt represented for the Catholic Church a dangerous rival. The dispute of Rhodon with Marcion's disciple Apelles conveys to us a picture of the public debate.

The above-named Apelles was, judging by the relatively large number of witnesses, the most significant disciple of Marcion.[74] He apparently seriously took issue with the ideas of his teacher and advocated the concept that the good God was the only principle of being; the Demiurge and the God of the Old Testament, viewed by Apelles as separate, are angelic beings created by the good God. Apelles' speculations about the body of Christ show that he had tempered Marcion's strict Docetism. An approximation to Gnostic ideas of the Valentinian type as well as to Catholic theology here becomes recognizable. Whereas we hear nothing of enthusiasm and spiritualism in Marcion, Apelles appealed to the revelations of the prophetess Philumene. With the emerging of a Marcionite prophecy, do we see a parallel phenomenon with the outset of Montanism, which shook the Catholic Church simultaneously?

As soon as the Catholic Church had taken up the dispute with the Marcionites on a broad front, the weaknesses of its theological position became apparent. The Catholic canon of the Bible fulfilled the demand to guarantee documentarily the tradition in a better way than the Marcionite canon, whose one-sided choices and severe textual omissions were easy to criticize. The Catholic theologians had not only church tradition on their side, they appropriated more justly philosophical arguments and knew how to interpret the reality of human experience more convincingly than the Marcionites. The Marcionite negation of the creation and its God had a certain grandeur—"a giant fighting against God," as Clement of Alexandria calls Marcion (*Strom.* III. 25.2)—but if one wanted to survive in this creation, one had to affirm it at least within limits; the Catholic polemicists inexorably reproached the Marcionites with this.

In the course of the third century, Marcionism fell more and more into the defensive position. In the West it even experienced a rapid decline, in fact, before the age of Constantine and before the beginning of state

---

[74] The fundamental studies on Apelles are from Harnack, *De Apellis gnosi monarchica* (Leipzig, 1874); see also Harnack, *Marcion,* pp. 177–196, 404–420. In addition, there are now the contributions by J.-P. Mahé, *Tertullien, La chair du Christ I* (Paris: Cerf, 1975), 94–110 and E. Junod, "Les attitudes d'Apelles, disciple de Marcion, à l'égard de l'Ancien Testament," *Augustinianum* 12 (1982): 113–133. I treat the relationship of Apelles to Marcion more thoroughly in the article "Apelles und die Entwicklung der marcionitischen Theologie," which is to appear in *Aufstieg und Niedergang der Römischen Welt.*

persecution of heretics. However, it was able to maintain itself longer in the East, above all in eastern Syria, where a favorable atmosphere prevailed for asceticism as well as for Gnostic speculative tendencies. The Marcionite church was able to assert itself into the fifth century, even at first against the growing competition of Manichaeism. The rapid recession of Marcionism in wide parts of the Roman Empire is not astonishing to us, but rather the fact that it possessed the energy to survive for centuries in the East.

Irénée et l'hérésie

Les conceptions hérésiologiques de l'évêque de Lyon

Il ne s'agit pas ici de donner une nouvelle description des diverses hérésies qui apparaissent dans l'oeuvre de saint Irénée: ce travail a déjà fait l'objet de nombreuses études. Il ne sera pas non plus question de chercher à découvrir les sources des hérésies mentionnées par l'évêque de Lyon, ni, non plus, d'en établir la généalogie critique. Notre but n'est pas de décrire la manière dont Irénée réfute chacune des hérésies qu'il rencontre, pas plus d'ailleurs que de dégager l'apologétique antihérétique que l'on trouve dans l'*Adversus Haereses* ... Ce que nous voudrions tenter de dégager, au delà de la figure de chaque hérésie particulière, c'est l'image même qu'Irénée se fait de l'hérésie en tant que telle, non pas l'image de telle ou telle hérésie, mais l'image globale de ce qu'est en soi l'hérésie. Autrement dit, il s'agit d'essayer de déterminer la manière dont Irénée perçoit l'hérésie, et sa conception du phénomène hérétique.

Pour donner une réponse à cette question, on pourrait essayer de dégager des deux premiers livres de l'*Adversus Haereses* ce qu'Irénée dit de l'hérésie en général et, à partir des analyses de détail, d'en brosser un portrait synthétique. C'est ainsi qu'on pourrait repérer les qualificatifs par lesquels notre auteur désigne les hérésies: *impia, falsa, blasphemia, apostasia, inanis stultitia, mendacium* ... A la vouloir exhaustive, la liste en serait fort longue et n'apporterait pas grand chose à notre compréhension profonde du fait hérétique. L'injure, depuis Homère, est entrée dans la littérature et les hérésiologues ne se sont pas fait faute de s'en servir et d'améliorer les modèles qui leur étaient proposés.

Il serait sans doute intéressant de relever les images par lesquelles Irénée décrit l'hérésie. Dans la Préface du Livre I, voulant montrer combien la gnose est difficile à détecter tant elle a l'apparence de la vérité, Irénée utilise l'image d'une fausse pierre précieuse ... Pour conclure son premier Livre,

l'évêque de Lyon compare l'hérésie à une bête sauvage cachée
dans la forêt et qui, de là, lance ses attaques. Celui qui abat
les arbres et dénude la forêt découvre la bête et peut, tout à
la fois, éviter ses assauts et lui décocher des traits meutriers.
Mais la comparaison ne nous apprend rien de bien nouveau:
l'hérésie est comme une bête sauvage, dévastatrice et nuisi-
ble ... pour en faire façon il faut la débusquer, autrement dit,
il faut connaître ses doctrines ... Un peu plus loin, en I,11,4, on
verra Irénée appliquer à l'hérésie l'image de la concombre, ce
qui revient à la traiter de « cornichon » ... Si ces images, comme
on l'a remarqué, montrent que la réthorique et ses procédés
ne sont pas inconnus d'Irénée, elles ne nous permettent guère
de cerner avec quelque précision l'image qu'Irénée se fait de
l'hérésie.

Pour tenter d'apporter une réponse à la question posée
par notre propos, il nous a semblé que la meilleure manière
de procéder était de faire une enquête sur les termes hérésie(s)-
hérétique(s) dans l'*Adversus Haereses* afin d'en déterminer la
signification exacte ainsi que le rôle qui leur est dévolu dans
les développements irénéens. Il devrait y avoir là une base
scientifique incontestable permettant d'aboutir à des conclusions objectives et valables. Nous étudierons donc d'abord
« l'usage et la signification des termes hérésie-hérétique » dans
l'*Adversus Haereses*. A partir des résultats obtenus nous cher-
cherons à dégager quelle est « l'origine de l'hérésie », puis ce
qu'est « le contenu doctrinal type de l'hérésie » et enfin ce que
pourrait être une « réfutation globale de l'hérésie ».

1. *Usage et signification des mots hérésie-hérétique.*

Une recherche lexicographique s'impose d'autant plus que
l'*Adversus Haereses* est le premier ouvrage hérésiologique qui
ait été conservé. Il est donc important de déterminer le sens
des termes utilisés pour désigner les dissidences à l'intérieur
du christianisme et d'en préciser l'usage. Pour le repérage des
termes nous avons utilisé le travail de B. Reynders qui donne
toutes les références nécessaires et constitue un instrument
de travail dont on ne saurait plus se passer (*Lexique comparé
du texte grec et des versions latine, arménienne et syriaque de
l'*Adversus Haereses *de Saint Irénée* [CSCO 141, Subsidia 5],
Louvain 1954).

La collation des différents passages où les termes *haeresis* et *haereticus* apparaissent permet l'établissement d'un tableau récapitulatif lourd de signification. Mais sa présentation appelle quelques remarques préliminaires:

1º À propos du terme *haereticus*, le lexique fait une distinction entre le nom utilisé au singulier et le nom utilisé au pluriel accompagné de l'adjectif *omnes*. Une telle distinction s'impose par le nombre des références. Or à propos du terme *haeresis*, le lexique ne reprend pas la classification ébauchée précédemment et ne distingue pas entre l'usage au singulier et au pluriel. Cependant l'examen des différents passages où apparaît le terme *haeresis* montre que dans nombre de cas l'adjectif *omnes* lui est adjoint. Dans ces conditions le tableau tiendra compte du parallélisme constaté entre l'usage d'*haereticus* et *haeresis* en distinguant chaque fois le mot au singulier et le mot au pluriel accompagné du qualificatif *omnes*.

2º Il a fallu distinguer les passages où Irénée parle de lui-même et ceux où les termes apparaissent dans des citations bibliques. On relève ainsi 2 textes néotestamentaires: *Gal* 5,19-21 pour le nom en V,11,1; *Tit* 3,10 pour l'adjectif en III,3,4.

3º À propos du mot *haereticus* on a distingué entre l'usage en tant qu'adjectif et l'usage en tant que nom.

4º Le tableau distingue entre l'utilisation des termes au pluriel ou au singulier.

Adversus Haereses		I	II	III	IV	V		
haeresis	Cit.					1	1	
	Sing.	2					2	4
	Pl.	1					1	
omnis haeresis	Sing.				1		1	4
	Pl.	2	1				3	
		5	1	0	1	1		8
haereticus	Cit.			1			1	
	Nom Sing.						0	
	Nom Pl.		5	6	6	9	26	31
	Adj. Sing.			1		1	2	
	Adj. Pl.					2	2	
omnes haeretici	Pl.	1	3	5	6	6		21
		1	8	13	12	18		52

Soit au total 8+52 = 60.

Ce tableau appelle une série de remarques:

1° Le terme *haeresis* apparaît assez rarement. Sur 8 mentions, 1 relève du Nouveau Testament. Irénée n'utilise donc le mot hérésie que 7 fois, alors que le terme hérétique revient 52 fois. De plus sur 7 mentions intéressantes, il faut remarquer que 6 appartiennent aux deux premiers livres de l'*Adversus Haereses*, livres essentiellement consacrés à la description des hérésies gnostiques. Il faut également remarquer que le mot est lié à l'adjectif *omnis* dans 50% des cas.

De cette première série de remarques est-il possible de tirer quelque conclusion? Il est manifeste qu'Irénée préfère au terme abstrait désignant la catégorie — l'hérésie — le terme concret désignant l'individu, l'hérétique. Cette préférence pourrait provenir du fait que le mot hérésie n'a, peut-être, pas encore acquis un droit de cité définitif dans la langue chrétienne et qu'il est, peut-être, en train de passer d'un usage neutre — le parti, l'opinion différente — à un usage qui va devenir technique et péjorativement nuancé, le mauvais parti, l'opinion fausse. On pourrait aussi se demander si cette préférence pour le terme concret ne provient pas du fait que l'évêque de Lyon, qui n'a pas un esprit spéculatif, est assez peu doué pour l'abstraction. Serait-ce aussi que l'intérêt d'Irénée n'est pas la réfutation en soi d'une doctrine abstraite, mais la réfutation d'opinions et d'erreurs prônées par des hommes, des communautés bien précises qu'il rencontre journellement? Sans doute chacune de ces raisons possède sa part de vérité. Au fond, Irénée pense difficilement l'hérésie, il pense plutôt aux hérétiques. Quand il pense hérésie, il dit hérétiques.

Ceci se confirme par le passage où Irénée parle de l'erreur de Tatien (III,23,8): Tatien n'a fait que combiner une série de doctrines erronées pour se forger sa propre théologie. Et Irénée écrit: « connexio quidem factus omnium haereticorum ». Autrement dit Tatien a fait une combinaison de tous les hérétiques, car ce qui intéresse l'évêque de Lyon dans son souci pastoral, c'est la personne même des hérétiques plutôt que leurs doctrines abstraites. Il est intéressant de constater que le traducteur français d'Irénée, F. Sagnard (*Irénée de Lyon, Contre les hérésies* III [SCh 34], Paris 1952, p. 397), a rétabli de lui-même le sens correct en traduisant: « après avoir fait une combinaison de toutes les hérésies ... ».

2° Notre deuxième remarque portera sur le terme *hae-reticus*. Celui-ci apparaît très fréquemment, 51 fois plus 1 citation biblique; mais ce qu'il y a de plus remarquable c'est l'usage presque constant de ce terme au pluriel: on ne trouve, sur les 51 récurrences, que 2 fois le singulier. De plus, la grande majorité des passages où apparaît le terme se trouve dans les 3 derniers livres de l'*Adversus haereses*: 9 fois dans les deux premiers Livres contre 43 dans les 3 derniers. Il faut également signaler que dans 21 cas l'adjectif *omnis* est lié au nom *haereticus*, ce qui dénote chez Irénée un effort de généralisation, un effort pour penser l'hérétique en général.

Est-il possible de dégager quelque conclusion de cette deuxième série de remarques? Si Irénée n'arrive pas à bien cerner la catégorie « hérésie », il s'intéresse très particulièrement aux « hérétiques » et ce qui lui importe c'est leur groupe, la communauté formée par les hérétiques qu'il cotoye. Naturellement il connaît les chefs de file des hérésies, Valentin, Basilide, Montan ..., mais ces individus qui appartiennent au passé ne l'intéressent guère, ce qui lui importe ce sont les groupes d'hommes qui se sont formés à la suite de ces promoteurs.

Irénée travaille avec la catégorie « hérétiques » plutôt qu'avec la catégorie « hérésie ». Néanmoins la fréquence des expressions *omnes haeretici* est le signe qu'en partant du concret et de l'individuel Irénée cherche à généraliser, à abstraire. Ici encore on est en plein processus d'évolution: Irénée est en train de se forger une image type de l'hérétique qui ne pourra faire autrement que de déboucher dans une image type et abstraite de l'hérésie en elle-même et pour elle-même, indépendante des doctrines concrètes, variables et contingentes par lesquelles elle se manifeste.

2. Origine et développement de l'hérésie.

Dans un certain nombre de textes, Simon le Magicien apparaît comme étant à l'origine même de l'hérésie (cf. *Act* 8,9-25).

« Simo autem Samaritanus, ex quo *universae haereses* substituerunt ... » (I,23,2). Irénée reprendra cette conception dans la préface du Livre II: « Et quoniam *omnes* a Simone *haeretici* initia sumentes ».

On peut encore citer I,27,4 à 28,1: « Il est nécessaire de nous rappeler de lui (Simon), afin que tu saches que tous ceux

qui déforment en quelque manière la vérité et la prédication
de l'Église sont les disciples de Simon le Mage et ses succes-
seurs ... tous ceux-ci sont les propagateurs de *nombreuses hérésies* et finissent par se séparer de *l'hérésie* dans laquelle ils
ont vécu ». Simon le Mage, ou le Magicien, nous apparaît ici,
une fois de plus, comme l'ancêtre unique des hérésies. Mais
il y a une idée nouvelle, les hérétiques ne forment pas un groupe unique, mais ils se séparent les uns des autres. Si l'hérésie
est séparation d'avec l'Église, la séparation et la division l'af-
fecte elle-même en sorte que derrière l'hérésie, il y a une multiplicité d'hérésies. Pour Irénée l'hérésie est caractérisée par
un processus de fractionnement et de division qui n'a point de
limite.

Ainsi les hérétiques ne présentent pas une doctrine unique,
mais ils professent des doctrines variées, diverses et opposées.
Et ceci l'évêque de Lyon ne cessera de le redire. En I,22,2 il
parlera de la « convictio varia et multifaria » des hérétiques.
En V,20,1, nous avons ce texte significatif : « Force est donc à
tous les hérétiques ci-dessus mentionnés, par là-même qu'ils
sont aveugles à l'égard de la vérité, d'aller de côté et d'autre
hors de tout chemin frayé, et, pour cette raison, les traces
de leurs doctrines sont éparpillées çà et là, sans accord et sans
suite. Il en va tout autrement de ceux qui appartiennent à
l'Église ... ». On le voit une des caractéristiques c'est un pulul-
lement de doctrines multiples qui se contredisent récipro-
quement.

De plus l'hérésie n'est pas seulement une division progressive à partir d'une unité primitive, mais elle est une combinaison de doctrines hérétiques, une « connexio omnium *haereticorum* » (Cf. III,23,8).

En fait Irénée nous met en présence d'une vision théologique de l'hérésie qui offre un parallélisme certain avec la
manière dont il conçoit l'orthodoxie. L'hérésie a un ancêtre —
Simon — comme l'orthodoxie a elle aussi ses ancêtres, les apôtres. En face des apôtres qui garantissent la vérité de la prédication de l'Évangile, il faut un hérétique, une sorte d'apôtre
défroqué qui soit à l'origine du contre-évangile que représente
l'hérésie. Et tout comme les apôtres seront au point de départ
de la transmission de l'Évangile, ce faux apôtre sera au point
de départ de la transmission de l'hérésie. Et l'on comprend
l'insistance d'Irénée sur les apôtres comme garants de la trans-

mission authentique de l'Évangile en face de Simon auteur et garant d'une mauvaise transmission de l'Évangile.

Plus encore, il semble bien que pour Irénée l'idée de succession soit aussi présente dans l'hérésie. Il existe une succession à partir de Simon qui est l'ancêtre des autres hérétiques, tout comme il existe une succession à partir des apôtres. Finalement l'orthodoxie et l'hérésie se développent parallélement, l'une et l'autre sont comprises dans un même schéma: le Christ, les apôtres, l'orthodoxie ou le Christ, le faux apôtres, les hérésies. Et naturellement un coefficient positif est affecté au premier schéma, tandisque le second est affecté d'une appréciation négative. Cependant et quoiqu'il en soit de l'appréciation, la structure de pensée est la même.

S'il y a un même processus à l'origine, le développement historique de l'hérésie et de l'orthodoxie ne suivent pas le même chemin. Car si l'orthodoxie apporte au cours de l'histoire une doctrine unique et homogène, l'hérésie est caractérisée par la multiplicité, la variation et même l'opposition de ses doctrines. Ici Irénée introduit un critère de différenciation: en face de l'unité de l'Église, on voit naître la diversité comme note de l'hérésie.

Ainsi s'ébauche une notion de l'hérésie où celle-ci se présente comme un antitype de l'Église, comme une image négative de l'orthodoxie. La note d'universalité est remplacée par celle de particularité, celle d'unité par multiplicité, celle d'apostolicité authentique par la fausse apostolicité. Il y a là une construction intéressante où le théologien qu'était Irénée se trouve à l'aise. Désormais on sait ce que représente l'hérésie sur le plan théologique, on peut la situer dans un système doctrinal et de ce fait elle perd son caractère inquiétant et insécurisant.

On trouve chez Irénée une autre conception de l'origine de l'hérésie et de son développement originel. Pour lui la gnose valentinienne qui est en fait le résumé de toutes les hérésies (IV, *préf.* 2), trouve son origine dans la philosophie à laquelle elle doit ses idées fondamentales. Au chapitre 14 du Livre II, Irénée, pour montrer que les doctrines hérétiques sont sans originalité, affirme qu'elles sont faites d'emprunts aux poètes et aux philosophes. Ce que les hérétiques présentent comme nouveau n'est en fait qu'un tissu de vieux dogmes philosophiques. Et Irénée prend la peine de détailler. Les hérétiques ont

emprunté à Thalès de Milet leur doctrine sur l'eau, cause et
origine de tout. Ils doivent à Anaximandre leur affirmation
que l'infini est le commencement de toutes choses. C'est Anaxagore qui leur a fourni l'idée que les êtres vivants provien-
nent de semences tombées du ciel ... Et Irénée de citer encore
Démocrite et Épicure, Platon, Anaxagore et Empédocle, les
Stoïciens, les Cyniques, Aristote et les Pythagoriciens. Il est
donc tout à fait clair que l'hérésie est le résultat d'une contamination de la vérité apostolique par la philosophie. Irénée
est-il à l'origine de cette conception qui fera fortune chez les
hérésiologues? On sait en effet qu'Hippolyte reprendra ce
thème et rattachera chaque hérésie à une école philosophique.
Irénée a-t-il déjà trouvé cette conception chez Justin ou Théo-
phile? Il est difficile de le dire.

Cette conception de l'origine de l'hérésie n'est pas du même
genre que la précédente et pourrait sembler en contradiction
avec elle. Pour concilier ces deux explications on pourrait peut-
être dire que Simon a été influencé par le philosophie et que
c'est pour cela qu'il est devenu hérétique. Mais ceci Irénée ne
le dit pas explicitement. Avec cette deuxième explication on
aurait une manière historique de rendre compte de la réalité
de l'hérésie tandisque la première explication serait plus théologique. Peut-être! Mais on peut penser que même dans cette
explication par la philosophie, la visée d'Irénée reste théologique. Pourquoi l'hérésie?, par suite de la contamination de la
philosophie. Autrement dit, l'hérésie relève du syncrétisme. Ainsi apparaît une caractéristique supplémentaire de l'hérésie, elle
est syncrétiste tandisque l'orthodoxie se veut pure de toute
contamination qui fausserait l'Évangile des Apôtres.

3. *Le contenu doctrinal de l'hérésie.*

À partir des passages où Irénée fait mention des termes
hérésie-hérétique, il va être intéressant de dégager l'image doc-
trinale globale que notre auteur se fait de l'hérésie. Celle-ci
peut être caractérisée par quatre éléments que l'on retrouve
partout. Il s'agit d'abord d'une conception de l'Écriture et de
la Tradition différente de celle de l'Église. Ensuite l'hérésie
refuse que le créateur et le sauveur soient le même Dieu. L'hérésie refuse l'incarnation. Enfin les hérétiques nient le salut
de la chair.

A. *Écriture et Tradition.* Les hérétiques utilisent l'Écriture et s'en servent comme base de référence pour leurs doctrines. « Chacun d'entre eux (*les hérétiques*) qui sort de l'Église cherche à se servir des Évangiles pour confirmer sa doctrine » (*confirmare doctrinam*) (III,11,8). Il y a donc chez les hérétiques la reconnaissance d'une autorité écrite, scripturaire qui sert de référence à la doctrine. Mais s'agit-il de la même Écriture que les orthodoxes? D'abord nombre d'hérétiques — sinon tous ceux combattus par Irénée — rejettent l'Ancien Testament en totalité ou en partie. De plus certains d'entre eux complètent les Évangiles reçus dans l'Église par d'autres récits évangéliques comme l'Évangile de vérité, tandisque d'autres ou bien corrigent les Évangiles ou les réduisent jusqu'à n'en recevoir qu'un. Ainsi l'Écriture, les Évangiles et même l'Apôtre sont des références qui confirment les doctrines dissidentes. Si donc les hérétiques font appel à l'autorité de l'Écriture, celle-ci n'a pas le même contenu que pour les membres de l'Église.

Mais même lorsque l'on se réfère à des textes identiques, les interprétations diffèrent et s'opposent. En effet celles-ci dépendent de traditions différentes: « On ne peut trouver la vérité si l'on ignore la Tradition. Car ce n'est pas par écrit que la vérité a été transmise, mais de vive voix » (III,1,2). C'est donc la Tradition orale gnostique, transmise par les successions de chefs de l'hérésie, qui est le principe herméneutique permettant une lecture vraie de l'Écriture.

Les normes d'autorité sont les mêmes pour l'hérésie, comme pour l'orthodoxie, à savoir l'Écriture et la Tradition. Mais l'extension de la première est différente et le cheminement de la seconde est autre.

B. *Le créateur n'est pas le sauveur.* Souvent les hérétiques sont mis en relation avec le créateur, le démiurge. Et l'on sent que, pour Irénée, un des aspects fondamentaux de l'hérésie est le problème de la création.

Voici quelques textes: « Presque *toutes les hérésies* affirment qu'il n'y a qu'un seul Dieu, mais ils transforment cette affirmation par leurs mauvaises idées et deviennent ingrats à l'égard de celui qui les a faits, tout comme les païens le font par leur idolâtrie » (I,22,1). L'hérétique n'est donc pas polythéiste, il affirme l'existence d'un seul Dieu. Cependant il comprend mal cette affirmation, puisqu'il ne reconnaît pas celui qui l'a créé. Autrement dit l'existence du Dieu créateur est mise en question. En II,2,5 Irénée déclare que les hérétiques débitent des choses insensées et inconsistantes sur la création. Dans la Préface du Livre IV Irénée se résume: « Car tous ces gens, quoique venant d'endroits divers et enseignant ces doctrines différentes, n'en aboutissent pas moins à la même thèse blasphématoire: ils blessent à mort, en enseignant à blasphémer Dieu, notre Créateur et Nourricier ... Car, quelques solennelles déclarations qu'ils fassent, *tous les hérétiques* aboutissent en fin de compte à ceci: blasphémer le Créateur » (IV, *préf.* 4).

Ainsi l'hérésie quelle qu'elle soit met en cause le Dieu créateur et en quelque sorte ne reconnaît pas son identité avec le Dieu sauveur. Certes, selon les diverses hérésies, cette mise en question ne se fait pas toujours de la même manière, comme en témoignent les doctrines de Valentin et de Marcion. Mais en fin de compte, c'est toujours le même processus: séparer le Dieu Sauveur du Dieu créateur et faire du démiurge un Dieu inférieur, secondaire (Cf. II,3).

Cette méconnaissance de la création conduit les hérétiques à méconnaître les économies de Dieu et son plan de salut: « Ils sont stupides tous les hérétiques, et ignorants de l'économie de Dieu, et bien peu au fait de son oeuvre relative à l'homme — aveugles qu'ils sont à l'égard de la vérité — lorsqu'ils contredisent eux-mêmes leur propre salut, les uns en introduisant un autre Père en dehors du créateur, les autres en prétendant que le monde et la matière qui le constitue ont été faits par des anges ... » (V,19,2). Cette apréciation négative de la création conduit les hérétiques à séparer l'Ancien Testament du Nouveau et les empêche de trouver dans l'Ancien Testament la prophétie du Nouveau: « Nous dirons donc à l'adresse de *tous les hérétiques,* et d'abord des disciples de Marcion et de ceux qui comme eux prétendent que les prophètes venaient de la part d'une autre Dieu: Lisez avec attention l'Évangile qui nous a été donné par les apôtres, lisez aussi avec attention les prophéties, et vous constaterez que toute l'oeuvre, toute la doctrine et toute la Passion de notre Seigneur y ont été prédites ... » (IV,34,1).

C. *La négation de l'incarnation.* Au delà des divergences des diverses hérésies relatives à la christologie, le grand reproche qu'Irénée fait aux hérétiques c'est de refuser l'incarnation. « De toutes façons pour aucun de ces *hérétiques* le Verbe de Dieu ne s'est fait chair. Si on examine à fond tous leurs systèmes, on verra que tous présentent un Verbe de Dieu et un Christ des régions supérieures qui sont sans chair, incapables de souffrir. Les uns pensent que ce Verbe ou Christ s'est manifesté sous une forme semblable à celle d'un homme, mais qu'il n'est pas né, ni incarné. Les autres disent qu'il n'a même pas pris la forme d'un homme, mais qu'il est descendu, telle une colombe, sur le Jésus né de Marie. *Tous* par conséquent sont convaincus de faux témoignage par le disciple du Seigneur, qui dit: Et le Verbe s'est fait chair et il a habité parmi nous » (III,11,3). Cependant ce refus de l'incarnation n'implique pas pour autant que les hérétiques refusent de confesser le crucifié: « Les *hérétiques* eux-mêmes confessent le crucifié » (V, 18,1), mais en fait ce crucifié n'est pas le Verbe de Dieu.

Ce refus de l'incarnation a comme conséquence que les hérétiques ne peuvent offrir l'eucharistie. On ne peut offrir à Dieu le pain et le vin de l'eucharistie si l'on ne croit pas que ce pain et ce vin sont l'oeuvre de Dieu, du Dieu créateur. Comment seraient-ils susceptibles de devenir le corps et le sang du Christ si celui-ci n'avait pas assumé une humanité faite de corps et de sang? « *Toutes les assemblées des hérétiques* ne l'offrent pas davantage. Les uns disent qu'il y a un Père autre que le Créateur: mais alors en lui offrant des dons tirés de notre monde créé, ils prouvent qu'il est cupide et désireux du bien d'autrui. D'autres disent que notre monde est issu d'une déchéance, d'une ignorance et d'une passion: mais alors en offrant les fruits de cette ignorance, de cette passion et de cette déchéance, ils pèchent contre leur Père et l'outragent plus qu'ils ne lui rendent grâce » (V,18,4).

D. *Le refus du salut de la chair.* Si le créateur n'a rien à voir avec le Sauveur, s'il n'y a pas d'incarnation, il est tout naturel que les hérétiques récusent le salut de la chair. « Vains, de toutes manières, ceux qui rejettent l'" économie " de Dieu, nient le salut de la chair, méprisent sa régénération en déclarant qu'elle n'est pas capable de recevoir l'incorruptibilité » (V,2,2). Mais ici Irénée se heurte à une grave difficulté. En effet l'Apôtre a écrit: « la chair et le sang ne peuvent hériter le royaume de Dieu » (*1Cor* 15,50) et ceci semble donner raison aux hérétiques dualistes. Il y a là un « texte que *tous les hérétiques* allèguent dans leur folie et à partir duquel ils s'efforcent de prouver qu'il n'y a pas de salut pour l'ouvrage modelé par Dieu » (V,9,1). Et l'évêque de Lyon est obligé de consacrer un très long développement à montrer que le texte de l'Apôtre Paul est mal interprété par les hérétiques (V,9-13).

Les quatres points que nous venons de relever caractérisent tous les hérétiques, ils sont donc communs à l'hérésie en tant que telle. Pour Irénée l'hérésie c'est donc l'usage d'une herméneutique différente de la sienne qui conduit à une négation du Dieu créateur, une négation de l'incarnation et un refus du salut de la chair. En fait l'hérésie c'est le dualisme sous-jacent à chacun de ces points.

4. La réfutation globale de l'hérésie.

On voit comment Irénée schématise peu à peu l'hérésie en dégageant ce qui fait le dénominateur commun de chacune des doctrines envisagées. Mais Irénée qui ne veut pas se laisser égarer dans des notions trop abstraites, va tenter de réduire les diverses hérésies à une seule qui les recapitulera toutes. On voit ici le thème de la récapitulation se manifester d'une manière originale par la recherche d'une hérésie qui résumerait toutes les autres. Cette hérésie n'est autre que la doctrine valentinienne. En II,21,1 il écrit: « Une fois les tenants de Valentin anéantis, *toute la multitude des hérétiques* est réfutée » (Cf. également II,19,8). Dans la Préface (2) du Livre IV, Irénée s'exprime on ne peut plus clairement: « Quinconque veut les convertir doit connaître exactement leurs systèmes. Impossible en effet de guérir des malades, si l'on ignore le mal dont ils souffrent. Voilà pourquoi nos prédecesseurs, pourtant bien supérieurs à nous, n'ont pu s'opposer de façon satisfaisante aux disciples de Valentin: ils ignoraient leur système — ce système que pour notre part nous t'avons communiqué avec toute l'exactitude possible dans notre premier livre. Nous y avons montré de surcroît que leur doctrine est la récapitulation de toute *hérésie*. C'est pourquoi aussi, dans notre second livre, nous les avons pris pour cible de toute notre réfutation: car ceux qui s'opposent à des telles gens comme il convient, s'opposent à tous les tenants d'opinions fausses, et ceux qui les réfutent réfutent *toute hérésie* ».

S'il en est ainsi, il suffit alors de réfuter l'hérésie des Valentiniens pour avoir réfuté toute les hérésies. Dès lors la réfutation des hérétiques peut se borner à la réfutation de la gnose valentinienne; ici encore on assiste à une réduction: une réfutation globale devient suffisante (Cf. IV,41,4; V, préf.; V, 14,4).

Dans les pages qui précèdent nous avons tenté de préciser la manière dont saint Irénée percevait les diverses doctrines des hérétiques. Et nous avons constaté que pour mieux appréhender le phénomène de l'hérésie il procédait à une réduction progressive. L'hérésie ce n'est finalement qu'une interprétation de l'Écriture et de la Tradition d'inspiration dualiste dans laquelle la chair n'est pas l'oeuvre de Dieu, n'est pas assumée par le Verbe de Dieu et n'est pas sauvée par la résurrection. Pour réfuter les hérésies il suffira de réfuter ces doctrines. Mais Irénée, pour se faciliter la tâche, procède à une autre réduction, il réduit toutes les hérésies à une seule, celle des Valentiniens qu'il suffira alors de réfuter pour avoir réfuté toutes les autres.

Ce faisant Irénée ne rend certainement pas justice à la diversité, et à la multiplicité des hérésies de son temps ainsi qu'aux nuances qui les distinguent. Mais, par contre, il élabore un cadre théologique bien déterminé qui lui permet de situer le phénomène hérétique et l'aide à en faire façon. Son propos est avant tout théologique.

A. BENOIT
Strasbourg

POPULAR CHRISTIANITY AND THE THEOLOGIANS IN THE EARLY CENTURIES

IT is possible to study the history of doctrine in any period simply as a movement of thought exhibited in the minds of its theological writers. The problems are posed, solutions are offered, discussion ensues, one school of thought is influenced by or reacts against another; the whole story unfolds at a purely theological level, with a minimum of reference to the historical setting in which the discussion occurs. For the systematic theologian in particular, as he seeks to set out a developed Christian theology as an ordered whole, this way of studying the history of Christian doctrine will be proper, and indeed all that he can find time for. But the historian of Christian doctrine cannot feel equally content to abstract the doctrine from its setting in the person of a particular teacher, who lived in a particular environment, both Christian and secular. Recent work in the liturgical field has shown what can be achieved in the way of historical understanding if one assumes that the study of the liturgy is concerned not merely with the arrangement and development of prayers and ceremonies, but with 'people praying'. The statements of the theologians are made similarly by 'people believing' and living more or less in the Christian community of the day, explaining, interpreting, or perhaps defying its tradition, and in any case in some direct relation to it. For historical purposes this fact, and indeed many of the parallel facts of context, cannot be passed over.

The purpose of this paper is to bring together some well-known facts concerning the period in which speculative and systematic Christian theology may be said to begin, in order to see this theology in relation to the popular Christianity of the day. Perhaps it is well to say that popular Christianity is a term used with no note of disparagement, to indicate Christianity as believed, thought about, and lived by the average Christian, and as taught by the average Christian teacher: the Christianity, in fact, of that *maior pars credentium* whom Tertullian, with not a little disparagement, described as *simplices, ne dixerim idiotae et imprudentes*, but whose faith and life he had presented to the pagans with passionate zeal in his Apology.

Tertullian's remark just quoted points to the fact that there is a problem. There are only three great theological writers in the West in the first half of the third century, Tertullian, Hippolytus, and Novatian, and all of them eventually parted company with the Christian com-

[Journal of Theological Studies, N.S., Vol. XIV, Pt. 2, October 1963]

munity in which they lived. In the East Origen was, until towards the end of his life, an isolated figure, driven from his native church and highly conscious of enlightenment denied to the multitude. In a sense the future belonged to these men, at least on theological issues, but they were all acutely aware of swimming against a tide, and their work passed into the future with its content and direction profoundly modified as the result of this force which opposed them. They stood in varying degrees for a new kind of interest in the faith which was not welcome to the great mass of Christians. Nor can this be wholly explained, as is sometimes believed, as a reaction of simple Christianity against the extravagances of gnostic speculation. At points the new learned theology seemed to endanger truths firmly held, such as the unity of God; it was equally important that it threatened to introduce new controversy and division, a new distraction from the main business of Christian living, and a church still at times called to martyrdom could not afford that luxury.

It is possible to look back at the second century and see there some general features of the Christian life and outlook which throw light on the situation confronting the pioneers of speculative theology in the early third century. Popular Christianity, in the century or so of which the work of Irenaeus is the term, was not untheological in the sense of having no definite beliefs. It was hardly possible for the simplest Christian to belong to a half-secret, unpopular, and persecuted body without being aware of the main grounds of his segregation from the religion and society of his day. Pagans did not die for their religious practices, let alone for beliefs on which the practices were grounded. The tenets of the average Christian were dogmas in the proper sense of that word, inasmuch as they were fundamental to his whole way of life, and belief in them was an obligation involved in his membership of the Church. But his attitude to them was one of affirmation and defence rather than reflection. His main effort lay in other directions. The documents known as the Apostolic Fathers illustrate this clearly. Theologically these documents seem poor and thin in comparison with much of the New Testament; in fact their most striking characteristic, as Harnack pointed out, is their relative independence of the more primitive literature of Christianity now embodied in the Canon. They represent the tradition as it had come down in the community; their authors and the churches in which they wrote, had as yet felt little impact from the theology of Paul or John or even the synoptic gospels. In this respect Clement of Rome is typical, and Ignatius a partial exception, because he does seem o have behind him a tradition of a marked Johannine quality, though ιot the fourth gospel itself. There is much to be said for the view that the Apostolic Fathers in their emphasis and direction of interest fairly represent the main bulk of popular Christianity throughout the second century and well on into the third. The evidence of credal formulations, acts of the martyrs, letters of bishops, and church orders goes to support this view. Three points emerge with some clearness.

First, there is the concentrated interest in moral questions. Christians were conscious of having divine commandments on conduct which separated them from the pagans. There were poignant questions to be decided about this separation, as the list of professions forbidden to the catechumens in Hippolytus's *Apostolic Tradition* indicates. The constant need for moral instruction of converts exercised the ingenuity of Christian teachers in ways amply illustrated by the allegories of Hermas and the curious speculations of Barnabas on the food laws of the Old Testament. Popular Christianity exercised earnest and concentrated thinking on these questions, which was more than it did on theological matters. Much ethical teaching of the current popular philosophy was painlessly absorbed, and loosely connected with the Jewish commandments, the stories of the Old Testament, and some of the Dominical utterances. Clement habitually goes to the Old Testament for the illustration as well as the formulation of moral theses, but he can use popular illustrations as well, and from time to time quotes the words of Christ. In general the nexus between specifically Christian beliefs and the moral teaching is extremely loose, as compared with the New Testament writings. It is no matter for surprise that theological speculation could not easily flourish where discipline and moral exhortation demanded so much attention. When Hermas or Second Clement spend a free half-hour in a little theological excursion it is sure to end abruptly in an earnest moral precept.

Secondly, popular Christianity was inevitably preoccupied with the institutional life of the Church. Whatever may be true about their teaching on matters such as the ministry, Clement and Ignatius are entirely typical in their concern for the organization, unity, and harmony of the common Christian life. The Church as a personified entity forms the background of all that Hermas has to say about morals and discipline. All through the second century the fragmentary evidence shows us the same interest manifested in the constant intercommunication between the scattered communities, giving information or exhortation, or assistance of a more tangible kind, or again in the growing definition of usage and custom and the desire to approximate these in the different communities. Hippolytus early in the third century brought the whole liturgical usage of his church under the heading of the Apostolic Tradition, and the Quartodeciman controversy, however it originated and developed, showed a widespread concern for a common observance of the Pascha. These matters of prayer, worship, and order affected the mass of Christians in the practical living of the Christian life. The instinct of self-preservation in a separated body beset by paganism does not altogether account for this concern of the Church with the orderly articulation of its own common life. The separateness itself was based on the consciousness of an exclusive faith in God and a divine calling of a chosen people, both of which go back to Jewish roots, and the old Israel familiar to the ordinary Christian in the pages of the Old Testament largely influenced the institutions of the new Christian ecclesia. But the fundamental theological convictions took concrete form in the actual organization of the Church, and in this form the questions at issue were of direct interest for the average Christian.

On the ministers of the Church the questions forced themselves. Since its earliest days the Church had experienced the rise of disruptive forces from within. At the bottom of such movements there was often a theological idea, but the movement became actual to the ordinary Christian only when a party was formed, or there was open opposition to the local ministry or a separate worship was set up or a familiar institution was attacked. In any case the reply to these internal threats during the greater part of the second century was far less the elaboration of theological refutation than the drawing together more closely of the institutional and practical life of the Church. The theological replies came when the danger had passed its zenith, as Irenaeus and Tertullian and Hippolytus dealt with Marcion and the gnostics when the great Church had demonstrably survived the impact of these movements for half a century or more. The main body of Christians had stood firm on what was no doubt ultimately a theological conviction, the unity and creatorship of God. But this meant concretely the faith embodied in the Old Testament scriptures, the familiar and loved sacred book. Marcion was not so much refuted, as defeated by the obstinate refusal of the ordinary Christian to abandon his Bible. He was dangerous because he offered his converts a Marcionite church with all the familiar institutions except that he substituted a new Bible for the old. As a result of the struggle with gnosticism and Marcion the Church emerged institutionally strengthened with a clearer idea of what it meant by the apostolic tradition, a greater zeal, if possible, than ever for the Old Testament scriptures, and a growing tendency to canonize the apostolic books. On the side of the gnostics there had been considerable literary activity, but with the exception of Justin's lost work against Marcion we do not know of any literary replies from churchmen until the period beginning with Irenaeus. In Asia Minor opposition to Montanism had been expressed in a number of writings which, to judge from the extracts given by Eusebius, were not of a very considerable scope. They illustrate the fact that the average Christian was more ready to respond to aspersions cast on the lives of the dissidents, their personal habits, their financial transactions, and their alleged unwillingness for martyrdom, than on arguments of a theological nature.

But thirdly, in spite of the main directions of interest we have indicated, it is clear that popular Christianity had a theological consciousness. There was a popular theology and we must be guilty of the folly of attempting generalizations about it. We know it mainly from the surviving works of those who were or considered themselves to be teachers, but it is possible to distinguish sufficiently between the writings which represented the average level and those which are of a more individual character. The acts of the martyrs, the accounts of Polycarp's martyrdom, and the letter of the churches of Lyons and Vienne provide us with some undoubted evidence with which to check the rest. And again the creed and the many summary formulations of a similar character which appear in second-century writers are all evidence of the main heads of current teaching and the way in which they were put together for practical purposes. The formation of such summaries goes back to apostolic practice and is indeed in itself an important theological fact. Christianity was from the first a teaching religion, with more fundamentals to teach than had Judaism. No examples of actual catechetical instructions have survived from the ante-Nicene age. The catechetical lectures of Cyril of Jerusalem, which later set a fashion for the West as well, are probably far more carefully constructed and elaborate in theological detail than anything that was usual in the earlier centuries. In his *Demonstration of the Apostolic Preaching* written by Irenaeus for an educated believer, it is of interest to note that after a brief exposition of the threefold Name, he passes to a summary of Old Testament history from the creation to David, and spends the rest of the work in illustrating and proving points of teaching already mentioned by appeal to Old Testament types and prophecies. We may infer from this, as well as from second-century documents in general, that normal catechetical instruction proceeded on the basis of the threefold Name with such positive statements as we have in the Old Roman creed. Elaboration, illustration, and proof were obtained not by discussion of problems arising out of the affirmations, but by acquainting the catechumen with the scriptures, mainly those of the Old Testament. To quote only one example, when Clement wishes to say something theological about the crucifixion he seems singularly unable to do so in his own words. He does not even use statements from Romans or 1 Corinthians which he certainly knew. What he does is to quote the whole of Isaiah liii. This was no doubt what he was accustomed to do as a *teacher*.

The result of this concentration on the scriptures was that the believer was given a conspectus of the divine activity embodied in *history*, God creating; Jesus Christ living, dying, redeeming, and judging; the Holy Spirit operating in the prophets of the old Israel and in the Church for the salvation of its members. This is what we have in the Old Roman creed. All its statements are of an historical character, concerned with the divine acts. It is, for instance, surely a mistake to regard its final section—belief in Holy Spirit, Holy Church, forgiveness of sins, resurrection of the flesh—as a collection of unrelated miscellanea added at the end. The last three members are a description of what the Holy Spirit does. He operates in Holy Church, brings forgiveness in baptism, and carries the believer to final salvation in the resurrection life. For our purpose the point is important because it helps to explain why the ordinary Christian was not interested in and was even alarmed by the problems and speculations which the theologians were soon to bring into the foreground, such as those concerning the supra-temporal relations of Father, Son, and Spirit and the constitution of human nature. In the Old Roman creed, for instance, the positive statements of the historical activity of each of the Three is not accompanied by any precise statement as to the relations existing between them. Of Jesus Christ we have simply that he is 'His only Son', and that he was born of Holy Spirit and Mary the Virgin. Whether the sonship here stated is more than historical is gravely open to doubt and is certainly not made clear; the birth 'of (ἐκ) Holy Spirit' in the light of second-century interpretation of the relevant New Testament passages probably does imply divine pre-existence, but in a form which is anything but precise as to the relation implied. While there seems to be no good reason to doubt that popular Christianity everywhere, and certainly in Rome, ascribed deity to Jesus Christ, the forms in which this belief was expressed were various and the problems arising out of it were not consciously apprehended. Thus Second Clement opens his homily with the impressive statement that we must think of Jesus Christ as of God, as of judge of living and dead, and later asserts that Christ the Lord, being at first spirit became flesh, in order to clinch an exhortation to keep the flesh pure and to believe that it will rise again for its reward. His statements illustrate both the quick translation of doctrinal affirmations into practical exhortation and also the unreflective way in which the primitive Christian mind made these affirmations. The letters of Ignatius would provide further illustration of both points.

If we have now fairly sketched the character of popular Christianity

301

with its moralism, institutionalism, and practical and historical interest in theology, it is not hard to understand the controversies and tensions which ensued when a more speculative theology made its appearance at the close of the second century and the opening of the third. The consciousness of the tension was very marked on both sides. At this point it is worth noting the principal factors which made such theological development inevitable. They seem to be three. First, during the second century Christianity attracted the attention of an increasing number of philosophically educated people, who became either converts or determined opponents. The work of the apologists is a symptom of the existence of both classes, and the ἀληθὴς λόγος of Celsus which had to wait for an answer for three-quarters of a century testifies to the degree of interest and inquiry aroused. Contemporary philosophical thought, in which Platonism and Stoicism were the dominating factors, was already deeply concerned with the doctrines of God and his relation to the cosmos, and the nature of the soul. If we leave the gnostics on one side, the full weight of the philosophical interest does not appear in Christian teaching until Clement and Origen. But in a more general form educated interest within the Church created a demand to supply which some attempt had to be made by giving attention to questions which interested contemporary thought, and the educated themselves began to write in explanation and defence of their new faith. Justin Martyr represents the latter class and in him the increased interest in cosmology and the human soul makes its appearance. But it was a modest beginning, chiefly of importance because of its influence on Irenaeus and Tertullian. The apologies of Justin to the pagans are consciously propagandist, and some of their prominent features are quite absent from the *Dialogue*. Justin's Christianity—and he is the only one of the Greek Apologists whose faith we can estimate as a whole—is still predominantly popular in character. Though he explicitly admits difference of view in the Church on points such as the millennium and the observance of the Jewish Law by Christians, he seems quite unconscious of any tension between his own version of Christianity and that of the mass of ordinary believers. On the other hand, Irenaeus is already conscious of the problem of the use which the Christian teacher may legitimately make of intellectual speculation which is likely to carry him outside the range of popular Christian knowledge. The second of our three factors, namely gnosticism, had begun to operate. Of this movement it is only necessary to say that, whatever modern historians may judge to be the truth about its general character, the anti-gnostic fathers consistently treat it as a system of speculative doctrine derived from philosophic sources and opposed to the gnosis expounded by the Church. In a passage of great explicitness early in his anti-heretical work, Irenaeus attempts to answer the question, how may an orthodox Christian use his intellect to extend the understanding of the Faith as commonly taught without falling into the errors of the gnostics? In dealing with his opponents he could not avoid that question. Before looking at his answer we should note a third factor in theological advance which became operative in the latter half of the second century, namely the formation of the New Testament canon. The general recognition of a body of inspired scriptures to set beside the Jewish books was in itself a notable doctrinal step. It is less often observed that it stimulated Christian thought in a new way. Books hitherto little read or used not at all in particular churches now came into prominence, not merely as books but as part of a corpus of inspired writings. Pauline and Johannine thought, so much more theologically profound than the bulk of popular Christian teaching in the first half of the second century, now impinged effectively upon the minds at least of those who considered it their business to study the scriptures. Comparisons and approximations between the different books of the New Testament corpus began to be made. New problems became apparent, and, in short, whereas the Church had hitherto mainly confined itself to enlightening its elementary theological tradition by the types and prophecies of the Old Testament, the period of New Testament exegesis now began. This is one of the facts which account for the striking increase in the range of theological interest and statement displayed in Irenaeus in comparison with all previous non-canonical writers. It has been said that 'his expositions are like a primitive forest through which it is hard to find one's way'. If this judgement has some truth, it is in part because of Irenaeus's habit of taking up a variety of New Testament ideas and developing them against Marcion and the gnostics without any determined attempt to systematize.

Irenaeus was in fact attempting to carry out the programme which he had himself laid down for the Christian theologian in Book I, chapter 10. He holds that if any Christian claims to have a deeper understanding of the Faith than others, he will not show it by overthrowing the fundamentals of the Faith taught throughout the world, or, like the gnostics, by prying into such mysteries of the divine being as the generation of the Son. Rather, he will expound the divine economy to men, the primal transgression, the Old Testament theophanies, why there are two covenants, why the Word became flesh and suffered, how the Gentiles have been brought in by God to be fellow heirs with the saints, what scripture says of the consummation and of the resurrection of the flesh, since it was of such themes as these that the apostle exclaimed, 'Oh the depth of the riches and wisdom and knowledge of God'. Irenaeus wishes to see the theologian occupied in developing the doctrine of God's saving work for man as expounded in scripture. It is better, he says, to seek for nothing in the way of knowledge but Jesus Christ crucified for us, than to fall into blasphemy by subtlety of speculation. In making this distinction between essential faith and theology—and his is the first attempt to make it—Irenaeus is not merely determined by anti-gnostic polemic; he is taking his stand as a Christian pastor on the ground of popular theology. He refuses to extend its range of interest into speculative questions, but sees the possibility and need of enriching its content by a deeper understanding of the biblical story of salvation. Irenaeus cannot contemplate any conflict with the faith of the ordinary Christian.

But in the next few decades this conflict was to become apparent and open. It is hardly an accident that it comes to light in Rome and Africa where popular Christianity was best organized, though exposed to constant currents of external influence, and also in Alexandria where intellectual ferment was most active. Tertullian gives us the first hint of the position in the West. Consistency was not a strong point with this great advocate. He shared with popular Christianity all its interest in morals, discipline, and worship, and eventually accepted the new prophecy to support his rigorism in these matters. In the *De Praescriptione* he exalts the merits of uninquiring faith in the articles of the *regula fidei*, with hardly a word of encouragement for anyone who exhibits *curiositas* even within the limits of the *regula*. In the same treatise philosophy is denounced as mere human wisdom, the mother of heresy and a hazardous interpreter of divine things. In spite of this typical intransigence of expression, Tertullian was deeply influenced by Stoic philosophy and became the founder of Latin theology. His two great speculative and dogmatic treatises are significantly enough on the doctrine of divine being and on the nature of the soul, two points on which popular Christianity at the time showed no disposition to reflect, but with which contemporary philosophic thought was constantly concerned. On the soul Tertullian borrows freely from contemporary medicine and physiology to expound his thorough-going materialism. He notes that his views will probably not find acceptance, but so far as we know, no one was sufficiently interested to make controversy out of them, and it is a tribute to the prestige of his name that the treatise was preserved at all. The position is very different with his Trinitarian treatise. Tertullian begins by admitting that the majority of the faithful have no sympathy with the discussion of these questions. To them his version of the 'economy' appears to be a doctrine of two or three gods; in fact his use of this term to describe the internal relations of the deity was a startling innovation. The many who, as Tertullian remarks, were asleep in the simplicity of doctrine (*dormientibus in simplicitate doctrinae*) raised loud cries of 'the one God' and 'the divine monarchy' and were prepared to accept modalism as a sufficient account of the one God, believing themselves to possess thus the plain truth, *meram veritatem*. That popular Christianity, nurtured on the Old Testament and imbued with a practical horror of pagan polytheism, should have shied at the posing of the Trinitarian question is entirely intelligible. Tertullian himself appeals to the fact that now, as an adherent of the new prophecy, he is *instructior per paracletum* on this issue. By the time the controversy reached Africa modalism had undergone some development from its earlier and more naïve form. The Father was now said to be the deity, the Son the humanity in the historical Christ. The movement, which can hardly have arisen directly from New Testament influence, had begun to buttress itself with New Testament texts on the unity of Father and Son, and even to offer its own exegesis of passages such as Luke i. 35. Whatever the origins of modalism may have been it could not now escape involvement with the complicated data of the New Testament. Tertullian taunts the modalists with the accusation that they try to interpret the whole of the Bible in the light of three or four isolated proof texts. The merits of the theological positions in question are not our present subject, but we may note that the popular faith, concerned for its firmly held belief in the unity of God and the deity of Christ, might well recoil in deep suspicion from Tertullian's doctrine of extended divine substance and subordinate sonship, and feel better satisfied with the simpler modalist statement. The mass of Christians had clearly not been taught to think of these questions, much less given a clear presentation of doctrine upon them. The writings of Cyprian would seem to indicate that Tertullian did not succeed in gaining the interest of African Christianity for his doctrine of the divine economy. Of Cyprian's three books of Testimonia the third, dealing with morals and discipline, is by far the largest. The first is concerned with the relation between the Jewish and the Christian church, and when in the second book the headings deal with Christ and his work, the Trinitarian question is not touched. Christ is stated to be God, the Word and the Wisdom of God, and to have been born of Mary, God, and Man. That is all.

In Rome, thanks to the evidence of Hippolytus and Eusebius, we can form a much more detailed picture of the course of the conflict and the factors at work in it. Under Pope Victor, before the turn of the second century, what is called dynamic monarchianism had appeared in Rome and received condemnation. The origin and precise teaching of this

H. J. CARPENTER

movement is obscure, but such evidence as we have suggests that at any rate in Rome, it was neither widespread nor popular in character. The quotation of Eusebius from the Little Labyrinth, a contemporary estimate, describes, no doubt with much exaggeration, the variety of studies pursued by the school, including logic, geometry, the works of Aristotle, Theophrastus, and Galen, and the application of these studies to the support of their tenets and the emendation of the text of the scriptures. The document, the date of which may be nearer the middle than the beginning of the third century, may describe a second stage in the movement, connected with the obscure figure of Artemon, but the evidence of Epiphanius who quotes some of the arguments of Theodotus, the founder of the school in Rome, suggests at least that a close and critical study of the New Testament was from the beginning a distinguishing feature of their teaching. Such a critical study was in the air at the time both in Rome and in Asia Minor. Gaius, the Roman presbyter, about 200, possibly with the so-called Alogi in the East behind him, was ascribing the fourth gospel to Cerinthus on the ground of its discrepancies with the synoptics. Epiphanius actually asserts a direct connexion between the Theodotians and the Alogi, but this can hardly be maintained since Theodotus appealed to texts in the fourth gospel. On the whole the dynamic monarchian movement and its development appears to be best understood as arising from concern with the new problems presented by the formation of the four-gospel canon and the application to them of methods derived from contemporary logic and literary science. The quick reaction against Theodotus and his followers by the leaders of popular Christianity in Rome, in spite of the concern of the monarchians for the 'one God', is a testimony to the strength of popular conviction of the inherent deity of Christ. The movement was regarded as abhorrent but not dangerous. The learning and dialectical skill of its supporters carried little weight in Rome.

A very different reception awaited the modalist teachers who arrived at the same time or a little later. Bishop Zephyrinus raised no objection to Epigonus and Cleomenes when they set up their school and they taught freely under Zephyrinus and his successor Callistus. All that the vehement reproofs of Hippolytus could accomplish was the excommunication by Callistus of Sabellius, a modalist whose name became a kind of symbol in later doctrinal discussion, perhaps simply because he had been excommunicated at Rome, but of whose specific teaching we know nothing beyond the fact that he was a modalist. The personal involvement of Hippolytus in the controversy, and his final break with Callistus, has resulted in our possessing a relatively complete picture of the forces at work.

Hippolytus was the first man of wide learning to emerge in Western Christianity, and, if Schwartz's view of the *Contra Noetum* may be trusted, was the first Christian teacher to publish sermons as an instrument of propaganda. The obscurity which overtook him within the century in which he died was so great that even Eusebius did not know where his episcopal see had been. Rome showed no interest in his works, though his name was commemorated as a martyr, and it was left to the East to perpetuate and use them. The fact of his schism, which is said to have been healed shortly before his death in Sardinia, partly accounts for this neglect at Rome, as does also the increasing Latinization of that church. But perhaps it is equally true that his apparatus of philosophy, history, chronology, and learned Bible commentaries found little welcome in a church which was preoccupied with more practical questions and was pursuing in these matters a policy which Hippolytus himself repudiated. His schism with the main Roman community, as Callistus shows, was on both doctrinal and disciplinary grounds. The first half of the third century was a period of expansion and consolidation for the church in Rome. It had successfully weathered the internal storms threatened by the gnostic and Marcionite movements in the last century; it had recently strengthened its leading position among the churches by Victor's initiative in the paschal question; and it now held property of its own near the city in the shape of a cemetery, one sign of its increasing wealth and influence. Bishops Zephyrinus and Callistus, whom Hippolytus judged to be respectively a fool and a knave, were bent on pursuing a conciliatory policy in both discipline and doctrine, and had, as Hippolytus admits, the great majority of the people to support them. The rigour of discipline was relaxed to admit to penance and final reconciliation those guilty of sins of the flesh; twice-married men were no longer excluded from the ministry; and Christian women were allowed to contract with their slaves marriages which were recognized as legal by the Church, though contrary to state law. If these changes are to be attributed to no deeper motives, they were at least an attempt to adapt discipline in a pastoral way to a situation which was already different from that of the primitive church. Hippolytus read the changes in the worst light and opposed them on grounds of principle. Appeals to Noah's Ark and the Parable of the Tares as scriptural warrant for the Church as a *corpus mixtum* only increased his wrath and contempt. The character of the controversy on discipline supports the view that on the doctrinal issue also all possible conciliation and tolerance was the policy of the Roman bishops. In the modalist question they could plead that where the unity of God and the deity of Christ was upheld no condemnation could be merited. Their own utterances on the subject, if

Hippolytus quotes them fairly and correctly, reveal them as men who are out of their depth in the questions raised in the controversy, and only clear that while asserting that Christ is God they will not assert two Gods.

It is going too far to say with Schwartz, 'it was men and not doctrines which were in conflict'. Such a conclusion might well be drawn from Hippolytus's later work, the *Refutatio*, when he gives full rein to his personal animus against Callistus. But in the earlier sermon, the *Contra Noetum*, which probably veils a direct attack upon Callistus during his lifetime, Hippolytus has to take note of the scriptural arguments adduced by the modalists and their supporters. Again, as with the followers of Praxeas in Africa, the fourth gospel is prominent in the debate. The modalists appeal to passages of the gospel which appear to assert the identity of Father and Son, and will not admit that the Logos in the prologue means the Son. John, they say, spoke of a Logos, ἀλλ' ἄλλως ἀλληγορεῖ, he is using a chance metaphor. No, answers Hippolytus, for he uses it again of Christ in the Apocalypse. Popular Christianity was finding the New Testament an unexpectedly puzzling document. The whole controversy cannot be reduced to a mere struggle for place and power. Nor were the Roman bishops indifferent to theological truth, even if they deserve the epithets, 'ignorant' and 'uneducated', which Hippolytus scornfully affixed to them. In their concern that the unity of their community should not be disturbed by unnecessary and dangerous theological speculations, they attempted to pursue a middle course which was clear upon the traditional and fundamental assertions of faith and abjured problems. In this policy they carried the majority of the community with them, as Hippolytus angrily admits, and their successors in the period between the death of Callistus and the outbreak of the persecution reaped the benefit of the policy in an unparalleled expansion and consolidation of the local church life and organization.

There was no further strictly theological controversy in Rome, or indeed in the West generally, until an alien Arianism for a time came in from the East. But from the security of its unspeculative faith Rome was ready to come to the support of foreign churches or groups in theological controversy. These interventions proved extraordinarily true to type and reveal Zephyrinus and Callistus as organs of a corporate policy and temper which lasted long after their deaths. When the Roman Bishop Dionysius about 260 intervened against his namesake of Alexandria at the appeal of some Libyan communities, his statement of the doctrine of the Godhead was a categorical pronouncement singularly innocent of proofs and explanations. The learned and critical Alexandrine must have smiled as he read the letter, but he thought it worth while to reply in four books in which he made handsome concessions about his earlier utterances. The Libyan Christians whom he had denounced as Sabellians may well have felt satisfaction with the Roman letter, if they ever knew its contents, for there is no evidence that they were upholding anything more extreme than was contained in its statements.

Before turning our attention to the East, we must not pass over the figure of the one considerable Latin theologian produced by the Roman church in the third century, namely Novatian. After he had initiated his schism his rival Cornelius, and Cyprian, both refer to his dangerous learning and eloquence, which are sufficiently attested by his works still preserved. It would be pressing a thesis too far to maintain that he failed to obtain election as bishop in Rome precisely because of his theological ability. Other factors of a more personal nature probably determined the issue. Yet it is a fact that the developed doctrine of his treatise now known as the *de Trinitate* is far more in line with the teaching of Tertullian and Hippolytus than with the utterances of contemporary Roman bishops. It is also a fact that before the schism Novatian was the leader of the Roman presbyters during the vacancy of the see and in their name wrote to Cyprian two majestic letters. They stand in striking contrast with the letter addressed to Africa shortly before this by a body of Roman clergy, which elicited from Cyprian a sharp complaint about its sentiments, its ungrammatical style, and the paper on which it was written. Nor can one who organized such a successful schism have been altogether devoid of administrative ability. In spite of these ostensible advantages he was not elected to the Roman see, and like Hippolytus set up a schism.

The corresponding tension in the East between popular Christianity and the theologians can be described more briefly and more broadly. Our knowledge of doctrinal development in the East in the third century is extremely scanty, except for Origen and his scool and some of the reactions against him, but the general characteristics of culture in the eastern empire, as well as some fragments of information, enable us to see how the situation for the theologians differed from that in the West. The long-standing, but by no means complete, fusion of Greek and indigenous eastern cultures meant that Christianity was from the beginning agitated by divergent tendencies of thought and speculation, and there was no recognized centre, as in the West, to provide a steadying influence. If it is an exaggeration to maintain, with W. Bauer, that the majority of Christians in the East during the second century were gnostics of one kind or another, it is clear that the fight against gnosticism was strenuous, and had to be conducted well on into the third century with theological weapons. Leadership in the churches passed rapidly to men of learning. Though Origen was banished from Alexandria, he was welcomed by the local bishops at Jerusalem and Caesarea, and within a few years of his death many of his pupils were seated on episcopal thrones. At Antioch between 260 and 270 there appears the significant figure of the Christian sophist Malchion, without whose assistance even a body of Origenist bishops could not confute Paul of Samosata. Before the end of the century Lucian had established his theological schools in the same church. Alexandria and Caesarea had long since had such schools. They were centres of teaching and study at a high level, hardly to be compared with the local διδασκαλεία of Rome in the second century, where informal instruction was given by individual teachers like Justin or Cleomenes. Again, Eusebius's account of the succession of bishops at Laodicea in the second half of the third century throws light on the way in which things were moving. Of three successive bishops of that church we read that Anatolius, an Alexandrian, was noted for his learning, secular education, and philosophy, being expert in arithmetic, geometry, logic, astronomy, physics, and rhetoric, and had established at Alexandria a school of the Aristotelian tradition; his successor Stephen had won widespread admiration for his knowledge of philosophy and other secular learning; the third bishop, Theodotus, had reached the first rank in medicine. The leading cities of the East evidently preferred men of learning for their bishops and there was no scarcity of supply. It does not follow that they were all theologians, but the character of the teaching given in the course of their pastoral work must have been profoundly affected by the nature of their intellectual interests. The soil was already being prepared in which the controversies of the next century were to flourish. In the third century—and we must confine our view within these limits—there is little direct evidence of opposition to the movements of theological learning. Among the quick-witted and heterogeneous populations of the East, opposition to a particular line of theological teaching could only be carried through by producing a rival system, as Paul of Samosata apparently attempted to do against Origenism. Solidarity of church life, even when it could be achieved, was not enough to restrain thought, and teachers moved from church to church to keep the ferment active. But we have already had a glimpse of what seems like popular opposition to Dionysius of Alexandria, and before the influence of Origen had done its work in the East the great teacher himself was fully conscious of the cleft between his own outlook and that of the mass of Christians.

Origen was by his own choice and desire fully involved in the church life of his day. He accepted the principle and the contents of apostolic tradition as that was then understood. He set his face as firmly as any in the contemporary church against the current heresies. Above all he aspired to be an exegete of the divine scriptures of both Testaments. In other words, he stood on common ground with popular Christianity. And yet, both as a Platonist philosopher and as a conscientious student of the scriptures, he was profoundly dissatisfied with the popular version of the faith. The root of his dissatisfaction lay in the problems of history. At the purely historical level Origen saw discrepancies in the Old Testament and in the four gospels; at the moral and rational level he found the literal utterances of scripture often in conflict with his idea of the divine nature. His resort to allegorical interpretation was in itself neither a novelty nor, in many of its detailed results, out of harmony with popular teaching. But for Origen the allegorical principle went very deep into his thought. History tended to become the symbol of eternal truth, rather than the sphere of divine action. It was the realm of faith beyond which the perfect Christian will try to rise to wisdom and knowledge and direct apprehension of the divine Logos as he is in himself. So we have in the commentary on St. John (ii. 3, 28, p. 56) a distinction between those who partake of the Logos as he was in the beginning with God and those who know nothing but Jesus Christ and him crucified, thinking that the Logos made flesh is the whole of the Logos, knowing only Christ according to the flesh. This latter class are the majority of believers.

Again, earlier in the same commentary, he says that just as Paul was a Jew to Jews, so the spiritual Christian must when necessary preach the 'bodily Gospel' among the fleshly and know nothing but Christ crucified, but when these are ready in spirit and desire for heavenly wisdom, they must then have imparted to them 'the Word, ascending from his incarnation to that which he was in the beginning with God'. The final goal of Christian wisdom for Origen is the piercing of the veil of history and the establishment of unrestricted communion between two eternal realities, God and his Logos on the one hand and the human soul on the other. Owing to his devotion to the Bible, it is only at times that this underlying principle of his theology becomes explicit even to Origen's own mind; but its influence is clear throughout his thought. The reactions against his teaching were all reactions directed to reintroducing time and history and the historical revelation to its place of decisive importance in Christian theology. Such reactions were the rejection of the eternal pre-existence of souls, of the eternity of creation, of the possibility of successive worlds, of what appeared to be the undue spiritualization of the resurrection body, and so far it was the popular, biblical, historical view of God's relation to man which reasserted itself.

At one point, however, Origen introduced into eastern thought a ferment which was not easily stilled. His defence of the pure eternity and incorporeality of God and the inferences which he drew as to the relations of Father, Word, and Spirit raised questions which finally issued in the Arian controversy and the eastern definition of the Trinity. In this controversy the influence of popular Christianity played an important part in the person of Athanasius. Moreover, the West became involved, and with a minimum borrowing of technical terms from the theologians asserted its traditional popular faith in the unity of God and the deity of Christ. The outcome of the fourth- and fifth-century controversies can only be understood as the result of a perpetual pressure exercised by popular Christianity in its Western and some Eastern forms which forced the speculations of the theologians into channels which they would not naturally have followed. But on the threshold of the fourth century, with its more complicated currents of influence, this over-long survey must be brought to an end.   H. J. CARPENTER

WERE ANCIENT HERESIES NATIONAL OR SOCIAL MOVEMENTS IN DISGUISE?

MOST modern historians of the later Roman Empire, whether secular or ecclesiastical, seem to agree that certain of the heresies and schisms of that period were in some sense national rather than purely religious movements.[1] They point to the fact that some heresies either were confined to certain areas, as was Donatism to Africa, or were at any rate particularly strong and persistent in some districts or among some peoples—as were Monophysitism in Egypt and Syria, or Arianism among the German tribes. They stress the fact that among these groups indigenous languages—Punic or Berber in Africa, Coptic, Syriac, or German—were adopted by the heretical or schismatic churches. Their general line of argument is that mere doctrinal differences, often of extreme subtlety, could not have engendered such powerful and enduring movements, and that their real and underlying cause must be sought in national sentiment. They often maintain that under the later Roman Empire long-dormant nationalism arose or revived in a number of areas, and was an important contributory cause in the downfall of the empire; for the dissident groups not merely stubbornly resisted the efforts of the imperial government to impose religious conformity upon them, but struggled to break away from the empire, supporting local pretenders or foreign invaders.

At the risk of a certain crudity I should like to state this thesis in more concrete terms. Did the average Copt say to himself, 'I am an Egyptian and proud of it. I hate the Roman oppressor, and will at the earliest opportunity cast off the alien yoke. Meanwhile I insist on speaking my native Coptic instead of Greek, the language of the foreign government, and I refuse to belong to its church. I do not know or care whether Christ has one or two natures, but as the Romans insist on the latter view, I hold the former'? This statement of the case appears to be implied by some historians, who speak of the heresies as a mere screen for nationalist aspirations. But if the last sentence seems to be too

[1] For a thoroughgoing statement of this thesis see E. L. Woodward, *Christianity and Nationalism in the Later Roman Empire* (London, 1916). The latest great historian of the period, E. Stein, *Geschichte des spätrömischen Reiches*, i (Vienna, 1928), *Histoire du Bas-Empire*, ii (Paris, 1949), is its strong advocate. It is also adopted by the latest history of the Church, A. Fliche and V. Martin, *Histoire de l'Église*, iii, *De la paix Constantinienne à la mort de Théodose* (J. R. Palanque, G. Bardy, P. de Labriolle, Paris, 1945), iv, *De la mort de Théodose à l'élection de Grégoire le Grand* (P. de Labriolle, G. Bardy, L. Bréhier, G. de Plinval, Paris, 1947).

[Journal of Theological Studies, N.S., Vol. X, Pt. 2, October 1959]

cynical even for the most private thoughts, one might substitute for it, 'The Romans anyhow are heretics, we Egyptians are clearly right in believing that Christ has one nature only. I will firmly reject any compromise which the Romans may offer, and even if they accept our view I will never be reconciled with them.'[1]

If they felt like this the heretics fairly certainly did not put their sentiments into writing. We are not, it is true, so well provided with heretical literature as we could wish: if the German Arians wrote anything, it has been lost. But we possess a considerable bulk of monophysite literature, including theological treatises, letters, and histories both ecclesiastical and secular. Some Donatist writings have been preserved, and others can be reconstructed from Augustine's elaborate refutations of them. In the vast amount of controversial literature on the orthodox side some reference would surely be found to the nationalist sentiments of their opponents if they had voiced them openly. What the sectaries actually said in public, so far as our record goes, was—to change the instance—'The Donatist church is the true Catholic church, and we will never communicate with *traditores*', but what they thought, we are asked to believe, was: 'We are Africans and hate the Rome government; we will have nothing to do with the Romans and will maintain our African church and if possible set up our African state.'

This is a thesis which is obviously difficult to prove or to disprove, for one cannot easily read the secret thoughts of men who lived 1,500 years ago. One can only examine their written words with care, in case they have inadvertently revealed their real thoughts, or endeavour to deduce their thoughts from their actions and policies.

It could also be held that the sectaries not only said, but in their conscious thought believed, that their quarrel with the government was purely religious, but that they really held their peculiar views because they were in harmony with their national temperament or were emotionally linked with their national group, and conversely really hated the orthodox because they were foreigners, though they genuinely thought that they condemned them as heretics. On this hypothesis the conscious thought of a Copt might be: 'We Egyptians are right in believing that Christ has one nature, and I abominate the Romans as heretics and hate them as persecutors. Rather than submit to their rule I would welcome a barbarian invader.' Or he might even say no more than: 'We hold the true orthodox faith, and I abominate the government because it is heretical and persecutes us', but really hate the Romans as foreigners.

In this attenuated form the nationalist hypothesis is even more difficult to prove or disprove. One can seek to discover whether hostility to

---

[1] The last clause is required by Stein's view, see below, p. 288.

the Roman government persisted even when it accepted the theological view of the dissident groups. One can inquire whether the theological views of the sectaries show any affinity with the pre-Christian beliefs of the group which held them. One can finally inquire how far adherence to certain theological views was coterminous with national groups, defined by criteria of language or religion.

To turn from generalities to special cases I will first consider the Donatists. Donatism was confined to the African provinces, and within that area it was both widespread and persistent, at all times commanding a wide following and at some periods dominating the whole country, and surviving despite many persecutions for close on three centuries to our certain knowledge, and probably longer. Many, if not most, of its adherents were Punic- or Berber-speaking, and its greatest strength lay in the least Romanized areas, especially southern Numidia. In some of its beliefs and practices, in particular in its morbid emphasis on martyrdom, it seems to show affinities with the pagan religion of the area. Its leaders co-operated with two native pretenders, Firmus and Gildo, and some of them are alleged to have had treasonable dealings with certain Goths in the early fifth century.[1]

To take their political activities first, the Donatists were certainly not anti-imperial at the beginning: they in fact appealed to the emperor against the Caecilianists.[2] When Constantine had finally rejected their cause, they raised the cry that the State should not interfere in religion[3] —as later the homoousian party did when Constantius II favoured the Arians.[4] But when Julian ordered the restoration of banished clergy and confiscated church property they were happy to accept imperial aid.[5] That they co-operated with Firmus[6] and Gildo[7] need mean no more than that the pretenders exploited local grievances to win support for their personal ambitions, and that the Donatists, who by now had little hope of obtaining what they wanted from the legitimate government, decided to risk backing a pretender who might be successful. With a good deal less excuse the Spanish bishop Ithacius, when Gratian, or rather his master of the offices, supported the Priscillianists, transferred

---

[1] The evidence for these statements is well stated in Mr. W. H. C. Frend's work, *The Donatist Church* (Oxford, 1952), from which I differ only in some points of emphasis and interpretation.

[2] Aug. *Ep.* 88; Optatus, i. 22.

[3] Optatus, iii. 3, 'quid imperatori cum ecclesia?'

[4] Hilary, *Liber I ad Constantium*, C.S.E.L., lxv, pp. 181–7.

[5] Optatus, ii. 16; Aug. *Contra Litt. Pet.* ii. 97. 224.

[6] Aug. *Ep.* 87. 10; *Contra Ep. Parm.* i. 10. 16, 11. 17; *Contra Litt. Pet.* ii. 83. 184.

[7] Frend, op. cit., pp. 208 ff.

his allegiance to the usurper Maximus;[1] and yet no one has suggested that the Catholic Ithacius was a Spanish nationalist. It may be claimed that Firmus and Gildo, unlike Maximus, were leaders of national rebellions, but beyond the fact that they came from a Moorish princely family, there is nothing to suggest that they were not usurpers of the normal type, that is, ambitious individuals seeking for personal power. The record of the members of the family certainly does not suggest zeal for any cause but their own. When Firmus rebelled, his brother Gildo took the Roman side, and received the promotion on which he had no doubt counted. When he in turn rebelled, another brother, Mascazel, led the army which crushed him. There is in fact no reason to believe that the rebellions of Firmus and Gildo were different in kind from that of Alexander the Phrygian before them, or those of Heraclian and Boniface after them.

The negotiations of the Donatists with the Goths are only known from a letter of Augustine to Count Boniface, who had inquired whether Donatism and Arianism had any points in common.[2] Augustine replied that they had none, but that 'sometimes, as we have heard, some of them, wishing to conciliate the Goths to themselves, because they see that they have some power, say that they have the same beliefs as they'. It seems very unlikely that the Donatists were in touch with the Visigoths settled in Aquitania, and Boniface's interest in the matter suggests that it was his Gothic federates who were approached. If so the Donatists were merely making propaganda among influential persons in the entourage of the Comes Africae, and perhaps trying to curry favour with the Comes himself, who, we learn from a later letter of Augustine,[3] married an Arian wife. Or was Boniface himself thinking of striking an alliance with the Donatists when he put his question to Augustine? Augustine answers the question with the utmost brevity, and goes on to expatiate for pages on the doctrinal and historical issues involved. It is hard to believe that if he had had any suspicion that the Donatists were plotting treason against the empire he would have dismissed the matter so lightly.

There is no evidence that the Donatists made common cause with the Vandals. All that Victor Vitensis can say against them is that one Donatist, Nicesius, was perverted to Arianism.[4] It is scarcely credible that if they had taken the Vandal side or even secured toleration from them, this would not have been trumpeted abroad by their persecuted Catholic adversaries.

There is in fact very little hint that the Donatists cherished dreams

---

[1] Sulp. Sev. *Chron.* ii. 48–49. [2] Aug. *Ep.* 185. 1.
[3] Aug. *Ep.* 220. 4. [4] Victor Vitensis, iii. 71.

of a national African state. How far was the movement, in any national sense, African in character? It is no doubt true that a large proportion of Donatists were Punic- or Berber-speaking, and that the Donatist clergy used the indigenous languages for instruction and exhortation. But since Africa was a predominantly rural country, and most rural Africans knew no Latin, it was inevitable that any church which wished to rally the mass of the population had to use the native languages. On the Catholic side Augustine too was anxious to secure Punic-speaking clergy to take charge of rural areas.[1]

Nor was Donatism by any means confined to the humble strata of society where the native languages were spoken. The leaders and apologists of the movement, men like Parmenian (who was not even an African),[2] the learned and eloquent Tyconius,[3] the lawyer Petilian,[4] came from the cultivated and Romanized classes, and the penal law of 412 specifies appropriate penalties not only for circumcellions and plebeians, *negotiatores* and ordinary decurions, but for the higher urban aristocracy, the *principales* and *sacerdotales*, and for senators, *clarissimi*, *spectabiles*, and even *illustres*, the cream of Roman imperial society.[5] There is, furthermore, no suggestion that the Donatists took any pride in the indigenous languages. Their literature, or what survives of it, was all written in Latin, not only the controversial or apologetic treatises which were aimed at Catholics, but popular works, such as the Acts of Martyrs, meant for the encouragement of the faithful. The inscriptions of Donatist churches are all in Latin, even the slogans and war-cries of the circumcellions, like the famous 'Deo Laudes', were in Latin, the language of the enemy.

That Donatism may in the course of time have acquired certain African characteristics, derived from the pre-Christian beliefs of the people, may well be true. Popular Christianity everywhere tended to absorb local beliefs and customs. But I wonder whether the Donatist fixation on martyrdom may not be due as much to their quarrel with the Catholics as to any survival of primitive pagan ideas. They claimed to be the church of the martyrs as against the Catholics who were *traditores*, and martyrdom was therefore to them the touchstone of the true faith.

The Donatists certainly believed that in Africa only did the Catholic church survive, but they seem to have felt somewhat uneasy at their isolation. They apparently made abortive efforts to spread their faith in

---

[1] Aug. *Ep.* 84; 209. 3.   [2] Optatus, i. 5, ii. 7.
[3] Gennadius, *De Viris illustribus*, 18; Aug. *Contra Ep. Parm.* i. 1. 1.
[4] Aug. *Contra Litt. Pet.* iii. 16. 19.
[5] *Cod. Theod.* XVI. v. 52, cp. 54.

Spain. They may have negotiated with the Arians of Sardica in the hope of finding churches unsullied by *traditio* in the East. It is significant that they maintained a pope of the true faith at Rome throughout the fourth and early fifth centuries.[1] The fact, however, remained that for all practical purposes their church was confined to Africa, and they were reduced to interpreting a phrase from the Song of Songs, 'ubi pascis ubi cubas in meridie', as a prophecy that such was God's will.[2]

That Donatism should have had so strong a hold throughout Africa and should have been confined to Africa can be explained by the historical circumstances in which the movement arose. It would appear that the African provinces were exceptional in that Christianity had already in the latter part of the third century captured the countryside.[3] They were also exceptional in the number of their confessors and martyrs in the Great Persecution. These two facts are not unconnected. It is clear from contemporary accounts that in both the Decian and Diocletianic persecutions upper-class Christians lapsed in very large numbers, and that the confessors and martyrs were mainly men and women of the lower orders. This was not unnatural. The upper classes feared for their property and position and could be more easily intimidated by the threat of torture, from which they were normally immune. The poor had less to lose and to them flogging was an everyday occurrence. It may be added that the poor might well hope to pass undetected if they failed to comply with the law, whereas the rich would be more likely to be denounced.

It would seem likely, then, that in Africa a larger proportion of Christians remained steadfast than in most parts of the empire. Not unnaturally they took a less charitable view of the lapsed than that which prevailed in other provinces. Throughout Africa feelings were tense, and a rupture was likely between the rigorist and the lenient groups. The dispute over the election of Caecilian fired the spark, and inevitably involved all Africa, for Carthage had for long been acknowledged as the primatial see of all the African provinces. But outside Africa the churches had no sympathy with the rigorist party, and having decided that Caecilian was the lawful bishop of Carthage they took no further interest in the affair.

Only in one other province do we hear of a similar movement. In Egypt, where as in Africa Christianity had in the third century spread to the rural areas, the resistance to the Diocletianic persecution was stubborn, and a rigorist party, the Melitians, refused to readmit the

---

[1] Frend, op. cit., pp. 164, 170.
[2] Aug. *Ep. ad Catholicos*, 16. 40; *Serm.* 46. 36–37, 138. 9–10.
[3] Frend, op. cit., pp. 83 ff.

lapsed to communion.[1] But the Donatists seem never to have made contact with the Melitians; they were too far away. Melitianism remained confined to Egypt, where it lasted into the eighth century at least.[2] But it never became a dominant force there. The claim of the Melitians to be the Church of the Martyrs must have been gravely shaken when Peter of Alexandria, whose lenient views they denounced, himself died as a martyr, and the see of Alexandria was filled by a succession of able and ruthless bishops, who quickly broke the spirit of the rebels.

That Donatism survived so stubbornly is hardly a matter for surprise. Throughout history religious feuds have been long-lived, and have often survived when the original cause of quarrel has been almost forgotten. The Donatists were from the beginning a large group, which it was difficult to stamp out, and the intermittent and not very efficient persecutions which they suffered served only to embitter them—in these circumstances the blood of the martyrs was the seed of the church.

The Copts have a priori a stronger case to be regarded as a nation than the Africans for, whereas the inhabitants of the diocese of Africa had never formed a political unit, Egypt had in the past been a national kingdom, and long after that kingdom had fallen had cherished a strong national sentiment based on the traditions of the past and fostered by its peculiar religion. Under the later Ptolemies there had been revolts which had aimed at expelling the aliens and setting up a native dynasty, and as late as the third century A.D. copies were circulating of the Prophecy of the Potter, which holds out apocalyptic hopes of a king who should deliver Egypt from the yoke of the foreigners, and destroy 'the city beside the sea' which was 'the nurse of all men; every race of men dwelt within her'.[3] Alexandria also had its patriotic anti-Roman tradition witnessed by the Acts of the Pagan Martyrs, in which the city is represented as the champion of Hellenism against Roman tyrants and their Jewish protégés.[4] The anti-Roman movements of Egypt and Alexandria were it may be noted quite distinct and mutually hostile; the Alexandrian documents refer with contempt to Egyptians, and the Egyptian reflect hatred of Alexandria.

There is no evidence that either tradition survived the triumph of Christianity. The Egyptian tradition was closely linked with old native religion, and the Alexandrian with pagan Hellenism. Certainly in Chris-

[1] Frend, op. cit., p. 86. For a full account of the Melitians see H. I. Bell, *Jews and Christians in Egypt* (London, 1924), pp. 38 ff.
[2] Bell, op. cit., pp. 42–43.
[3] *Hermes*, xl (1905), pp. 544 ff.
[4] Collected in H. A. Musurillo, *The Acts of the Pagan Martyrs* (Oxford, 1954).

tian Egypt no trace survived of the old antagonism between Egypt and Alexandria; Alexandria was the undisputed religious capital of Egypt. This fact seems decisive proof that there was no conscious survival of the old Egyptian nationalism in the Christian period.

The nationalist thesis in the case of Egypt is based on much the same arguments as in that of Africa.[1] It is àrgued that the stubborn and unanimous devotion of the Egyptians to the monophysite doctrine must have been derived from some other cause than the very subtle theological issues involved, and was in fact an expression of national Egyptian sentiment and hatred of the Roman empire. In support of this hypothesis two pieces of evidence are produced, the use of the Coptic language by the Egyptian church, and the alleged welcome given by the monophysite Egyptians to the Persians and to the Arabs.

The linguistic point is not convincing. Coptic was the normal language of the great majority of rural Egyptians, very many of whom knew no Greek. It was naturally adopted by the church as soon as Christianity spread to the countryside, and was employed long before the Egyptian church became heretical. Long after the split the intellectual leaders of the monophysite church continued to be Greek-speaking, and the literature of the movement was written in Greek. Ultimately, it is true, the monophysite church became purely Coptic and the Orthodox purely Greek; but this was only after the Arab conquest, when Greek gradually died out in Egypt and the native church naturally abandoned its use, while on the other hand the Orthodox patriarch was a nominee of the Byzantine government, often non-resident.

In the sixth century there is no very convincing evidence that Greek-speaking Egyptians favoured Chalcedon and Copts opposed it. Alexandria, where the Greek element was strongest, was a stronghold of monophysitism: John the Almoner, when he became patriarch in the early seventh century, found only seven churches in the hands of the Chalcedonians.[2] It may well be that in periods when the penal laws were enforced, members of the local aristocracy conformed for prudential reasons. Flavius Apion was persuaded by 'the most pious and faithful emperors', Justin and Justinian, to adopt the Chalcedonian faith: if he had not he might well have forfeited his patrician rank and his great estates. But until the change of emperors made a change of faith

---

[1] For scholarly and moderate statements of the case see J. Maspero, *Histoire des patriarches d'Alexandrie depuis la mort de l'empéreur Anastase jusqu'à la réconciliation des églises jacobites, 518–616* (Paris, 1923); E. R. Hardy, 'The Patriarchate of Alexandria: a Study in National Christianity', *Church History*, xv (1946), pp. 81–100; idem, *Christian Egypt: Church and People* (New York, 1952).

[2] Sophronius, *Vita Ioh. Eleemos.* 5.

expedient, Flavius Apion, great aristocrat though he was, had been a monophysite,[1] and his descendants later returned to that faith.[2]

There is no hint of any anti-imperial movement, much less any rebellion, during the period of close on two centuries that elapsed between the Council of Chalcedon and the Arab conquest. The Alexandrians, of course, frequently rioted when the imperial government forced Chalcedonian patriarchs upon them, and considerable bodies of troops had to be used to suppress them. But during the periods when the emperors favoured or tolerated monophysitism, the Egyptians seem to have been content. Ernst Stein has made much of one incident.[3] When in 516 Anastasius, whose monophysite sympathies were by now quite undisguised, appointed Dioscorus II to succeed John III as patriarch of Alexandria, the people objected that he had been uncanonically installed by the secular authorities, and insisted on the clergy, who had acquiesced, going through the form of electing him again. Next day they lynched the Augustal prefect, for praising Anastasius, according to Theophanes; Malalas says that it was a food shortage that provoked the attack on the Augustal.[4] This incident, Stein argues, proves that the Egyptians were unwilling to receive a good monophysite patriarch from a monophysite emperor: they were not really interested in the theological issue but wanted a patriarch of their own choice. The story certainly shows that the people of Alexandria were jealous of the canonical rights of their church, and resented the interference of the secular authorities: but this hardly proves hostility to the imperial government.

That the Copts welcomed the Persian invaders there is no evidence. They were certainly later remembered as cruel oppressors and persecutors, as appears from a prophecy attributed to Shenuda by a seventh-century biography.[5] Nor is there any good evidence that the Copts welcomed the Arabs.[6] The sources are most unreliable and confused, but from the best of them, John, bishop of Nikiu, who wrote about two generations after the event, it is evident that the rapid subjugation of Egypt by the Arabs was mainly due to the defeatism of Cyrus, the Chalcedonian

[1] Acta Conc. Oec. IV. ii. 170.

[2] J. B. Chabot, Chronique de Michel le Syrien, ii. 385 (read 'Strategios the patrician'). [3] E. Stein, Histoire du Bas-Empire, ii, p. 164.

[4] Theophanes, D.C. 6009; Malalas, p. 401 (Ed. Bonn.), fr. 41 (de Boor).

[5] M. Amélineau, Monuments pour servir à l'histoire de l'Égypte chrétienne (Paris, 1888); cp. idem, Étude sur le christianisme en Égypte au septième siècle (Paris, 1887), for a seventh-century Coptic life of Pisentios, bishop of Coptos, who fled into the desert on the advent of the Persians, and wrote to his flock, 'Because of our sins God has abandoned us: he has delivered us to the nations without mercy'.

[6] See A. J. Butler, The Arab Conquest of Egypt.

patriarch and prefect, and to the dynastic disputes which paralysed the government at Constantinople after the death of Heraclius. He records, it is true, that the Arabs were encouraged not only by the weakness of the Roman troops, but by the hostility of the people to Heraclius on account of the recent persecution.[1] But the reaction of the Egyptians seems to have been confused and uncertain, some fleeing in panic,[2] others deserting to the Arabs,[3] others resisting to the best of their ability.[4] The people of Alexandria were certainly horrified when they learned that they were to be surrendered to the Arabs under the final treaty.[5]

John's own attitude is significant. He regards the Arab conquest not as a deliverance, but as a calamity, the judgement of God upon the emperor Heraclius for persecuting the orthodox. It is to him strictly comparable with the earthquakes and plagues whereby God punished the previous apostasy of Justin and Justinian. But even more significant is the whole tone of John's history. If there had been anything that could truly be called a Coptic national movement, one would have expected it to develop its own version of history, in which the Egyptian people would play a heroic or at least a central role, and its resistance to the alien oppressor would be glorified. John in fact produces a standard history of the Roman Empire, merely reversing the Chalcedonian judgements on the merits of the successive emperors. He denounces Marcian and Pulcheria, Justin and Justinian, and above all Heraclius, the arch-persecutor. But he praises Anastasius, and even Tiberius who was merely tolerant of monophysitism. He betrays no hatred of the Roman Empire as such, and so far from rejoicing in its fall, laments the disasters which the apostasy of certain emperors brought upon it.

It remains true, of course, that the Egyptian church almost throughout its history maintained a remarkable solidarity, tenaciously supporting the doctrines of its chiefs, the patriarchs of Alexandria, through thick and thin; provided, of course, that these patriarchs were canonically elected and upheld the doctrines of their predecessors. To usurpers, who were intruded by an external authority and betrayed the traditions of the see, it maintained uncompromising resistance. The Egyptian church never wavered in its devotion to the homoousian doctrine enunciated by Alexander and Athanasius, and the monophysite doctrine of Dioscorus.

This monolithic solidarity may be attributed to national sentiment, but it is more simply explained by the structure and traditions of the Egyptian church. From the earliest times the bishop of Alexandria had

---

[1] R. H. Charles, *The Chronicle of John bishop of Nikiu*, cxv. 9.
[2] Op. cit. cxiii. 6, cxv. 6, cxx. 28.   [3] Op. cit. cxiii. 2, cxix. 1
[4] Op. cit. cxv. 1–3, 10.   [5] Op. cit. cxx. 24–26.

virtually appointed all the other bishops of Egypt, and by tradition he exercised an absolute authority over them. As the Egyptian bishops at Chalcedon protested, when they were ordered to sign the statement of the dyophysite faith: 'the ancient custom has prevailed in the Egyptian diocese that all the bishops obey the archbishop of Alexandria'.[1] In these circumstances the Egyptians never heard any view but that of their patriarch, and they naturally accepted it as gospel. That it was the supremacy of the patriarch and not any national spirit of unanimity which produced the solidarity of the Egyptian church is strongly suggested by the fact that when under Justinian there was for a long period no genuine patriarch in Egypt, the unity of the church broke down and rival parties formed within it.[2]

The people of Egypt—whether they spoke Greek or Coptic—naturally took great pride in the renown of their patriarchal see. The bishops of Alexandria claimed a pre-eminent position in the church and plumed themselves on being unerring champions of orthodoxy. They resented the rival pretensions of the see of Constantinople, and took a certain malicious pleasure in humbling its successive occupants—John Chrysostom, Nestorius, Flavian—whenever they could catch them out in canonical or doctrinal deviations. The people of Egypt rejoiced in their triumphs and were bitterly chagrined at their defeats. The sullen refusal of the Egyptian church to accept any compromise on the monophysite issue was probably due not so much to the doctrinal differences involved, which were very minute, as to loyalty to Dioscorus' memory. Hence their insistence that Chalcedon, which had condemned him, must be explicitly anathematized; the Henoticon, which hedged on this point, was not satisfying to their pride. The Council's recognition of the patriarchal authority and primacy of Constantinople must also have contributed to Egyptian hatred of Chalcedon.

To turn to the Jacobite church of Syria,[3] the picture of a Syriac-speaking national monophysite church opposed to a Greek-speaking imperial orthodox church does not seem to be true for the period before the Arab conquest. In the first place the monophysite heresy was in the sixth century by no means confined to Syriac-speaking areas. John of Ephesus records that John of Hephaestopolis journeyed throughout Asia Minor, ordaining priests for the monophysite congregations, from Tralles and Ephesus in the west as far as Tarsus, and also visited Cyprus and Rhodes.[4] The journeys of James Baradaeus covered not only Syria and Armenia, but Cappadocia, Cilicia, Isauria, Pamphylia, Lycaonia,

---

[1] *Act. Conc. Oec.* II. i. 309.   [2] See Maspero, op. cit.
[3] See R. Devreesse, *Le Patriarcat d'Antioche* (Paris, 1945).
[4] John of Ephesus, *Lives of the Eastern Saints*, xxv.

Phrygia, Lycia, Caria, and Asia, as well as Cyprus, Rhodes, Chios, and Mitylene. Of the twenty-nine sees to which he consecrated bishops thirteen were in Egypt, seven in Syria and Mesopotamia, and nine in Asia Minor, Ephesus, Smyrna, Pergamum, Tralles, Aphrodisias, Alabanda, Chios, Tarsus, and Seleucia on the Calycadnus.[1] Later John speaks of the spread of the schism in the monophysite church from Syria into Armenia, Cilicia, Isauria, Cappadocia, and Asia.[2] Elsewhere he describes the flourishing monophysite churches of Pamphylia,[3] and he incidentally mentions monophysite bishops and communities in several other cities of Asia Minor, Sardis, Chalcedon, Nicomedia, Cyzicus, Prusias, Heraclea.[4]

In the second place the heresy did not establish itself in all Syriac-speaking areas. In Syria itself there was, and has been ever since, a strong Chalcedonian church, and in Palestine monophysitism after initially sweeping the field was soon stamped out. Ernst Stein cites the orthodoxy of Palestine as evidence for the nationalist thesis.[5] Palestine was, he argues, a more Hellenized land than Syria, and such non-Hellenized inhabitants as it had were Jews and Samaritans who stood outside the conflict. This picture is very questionable. The Samaritans were mainly concentrated in the territory of Neapolis, though they spilled over into neighbouring cities like Caesarea and Scythopolis.[6] The Jews were dominant in Galilee, where Sepphoris and Tiberias were completely Jewish cities,[7] but seem to have been eradicated from Judaea proper after the revolt of Barcochba, and had never been particularly numerous in the coastal plain or beyond the Jordan. Palestine was no more, and probably less, Hellenized than Phoenicia and Syria, and we have evidence of Syriac-speaking Christian townsfolk, who knew no Greek, at Scythopolis[8] and Gaza,[9] the latter a great centre of Hellenic culture.

---

[1] John of Ephesus, *Lives of the Eastern Saints*, l.

[2] John of Ephesus, *Eccl. Hist.* iv. 19, cp. i. 39 (Cappadocia), ii. 32 (Asia and Cappadocia).

[3] Op. cit. v. 6.

[4] Op. cit. i. 15 (Sardis), *Lives of the Eastern Saints*, xlvi (Chalcedon, &c.).

[5] *Histoire du Bas-Empire*, ii, pp. 174 ff.

[6] This may be inferred from the story of the various Samaritan revolts, which were always confined to this area (Malalas, pp. 382–3, 445–7, 487–8 (Ed. Bonn.); Procop. *Aed.* v. vii; *Anecd.* xi. 24–30; Cyril. Scythop. *Vita Sabae*, 70).

[7] Epiphanius, *Adv. Haer.* 30. The Jewish revolt under Gallus was apparently in Galilee, its principal stronghold being Sepphoris (Soc. *H.E.* ii. 33; Soz. *H.E.* iv. 7).

[8] Eusebius, *Martyrs of Palestine*, i. 1, cited in Schürer, *Gesch. Jüd. Volkes*, ii, p. 381, n. 139.

[9] Marcus Diaconus, *Vita Porphyrii*, 66–68; Jerome mentions Syriac-speaking townsfolk at Elusa (*Vita Hilarionis*, 25).

The monophysite and Syriac-speaking areas therefore by no means coincided in the sixth century. Monophysitism gradually died in Asia Minor, which remained under the control of an orthodox government, whereas it survived and prospered under the toleration accorded by the Arabs in Syria, though it never ousted orthodoxy there and never penetrated again to Palestine.

Nor until after the Arab conquest was the Syriac language particularly associated with monophysitism. East of the Euphrates Syriac had a continuous history as a literary language, and here it was used by the churches both orthodox and heretical from the fourth century onwards. In Syria and Palestine Syriac survived only as the spoken language of the lower classes, especially in the country, and Greek was normally used by the churches, though for the benefit of the lower classes some concessions were made to Syriac. At Scythopolis there were at the beginning of the fourth century readers whose duty it was to translate the service into Syriac,[1] and later Publius of Zeugma, when Syriac-speaking postulants sought admission to his Greek-speaking monastery, allowed them to sing the service in their own tongue.[2] The same linguistic division existed in the monophysite church. Those of its apologists who came from east of Euphrates, Philoxenus of Hierapolis for instance, and John of Ephesus, wrote in Syriac. Severus of Antioch, who was by origin a Pisidian,[3] wrote both his theological works and his letters in Greek, and Zacharias of Mitylene, who came from Gaza,[4] composed his ecclesiastical history and his life of Severus in that language.

There is no evidence that the monophysites of Syria were politically disaffected to the empire. The only bishop who collaborated with a rebel in these parts was Calandion, the Chalcedonian patriarch of Antioch, who accepted the support of Illus at a time when the legitimate emperor, Zeno, had by the issue of the Henoticon proclaimed his sympathy with the monophysite cause.[5] We possess very long and detailed accounts of the wars waged under Justinian, Justin II, Tiberius, and Maurice between the Persian and the Roman empires in the very areas where monophysitism was strongest, but there is no hint in them that the monophysites gave the Persians any aid or comfort, or indeed regarded them with anything but fear and detestation. Nor is there any suggestion in the monophysite historians that they ever envisaged secession from the empire, or regarded the Romans as alien oppressors. Of the attitude of the Syrian monophysites in the later Persian wars under

---

[1] See p. 291, n. 8.
[2] Theodoret, *Hist. Rel.* 5.
[3] Zacharias, *Life of Severus, Patr. Or.* II. i, p. 10.
[4] Ibid., pp. 23-24.
[5] Evagrius, *H.E.* iii. 16.

Heraclius or during the Arab invasion we have no contemporary evidence.

The case of the Armenians is different. Armenia had been an independent kingdom down to the reign of Theodosius the Great, when it was partitioned between Rome and Persia, the latter getting the lion's share. Under alien domination the Armenians continued to feel and act as a nation. They had possessed their own church, which might truly be called national, since the early fourth century. In the middle decades of the fifth century they were involved in a struggle with Persia, which was endeavouring to impose Zoroastrianism on them, and took no part in the councils of Ephesus and Chalcedon. As late as 506 they were unaware of the issues involved, and learned of them only from certain Mesopotamian monophysites who were being persecuted, at the instigation of the Nestorians, by the Persian government. They naturally accepted the views of their fellow-sufferers, and affirmed their unity with the Romans, condemning Nestorius and the council of Chalcedon, and approving 'the letter of Zeno blessed emperor of the Romans'. When Justin and Justinian reversed Anastasius' ecclesiastical policy, they were apparently not consulted, and did not follow suit. This implied no hostility to Rome, however, for when in 572 they revolted against Persia they appealed to Justin II. He insisted on their subscribing to Chalcedon as a condition of aid, but they soon went back to their old beliefs. Maurice again attempted to impose the Chalcedonian position upon them, but the bishops of Persian Armenia refused to attend his council, and excommunicated the bishops of Roman Armenia, who had conformed. It was thus not hostility to Rome which led the Armenians into heresy; on the contrary they conformed to what was at the time the official Roman position. But having got used to this position they were unwilling to move from it, though they still regarded Rome as their natural ally and protector.[1]

The Arian German tribes are in a way a parallel case. There is, of course, no doubt that the Ostrogoths, Visigoths, Vandals, Burgundians, and Lombards were conscious national or tribal units. The Goths became Arians because they were evangelized at a time when Arianism was the official and dominant doctrine of the eastern part of the Roman Empire, and the other tribes seem to have learnt their Christianity from them. The question is why did the German tribes cling so tenaciously to their long out-moded heresy. Was it from national pride or because they believed that it was the true faith? In fact no doubt they remained Arians from mere conservatism, but they certainly were convinced that

[1] See V. Inglisian, 'Chalkedon und die armenische Kirche', in A. Grillmeier and H. Bacht, *Das Konzil von Chalkedon* (Würzburg, 1953), ii, pp. 361–417.

Arianism was true and pleasing to God. A remark of Sidonius Apollinaris about the Visigothic king Euric is revealing.[1] Euric was, Sidonius says, a fanatic and a persecutor, so much so that 'one might be in doubt whether he is leader of his tribe or of his sect'. 'His mistake is', he goes on, 'that he believes that success is granted to him in his dealings and plans in virtue of true religion, whereas he really obtains it in virtue of earthly good fortune.' Euric, in other words, like most Christians of his day, believed that God rewarded with worldly success those rulers who held the true faith and stamped out heresy, and attributed his own success to his zeal in promoting Arianism and crushing the heresy of the homoousians.

Of one sect only, so far as I know, has it been claimed that it was at bottom a social movement. Donatism has been represented as a revolutionary uprising of the poor against the rich.[2] For this view there is some solid evidence. Both Augustine and Optatus depict in vivid and circumstantial terms the activities of the circumcellions.[3] They gave their protection to tenant farmers against their landlords, to debtors against their creditors, and to slaves against their masters. 'No one was allowed to be safe on his estates. The bonds of debtors lost their force, no creditor was free to exact his money at that time.' Those who dared to disobey the letters of the Leaders of the Saints suffered dire penalties. Their houses were burnt down, they themselves were forced to work at the mill like slaves, or torn from their carriages and compelled to run behind while their slaves drove.

That circumcellion bands did from time to time exercise such a reign of terror in some areas cannot be doubted. The circumcellions were recruited from the poor peasantry, and were no doubt not averse from paying off old scores against oppressive landlords and extortionate moneylenders when they had a good excuse for doing so in the name of religion. But the circumcellions must be distinguished from the Donatist church; they were the storm-troopers of the movement, whom its official leaders did not always find it easy to control, and some of whose activities they may not have approved.[4] There is, so far as I know, no evidence that the Donatist church ever proclaimed any revolutionary programme of community of goods or freeing of slaves or remission of debt. In general, moreover, the activities of the circumcellions were inspired by religious zeal, and their victims were renegades who had

---

[1] Sid. Apoll. *Ep*. vii. 6. 6.
[2] F. Martroye, 'Un tentative de révolution sociale en Afrique', *Rev. quest. hist*. lxxvi (1904), pp. 353–416; lxxvii (1905), pp. 1–53.
[3] Aug. *Ep*. 108. 6. 18; 185. 4. 15; Optatus, iii. 4.
[4] Aug. *Contra Litt. Pet*. i. 24. 26; cp. ii. 23. 53, and *Contra Ep. Parm*. i. 11. 17.

deserted to the Catholic fold, or Catholics who had exercised pressure on Donatists to abjure their faith. There is an interesting letter of Augustine to the great senator Pammachius, who owned estates in Numidia, in which he heaps the most fulsome praise upon him for having had the courage to convert his Donatist tenants to catholicism, and expresses the hope that other senatorial landlords will be encouraged to follow his example.[1] From this it would appear that Donatist peasants were generally content to pay their rent to their landlords even if they were Catholics, and that the circumcellions would normally only take action against Catholic landlords if they tried to seduce their tenants from the faith.

The nationalist and socialist theories which I have been discussing seem to me to be based on a radical misapprehension of the mentality of the later Roman Empire. Today religion, or at any rate doctrine, is not with the majority of people a dominant issue and does not arouse major passions. Nationalism and socialism are, on the other hand, powerful forces, which can and do provoke the most intense feelings. Modern historians are, I think, retrojecting into the past the sentiments of the present age when they argue that mere religious or doctrinal dissension cannot have generated such violent and enduring animosity as that evinced by the Donatists, Arians, or Monophysites, and that the real moving force behind these movements must have been national or class feeling.

The evidence for nationalism of any kind in the later Roman Empire is tenuous in the extreme. It has been argued that when the imperial government in the fifth century tended to appoint senators of Gallic domicile to posts in Gaul, it was placating a sentiment of 'Gaul for the Gauls', which later found expression in the election of Avitus by the Gallic nobility.[2] But these facts imply no more than that Gallic senators expected their share of offices and naturally preferred to serve near home, and that in the anarchy which followed the death of Petronius they saw an opportunity of electing one of themselves to be emperor. Neither Avitus nor his backers had any intention of setting up a Gallic state; he intended to be emperor of the western empire. No one who has read the letters, poems, speeches, and histories which they wrote can doubt that the literate upper classes of the empire regarded themselves as Romans, as was only natural, seeing that they all shared the same cultural tradition. Of the lower classes we know little, since they were inarticulate. Very many of them spoke indigenous languages, but if they possessed any national traditions, they have not come down to us. In their actions, while they rarely displayed any positive loyalty to the

[1] Aug. *Ep.* 58. [2] Sundwall, *Weströmische Studien*, pp. 8–26.

empire, neither did they show any positive hostility. Usually they accepted Roman or barbarian with equal apathy.

Nor again, though there was much misery and some discontent among the lower classes, is there much sign of a class-conscious hatred of the rich. In times of famine the urban populace sometimes rioted and lynched unpopular officials or rich men who were hoarding stocks of corn, but such outbursts were sporadic and unorganized. Peasant revolts were very rare. The most notable were those of the Bacaudae in Gaul and later also in Spain.[1] Three rebellions are known in Gaul, one under Diocletian, the second under Honorius, and the third under Valentinian III. All reached formidable proportions, and required large-scale military operations to suppress them. They each lasted for a number of years, were commanded by recognized leaders, and controlled substantial areas—the two last Armorica, that is the territory between the English Channel and the Loire. Unfortunately we have very little information about their inner character save that the Bacaudae are characterized as peasants, brigands, and runaway slaves, and that Exsuperantius, who suppressed the second outbreak in 417, is said to have 'restored the laws and brought back liberty, and not suffered them to be slaves of their own servants'. Here we seem to have something more organized than sporadic jacqueries, but these revolts find no parallel in the rest of the empire.

On the other hand there is abundant evidence that interest in theology was intense and widespread. The generality of people firmly believed that not only individual salvation but the fortunes of the empire depended on correct doctrine, and it was natural that they felt passionately on the subject. Not all, of course, were well informed. Many humble Donatists shouted 'Deo Laudes' and denounced the Catholics as *traditores* without any clear understanding of the issues, or at best sang with gusto the songs which Parmenian had composed for their instruction.[2] Many an Egyptian monk could not have explained the subtleties of the monophysite doctrine, and was content to chant 'who was crucified for us' after the Trisagion, and to curse the Chalcedonians as Nestorians. But even uneducated people argued theological points with zest, and could cite the key texts and repeat the stock arguments. I need hardly

---

[1] The evidence is assembled by Thompson in *Past and Present*, ii (1952), pp. 11 ff.

[2] Aug. *Ep.* 55. 18. 34; Praedestinatus, *de Haer.* 43. Other examples of popular songs for the instruction of the ignorant on theological issues are Augustine's *Psalmus contra partem Donati* and Arius' *Thaleia*. If the latter was really, as Athanasius implies (*Or. c. Arianos*, i. 4), sung in the bars of Alexandria, the proletariat of that city must have had a strong taste for theological controversy: the surviving verses (cited in Athanasius, *de Syn.* 15) are not very inspiring.

remind you of Gregory of Nyssa's description of Constantinople during the Arian controversy. 'If you ask for your change, the shopkeeper philosophizes to you about the Begotten and the Unbegotten. If you ask the price of a loaf, the answer is "the Father is greater and the Son inferior"; if you say "Is my bath ready?", the attendant declares that the Son is of nothing.'[1] And finally thousands of people were prepared to face deportation, pecuniary loss, torture, and even death on theological issues for most of which no national or social undertones can be discovered.

I would contend that under the later Roman Empire most people felt strongly on doctrinal issues and a high proportion had sufficient acquaintance with theology to argue about them with zest if without any deep understanding. It does not, of course, follow that they adopted whatever doctrinal position they held from a rational evaluation of the arguments for and against it. As today and in all ages most people's religious beliefs were determined by a variety of irrational influences. Some were swayed by the authority of a revered theologian, or more often by that of a holy man whose orthodoxy was guaranteed by his austerities and miracles. The great majority accepted what they had been brought up to believe as children, or the dominant belief of their social milieu. Some doctrines made a special appeal to certain classes of society. It has been claimed that in Asia Minor the areas where the rigorist sects prevailed coincided with those where native languages survived. This is not the whole truth, for, as we know from Socrates, there were in Constantinople, Nicomedia, Nicaea, and other great cities cultivated Novatians, like their delightful bishop Sisinnius, who when asked by censorious members of his flock why, being a bishop, he took two baths a day, replied: 'Because I have not got time for a third.'[2] But the bulk of the more fundamentalist Novatians were Phrygians and Paphlagonians, and Socrates is surely on the right lines when he explains this fact by saying that these people were naturally not addicted to the horse races and the theatre, and regarded fornication with horror.[3] He holds that the austerity of the Phrygians and Paphlagonians is due to the climate—they lie in the zone between the Scythians and Thracians, who are inclined to violent passions, and the peoples of the East, who

---

[1] Greg. Nyss., *Or. de deitate Filii et Spiritus Sancti* (*P.G.* xlvi. 557).

[2] Socrates records a number of cultivated Novatian bishops of Constantinople: Marcian (iv. 9), Sisinnius (vi. 22), Chrysanthus (vii. 12), Paul (vii. 17), and also Ablabius, bishop of Nicaea, a rhetorician (vii. 12). The synod of Pazos, where the rural Novatians adopted the Quartodeciman heresy, was not attended by the leading bishops of the sect, those of Constantinople, Nicaea, Nicomedia, and Cotyaeum (iv. 28).

[3] Soc. *H.E.* iv. 28.

are subject to their appetites. The truth surely is that they were simple countryfolk, whose life was necessarily somewhat austere, and that they were naturally attracted by a severe doctrine which condemned indulgences to which they were not prone. The fact that they spoke an indigenous language is an index merely of their rusticity, and not of any mysterious affinity between Novatianism and Phrygian national culture.

In brief I would maintain that when the sectaries declared, as they did on our evidence declare: 'We hold the true faith and are the true church; our opponents are heretics, and never will we accept their doctrine or communicate with them, or yield to the impious government which supports them', they meant and felt what they said. Why they held their particular beliefs we in many cases cannot divine. Who can tell why in A.D. 450 out of the 800 villages in the territory of Cyrrhus one was Arian, one Eunomian, and eight remained stubbornly faithful to the doctrines of Marcion which had been generally condemned for some three centuries?[1] In some cases the sects more or less coincided with social or regional groups, and I have endeavoured to explain how this may have come about. But the line of demarcation between orthodoxy and heresy never, except in the case of the Armenians and the Germans, corresponded with anything that can legitimately be called a national, as opposed to a regional, division. It was inhabitants of Egypt, and not Copts, who were monophysite, and even in Africa, though Donatism made a greater appeal, as a rigorist sect, to the Punic- or Berber-speaking peasantry, many Romanized Africans were found on the Donatist side. And finally the sects never pursued political aims, whether national or social.

A. H. M. JONES

[1] Theodoret, *Ep.* 81, 113.

THE HERESY OF THE PHRYGIANS.[1]

IT may be well at the outset to make clear the purpose with which this paper has been written. For some time the suspicion has forced itself upon me that a good deal that has been published on the subject of Montanism has been based on investigations which proceeded on a faulty method. I propose to set forth the reasons which have led me to entertain this suspicion. My hope is that, if my argument is not accepted, it may elicit criticism which shall suggest a truer interpretation of the evidence which is here presented.

The most illustrious adherent of the Montanist movement was undoubtedly Tertullian of Carthage. And for the purpose of the enquirer into the inner meaning of Montanism Tertullian has the advantage of being a voluminous writer, of whose treatises moreover many have survived. The later writings of Tertullian are in fact—if we except a few oracles of the Phrygian prophets not quoted by him—the only source from which we can acquire a first-hand knowledge of Montanist principles and practice. Historians can scarcely be blamed if they have given them a very high place among the materials now available for ascertaining the character of the Phrygian heresy. And the procedure usually adopted by investigators has, if I am not mistaken, been suggested by an unquestioning assumption of their primary authority for the purpose in hand. It has been assumed that what Tertullian reckons as Montanist doctrine and custom is really such. The evidence supplied by him has been accepted as indisputably reliable: the statements of Catholic writers which appear to conflict with it have either been tortured into agreement

---

[1] A paper read before the Cambridge Theological Society on Friday, January 31, 1908.

with his *dicta*, or have been rejected as calumnies.   It has thus come to pass that what passes current as Montanism is in the main identical with the later theology of Tertullian.   We seek a description of a system which penetrated from its first home in Phrygia into many regions; and we have been content to accept instead an account which we have no assurance for believing to be more than the picture of a local developement of the movement, or even of its embodiment in a single individual.

The hypothesis which is the ground of this method is the homogeneity of Montanism.   Phrygian Montanism and African Montanism are assumed to be, in great measure, the same thing.   But is this assumption justified?   Was Montanism really homogeneous?

It seems to me that *a priori* we should scarcely expect this to be the case.

The movement began, as we learn from early documents preserved by Eusebius and Epiphanius, at an obscure village called Ardabau in Mysia, not far from the border of Phrygia. There, probably in the fifties of the second century, Montanus, a new convert to Christianity, who had been a priest of Cybele, began to prophesy.   And his prophesyings were accompanied by strange phenomena closely resembling those associated with demoniacal possession.   He spoke in an ecstasy, as his followers would have expressed it.

Montanus was soon joined by two women, Maximilla and Priscilla or Prisca, who also claimed to possess the prophetic charisma, and whose utterances were similar in matter and in manner to those of their leader.   Before long the movement acquired a local centre at Pepuza and Tymion, villages of Phrygia, to which the name of Jerusalem was given.   Its adherents were by and by excommunicated by many synods, and Montanism became a sect with a definite organization.   The prophecies of Montanus, Maximilla, and Priscilla were committed to writing, were widely circulated, and were regarded by friends and foes as authoritative statements of all that distinguished the Montanistic teaching from current Christianity.   By the Montanists themselves the prophetic oracles were placed at least on a level with the Gospels and the Apostolic Scriptures.

Now it is evident that the moment the oracles of the original exponents of the New Prophecy were written down, and read without the explanations of the prophets, they became, as truly as the Scriptures which they in part superseded, 'a nose of wax'. All depended on their interpretation. And as Montanism spread into different countries, and was accepted by men of different environment and mental training, the interpretations put upon them were certain to be diverse. From this we have ample warrant for the expectation that Montanism would, in some degree, display a divergent type in each country to which it gained admission.

It may, perhaps, make the meaning of what I have said clearer, and at the same time justify the conclusion which I have reached on *a priori* grounds, if I proceed to give what may be termed an example of the forces of disintegration at work.

Didymus of Alexandria,[1] or rather the early and valuable document on which he bases his account of the sect, charges the Montanists with three errors. The first of them is, that on the plea of a prophetic revelation, supported by certain passages from the latter chapters of the fourth Gospel, they affirmed ($\dot{a}\pi o\mu a\nu\tau\epsilon\acute{v}o\nu\tau a\iota$) that there is one $\pi\rho\acute{o}\sigma\omega\pi o\nu$ of the three divine $\acute{v}\pi o\sigma\tau\acute{a}\sigma\epsilon\iota s$. That is to say, they taught what later came to be known as Sabellianism. The oracle on which they relied for this teaching, according to Didymus, was a saying of Montanus, 'I am the Father and the Son and the Holy Ghost.' This certainly sounds like Monarchian heresy. So also does a saying of Maximilla recorded by Asterius Urbanus,[2] 'I am Word and Spirit and Power'—for the words $\acute{\rho}\eta\mu a$, $\pi\nu\epsilon\hat{v}\mu a$ and $\delta\acute{v}\nu a\mu\iota s$ must be taken as equivalent to Montanus's Son, Spirit, and Father. And in support of the inference drawn from these, appeal might have been also made to some other oracles among the few that remain. If we had only the statement of Didymus and the oracles to which I have referred we might have confidently classed the Montanists with the Sabellians. But we turn to Tertullian. There is no need to say that he, whether as Catholic or as Montanist, did not deviate from orthodoxy. He was an ardent opponent of the Monarchian Praxeas. And he declares that it was exactly his Montanism which specially fitted him to be the champion of the true faith.[3] For the Paraclete had made

<hr>

[1] *De Trin.* iii 41.   [2] *Ap.* Eus. *H. E.* v 16. 17.
[3] *Adv. Prax.* 13, *De Carn. Res.* 63.

I i 2

use of expressions which, without any such ambiguity as was found in the phrases of Scripture, denounced the teaching of Praxeas as false. It is true that the only oracle which he quotes in this connexion rather tells against his contention;[1] but he refers to another, which, if his paraphrase of it is reliable, must have been emphatically orthodox.[2] Moreover he vouches for the orthodoxy of the entire body of the Montanists. No one, he assures us, had ever accused them of heresy.[3] Their rules of discipline—such is his argument—cannot be corrupt, for error in doctrine always precedes error in discipline.[4]

The fact is that, in spite of the vehemence of Tertullian, the Montanists were as much divided as their opponents on the question of the Divine Monarchy. Besides the orthodox party among them, to which Tertullian himself belonged, known as the Cataproclans, there was a heterodox party, which he was ignorant of, or, more probably, chose to ignore—the Cataeschinites. This we may gather from the *Philosophumena* of Hippolytus, and from the treatise *Against Heresies* of Pseudo-Tertullian, who, no doubt, here as elsewhere, derives his information from Hippolytus's *Syntagma*.[5] It is unnecessary to cite other authorities in confirmation of the statements of Hippolytus. The remarkable fact is that both the orthodox and the heterodox parties among the Montanists sheltered themselves behind the oracles of the prophets.

But it was not only the difficulty of interpreting the oracles, and applying them to controversies which did not belong to the place and period of the original prophets, which tended to divide the Montanists. There were at least three other influences, all closely related to each other, which might well lead to this result.

The first of these was the oracles of later prophets. For the charismata were by no means confined to the first three. Theodotus, 'the first steward of the New Prophecy,' was a fellow-worker of Montanus, and he was almost certainly a prophet.[6] Apollonius, about the year 200, mentions both a prophet and a prophetess;[7] and, notwithstanding the opinion of so eminent a historian as Harnack,[8] one can hardly suppose that they are to be identified with Montanus and Maximilla or Priscilla.

---

[1] *Adv. Prax.* 8. [2] *Ib.* 30. [3] *De Ieiun.* 1. [4] *De Moneg.* 2.
[5] Hippol. *Philos.* 19, Ps.-Tert. *Haer.* 7. [6] Anon. *ap.* Eus. *H. E.* v 16. 14.
[7] *Ap.* Eus. *H. E.* v 18. 4, 6, 7, 10. [8] *Chronologie* i 370.

In any case Apollonius implies that Maximilla and Priscilla had successors by his remark that they were the *first* prophetesses to abandon their husbands.[1] Firmilian, in his letter to Cyprian, speaks of a prophetess (probably a Montanist) who appeared in Cappadocia about 236 A.D.[2] And finally Epiphanius tells of a prophetess named Quintilla.[3] Whether she was one of those already mentioned we cannot determine.[4] She was certainly not a member of the original group. There is no evidence that the inspired utterances of these later prophets were circulated in writing. Certainly none of them is quoted in writings now extant. They probably had no more than a local celebrity. The same remark may be made about Themiso, whose Catholic epistle, written 'in imitation of the Apostle',[5] claimed, we cannot doubt, to have been inspired. But that they furthered the developement of Montanism in the districts where they were known it is impossible not to believe. And the narrower the sphere of their influence so much the more their sayings tended to generate purely local forms of the system.

In the West, so far as I know, there is no mention of later prophets. But Tertullian several times refers to the visions of sisters,[6] and he appeals on one occasion to the vision of Saturus, which we can still read in the Acts of Perpetua.[7] In each case the vision is used as giving authority to a disciplinary custom or a doctrine advocated by the writer. Thus in the West, as in the East, the means was at hand of explaining or adding to the original deposit of the New Prophecy by an authority which was held to be divine.

A second agent of developement which must be taken into account is the weight of influence exerted by prominent members of the sect, who were not themselves prophets, or possessed of charismata which involved the capacity for receiving revelations by visions or otherwise.

---

[1] Eus. *H. E.* v 18. 3 δείκνυμεν οὖν αὐτὰς πρώτας τὰς προφήτιδας ταύτας . . . τοὺς ἄνδρας καταλιπούσας.   [2] Cyp. *Ep.* 75. 10 (Hartel, p. 817).   [3] *Haer.* 49.

[4] Bonwetsch (*Die Geschichte des Montanismus,* Erlangen, 1881, p. 171) suggests that she may have been the prophetess mentioned by Firmilian, Salmon (*Dict. of Christ. Biog.* iii 939) that she was the prophetess referred to by Apollonius.

[5] Apollonius *ap.* Eus. *H. E.* v 18. 5.   [6] e. g. *De An.* 9, *De Virg. Vel.* 17.

[7] *De An.* 55.

Tertullian, in his own person, notably illustrates the power of this influence. He nowhere claims to have had revelations. He was simply, in his own view, an adherent of the Paraclete. Yet his influence in determining the form of Montanism in Africa must have been immense. Dr Rendel Harris and Professor Gifford, in the introduction to their edition of the *Acts of the Martyrdom of Perpetua and Felicitas*,[1] direct attention to ' the difficulty with which any of his writings, except a very few tracts, can satisfactorily be labelled non-Montanist '. They have themselves transferred what previous writers had regarded as ' probably Tertullian's earliest existing writing '[2] to the Montanistic period of his life. The fact is that the unquestionably Montanistic treatises are recognized merely by more or less explicit allusions to the revelations of the Paraclete. The doctrines and practices advocated in his latest works are, for the most part, essentially the same as those upheld in the earliest now extant. If there is any difference between them it is amply accounted for by the developement of opinion which would inevitably take place in a man of Tertullian's character. They are presented from new points of view and under new sanctions, but in their main substance they are unchanged. Of this fact it is superfluous to give proof, and the inference from it is irresistible. Tertullian brought far more to Montanism than he found in it. It is an inference which might have been drawn if we knew nothing more of the man than what his writings reveal of his masterful personality. But if African Montanism was largely made by Tertullian, it must have differed widely from the Montanism which in his day, or at any other time, existed in Phrygia.

We have from Tertullian himself a story which well illustrates how the influence of later revelations and the influence of personality helped each other in producing the local developement of Montanism. In his treatise *de Anima* 9 he speaks of a certain sister, who had the charisma of revelations. The material for visions was often supplied by the lessons, psalms, discourses, &c., of the church service. During service, on one occasion, when Tertullian was discoursing on the soul, the sister fell into an ecstasy and saw a vision. Subsequently, when service was over, and the congregation dismissed, she was invited to describe her vision.

[1] Cambridge, 1890, p. 28 ff.   [2] *Dict. of Christ. Biog.* iv 822.

Among other things she declared that she had seen a soul which displayed all the signs of a corporeal nature. Thus was established a favourite doctrine of the preacher, on which he had no doubt been insisting in his sermon. I shall have occasion to refer to this story again. For the present it is sufficient to observe that the preacher obviously, though he was unconscious that he had done so, produced the vision, while the vision in its turn was adduced to impart divine sanction to the preacher's doctrine. A new tenet was thus added to the official teaching of African Montanism, nominally by a revelation, really by the personality of Tertullian.

The third power which co-operated with revelations and personal force in the moulding of Montanism need only be mentioned—the power of local environment. This always exercises its subtle influence on a transplanted faith. It has in no small degree affected Christianity itself. And wherever its influence is effective it produces a change of form.

The conclusion to which these considerations compel us is, I believe, that any large measure of homogeneity in Montanism is a thing which could not be looked for beforehand. Any method of investigation which assumes it must therefore be radically wrong. The only way to arrive at a true conception of Montanism is to begin by examining Phrygian Montanism and African Montanism apart. It may be urged that the only Montanism of which we can learn anything is a developed or a decadent Montanism. That may be in part true. But we can reach a knowledge of its inner principle in no other way than by a preliminary study of the later forms, each by itself, and by tracing them back to their common root. By combining them merely we can attain no sure result. And for this purpose an enquiry into Phrygian Montanism—the heresy of the Phrygians in its original home, shaped only by its original environment— scanty and unsatisfying as the materials for such an enquiry are, is immeasurably more important than an enquiry into the exotic Montanism of Tertullian.

It remains to point out one or two very striking instances of dissimilarity between Phrygian Montanism and the current conception of Montanism, mainly drawn from Tertullian, which such a study seems to me to reveal.

Let us note, in the first place, what we may learn from the

earliest documents as to the conception which was held in Phrygia of the nature of the New Prophecy. It is well known that Montanus and his companions prophesied in ecstasy, and that their utterances were accompanied by strange ravings.[1]   The Catholics laid hold of this fact as demonstrating that they were inspired by an evil spirit ; and the defenders of Montanism replied that being in a state of ecstasy was a condition of the exercise of the prophetic gift. But all this seems to me to have been an afterthought. The Catholics made much of the frenzy of the prophets merely as a way of evading an argument of the Montanists which, without bringing in this other issue, was not easily disposed of. This earlier argument is revealed by the anonymous writer quoted by Eusebius.[2]   The Montanists, he says, evidently quoting from one of their books, boasted of Agabus, Judas, Silas, the daughters of Philip, Ammia of Philadelphia and Quadratus; and from the last two they claimed to have received the prophetic gift *by way of succession* (διεδέξαντο).[3]   That is to say, they received their charismata as successors in the line of New Testament prophets, which all believed would remain until the end, just as the Bishops had received their office from a line of predecessors which went back to Apostolic days. They were the last prophets, no doubt ; they had the gifts in a pre-eminent degree ; in them was fulfilled the promise of the Paraclete. All Montanist writers maintained that position. But still, they were the last and the greatest *in a line of succession.*

It is hazardous to assert a negative. But I cannot recall any trace of this notion of a prophetic succession in the West. Tertullian seems consistently to ignore all prophecy between the Baptist, or at any rate the Apostles, and Montanus.[4]

And I may here observe that the impression left by a perusal

---

[1] Eus. *H. E.* v 16. 7, 9.

[2] Lightfoot (*Ignatius* i 482 f) and Harnack (*Chronologie* i 364 f) agree in dating the anonymous treatise A. D. 192–193.   It was undertaken at the request of Avircius Marcellus of Hieropolis in the Phrygian Pentapolis (Eus. v 16. 3), and the writer speaks of Avircius and Zoticus of Otrous, a neighbouring town, as his fellow pres-byters (§ 5).   It is probable therefore that all three were bishops of the Pentapolis, and that Miltiades, against whose followers the treatise was directed, was a Montanist leader of the same district.

[3] Eus. *H. E.* v 17. 3, 4.

[4] *De An.* 9, cf. *De Virg. Vel.* 1, *De Monog.* 3, *De Ieiun.* 12.

of the extant passages of Tertullian [1] in which he refers to ecstasy as a condition of prophecy is that the ecstasy which he contemplated was something very different from the violent and uncontrolled ravings of the Phrygian prophets as reported (possibly not without exaggeration) by the Anonymous.[2] Epiphanius says truly that the word ἔκστασις has different meanings,[3] and I am inclined to think that Western Montanists used it in one sense, and their Phrygian brethren in another. The account of the sister whose ecstasy was kept so well in hand that she could wait patiently till service was over before relating her vision stands in curious contrast to the narrative of the proceedings at Ardabau.

A comparison of these two stories recalls also another marked difference between the Montanism of Phrygia and that of Africa. In Phrygia women were given a high position in the native cults. And among the Montanists they retained it. Montanus evidently prophesied in the midst of a congregation. There were large numbers present (ὄχλοι), some of whom would have silenced him, while others opposed their efforts. And it seems to be suggested that Maximilla and Priscilla likewise addressed a Christian assembly.[4] But however that may be, Firmilian, as we have seen, makes mention of a third-century prophetess, probably a Montanist, of whom he states that she baptized and celebrated the Eucharist.[5] Epiphanius describes a curious service of the Quintillians (who were obviously the Montanists under another name) at Pepuza, in which the officiants were seven virgins, who prophesied to the people; and he declares that they had female bishops and priests.[6] We are not surprised to find Catholics

---

[1] See especially *De Anima* 45, where he makes use of the favourite Montanist text, Gen. ii 21. The whole chapter should be compared with Epiph. *Haer.* 48. 3, 4. In several respects Tertullian appears to be more in harmony with the Catholic writer used by Epiphanius than with the Montanist opinions which that writer combats. See also *De Anima* 11, 21, *De Ieiun.* 3.

[2] *Ap.* Eus. *H. E.* v 16. 7, 8 ; 17. 2. It will be observed that the Anonymous substitutes for ἔκστασις the stronger word παρέκστασις. [3] *Haer.* 48. 4.

[4] They spoke in the same way as Montanus (§ 9). And it is added, by way of explanation, that they did so ἐκφρόνως καὶ ἀκαίρως καὶ ἀλλοτριοτρόπως. There is nothing corresponding to the second adverb in the description of Montanus's utterances. It may perhaps indicate that they spoke during a Church service ; which would be an improper occasion for speech for women, though not for a man.

[5] Cyprian *Ep.* 75. 10 (Hartel, p. 818 f). [6] *Haer.* 49. 2, 3.

indignantly quoting St Paul's injunction about women keeping silence in the Church.

This peculiarity of Montanism certainly never found its way into the West. It is not a Catholic, but Tertullian, in one of his most distinctly Montanist writings, who says, ' It is not permitted to a woman to speak in Church, nor yet to teach, nor to baptize, nor to offer, nor to assume any office which belongs to a man, least of all the priesthood.' [1]

Not much is known of the penitential discipline of the Eastern Montanists. But there is ground for believing that in this matter also they differed from the Africans. Apollonius [2] discusses the case of one Alexander, whom the sectaries regarded as a martyr, but whom he affirmed to have been tried not for the Name but for robbery.[3] After his release he spent some years with a prophet. Apollonius sneers after his accustomed fashion : ' Which of them forgives the sins of the other? Does the prophet forgive the robberies of the martyr, or the martyr the extortions of the prophet?' This implies that prophets were supposed by the Montanists to have the power of absolution. And in this insinuation Apollonius is confirmed, not only by Tertullian, but also (which is more to the purpose) by an oracle which Tertullian quotes.[4] We have therefore no reason to doubt the further insinuation that martyrs were regarded as possessed of the same power.[5] But the African Montanists allowed no such prerogative to the martyrs. In Carthage it was only the Catholics who admitted the validity of their absolutions, and Tertullian heaps much scorn upon them for so doing.[6]

But we must now proceed to discuss two questions which will be recognized as of fundamental importance. Did Montanism

---

[1] *De Virg. Vel.* 9.

[2] Apollonius says that he wrote forty years after the beginning of Montanism (Eus. *H. E.* v 18. 12). Hence Harnack (*Chronologie* i 370–375) dates his treatise A. D. 196–197. But, though it is probable that Montanus prophesied for the first time in 156, we cannot be sure that Apollonius was accurately informed on that point, neither are we certain that he did not use round numbers when he spoke of the forty years that had elapsed since the New Prophecy began. The recrudescence of prophecy to which he bears witness seems to indicate a longer period than four years between the Anonymous and him. Possibly therefore he wrote as late as A. D. 200. He was certainly an Asian, and possibly, as Praedestinatus says, bishop of Ephesus.

[3] *Ap.* Eus. *H. E.* v 18. 6-9.   [4] *De Pud.* 21.   [5] Cf. Bonwetsch, p. 112.
[6] *De Pud.* 22.

inculcate asceticism? No one can doubt that, as expounded by Tertullian, it did. But we are concerned with Phrygian Montanism. What evidence have we as to asceticism among the adherents of the New Prophecy in Phrygia?

The writer who gives us most help in answering this question is Apollonius. In the passages quoted from him by Eusebius he insists that the lives of the Montanist martyrs and prophets do not conform to the requirements of the Gospel. He roundly charges them with covetousness. Montanus himself, he tells us, appointed πρακτῆρας χρημάτων, agents for the collection of money (Eus. *H. E.* v 18. 2), and out of the fund raised by them he actually paid salaries to the teachers who propagated his doctrine. Moreover he devised a system of receiving gifts under the name of 'offerings'. Accordingly the prophets took gifts (*ib.* § 11), and both prophets and martyrs made gain not only from the rich, but from the poor and orphans and widows. Prophets and prophetesses and martyrs, unmindful of the saying of our Lord: 'Ye shall not take gold or silver or two coats,' accepted offerings not only of gold and silver, but also of costly garments (§§ 4, 7). Themiso, a leader of the sect, who claimed to be a 'martyr', or as we should say, a 'confessor', was rich enough to purchase his liberation from prison with a large sum of money (πλήθει χρημάτων). Themiso was, in fact, clothed with covetousness as with a garment (§ 5). Another, who was counted as a prophet, was a money-lender (§ 11). And, finally, Apollonius asks the scornful questions, 'Does a prophet dye his hair? Does a prophet paint himself? Does a prophet delight in self-adornment? Does a prophet play with tables and dice? Does a prophet lend money at interest?'; and he offers to prove that all these things were done by the Montanist prophets (§ 11).

In some of these statements and insinuations—those namely which relate to the financial organization of the sect—Apollonius is confirmed by the Anonymous. For when he calls Theodotus the 'first steward' of the new prophecy (τὸν πρῶτον τῆς ... προφη-τείας οἶον ἐπίτροπόν τινα [1]) I do not see why we may not take his words in their literal sense. And indeed the very innocency of some of the things laid to the charge of Montanus is a strong guarantee that the accusations are true. For who nowadays

[1] *Ap.* Eus. *H. E.* v 16. 14.

would find fault with a man who provided preachers with salaries, or who organized the collection of money for the purpose? And we shall not greatly blame prophets and confessors for taking the gifts which were offered to them, nor be greatly surprised if the more eminent and popular leaders became rich. There is really no need for Bonwetsch's suggestion that what Montanus aimed at was the establishment of a community of goods.[1] The statements about salaries and the wealth of certain individuals is quite inconsistent with such a supposition.

What scandalized Apollonius was perhaps the fact that Montanus was making the clerical and even the prophetic office into a profession. His preachers no longer worked at secular trades, as, in all probability, most bishops and priests at that period did: they derived their income solely from the payment made to them for the exercise of spiritual functions. One who is not a member of an established Church may perhaps be allowed to express sympathy with him if he also felt that absorption in financial organization is not conducive to the highest spiritual interests of Church or sect.

We may take it, at any rate, that Montanus desired that the officials of his sect should live, not indeed in luxury, but in ordinary comfort.

The remainder of Apollonius's charges Bonwetsch[2] asks us to disbelieve, on the ground that Socrates (iv 28) bears testimony to lack of zeal among the Paphlagonians and Phrygians of his day for the hippodrome and the theatre. The argument is scarcely convincing. He further reminds us, indeed, of Jerome's statement that in the lost work *De Ecstasi* Tertullian exposed the falsity of all Apollonius's assertions.[3] But even if we are bound to interpret rigorously the words of Jerome, we must still remark that an Asian writer is more likely to have known the facts than one who lived in Africa, and that if the probable prejudice of Apollonius is to be taken into account, the prejudice of Tertullian must not be left out of consideration. The explanation devised by Bonwetsch, for the benefit of those who are not disposed utterly to reject the witness of Apollonius—that the

[1] p. 165.　　　　　　　　　　　　　　　[2] p. 100.
[3] *De Vir. Ill.* 40 'septimum [volumen] proprie adversus Apollonium elaboravit in quo omnia quae ille arguit conatur defendere '.

Montanists, in order to express their spiritual joy as Christians, indulged in an 'apparent worldliness' which as the symbol of mere earthly merriment would not have been permitted ; and that the gay clothing of the prophetess served only to enhance her dignity, and to enforce the festive character of her utterances —need not detain us.

I am willing to grant that the statements of Apollonius are exaggerated. But is it possible that such charges could have been publicly made in Asia, and have been accompanied by an express challenge to the Montanists to disprove them, if they had not considerable foundation in fact? Could they have been made at all by him against the leaders of a numerous Asian community, of which asceticism was one of the most prominent characteristics? And would Tertullian have answered them if they were so contrary to the truth that no one could have believed them?

But Apollonius makes two statements about Montanus which may seem to imply that he inculcated an asceticism which exceeded that of the Catholic Church. 'This,' he says, 'is he who taught dissolutions of marriages, and made laws of fasting' (ὁ διδάξας λύσεις γάμων, ὁ νηστείας νομοθετήσας).[1] It is scarcely probable, indeed, considering the context in which this sentence occurs, that it was intended to convey the idea of special austerity on the part of Montanus. For it is immediately followed by accusations of extortion and gluttony. But let us examine the statements in their order.

1. Montanus taught 'dissolutions of marriages'. It is quite certain that in the East as in the West, Montanism was so far ascetic as absolutely to reject second marriages (Epiph. *Haer.* 48. 8, 9,[2]

---

[1] Eus. *H. E.* v 18. 2.

[2] Epiphanius evidently bases this part of his account of Montanism on a very early document. Bonwetsch (p. 36) argues, not altogether convincingly, that it was a treatise of Hippolytus. Its date seems to be earlier than the work of Apollonius, for the writer still asserts (§ 2) that there have been no prophets since the death of Maximilla, a statement which in the time of Apollonius would have been untrue. To connect it with Phrygia we have the statement (§ 11) : 'Immediately after Montanus had said this '—viz. an oracle which he had quoted—['God] gave us a suggestion to remember the words of the Lord ', &c. (ὅτε γὰρ εὐθὺς τοῦτο εἶπε Μοντανὸς ὑπόνοιαν ἡμῖν δίδωκεν ἀναμνησθῆναι κτλ). This seems to imply that the writer had actually heard Montanus. Moreover, several of his arguments resemble those of the Anonymous.

Tert. *De Monog.* 3, &c.). But this can hardly be referred to here. The words λύσεις γάμων have sometimes been rendered 'dissolution of marriage', leaving one to infer that Montanus was so strenuous an advocate of virginity as to lay it down that married couples on their acceptance of the new prophecy were bound to separate for the purpose of living in strict continence. And there is certainly an oracle of Priscilla, which Tertullian quotes and understands as a commendation of chastity.[1] We only know it in Tertullian's Latin rendering, which is not free from ambiguity. But it certainly does not enjoin the annulling of marriages already contracted. And if Apollonius had wished to indicate the sanction by Montanus of such an annulling in all cases, would he not have used the singular, λύσις? At any rate his language is easily explained as a rhetorical allusion to the fact, for which a somewhat later passage in his treatise[2] is our sole authority, that Maximilla and Priscilla (and probably other women also) deserted their husbands when they became prophetesses. Montanus must of course have sanctioned their conduct: he could not well have done otherwise, if it was his wish that prophetesses as well as preachers should give undivided attention to their spiritual work. But abandonment of married life under such circumstances does not necessarily imply an ascetic view of the relation between the sexes. It is true that it seems to be implied by Apollonius that the Montanists recognized an order of virgins. For after asserting that the prophetesses had left their husbands to join Montanus, he adds, 'How then did they speak falsehood, calling Priscilla a virgin?' But the existence of such an order did not strike the anti-Montanist writer as unfitting: what he counted outrageous was not the ascetic tendency of his opponents, but their laxity in giving one the rank of a virgin who had been married. So far as these indications go it would seem that the Montanists were *less* ascetic in their opinions about marriage than the Catholics.

2. But then Montanus 'made laws for fasting'. Does not this imply an unusually rigorous asceticism? Tertullian in his *De Ieiuniis* contrasts the Montanist fasts with those of the Catholics, and actually accuses the latter of gluttony because their fasts were less frequent and less severe. But how much meaning there

---

[1] *De Exhort. Cast.* 10. [2] Eus. *H. E.* v 18. 3.

is likely to be in such rhetoric may be judged when we find Apollonius making the same accusation against the Montanists because they had salaried preachers. The truth is that when we fix our thoughts on the facts which Tertullian mentions and not on the rhetoric beneath which they are buried, we perceive that the difference between him and the Catholics concerned far less the frequency and duration of fasts [1] than the principle on which they rested. The Catholics held that, with certain exceptions, they were 'ex arbitrio', Tertullian held that they were 'ex imperio novae disciplinae'.[2] And similarly in Epiph. *Haer.* 48. 8, where apparently Montanists and Gnostics are classed together, there is no allusion to difference in the amount of fasting, but only to difference in the principle which lies behind it. And nothing more is implied in the words ὁ νηστείας νομοθετήσας. The fasts were reduced to rule, no doubt by command of the Paraclete; but it does not follow from this that they were increased in number or in severity. That would depend on the frequency and rigour of fasting in the already existing usage of Catholic Christians. The Montanist rule may even, in this matter, have fallen below the standard of Phrygian Catholic custom. It is at least remarkable that when Sozomen enumerates the local differences as to the duration of Lent, the shortest Lent which he mentions is that of those who 'minded the things of Montanus', and who kept but two weeks.[3]

The remark about marriage and fasting therefore leaves unimpaired the impression produced by the charges of greed and worldliness brought by Apollonius against the Montanists. We cannot regard those whom he had in view as an ascetic community.

Not unconnected, in the mind of Tertullian, with the question of asceticism, was the eagerness for martyrdom to which as a Montanist he urged his readers. It is necessary therefore to enquire what we can learn as to the attitude towards martyrdom of the Phrygian Montanists.

Tertullian quotes oracles of the prophets in favour of his view

---

[1] Bonwetsch (p. 96) scarcely succeeds in proving that in these respects the Montanists (in Africa) differed to any considerable extent from the Catholics. He shews (p. 95) that Jerome exaggerated the number of fasts peculiar to the Montanists.

[2] *De Ieiun.* 2, 13.   [3] *H. E.* vii 19.

that Christians should seek rather than evade martyrdom;[1] but they are not appreciably stronger than words spoken by our Lord, upon which at least one of them is plainly founded. Both alike are patient of different interpretations by different men. What then was the actual practice of the Montanists of Phrygia? Did they court martyrdom or did they avoid it? The answer must be, I think, if we are to be guided by the available evidence, that they behaved much in the same way as Catholic Christians did under similar circumstances.

A passage of the Anonymous has been interpreted to mean that the Montanists had no martyrs. 'Is there any,' he asks,[2] 'of those who began to speak, from Montanus and the women on, who was persecuted by Jews or slain by lawless men?' And he answers, 'Not one.' It is instructive to observe the use which has been made of these words, and some others like them which follow. Mr McGiffert, in the notes to his English translation of Eusebius,[3] affirms that 'there is a flat contradiction' between them and a subsequent passage of the same writer, in which he admits that the Montanists had many martyrs; and he infers that the Anonymous had 'no regard whatever for the truth'. He adds that 'we know that the Montanists had many martyrs, and that their principles were such as to lead them to martyrdom even where the Catholics avoided it', referring to Tertullian's *De Fuga*. In the latter remark he assumes that African and Phrygian Montanism were identical in principle. And all that precedes it is based on a misinterpretation of the Anonymous.

For that writer is answering the argument—based on Matt. xxiii 34, 'I will send unto you prophets and wise men and scribes; some of them ye shall kill and crucify'—that because the Catholics had not received Montanus and his companions they were slayers of the prophets. Any one who reads the whole passage with attention will perceive that his answer amounts to this: The text must be taken literally; and in its literal sense it has not been fulfilled in the Montanist prophets. None of them has been put to death by any one, still less by the Jews, to whom Christ was speaking. Montanus and Maximilla and Theodotus were all dead, but not one of them had died as a martyr. The

---

[1] *De Fuga* 9; cp. cap. 11; *De Cor.* 1.   [2] *Ap.* Eus. *H. E.* v 16. 12.
[3] p. 232 f.

Anonymous makes no reference to the general body of Montanists. He neither denies nor affirms that they had martyrs. Hence his words cannot contradict the later passage in which he allows that the sect had numerous martyrs.

But it is not without significance that, if we may believe him— and I see no reason why we should not—none of the early Phrygian prophets had suffered for the faith. Is it likely, if they preached, with the vigour of a Tertullian, that the glory of martyrdom should be eagerly sought, that all of them should have passed through the persecution of Marcus Aurelius unscathed?

But let us proceed to consider the second passage of the Anonymous to which Mr McGiffert refers. In it he tells us that when all other argument failed them the Montanists fell back on their martyrs. And he admits the truth of their contention that their martyrs were many in number.[1]

What was the argument based on this fact? The Anonymous only says that they regarded it as 'a proof of the power of the prophetic Spirit that was among them'. We may perhaps guess that what they meant was something of this kind. The Anonymous plainly refers to the persecution of Marcus Aurelius; for after it according to him the Church had enjoyed continuous peace up to the time when he wrote.[2] Now the martyrs of Lyons had during that persecution testified by their letters in favour of the Catholic party in Phrygia.[3] Their judgement would have had great weight with all Christendom. Just in the same way we cannot doubt that the arguments of Praxeas against the Montanists were the more readily listened to by the Bishop of Rome because of his 'martyrdom' of which he made such proud boasting, and the reality of which Tertullian so eagerly disputed.[4] By way of reply the Montanists may have appealed to their own martyrs: 'We too had then many martyrs who testified on our behalf.'

But, however that may be, the Anonymous gives us no reason to suppose that there was any balancing of one set of martyrs against another in regard either to their number or their eagerness and stedfastness. As yet we have nothing to guide us to a sure

[1] *Ap.* Eus. *H. E.* v 16. 20 f.
[3] Eus. *H. E.* v 3. 4.
[2] *Ib.* § 19.
[4] *Adv. Prax.* 1.

judgement about the attitude of the Phrygian Montanists towards martyrdom.

We turn to the treatise of Apollonius. Here at length we find a hint. Apollonius tells us that Themiso purchased his liberation from bonds with a large sum of money, and thereafter boasted as a martyr.[1] This statement may of course be false; but it is not proved to be false because Tertullian in his *De Fuga* denounced the practice of purchasing release.[2] And it is worthy of remark that in this case it is not a Montanist but a Catholic who says that Themiso's act of cowardice ought to have humbled him. Moreover the statement (whether true or false) would hardly have been made if it had admitted of an easy retort. So far as it goes it indicates that in Phrygia the Montanists were more inclined to avoid martyrdom than the Catholics.

This is confirmed by a document of later date. Under Decius one Achatius, apparently bishop of Melitene in Armenia Minor, was examined by a governor named Martianus. The record of the examination was printed by Ruinart,[3] and has many marks of genuineness. In it the governor is represented as urging Achatius to sacrifice by an appeal to the example of the Cataphrygians, 'homines religionis antiquae,' who had in a body abandoned Christianity and made their offerings to the gods. This address cannot have been put into the mouth of Martianus by an orthodox writer. For such a one would not have made him speak of the Montanists as men of an ancient religion; and still less would he have made him immediately afterwards contrast their faith with the 'nouum genus religionis' of their Catholic rivals. The governor is struck by the difference between the faint-heartedness of the Montanists and the courage of the Catholics.

Another indication of the position taken by the Eastern Montanists in the matter of martyrdom remains to be noticed. The sect which was commonly known as 'the heresy of the Phrygians' must have included among its members a large number—perhaps the majority—of the Christians of Phrygia. And we have direct testimony that this was so even as late as the

---

[1] *Ap.* Eus. *H. E.* v 18. 5.   [2] Bonwetsch, p. 163.
[3] *Acta sincera*, ed. Amsterdam, 1713, p. 152.

fifth century (Soz. *H. E.* ii 32). But Sir William Ramsay[1] points out that in Phrygia as a whole martyrdoms in the latter part of the second, and throughout the third, century were rare. From a study of the inscriptions he is able to suggest a reason for this fact. The Christians lived on good terms with their heathen fellow countrymen, and did not obtrude their Christianity unnecessarily; and, speaking generally, a spirit of compromise and accommodation in matters religious prevailed. If this description is at all near the truth the attitude of the Phrygian Christians towards paganism and towards persecution must have been as different as possible from that which is enforced in Tertullian's Montanist treatises, and, for that matter, in many other writings which have never been suspected of Montanist leanings. So far from courting persecution the Phrygian Christians sought to avoid it, and succeeded. If the Montanists had not been in this point in agreement with the Catholics such a result would have been impossible.

But this paper must be brought to a close. Professor Harnack, following many other writers, has said that 'what is called Montanism was a reaction against secularism in the Church'.[2] The considerations which I have now adduced seem to me to prove that, if this be true, Montanism, in the place of its birth, must have departed from its original standpoint far more rapidly than the Montanism which, in the last years of the second century, established itself at Carthage, and is represented, for us, by Tertullian.

H. J. LAWLOR.

[1] *Cities and Bishoprics of Phrygia* ii (1897) chaps. xii, xvii, esp. p. 501.
[2] *Encycl. Brit.* xvi 777.

K k 2

Acknowledgments

La Piana, George. "The Roman Church at the End of the Second Century." *Harvard Theological Review* 18 (1925): 201–77. Courtesy of Yale University Sterling Memorial Library.

Mitros, Joseph F. "The Norm of Faith in the Patristic Age." *Theological Studies* 29 (1968): 444–71. Reprinted with the permission of *Theological Studies*, Georgetown University. Courtesy of *Theological Studies*.

Walls, A.F. "Papias and Oral Tradition." *Vigiliae Christianae* 21 (1967): 137–40. Reprinted with the permission of E.J. Brill. Courtesy of Yale University Seeley G. Mudd Library.

Hanson, R.P.C. "Origen's Doctrine of Tradition." *Journal of Theological Studies* 49 (1948): 17–27. Reprinted with the permission of Oxford University Press. Courtesy of Yale University Seeley G. Mudd Library.

Hanson, R.P.C. "Basil's Doctrine of Tradition in Relation to the Holy Spirit." *Vigiliae Christianae* 22 (1968): 241–55. Reprinted with the permission of E.J. Brill. Courtesy of Yale University Seeley G. Mudd Library.

Ammundsen, Valdemar. "The Rule of Truth in Irenaeus." *Journal of Theological Studies* 13 (1912): 574–80. Courtesy of Yale University Seeley G. Mudd Library.

Smulders, P. "Some Riddles in the Apostles' Creed." *Bijdragen* (1970): 234–60, (1971): 350–66. Reprinted with the permission of Stichting Bijdragen. Courtesy of Stichting Bijdragen.

Koester, Helmut. "ΓΝΩΜΑΙ ΔΙΑΦΟΡΟΙ: The Origin and Nature of Diversification in the History of Early Christianity." *Harvard Theo-*

logical Review 58 (1965): 279–318. Copyright 1965 by the President and Fellows of Harvard College. Reprinted by permission. Courtesy of *Harvard Theological Review.*

Norris, Frederick W. "Ignatius, Polycarp, and I Clement: Walter Bauer Reconsidered." *Vigiliae Christianae* 30 (1976): 23–44. Reprinted with the permission of E.J. Brill. Courtesy of Yale University Seeley G. Mudd Library.

May, Gerhard. "Marcion in Contemporary Views: Results and Open Questions." *The Second Century* 6 (1987–88): 129–51. Reprinted with the permission of the Second Century Journal, Inc. Courtesy of Yale University Divinity Library.

Benoit, A. "Irénée et l'hérésie: Les conceptions hérésiologiques de l'évêque de Lyon." *Augustinianum* 20 (1980): 55–67. Reprinted with the permission of Instituto Patristico Augustinianum. Courtesy of Yale University Divinity Library.

Carpenter, H.J. "Popular Christianity and the Theologians in the Early Centuries." *Journal of Theological Studies,* n.s.14 (1963): 294–310. Reprinted with the permission of Oxford University Press. Courtesy of Yale University Seeley G. Mudd Library.

Jones, A.H.M. "Were Ancient Heresies National or Social Movements in Disguise?" *Journal of Theological Studies,* n.s.10 (1959): 280–98. Reprinted with the permission of Oxford University Press. Courtesy of Yale University Seeley G. Mudd Library.

Lawlor, H.J. "The Heresy of the Phrygians." *Journal of Theological Studies* 9 (1908): 481–99. Courtesy of Yale University Seeley G. Mudd Library.